NIZAM-BRITISH RELATIONS

About the Author

Prof. **SAROJINI REGANI** is the Dean of the Faculty of Social Sciences at the Osmania University, Hyderabad. Earlier, she was the Professor and Head, Department of History at the Osmania University, Hyderabad. She is also the founder Editor of the Research Journal of the A.P. Archives called 'Itihas' and a member of the Indian Council of Historical Studies. She is the author of the work 'Highlights of the Freedom Struggle' in Andhra Pradesh' and also Editor of the three volumes on 'Who is Who in Freedom Struggle in Andhra Pradesh'.

NIZAM-BRITISH RELATIONS 1724-1857

SAROJINI REGANI

CONCEPT PUBLISHING COMPANY PVT. LTD.
NEW DELHI-110059

The publication of this book was financially supported by the Indian Council of Historical Research.

ISBN: 978-81-7022-195-1

Edition 2026

Published and Printed by

Concept
Since 1974

Concept Publishing Company Pvt. Ltd.
A/15-16, Commercial Block, Mohan Garden,
New Delhi-110059 (India)
T: 91-11-41101460
E: publishing@conceptpub.com, *W*: www.conceptpub.com

Foreword

I have read with interest Sarojini Regani's study of Nizam-British Relations (1724-1857).

Hyderabad played a very important role in the development in India in the eighteenth century. Its early identification with the British had far-reaching consequences not only on the fortunes of the Nizam's State but the whole of India.

Sarojini Regani has based her study on all available documents and justifies everyone of her statements with reference to original sources. I am sure her study will be of great interest to all who want a more detailed study of Indo-British relations from the beginnings of British connection with this country.

Humayun Kabir

Contents

New Introduction

The political relations of the Nizams of Hyderabad with the British East India Company are a matter of considerable interest to a student of Indian history. The condition of Hyderabad in the early 19th century bears close resemblance to that of other States in India. In the words of M.S. Mehta "The main features of the Indian States at this time were passion for independence, and secondly, their burning hatred of their rivals. It is a sad commentary of their sagacity and judgement that they should have failed to understand the simple phenomenon that mutual enemity and disunion were bound to destroy the sovereignty and independence which they so proudly wished to preserve."

The mutual dissensions of the Indian Princes in the Carnatic drew the two commercial companies, the French and the English East India Companies into the vortex of Indian politics.

In the Deccan the death of Nizam-ul-Mulk Asaf Jah I in 1743 unleashed the forces of disruption in the Deccan and the Carnatic and acted as a signal for the outbreak of civil war and chaos. Obsessed by feelings of jealousy and petty notions of independence, the Indian princes did not hesitate to appeal to the foreign commercial companies to join them and Dupleix the French Governor was quick to take advantage of the situation. Inspired by dreams of French hegemony in the South and encouraged by early success, Dupleix proudly wrote to the English Governor Saunders after the battle of Amboor, "Our forces were not on the footing of auxiliaries.

They acted as principals." Saunders declared that "it might have been better for trade if the country powers had been left to decide their own quarrels", but was quick to add that "the company's affairs depend on a strong force to curb the French". The British were the last to enter the political arena but they ultimately ousted the French and in a century became the Paramount Power in India.

The Nizam's hatred of the Marathas and his contempt for Hyder Ali and Tippu Sultan of Mysore were so great, that in spite of several overtures from the latter to form a common alliance against the British, he preferred to adhere to the English alliance, and ceded to them once and for all not only the Northern Sarkars but also the territories that he acquired by the Mysore wars. He even entered into a Subsidiary Treaty with the British on the 20th October 1800 and lost his independence in external affairs. Hyderabad was reduced to the position of a "Protected State."

The British knew that the Marathas were their only rivals for political power in India and so, realised "that the preservation of the Nizam's power is of importance to the Company and that it was in their interest to support his Government."

This was their real motive in entering into subsidiary alliance with the Nizam. That is why, although they had declared solemnly that they had "no manner of concern with any of His Highness's children, relations, subjects or servants with respect to whom His Highness is absolute", from the moment the Subsidiary Treaty was concluded they tried to subvert the internal sovereignty of the Nizam and insisted on the appointment of a Diwan who would be a pliable instrument in the hands of the British.

The Governor General Barlow categorically stated in a letter to the Resident at Hyderabad "I can no more admit the right of the Nizam to withdraw from the alliance than under the obligation of it to adopt any other measures which would expose to imminent hazard the very existence of the Company's dominions. I have no hesitation therefore in proposing the adoption of measures calculated to replace the alliance on its just and proper function. I am aware that the adoption of such measures involves a deviation from that system of non-interference in the internal concern of His

Highness's administration...but the adoption of that system necessarily pre-supposed a just conception on the part of His Highness of the true principles and solid advantages of the alliance...."

Anxious to preserve their internal sovereignty and to free themselves from the irksome interference of the Resident, the Nizam tried in vain to procure Ministers of their own choice. A striking feature of the History of Hyderabad from 1857 is a persistent endeavour on the part of the monarch to assert his independence internally in the State; in the silent but acrimonious tussle, the Resident backed by the power of the India Government was bound to emerge successful. Nawab Sikandar Jah withdrew in disgust from taking part in the administration of the State. Nasir-ud-Doula pathetically tried to dispense with the institution of Diwanship and Afzal-ud-Doula gave vent to his irate feelings by making perverse remarks about his ministers' ancestry. But the Nizam had to accept defeat. The Residency Correspondence preserved in the National Archives at Delhi throws a flood of light on their silent struggle between the British and their "Faithful Ally", the Nizam. The creation of the Hyderabad Contingent, the plunder of the Nizams by the Palmer and Company and the subsequent cession of Berar can all be traced to the constant interference of the Resident and his backing of the Diwan, whose primary aim was to please the British Resident.

The Residency Correspondence further reveals that Hyderabad was far from being free from the great rebellion of 1857. The British alliance was never accepted whole-heartedly either by the ruler or by the people of Hyderabad. The intrigues of Mahipat Ram and the Wahabi Movement headed by prince Mubariz-ud-Doula are a sure pointer in this direction; but the Nizam realised that each trial for power only resulted in making the position of the Resident more clear and powerful. The Nizam had no alternative but to accept the situation, a fact that is testified to, by the remark of Nasir-ud-Doula to his Minister, "I am aware that the days when my alliance was useful or desirable to the British Government are well-nigh at an end, but I fully rely on the performance of the different articles of the treaties existing between the two Governments". The Nizams realised their weakness and that is why Afzal-ud-Doula and Salar Jung co-operated with the British in putting down the movement of 1857.

The lack of proper leadership was responsible for preventing the people of Hyderabad from offering an organized resistance to the British. Even the humble and sporadic attempts they made, occasioned the "Englishman" to comment, "it is curious to observe that easy transition with which Mohammadans who above all things are instructed by the precepts of their *Koran* to abhor idols and infidels in regard to the last of which they have given us a bumper benefit, have passed into sympathising with the Hindus. How absurd to think that, notwithstanding their doctrines and their antecedents past and present, they expect to be believed, they certainly will be. Our taxes will improve in regard to all that they make against us, the easy credulity of the Hindus...the Hindus will begin to hate us, they will begin to love the Mussulmans."

The sporadic attempts made by the common people, the general feeling of dislike towards the Company's rule and widefelt desire that the Nizam should co-operate with Nana Sahib in carrying on the war against the British show that the war of 1857 would have taken a very different course had proper leadership been forthcoming. Handicapped by a feudal setting, the humble efforts made by the people to drive away the foreign power from India throws considerable light on the History of Freedom Movement in Hyderabad during this period.

I am grateful to Dr. Loksh Chandra and the I.C.H.R. for the help they rendered in bringing out the 2nd edition of this book. I also thank Sri. P.K.V. Kaimal, Research Officer of the I.C.H.R. for the interest he took in seeing that the book is published.

I thank the Concept Publishing Company for having brought out this book.

Sarojini Regani

CHAPTER I

Nizamu'l-Mulk Asaf-Jah I And The English

The Asaf-Jahi dynasty was established in the Deccan in the year 1724, when Nizamul-Mulk Asaf Jah emerged as the Victor, in the field of Shakar-Kheda against Mubariz Khan, the Mughal Emperor's nominee.

The Mughal Emperor had to accept this *fait accompli* with apparent good grace, and he, not only confirmed Nizamul-Mulk in the Deccan Subedari, but also bestowed on him the title of Asaf-Jah[1].

From this time onwards, the Asaf-Jahi's ruled over the Deccan, nominally acknowledging the suzeranity of the Mughal Emperor. The Hyderabad State founded by them continued to flourish in the Deccan, long after the disappearance of the Mughal Empire in India.

Though the *de-facto* sovereign of the Deccan, his strong sense of loyalty prevented Nizamul-Mulk from severing his connection with the Mughal Empire. He was content to call himself the Deccan Subedar of the Mughal Emperor.

While Nizamul-Mulk was strengthening his hold on the Deccan, the other Deccan power, the Marathas under their redoubtable leader Baji Rao, were undertaking campaigns in Central and Northern India with a view to extend the Maratha sphere of influence. This preoccupation of the Marathas enabled Nizamul-Mulk to consolidate his position in the Deccan and the Carnatic; the latter region acknowledging the Deccan Subedar as the liege lord.

Conditions in the Carnatic during this period were far from peaceful. The administration in the Carnatic was in a state of disorder. The chaotic conditions there were all the more augmented by the keen rivalry evinced by the English and the French East India Companies on the Coramandal Coast. The primary cause of discord in the Carnatic was sown by the marriage alliances of Nawab Dost Ali Khan.

Sadat-ullah Khan, the Nawab of Carnatic, had no issues of his own. Hence, he adopted his two nephews Dost Ali Khan and Baqar Ali. Sadat-ullah Khan also obtained the necessary sanction for Dost Ali Khan's succession to the masnad, directly from the Mughal Emperor without any

1. Maasir-ul-Umara., Vol. II.

reference to his immediate liege lord Nizamul-Mulk the Subedar of the Deccan[2].

Dost Ali Khan, after his accession to the masnad of the Carnatic, neglected to pay the yearly tribute due to the Subedar of the Deccan. The administration in the Carnatic also began to deteriorate rapidly.

Seeing the deplorable state of affairs in the Carnatic, Nizamul-Mulk decided to intervene personally in the Carnatic affairs and take Dost Ali to task. While he was still contemplating to proceed to the Carnatic and restore his authority there, the Marathas under the leadership of Raghoji Bhonsla and Fateh Singh entered the Carnatic in 1740 to levy Chouth in that region.

The Marathas laid seige to Arcot, the Capital of the Carnatic Government, and later on invested Trichinopoly which at that time was held by Chanda Sahib the son-in-law and Diwan of Dost Ali Khan[3]. The Marathas after taking Trichinopoly took Chanda Sahib a prisoner to Satara leaving Murari Rao Ghorpade in charge of Trichinopoly[4].

Nawab Dost Ali Khan lost his life at the pass of Damarla Cheruvu in defence of Arcot, and Arcot was occupied by the Marathas[5]. They recognised Safdar Ali, the son of Nawab Dost Ali Khan, as the Nawab of the Carnatic, on condition, of his agreeing to pay Chouth to the Marathas and also an indemnity of forty lakhs of rupees[6].

On Safdar Ali becoming the Nawab of the Carnatic Nizamul-Mulk once again demanded the payment of the arrears due to the Subah of the Deccan[7].

But Safdar Ali, was hardly in a position to meet the demands of the Nizam his treasury was greatly depleted on account of the indemnity he had to pay to the Marathas. Hence to meet these double expenses he started to levy contributions from every town and fort in the Carnatic[8], thus adding greatly to the distress of the people, whose sufferings have been graphically described by an agent of the British East India Company in the following words[9];

2. Tuzuk-i-Walajahi.
   Wheeler-"Early records of British India"., p. 135.
3. Robert Sewell and S. K. Aiyangar.-"Historical Inscriptions of South India"., p. 296.
4. Ibid., p. 297.
5. Ibid., p. 297.
   Tuzuk-i-Walajahi.
6. Correspondence du conseil superieur de Pondicherry.,
   Tome I, (1726-1730).
   "Vestege's of Old Madras"., Vol. III., p. 280., (The Indemnity was 32 lakhs).
   Robert Sewell & S. K. Aiyangar-"Historical Inscriptions of South India"., p. 297.
7. Malleson-"History of the French in India"., p. 94.
8. Wheeler-"Early records of British India"., p. 136.
9. Robert Sewell and S. K. Aiyangar.-"Historical Inscriptions of South India", (1728-1803)., p. 296.
   Love's-"Vestege's of Old Madras"., p. 278.

"The exactions of the Havildars have been so vexatious and intolerable------that the several towns and villages have been deserted by the inhabitants. In a word the confusion and disorder of the country is exceeding great".

The people were not only the victims of constant harassment and oppression at the hands of their rulers, but they were also the constant prey of dacoits and Thugs.

Nawab Murtiza Ali Khan of Vellore, a brother-in-law of Safdar Ali refused to pay the usual contributions that were levied from the poligars by Safdar Ali. Thereupon Safdar Ali threatened to dispossess him of his fief. Murtuza Ali Khan taking advantage of Safdar Ali's visit to Vellore, contrived to murder him with the connivance of his wife who was a sister of Safdar Ali[10].

After disposing off Safdar Ali in the above manner. Murtiza Ali Khan tried to proclaim himself as the Nawab of the Carnatic. This roused the ire of the nobles and the people of the Carnatic and they proclaimed Sa-ed Muhammad Khan, a young son of Safdar Ali as the Nawab of the Carnatic in 1742.

While matters were in such a fluid state in the Carnatic, Nizamul-Mulk reached that country in the beginning of 1743, at the head of 80,000 horse and 200,000 foot[11], and stayed in the Carnatic Country till the end of March 1744, during which period he devoted his time and energies in restoring order in the Carnatic.

These years, were also important for the Anglo-French commercial rivalries and struggle in the Carnatic, that ultimately turned out to be a battle for supremacy.

The English and the French East India Companies on the Coramandal Coast tried to checkmate each other and secure power by allying themselves with the Powers of Southern India.

While the Marathas were engrossed in North Indian affairs, and in their dreams of an Empire of Hindustan,these alien traders slowly and almost imperceptably established their spheres of influence in the Carnatic.

Europe, about this time was on the eve of the Austrian Succession War. England and France were participants in this war, on the opposite sides, and they carried their antagonism on all fronts at home and abroad.

In the meantime in India the bold and ambitious Dupleix, had succeeded Dumas as the French Governor.

---

10. Orme-Vol. I., page 48.
    Tuzuk-i-Walajahi.

11. Wheeler-'Early Records of British India'., p. 137.

Mons.Dupleix was anxious to show to the princes of India, the genius and superiority of the French Nation, much to the chargin and jealousy of the English East India Company. The mutual jealousy between the two Companies led to a keen competition on their part to secure the support of the Indian Princes.

Both the Companies, felt the imperative need of acquiring territories, if they wanted to establish their trade on a permanent basis in India. Hence they tried to cultivate the friendship of the Native Powers and vied with each other to enlist the sympathy of the Subedar of the Deccan and of his son Nasir Jung.

After his arrival in the Carnatic, Nizamul-Mulk confirmed Sa-ed Muhammad Khan as the Nawab of Arcot and appointed Anwar-ud-din Khan as the regent[12]. During his stay in the Carnatic, Nizamul-Mulk also got the fortress of Trichinopoly evacuated by the Marathas.

The French had a strong friend in the person of Ghulam Imam Hussain at the Court of Nizamul-Mulk[13]. It was through his intercession and influence the French acquired the right of minting Pondicherry Rupees and later on in 1734 obtained from the Nizam four Canis of land (40 bighas) at Masulipatam for building a factory and a village[14].

To gain the good will of the Nizam, the French, on his arrival in the Carnatic sent valuable presents to him.

Their erstwhile rival the English East India Company, not to be outdone in the demonstrations of loyalty to the Subedar decided to send presents worth about 13,000 pagodas to the Nizam and his son Nasir Jung, through Khwaja Addullah Khan.

They also sought the intercession of Imam Sahib with the Nizam in this matter[15].

Richard Benyon, was the English Governor at Madras during this time. The English had an ulterior motive in sending the presents to the Nizam, namely, to get a confirmation of the rights granted to them by Sa-ed Muhammad Khan on his becoming the Nawab of Arcot.

During the Maratha invasions the Nawab of Arcot, Dost Ali Khan and his son-in-law Chanda Sahib had sent their respective familes and treasury

12. Robert Sewell & S. K.Aiyangar-'Historical Inscriptions of South India', pp. 297-88., Hadiqatul Alam.

13. He was originally the Foujdar of Alambur but when Safdar Ali became the Nawab of Carnatic he fled to the Nizam and was appointed by him as the Foujdar of Masulipatam. Later on he was placed about the person of Nasir Jung.

14. Dr. Yusuf Hussain Khan-'Nizamul-Mulk Asaf Jah', p. 277.

15. Wheeler-'Madras in the Olden Times'., p. 612.

for safety to the French settlement of Pondicherry[16]. In the beginning Safdar Ali had also sent his family to Pondicherry but later on they were sent to Madras, according to Orme, on the advice of Mir Asad. Hence it happened that at the time of Safdar Ali's murder and the subsequent turmoil in the Carnatic, his wife and his son Sa-ed Muhammad Khan remained at Madras.

On his becoming the Nawab of Carnatic Sa-ed Muhammad as a mark of his gratitude to the English, granted the following to the English East India Company on the 4th November 1742[17].

(1) The villages of Eravanore, Sandian, Copang, Vepery and Pandu Pack

(2) A grant for the liberty of coining Arcot Rupees and Pagodas according to the usage and practice of the country mints.

(3) Lessening of duties on sundry goods brought in and out of Chintra-dripeta and for the abolition of duties on other goods.

(4) A grant of one adda on evey Collum of paddy produced in the countries of Poonamalle, Manin Congalon, Peddapalam and Perambak to be applied to the maintenance of Pagodas of Chintradripeta.

Sa-ed Muhammad also sent the necessary Sanads to all the 'Mutassady's in his dominions intimating the grant of the above privileges to the English East India Company.

But Ghulam Imam Hussain popularly known as Imam Sahib intimated to the English that Sa-ed Muhammad Khan was not empowered to give away lands, nor the permission to mint Arcot Rupees without the prior concurrence of the Nizam, the Subedar of the Deccan and overlord of the Nawab of Carnatic.

In view of this intimation the English Governor Benyon sent his agents Coja Petrus and Venkatachellum to Imam Sahib at Arcot to induce him to obtain the necessary official recognition for the grants made to the English East India Company. Venkatachellum was asked to impress upon Imam Sahib that it would be a disgrace if the villages were to be taken away from the English East India Company[18]. Imam Sahib's advice and opinion were also sought concerning the type of presents that were to be sent to the Nizam.

On Imam Sahib advising them to send presents not only to the Nizam, but also to his son Nasir Jung and to Khwaja Abdullah Khan who at that time was expected to become the regent of Sa-ed Muhammad Khan, the

---

16. Robert Sewell & S. K. Aiyangar—"Historical Inscriptions of South India", p. 297.
17. Wheeler "Madras as in the Olden Times", pp. 604,605,606.
Love's—"Vestege's of Old Madras", Vol. III., p. 285.
18. Love's—"Vestege's of Old Madras", Vol. III., p. 285.

English decided to send presents worth in all about thirteen hundred pagodas, leaving it to Imam Sahib's discretion to apportion them according to the rank of each dignitary, keeping some for himself.

Hodjee Adee[19] was entrusted with the task of carrying the President's letter to Nizamul-Mulk.

Messrs Thomas Eyre, Samuel Harrison and Lieutenant Holland were chosen to lead the mission[20]. They also carried the President's seal with them so that they could duly seal the list of presents chosen by Imam Sahib.

The English Governor Benyon made it clear in his letter to Imam Sahib that they hoped to get, through the mediation of Imam Sahib a confirmation of the grants and privileges made by Sa-ed Muhammad to the English East India Company and a Dustak (Official Permit) for transport of the Company's calicoes free of duties through the country[21].

The Mission was instructed to be polite in their demeanour and to impress upon the Nizam that they are entirely dependent on his favour for enjoying the privileges conferred on them by Zulfikar Khan, the general of Aurangzeb, during the course of his conquest of the Carnatic[22]. While they were asked to ingratiate themselves with the Nizam at the same time, the mission was also strictly instructed to answer in general terms, if the Nizam were to ask particulars of their trade.

The deputation was given 630 Rs., two hundred Pagodas in gold and two hundred Pagodas in Fanams for paying batta to the peons and coolies, five hundred gold Mohurs, five hundred Pagodas in Rupee, Fanams and Pagodas towards Durbar expenses.

They were also given a letter of credit on the firm of Kasidas Bukkanji to draw the necessary money in case of emergency[23].

Contrary to their expectations the English had to prolong their stay at the Nizam's camp. By the time the mission could start the Nizam left Arcot to invest the fortress of Trichinopoly. The deputation was instructed to follow the Nizam and reach his camp somehow or other where the French had already preceded them[24]. The Nizam was constantly on the move and the mission had to undergo many hardships to reach the Nizam's camp. The coolies that accompanied the English, to carry the baggage were unable to cope up with the arduous journey and many of them deserted. Some of them fell sick

19. Ahmedji Hadi–Dodwell (calls him).
20. Diary and Consultation Book, (1743).
21. Wheeler–"Madras in the Olden Times", p. 613.
22. Ibid.
23. Diary and Consultation Book, (1743).
24. Wheeler–"Madras in the Olden Times", pp. 614, 615.

during the course of the journey. Sometimes they found it difficult to get even water to quench their thirst. Faced with such hardships they found it difficult to muster the necessary oxen and coolies to carry their baggage.

The frequent absconding of the coolies,and the distance having far exceeded their original estimation the mission found itself running short of money, to pay the wages of the coolies. This made them borrow two hundred Arcot Rupees from the Qiledar of Ginjee. At Ginjee they heard that the French had already preceded them to Trichinopoly and also had an audience with the Nizam.

The English Governor sent them instructions to proceed to Trichinopoly. So, having replenished their train with a fresh supply of coolies and oxen they hastened towards Trichinopoly and reached that place on the 28th of March 1743[25].

The next day Imam Sahib visited their camp, where he was received with due honour and was presented with the usual *nazrana*. Imam Sahib informed them that the Nizam on hearing of their arrival had ordered Mir Mucktada Khan to conduct them to his presence[26].

On the 30th March 1743, Mir Mucktada Khan visited the English camp with a guard of horse and foot and two elephants, and conducted the mission to the Public Durbar with drums and colours. There they were shown the places that were already assigned to them.

After the Durbar was over, the Nizam received them in his private apartment and they were served coffee with the honour of the fans, a privilege enjoyed by the most distinguished persons of the realm. The interview lasted for nearly an hour when the Nizam discussed sundry matters with them and the mission was dismissed with proper decorum.

In the evening both the Nizam and Imam Sahib sent them dinner[27]. The next day presents were sent to the Nizam's tent, and a private audience was granted to the English when the Nizam expressed his pleasure on having received the presents and told them he would send the presents to the Emperor at Delhi, keeping some for himself*.

---

25. Diary and Consultation Book, (1743)., (Records of Fort St. George).
26. Wheeler-"Madras in the Olden Times"., p. 617.
    Gribble-"History of the Deccan." Vol. II., p. 13.
27. Dr. Yusuf Hussain Khan Nizamul-"Mulk, Asaf Jah I"., p. 250.

* The following is a list of the presents sent to the Nizam as found in the Fort St. George Records, (Diary and Consultation Book, 1743).

	PS	PFC	PF
Nankin gold flowered silk double pieces.	35 @	25	875
Gold and Silver flowered silks European pattern.	22	33	726
Velverts flowered silks with gold.	35	15	525
Brocade, white and silver grounds P. S.	124½	7	169·27
Brocade purple and silver.	124	8	192
Brocade Europe.	116¾	10.13	170

Imam Sahib while sending the presents to the Nizam strangely enough, omitted, to send the President's letter to him. This roused the suspicions of

---

Persia Brocade viz. 59

10	PS	6 yds. long	80—800
2			55—110
2			60—120
2			80—160

Persia Carpets. Viz.

2	27½	yds. long and	12 yds. broad	300
2	28½	yds. long and	9¼ ,,	250
2	28		10½	150
2	21		13	150
2	37½		14¾	350
2	31½		9	250

A gold Mussnud			1450
Filagree Plate viz.			216
Ottardans 3 Ps	372¼ RWT		
Collumdans 2	297¼		
Pandans 4	565 3/16		
An equippage for coffee cups	148		
A rose water bottle in shape of a bird	87 7/16		
Rose Water bottles 6	304⅞		
	1775		
Workmanship	1775		
Rupee wt 3550 at 320 per 100 pagodas			1109-13-40
Large painted looking glass 2 prs. at 150			300—0—0

China Ware

Large China Cisterns 1 pr. corge		40—0—0
Japan dishes 8.3		
" plates 43.8		
" Button pots 8.8		700—0—0
Plates 2.18		35—0—0
Sneakers and plates 1000 pr. at Ps. per 100 Pr.		100—0—0
Large gold dishes 4	30	
" Bowels 4		
Large gold dishes 4	80	110—0—0
" Bowels 4		
Carried forward Pagodas		7908—4-40

Brought forward:–

Velvets	P.S.	Yds.		Qt.
Green	6 ft.	[illegible]	at	2.18 409-24-60

the English and they began to doubt his sincerity towards them. They began to press Imam Sahib to present the President's letter to the Nizam but the

Item				Amount	Total
Crimson	3	73½	3	220-18-0	
Embossed cloth					630-6-60
Aurora 3 at 30 Ps per P				90- 0-0	125-0- 0
Green 1				35- 0-0	
Board Cloth fine yds.					
Scarlet and blue 3qts. 60¾ at Ps. 3					182-0-0
Almonds.					
10 Candy at Pags 26 per candy		260			
9¼ maund at 8 per maund		74			334-0-0
Kismish 1 candy					22-0-0
Candles 1 candy					110-0-0
Rose Water.					
1St. 15 chests at Pags 8 per chest		120			
2St. 15 chests at Pag 6½ per chest		97-0-0			276-0-0
3St. 9¾ chests at Pag 6 per chest		58-0-0			
A Silver mounted gun		50-0-0			
A gun and pair of pistols double barrels		80-0-0			
A fowling piece, silver mounted		35-0-0			
A long gun silver mounted		20-0-0			249-9-0
A pair of pistols silver mounted		20-0-0			
do		26-9-0			
Crimson Velvet cushions at p. 37-18 each	8				300-0-0
Young Arab Horses	2				800-0-0
White aniseed water	5	doz	15—0—0		
Orange Water	15	,,	30—0—0		
Empty bottles corks etc.			5-11—0		50-11-0
Dram cases					
No. 1	2 cases at 4 Pags		8-0-0		
No. 2	2 cases 4.18, Pags		9-0-0		
No. 5	1 ,,		7-0-0		24-0-0
Broad cloth fine					
	PS	PF			
Scarlet	14	34.18		483—0—0	
Green	6	26.18		159—0—0	
Yellow	6	26		156—0—0	1254-0-0
Aurora	24	19		456—0—0	
Red	18	12.18		225—0—0	
Green	18	12.18		225—0—0	450-0-0

latter always tried to put them off. Seeing this attitude of Imam Sahib, the English decided to present the letter themselves and on the 7th of April, Eyre who was sent at the head of the English mission presented it in open Durbar to the Nizam.

The Nizam deputed Imam Sahib to enquire about the grants made by Sa-ed Muhammad Khan to the English. Imam Sahib visited the English

Broad cloth	Yds.	P.F.		
Scarlet fine	$4\frac{1}{8}$	2- 1	8-13-10	
Green fine	$4\frac{1}{2}$	1-27	7-31-40	23—22—10
Aurora fine	3	1	3—0—0	
Green middling	5	31-40	4-13-40	
Carried over Pagodas				1,27,38-26-40
Charge of package etc.				215- 6-37
			Pagodas	1,29,53-32-77

Besides this the accounts of sundry glasses bought and sent to Nizamul-Mulk's camp were as follows

1. Large concave glass bought of Mr. Solomons		20—0—0	
6. Pictures with black frames gilded		14—0—0	
		34- 0—0	
1. Large conclave glass 27. Pictures without frames **Bought of** Mr. Savage		20—0—0	
3. double oval glasses convex and concave 4 pags		12—0—0	
1. Square Do. sent hither as a Muster, new covered with Velvet		18—0—0	
Green velvet 2 yds. for covering the 2 large and 3 small glasses at $3\frac{1}{2}$ per yard 7			
Silver for Hoops, Rings and Studs			
Arcot Rupees	$93\frac{5}{8}$		
	2		
Wasted in working	$95\frac{5}{8}$ at 327	29—9—40	
Silver smith......		4—0—0	
		40—9—40	66—27
Two wooden cases for the large glasses	1—16		
Yellow perpets for lining	1—0	2—16—00	
Workmen employed		3— 0—00	
		45—16—40	
	Pagodas		112—16—40
Charge of Package 4—12—73	Pagodas		116—29—33

camp the same afternoon and questioned them closely regarding the village grants and the effect of taxes on the Company's goods[28].

Since the mission was instructed to avoid going into details and answer in general terms about their trade, their answers were necessarily vague. Finding their answers unsatisfactory Imam Sahib asked them to write to the President for particulars. Thus the English could not make any headway in achieving the purpose of the interview.

It was nearly a month since the misson had started from Madras and fifteen days since they were presented to the Nizam. They found it exceedingly difficult to adjust their finances in relation to the exorbitant Durbar charges. The high expenses at the Durbar reduced them to such sore straits that they were once again compelled to borrow from Kasidas Bukkanji amounts worth two thousand and one thousand Arcot Rupees on two separate occasions. After this, even the banker refused to advance further sums of money. Hence the next time they needed another two thousand Arcot Rupees they approached the firm of Govardan Das[29].

Apart from financial difficulties the English had to face many other troubles also. Many among the men who had accompanied the deputation fell sick, while some died unable to face the hardships of the journey. This cast a gloom on the English camp and the men threatened to leave the camp. So the English urged Imam Sahib to procure permission for their departure from the Nizam's court.

The permission to leave Trichinopoly was obtained for them by Imam Sahib on the 17th April 1740[30].

Before their departure the Nizam asked them to send some guns, mortars and shells with a gunner. As regards the main purpose of their visit, to obtain the confirmation of the grants made to them by Sa-ed Muhammad and for which the English had to undergo so much trouble, they were informed by Imam Sahib that the Sanads concerning the grants would be sent to them later.

Since waiting for the actual issue of the Sanads would have meant a further delay, the English readily agreed to Imam Sahib's proposal and started for Madras where they arrived on the 1st May 1743.

Nizamul-Mulk sent a horse and "Sarpich"* by way of presents to the English Governor at Fort St. George along with the mission and the latter received them with due honour.

---

28. Diary and Consultation Book, (1743)., (Records of Fort St. George.), p. 10. Wheeler-"Madras in the Older Times"., p. 619.
29. Ibid.
30. Ibid.

* An ornament of gold and silver placed in front of the turban.

As a gesture of friendship and amity Nizamul-Mulk once again sent a dress of honour and a suitable present to Nicholas Morse when he succeeded Benyon in 1744 as the President[31].

It was nearly a year since the English mission had returned from the Nizam's camp at Trichinopoly and yet the sanads confirming the grant of villages by Sa-ed Muhammad to the English East India Company had not arrived. Now the English heard with dismay that the Nizam was returning to Golconda. This made them doubtful about Imam Sahib's professions of friendship towards them.

Hence, Governor Morse decided to appeal directly to the Nizam and he wrote the following letter to him[32].

The letter of Governor Morse to Nobob-ul-mulk Asaf Jah Bahadur-Sepa Santam;

"Your Excellency's appearance in these parts the English had looked upon as the most favourable circumstance that would possibly happen to them; That thereby they might have the great honour of paying their respects to you, and that you might be informed of the assistance they have of late years given to on many occassions to the subject of His Majesty's when the commotions in the country rendered their lives as well as fortunes very unsafe without the walls of Chennapatnam.

They persuaded themselves that these services would be acceptable to your Excellency and that they would entitle them to your favour and regard. This they had the great pleasure to find by the reception and kind treatment the gentlemen met with when they had the honour of being in your presence at Trichinopoly.

By the blessings of God the affairs of the province are now settled and your Excellency as I am informed of your departure from us, before which I beg leave to hope your Excellency will grant us some mark of your favour as shall be agreeable to your great wisdom and generosity. This will show to the world of your kind acceptance of our services to the Circar, and is what I have waited for the most earnest desire and which I should not have doubted to have been honoured with before now, had the English been so fortunate as to have an advocate to put your Excellency in mind of us when matters of greater consequence would have admitted. Since I have failed in that point I humbly presume to ask it myself of your Excellency, whose goodness now we rely on without any intercessor. This will be an addition to my happiness, as it will give an opportunity of making this particular address to so great a personage as your Excellency, of whom I beg favourable

31. Diary & Consultation Book, (1743)., (Records of Fort St. George.).

32. Wheeler—"Madras in the Olden Times"., p. 634.

ear to what I am now about to represent; and that the English Company provide goods in several parts of this country which is well known to be a great advantage to the Circar, as well as the inhabitants and that these are brought at different times at Chennapatnam and other places. The Jamadars of this country frequently stop them and make unreasonable demands from us on this account. Though we have His Majesty's Royal Firman for passing our goods custom free to which a great regard is always paid in Bengal. Yet the Foujdars in this province have not shown the same but have always acted in opposition to the Royal Order. I, therefore humbly entreat your Excellency, would be so gracious to grant a "dustuck", that by virtue thereof the English Company goods may be always freed from paying any custom. This will strengthen and support us in asserting our right to the enjoyments of what His Majesty has so graciously favoured us with; and I beg your Excellency would be pleased to send down your perwanah to the Governor of this Province to the following effect".

"That in consideration of the Royal Firman and the service done to the Circar by the Governor of Chennapatnam I have freed the English Company from paying any customs on their goods which they purchase in several parts of the country, and carry it to Chennapatnam and other settlements."

May it please your Excellency that the intent of my mentioning the service to the Circar,is,that the copy of the Sunnud which you in your goodness may favour me with will be sent to England to be laid before our Honourable Masters, who will be pleased with my behaviour in that respect and it will recommend me to them"; But even this appeal of Morse was of no effect, and by now the English were completely disillusioned about Imam Sahib's professions of friendship towards them.

As a matter of fact, Nizamul-Mulk objected to the privilege granted to them of coining Rupees at Chintradripeta. Taking advantage of this, Imam Sahib asked the English not to coin money without the sanction of the Nizam. Nizamul-Mulk had issued an order forbidding the minting of coins at different places except at St. Thome and Covelong. But one of the first acts of Imam Sahib soon after Nizamul-Mulk's arrival in the Carnatic was to obtain the latter's sanction for re-opening his own mint at St. Thome.

Thus Imam Sahib had his own reasons in preventing the English from minting coins. This attitude of Imam Sahib made the English seek the help of his sister who was living at Madras. This lady wielded great influence over her brother, and owing to her intervention Imam Sahib gave an order to the Havildar at St. Thome to behave in such a way that for all outward appearances it might appear as though the villages were in actual possession of the English till such time as he obtained formal sanction from Nizamul-Mulk confirming the grant of the villages.

Soon after this he informed his sister that he had succeeded in obtaining the Sanads confirming the grant of the villages to the English East India Company[33].

One of the interesting features about the Sanad was that it was silent about granting the power of coining money to the English East India Company, but the Company surreptitiously continued to mint Arcot Rupees.

Imam Sahib was more inclined to favour the French than the English. Owing to his machinations the French influence was preponderent at the Nizam's court, and taking advantage of these favourable factors, Dupleix the French Governor at Pondicherry sent Monsieur Du' Bausset to protect the French interests at the Deccan court.

Nizamul-Mulk returned to the Deccan from the Carnatic in 1744. But meanwhile, war broke out between the French and the English East India Companies on the Coromandal Coast and the French captured Madras in 1746[34].

The Nawab of Arcot, Anwar-ud-din Khan, had sent his eldest son Mahfuz-khan to the assistance of the English, but Mahfuz Khan was defeated by the French and he soon came to terms with Dupleix leaving the English to their fate. Nizamul-Mulk, owing to his pre-occupations with the Marathas could not once again proceed to the Carnatic to restore order there[35]. Hence in 1747 he appointed his son Nasir Jung as the Nawab of Kondanur, Cudapah and Arcot, empowering him to collect the arrears of tribute from Mysore.

Dupleix, after the capture of Madras, wanted to exchange that place for the districts of Villiyanallur and Valudavur which were contiguous with Pondicherry. They sought the intercession of Imam Sahib in this matter, and the latter readily agreed to exert his good offices on their behalf, with the Nizam.

When Nasir Jung arrived in the Carnatic, Dupleix sent Subbaiyan, his native agent, to Nasir Jung at Arcot with a letter of congratulations and a *nazrana* of 21 Mohurs[36]. Through Subbaiyan the French came to know that the Governor of Fort St. David had written to Nasir Jung requesting him to restore Madras to the English and that Nasir Jung had sent word to the English, through Fazl-ulla Beg and Haji Muhammad that he would be coming to their succour soon.

On learning this Dupleix instructed Subbaiyan to acquaint Anwar-ud-din Khan about the doings of the English.

On being apprised by Subbaiyan of Nasir Jung's intentions, Anwar-ud-din at once sent instructions to his eldest son Mahfuz Khan who was in the camp

33. Diary and Consultation Book, (1743).
34. Robert Sewell and S. K. Aiyangar–'Historical Inscriptions of South India'., p. 298.
35. Ananda Ranga Pillay's Diary., Vol. IV., pp. 70, 72.
36. Ibid., page 72.

of Nasir Jung to see to it that the latter did not go to the help of the English[37]. The country was already in the grip of famine owing to the devastations of the Anglo-French wars, and Anwar-ud-din feared that it would not be able to bear the further expenses of Nasir Jung's army[38]. Owing to these manipulations Nasir Jung did not go to the help of the English. On the other hand, on receiving the letter of congratulations from Dupleix, he sent him a sarpich set with an emerald plume which had a diamond set between two rubies and a pendant consisting of three pearls. Imam Sahib also sent to Dupleix a horse and four jewels.

Yet the English did not despair of convincing Nasir Jung about the justness of their cause, and we find Commodore Griffin in his letter dated 6th March 1747 writing to Nizamul-Mulk dilating on the sufferings of the English at the hands of the French and imploring him to restore Madras to the English[39];- Commodore Griffin wrote[40];

"I shall not enter into a particular detail of all the robberies, cruelties and depredations committed on shore upon the King, my Master's subjects by that insolent perfiduous nation the French; connived at and abetted by those your Excellency (the Nabob of Arcot) whose duty it was to have preserved the peace of your country instead of selling the interest of a nation with whom you have had the strictest friendship time out of mind; a nation that has been the means of not only enriching this part of the country but the whole dominions of the Grand Moghul; and that to a people who are remarkable all over the world for encouraging upon and giving disturbances and disquiet to all near them; A people who are strangers in your country in comparison to those who have been dropped by them of that most important fortress and factory Madras and now they are possessed of it, have neither money nor credit to carry on the trade-----And now excellent Sir, we have laid this before you for your information and consideration and must entreat you in the name of the King of Great Britain, my Royal Master, to call the Nabob to an account for this past transactions and interpose your power to restore as near as possible in its original state what has been unjustly taken from us".

The English also appealed to Nasir Jung to intercede on their behalf with the Nizam. Nizamul-Mulk gave a favourable reply to the above letter of Griffin and sent a mandate to Anwar-ud-din Khan ordering him to desist from helping the French and to help the English in recovering Madras"[41]. He wrote to Anwar-ud-din;

37. Ibid; Vol. IV., p. 72.
38. Ibid; (Vol.) IV., p. 174-175.
39. Country Correspondence., (1748)., (Records of Fort St. George).
40. Mill.—"History of British India"., Vol. III., p. 74.
41. Ibid.

"The English nation from Ancient times are very obedient and serviceable to us, besides which they always proved to be a set of true people and it is very hard that they met with these troubles, misfortunes and destruction. I do, therefore, write you to protect, and assist them in all respects, and use your best endeavours in such a manner that the French may be severely chastised and rooted off, that his Majesty's seaport towns may be recovered and that the English nation may be restored, to their right, establish themselves to their former places as before and carry on their trade and commerce for the flourishment of the place".

Apart from appealing to Nasir Jung to intercede on their behalf with Nizamul-Mulk, the English also in 1747, sent one Bondla Mutyalu Naikan to Nasir Jung to procure his help in recapturing Madras.

Mutyalu was favourably received at Nasir Jung's camp mainly, due to the exertions of Imam Sahib who at this time had reasons to be offended with the French[42].

On his arrival at Nasir Jung's camp, Mutyalu, exerted himself in winning over Nasir Jung and his friends. He agreed to pay two thousand rupees to Nizamul-Mulk and offered similar monetary inducements to other Mughal officers in return for their supplying 1000 horsemen to the English, to enable them to recover Madras. He also wanted Nasir Jung to issue a Firman to Anwar-ud-din Khan and the polygars of the Carnatic forbidding them to help the French with provisions and men, and to write to Dupleix asking him to restore Madras to the English[43].

Nasir Jung at first showed his willingness to assist in retrieving Madras for a consideration of three lakhs of Rupees[44], but later on due to the influence of the pro-French faction at the Court the sum was raised to 10 lakhs.

Later on, this figure was reduced to five lakhs, as Nazir Jung demanded advance payment the English declined to take his assistance[45]. However after a great deal of haggling it was decided that Nasir Jung should supply the English with one thousand horse on receipt of a sum of 1 lakh of rupees. Nasir Jung also sent firmans to Anwar-ud-din and to the polygars in the Carnatic asking them not to help the French.

In spite of the above understanding, owing to the intrigues of the pro-French faction in Nasir Jung's camp, Mutyalu had to leave Arcot in the end with only 55 Mughal, 50 Maratha troopers and 300 peons, having spent 3 lakhs of rupees in trying to propitiate the nobles around Nasir Jung[46].

42. Ananda Ranga Pillay's Diary., Vol. IV., p. 189.
43. Country Correspondence, (1748), p. 4., (Records of Fort. St. George).
44. Ibid.
44. Ibid., Letter No. 5.
45. Dodwell.—"Madras Despatches"., p. 48.
46. Country Correspondence, (1748)., pp. 4, 5., (Records of Fort. St. George).

Nasir Jung despatched along with Mutyalu, 5 dresses of honour and 2 horses for the two chief people at Fort St. David. Mutyalu reached Fort St. David on the 9th March 1747 after having narrowly escaped from being way-laid by the French[47]. But there, poor Mutyalu had a cold reception at the hands of Floyers the Governor of Fort St. David, who was angry with him for having spent so much and got so little in return[48].

Soon after Mutyalu's departure, Nasir Jung left for Aurangabad having heard the news of Nizamul-Mulk's illness.

Mutyalu strove hard to win the sympathy and support of Nasir Jung, but the French partisans in Nasir Jung's camp were too strong. The French were also very active in their efforts to undermine Mutyalu's mission to Nasir Jung. Under the influence of the pro-French faction in his camp, Nasir Jung, in reply to their complaint against Anwar-ud-din, wrote to the English that Anwar-ud-din was not to be blamed. In fact he had tried to help them by sending Mahfuz Khan but the English help to Mahfuz Khan was tardy and so the latter came to an understanding with the French[49].

The French on the advice of Imam Sahib sent to Nasir Jung and Nizam-ul-Mulk, two powerful telescopes and a book on physiology and anatomy as presents[50]. While thanking the French for the beautiful telescopes Nasir Jung also wrote that the fact he had not treated Mutyalu with favour was a proof of his affection for the French.

Imam Sahib even tried to persuade Nizamul-Mulk to write a letter to the Emperor at Delhi justifying the French action in capturing Madras, but the Nizam was not to be persuaded so easily[51].

In the meanwhile Nizamul-mulk died in June 1748 at Aurangabad[52]. Peace was also restored between the English and the French nations in 1748 by the treaty of Aix-la-Chapelle, and by this treaty Madras was restored to the English.

Though Nizamul-Mulk was inclined to view the French with sympathy, he remained so vague till the last that the representatives of the two nations in the Nizam's Court were kept guessing whom he favoured most,---- a policy he adopted deliberately.

He suspected that these foreign settlers were out to take full advantage of the internal dissensions among the Indian Princes and tried to see that they did not take undue advantage by keeping himself aloof from their quarrels.

What he avoided, his descendants could not avoid. No sooner did his restraining influence disappear, than the whole of the Carnatic and later on the Deccan became a cockpit of Anglo-French struggle for power.

47. Ananda Ranga Pillay's Diary., Vol. IV., p. 420, 472.
48. Ibid.
49. Forrest—Bengal and Madras Papers, Vol. II., p. 7.
50. Ananda Ranga Pillay's Diary, Vol. V., p. 48. Ibid., p. 263.
51. Martineaw Dupleix et; Inde. Francaise, Vol. II., p. 283
52. Robert Sewell & S.K. Aiyangar.—Historical Inscriptions of South India, p. 298.

CHAPTER II

French Influence In The Deccan

The first phase of the Anglo-French rivalry in India came to an end by the treaty of Aix-la-Chapelle, but this treaty at best brought about only a truce and not a lasting peace between the two rival companies. The bitter animosity that existed between the two companies required only a spark to burst into a conflagration, and this spark was provided by the death of Nizam-ul-Mulk Asaf Jah I in 1748.

The death of Nizamul-Mulk Asaf Jah I released all the latent disruptive forces in the Deccan and the Carnatic that were hitherto kept in abeyance by the powerful personality of the first Nizam. His death marked the signal for the outbreak of the war of succession in the Deccan and the Carnatic, that plunged the Deccan peninsula in civil war and turmoil.

In the Carnatic the Hindu Rulers of Mysore and Tanjore aspired to become independent, while Dupleix the French Governor though still vauge about his ambitions and designs dreamed of active French intervention in the chaos created by the jealousies of the princes in the Carnatic.

Nizamul-Mulk Asaf Jah I died leaving behind him six sons and six daughters. The names of the sons are as given below in the order of their birth; Ghazi-ud-Din Khan Feroze Jung, Nizamud-Doulah Nasir Jung, Salabat Jung, Nizam Ali Khan Bahadur, Basalat Jung and Mughal Ali Khan. He had also a grand-son, by name Hidayat-Muhui-ud-din Khan popularly known as Nawab Sadat Ullah Khan Bahadur Muzaffar Jung by one of his daughters Khair-un-Nissa Begam[1]. This title was conferred on Hidayat Muhui-ud-din-Khan by his grand-father.

At the time of Nizamul-Mulk's death, the eldest son, Ghazi-ud-din Khan Feroze Jung, who was holding the office of Amir-ul-Umara in the Mughal Court was in Delhi, while Nasir Jung was near his father. As Nasir Jung also happened to be the commander of the troops, he lost no time in proclaiming himself as the Subedar of the Deccan.

To give an appearance of legitimacy to his claims he also declared that his elder brother had renounced his claims to the Deccan Subedari.

But very soon Nasir Jung realised that he was not the sole aspirant to his father's masnad. Muzaffar Jung the grandson of Nizamul-Mulk also put forth

---

1. Dr. Yusuf Hussain-Khan-Nizamul-Mulk Asaf Jah I., p. 81.

his claims to the Deccan Subedari on the strength of an alleged Firman from the Mughal Emperor[2].

As a matter of fact the title of Muzaffar Jung and the government of Raichur and Adoni were conferred on Hidayt Mohui-ud-din Khan by the Mughal Emperor on Nizamul-Mulk's recommendation[3].

Nizamul-Mulk had at one time contemplated the conferring of the Deccan Subedari on his grandson when Nasir Jung's conduct was none too satisfactory, but he gave up the idea in view of the possible grave repercussions, that might occur in the state and became reconciled to Nasir Jung[4].

In view of these events it is not surprising that Muzaffar Jung should have laid claim to the Deccan Subah, but his claim that he was aspiring for the Deccan Subedari on the basis of a Firman from the Mughal Emperor appears to have been dubious.

We have only the authority of the French and Chanda Sahib in this respect and both of them were partisans of Muzaffar Jung[5]. The only other person who mentions this is Higne, the Maratha agent at Delhi, from whose letter we come to know that the Marathas were planning to secure a candidate of their own to the Deccan Subedari through whom they hoped to control the whole of the Deccan[6]. The rapid succession of events in the Deccan brought the Maratha plans to naught.

Muzaffar Jung on the pretext of putting down recalcitrant polygars in his dominions, collected an army of 25,000 men and waited for a suitable opportunity to strike at his uncle.

Nasir Jung in the beginning tried to win over his nephew by adopting a conciliatory attitude, but the latter remained obdurate, and started levying tribute from the polygars in Raichur and Adoni in order to equip himself in an efficient manner.

Meanwhile Nasir Jung also sent an emissary to Delhi to obtain a Firman from the Mughal Emperor, confirming his claims to the Deccan Subedari. The Emperor instead of sending him the Firman asked him to proceed to Delhi immediately in order to humble the pride of his Vizier Safdar Jung and put down the other refractory nobles at the Imperial Court[7]. Besides the Em-

2. Records of Fort St.George., C. C. 1749., L. No. 98.
3. Ibid., Tarikhi-Zufra., p. 113.
4. Ibid.
5. Martineaw Deuleix-et-l' Inde Francaise, Vol. III., p. 83.
   Malleson. History of the French in India., p. 241.
   Records of Fort St. George. C. C. L. No. 105., p. 29.
6. Selections from the Peishaws Daftar, Vol. I., L. No. 79.
7. Tarikhi Rahat, Afza, Maathiral Kiram., p. 186.
   Wilks: (Historical sketches of South India., Vol. I., p. 259.
   (Wilks says that Nasir Jung was summoned to Delhi to fight Ahmed S[illegible] Abdali).

peror, Nasir Jung's elder brother Ghazi-ud-din Khan and his cousins, the sons of the late Vizier Imtiaz-ud-Doulah also pressed Nasir Jung to come to the assistance of the Emperor. All these events tend to show that Muzaffar Jung's pretentions to the Deccan Subedari were based on flimsy grounds. The letter of Monsieur De. Basset and Delarche to Dupleix dated 22 April 1750 further confirms the above suspicions. They wrote, "We have learnt from reliable sources that Muzaffar Jang has based his claims which are well known to you, on a mere letter of Mansur Ali (Safdar Jang) Vizier to the great Mughal who has promised him to render service on this occasion. This young man was little content with Nasir Jang for having prevented his grand-father from giving him the kingdom of Golcondah after his death. That no other nawabs of the Deccan have accompanied Muzaffar Jang in his expedition is a definite proof of the fact that he did not receive any firman from the Mughal Emperor. If he had received any firman from the Emperor all the nawabs of the Deccan would have received instructions from Delhi to join Muzaffar Jang and Nasir Jang would not have been in a position to offer him resistance[8]".

Soon after, proclaiming himself as the Subedar of the Deccan, Nasir Jung made the following appointments[9].

Mir Abdul Razaq the Diwan of Berar was appointed Chief Diwan with the title of Shah Nawaz Khan, while Ramdas Pandit was made the Peshcar[10]. Qaze Dayem was appointed Sadr-i-Sudur. In spite of the urgent messages from Delhi, Nasir Jung could not proceed to the North because of the belligerent activities of Muzaffar Jung. The latter had at this time come to an understanding with Chanda Sahib early in 1749 and it was decided that they should go on a campaign to the Carnatic against Nawab Anwar-ud-din.

Nasir Jung, after having nominated Shah Nawaz Khan as the commander-in-chief of his forces, left Aurangabad for Bidar in April 1749 and thence to Burhanpur. While on the banks of the Narbada he received a message from the Emperor asking him to return to the Deccan, as an amicable settlement, had been reached between the Emperor and his Vizier[11].

So, Nasir Jung returned from Burhanpur to Aurangabad on the 23rd June 1749, and after his arrival he received a Firman from the Mughal Emperor conferring on him the Subedari of the Deccan and the Carnatic and also the title of Nizam-ud-Doulah[12].

---

8. Ibid. , , , , , , , p. 259.
9. Tarikhi Rahat Afza-(Asafia Library. Pcs. M.S. History No. 1001).
10. Eng. Trans. Tuzuki-Walajahi of Burhan-ud-din.
    Rahsaare Farooqi-Nasir Jung Shaheed.
11. Wilks-Historical sketches of South India., Vol. I., p. 259.
    Rahsaare Farooqi-Nasir Jung Shaheed.
12. Records of Fort St. George., C. C. 1749., L. No. 25., p. 7.

The Firman was received by Nasir Jung with great ceremony, and he also sent a copy of the Firman to the French Governor Dupleix through Khwajah Namatullah Khan the Foujdar of Rajahmundry[13].

The English Governor Floyer, after the death of Nizamul-mulk sent a letter of condolence to Nasir Jung, and soon after the latter's accession to the masnad, Floyer sent a letter of congratulations also[14]. The English Admiral Boscawen also wrote the following complimentary letter to Nasir Jung on his accession[15]

"Admiral Griffin being gone for Europe the letter you sent him came into my hands in which I had the great satisfaction to hear of your health and also to be acquainted that you had succeeded to the honour and titles of your illustrious father on which I now congratulate you and wish they may be attended with all happiness.

His Majesty of Great Britain sent me last year to these parts, to command his sea and land forces and on my landing here I marched to attack the French at Pondicherry in order to take satisfaction of that people for the outrages and violence they had committed against the subjects of his Majesty residing in the province Act of which had reached Royal Ear and was the more surprising to him in as much as they were perpetrated by them in the territories of a Prince with whom he was in perfect amity. My arrival from Europe being so late and the rainy season setting in more early than usual prevented the carrying on any further attacks till that was over, and thereupon a cessation of Arms had been declared on the parts of the respective provinces engaged in the war the issue of which I am now waiting for, and the further commands of my Royal master. I have great pleasure in observing the regard and attachment you have shown my nation in the orders your officer the nabob of Arcot and also from what Mootal has told me, as soon as the expected advice from Europe come to my hands I shall not fail to communicate to you what may be necessary according to the circumstances of affairs I have recommended to the governor of this place to send you the colours and shells agreeable to you later and am to desire you will accept of 50 Mohurs as a token of the respect I have for your person. What can I say more" ------.

On the advice of Imam Sahib Dupleix, also sent the customary nazrana and a congratulatory letter to Nasir Jung[16]. Dupleix, who had captured Madras from the English, was anxious to get that exchanged for Valudavur and Villiayanallur and he solicited the help of Imam Sahib in this matter. He

13. Ananda Ranga Pillay's Diary. Vol. V., p. 247.
14. Records of Fort St. George, C. C., p. 11., L. No. 39.
15. Ibid., No. 38.
16. Diary of Ananda Ranga Pillay. Diary Vol. V., pp. 108, 109.

urged Imam Sahib to impress on Nasir Jung the effectiveness of French resources and valour[17]. The letters written by Dupleix to Imam Sahib in this regard strike an ominous note and give a glimpse of his mind at the time. He writes[18], "As Mahammad Shah Padshah and Nizam-ul-Mulk have died, all law and order have vanished and each is seizing as much of the kingdom as he can. I too could have seized territory if I had wished but that would be wrong. It will be well if you obtain and send Nasir Jang's Perwannah for the countries of Villianur and Valudavur about which I had already written. Otherwise I must act like the other people. Please do your best in the matter." In another letter he wrote;

"You desire that I should send 1000 gold mohurs to procure the diamond Kalgi, Sarpech, quiver, bow-cross, hilted dagger set with precious stones, swords, shields, spears etc., to be presented to me by Nasir Jang, but this is a behaviour befitting a hunckstar not a gentleman. When I reported to you the nominal and actual collections of the Valudavur and Villayanallur Jagirs, and requested the grant of the villages attached to it on condition of this never being restored to the English unless at the same time Kunnimedu and 75 villages including the waste lands to be granted to us in addition. Otherwise we will take them by force. As Anwar-ud-din Khan and Abdul Jalil helped the English when we attacked them we seized the country as far as Arcot but forgave him out of respect for the Padshah and Nasir Jang. But now if you do not act as written above, we will take the country by force".

One is not so much surprised at the above tone of Dupleix's letter when one remembers that as early as 1743 Dupleix was in communication with Chanda Sahib at Satara, the Nawait Candidate to the Nawabi of Arcot[19].

Chanda Sahib, the son-in-law of Nawab Dost Ali Khan, was taken prisoner by the Marathas in 1741, during the latter's invasion of Trichinopoly and was confined at Satara.

Chanda Sahib, had sent his family to Pondicherry during the time when Trichinopoly was invested by the Marathas, the family was still in Pondicherry when Dupleix went there as its governor.

After the death of Sa-ed Muhammad, Nizamul-Mulk nominated Anwar-ud-din as the Nawab of Arcot. But this choice was not to the liking of the people and the nobles of the Carnatic. They wanted a member of the old Nawait family to rule over them. The Nawait family at this time was represented by Chanda Sahib and Nawab Murtiza Ali Khan of Vellore, both sons-in-law of Nawab Dost Ali Khan. Of the two, Chanda Sahib was the more popular.

17. Ibid., Vol. VI., p. 150.
18. Ananda Ranga Pillay's Diary. Vol. VI., p. 15.
19. Dodwell - Dupleix and Clive., p. 34.

After becoming the governor of Pondicherry, Dupleix succeeded in establishing close and cordial relations with the family of Chanda Sahib through Madame Dupleix, who was well versed in the native languages. He also succeeded in opening communications with Chanda Sahib at Satara through the latter's son, Raza Sahib[20].

From Chanda Sahib's letters Dupleix, formed a shrewd estimate of his character. He found out that Chanda Sahib was not only ambitious but also possessed daring and political ability. Hence Dupleix did not hesitate to interfere on his behalf in the Carnatic affairs. By doing so he sought to gain commercial and political advantages for the French in India. Flushed with his recent victories against the English and Anwar-ud-din, Dupleix dreamed of making the Carnatic a French sphere of influence; he even persuaded the Pondicherry Council to collect one lakh of rupees for Chanda Sahib's release from Satara[21], which was later on raised to 3 lakhs by Dupleix[22].

Chanda Sahib, a subtle diplomat, in the mean-while, made many specious promises to the Peishwa and persuaded him to believe that his release would be of great advantage to the Marathas, that the Peishwa ultimately connived at his escape in June 1748 and ere long Chanda Sahib was marching towards the Carnatic at the head of 12,000 horses[23]. The Peishwa who hoped to exercise considerable influence in the Carnatic through Chanda Sahib and Muzaffar Jung, also supplied 3000 men to Chanda Sahib[24].

Having collected a respectable force Chanda Sahib joined Muzaffar Jung, with whom he was in communication while in prison. He now engaged himself in collecting tribute from the polygars of Adoni and Bijapur on behalf of Muzaffar Jung, during the course of which he came in conflict with the Rani of Bednore[25].

Chanda Sahib soon persuaded Muzaffar Jung that he could deal an effective blow to the power of Nasir Jung by striking at the Carnatic first, for they could have at their disposal the resources of the Carnatic as well as the French help. Muzaffar Jung's own position in the Deccan was rather precarious. Nasir Jung had on the eve of his departure to Delhi, instructed Shah Nawaz Khan his Diwan and Syed Lashkar Khan to station forces on the banks of the Krishna to forestall any possible movement by Muzaffar Jung's forces.

After stationing forces on the banks of the Krishna, Shah Nawaz Khan and Syed Lashkar Khan warned Muzaffar Jung not to persist in war-like activities against his uncle[26].

---

20. Ananda Ranga Pillay's Diary. Vol. VI., p. 84.
21. Dodwell - Dupleix and Clive., p. 34.
22. Records of Fort St. George. C.C. 1748., p. 54.
23. Ananda Ranga Pillay's Diary. Vol. V., p. 245.
24. Ibid., Vol.III & IV., p 140 & 124.
    Orme. Vol. I., p. 257.
25. Dodwell – Dupleix & Clive., p. 37.
26. Tuzuki-Walajahi (Nainar's Engl. Trans.)., Vol. I.

Muzaffar Jung did not take a long time to be persuaded by Chanda Sahib to launch into hostilities in the Carnatic. Muzaffar Jung nominated Chanda Sahib as his Diwan, and conferred on him the Nawabship of Arcot, Gingee, Tanjore, Trichinopoly and Madura, besides the title of Khuda Nawaz Khan[27].

Before starting for the Carnatic, Chanda Sahib appealed to Dupleix for help, and the latter readily despatched a body of 420 French soldiers, 2,000 sepoys, 100 topass and coffrees under the command of d' Auteuil[28].

Nawab Anwar-ud-din Khan, on hearing this, sent a message to Dupleix to desist from helping Chanda Sahib[29], at the same time his son Muhammad Ali wrote to the English Governor, Floyers, to dissuade the French from helping Chanda Sahib and Muzaffar Jung[30]. But Anwar-ud-din's efforts in this direction proved abortive. Hence he decided to give battle to Chanda Sahib and Muzaffar Jung.

On the 3rd August 1749 in a battle fought at Amboor, Anwar-ud-din lost his life fighting against the forces of the French and their allies Chanda Sahib and Muzaffar Jung. His second son Muhammad Ali on hearing of Anwar-ud-din's death fled to the Fortress of Trichinopoly. The French played the principal part in the battle of Amboor. It was mainly due to their help that Chanda Sahib and Muzaffar Jung were able to effect their entry into Arcot on the 7th August 1749[31].

The battle of Amboor was one of the decisive battles fought in India. It is in this battle that we hear for the first time about the exploits of Mon's. Bussy, the future hero of the Deccan under whose command the French forces defeated and killed Anwar-ud-din Khan. For the first time in this battle we see Europeans playing the part of principals while Indian soldiers remained in the background. Writing about this battle to the English Governor, Dupleix says, " our forces were not on the footing of auxiliaries. They acted as principals; former insults authorised it and during the whole course of the war we have never looked ourselves in any other light[32]".

This battle gave a concrete shape to the hitherto fleeting visions in the mind of Dupleix. Hitherto Dupleix could only think of the possibilities of increasing the French influence by co-operating with the Indian princes, but now the battle of Amboor fully revealed to him the extent to which decay had set in, in the body politic of India, and the possibility of the French becoming supreme.

27. Records of Fort St. George., C. C., p. 25., L. No. 98.
28. Ibid., Fort St. David Consultations., p. 134.
29. Dodwell-Dupleix and Clive., p. 38.
    Ananda Ranga Pillay's Diary., Vol. VI., p. 102.
30. Records of Fort St. George., C. C., p. 36., L. No. 125.
31. Records of Fort St. George - Fort St. David Consultations, 1749., p. 137.
32. Ibid. French Correspond

The death of Nizamul-Mulk resulted in a struggle for power between Nasir Jung and Muzaffar Jung, and this struggle ultimately developed into a scramble for power in the Deccan between the Nizam, the Marathas, the English and the French. Dupleix's original intention was to establish the French influence in the Carnatic by reinstating Chanda Sahib at Arcot, but he soon realised that Chanda Sahib's position was untenable without the requisite support from the Subahdar of the Deccan. Since Chanda Sahib's receiving the support of Nasir Jung was out of question, the only logical thing under the circumstances for Dupleix was to support Muzaffar Jung the rival of Nasir Jung; By following such a policy Dupleix was ultimately able to establish French influence to a preponderant degree even at Hyderabad.

According to the original understanding with the French, Chanda Sahib was expected to grant them, for the help received, the villages of Villiyanallur and Valudavur, territories that the French had failed to obtain from Nasir Jung, but Chanda Sahib out of gratitude to the French also conferred on them other vast territories besides the above villages[33].

Chanda Sahib proceeded from Arcot to Pondicherry where he was received with great pomp by Dupleix on the 28th September. He was joined there by Muzaffar Jung on the 30th September.

There, after nominally obtaining the permission of Muzaffar Jung, Chanda Sahib conferred on Dupleix not only the villages of Villiyanallur and Valudavur but also Bahur along with the 81 villages in its neighbourhood.

Muzaffar Jung conferred on the French the sea port of Masulipatam and Divi Island an area of 22 miles yielding an annual revenue of 8 lakhs of rupees[34].

The Government of Madras viewed the above grants with great misgiving. The thirty six villages of Bahur lay in the vicinity of Fort St. David, and if the French so desired, they could cut off all communications to Fort St. David with impunity.

The English resented in particular the granting of the following places, which brought their trade and commerce in jeopardy, namely Covelong to Monsieur Dupleix, Porto Nova to Madame Dupleix, St.Thome to Padire and Alampara to Monsieur d'. Auteuil. Mentioning this to the Court of Directors they wrote to the following effect[35]. "......So that we are surrounded in such a manner as for the French to have it entirely in their power to stop our trade or debar us from any supplies of provisions from the country

33. Ananda Ranga Pillay's Diary., Vol. VI., p.185.
Cultru., pp. 234-36.
34. Forests - Bengal & Madras Papers., Vol. II., - (Despatches from Fort St. David, 1751)., p. 179.
Archives - Vol. II., pp. 3-8.

and we have great reason to believe from what has already happened, they will not be waiting to make use of their advantage"[35].

Realising the danger in which they stood, the English while sending the customary congratulatory letter to Chanda Sahib on his success, sent at the same time a secret message to Muhammd Ali at Trichinopoly offering their help on condition that he should procure for them a mansab and a Jagir from Nasir Jung to match the possessions that the French had acquired from Muzaffar Jung and Chanda Sahib.

They also forestalled the occupation of San Thome and Mylapore by the French, as part of Bahur villages, by ordering Admiral Boscawen to take possession of them on the authority of a separate firman from Muhammad Ali[36]. Boscawen duly occupied these villages on the 11th October 1749.

The English also wrote pressing letters to Nasir Jung to come to the Carnatic and relieve that country from distress.

On hearing, that Nasir Jung, was proceeding to the Carnatic with the Marathas, Chanda Sahib and Muzaffar Jung left Pondicherry towards the end of October, and tried to raise their already depleted funds by laying siege to Tanjore on the way[37].

On hearing that his uncle was advancing on the Carnatic with a large army and that the Pathan Nawabs of Cuddapah and Kurnool who formed a part of Nasir Jung's entourage, had already advanced to Adoni to seize it, Muzaffar Jung lost heart and thought of asking his uncle's pardon; But Chanda Sahib by his subtle persuasion succeeded in preventing him from doing so and Muzaffar Jung decided to carry on the struggle. To express their fraternal feelings for each other Muzaffar Jung and Chanda Sahib vowed by the Qoran that whatever might be the fortunes of war they would support each other[38]. Fortified by these fresh vows of friendship they both proceeded and laid seige to Tanjore[39].

After his arrival at Hyderabad on 14th June 1749 Nasir Jung on hearing of his nephew's movements, instructed Shah Nawaz Khan to march in advance to the Carnatic to the succour of 'Anwar-ud-din Khan. Shah Nawaz Khan hastened to the Carnatic via Kalyan and Chincholi and while he was still near the village of Gurumatkal he heard about the fatal battle of Amboor and the death of Nawab Anwar-ud-din Khan.

---

35. Ibid., p. 1688.
    Gae Belle - Archives of the French Historical Society., Vol. No I., pp. 3-8.
36. Records of Fort St. George. French Correspondence, 1752.
37. Ananda Ranga Pillay's Diary. Vol. VI., p. 217.
    Records of Fort St. George. French Correspondence, 1752 ., p.4.
38. Vol. VI., p.236.
39. Ibid.

In the meantime Nawab Muhammad Ali Khan from Trichinopoly apprised Nasir Jung who was at Aurangabad, of the result of the battle of Amboor and the events that followed it[40]. Nasir Jung immediately despatched a letter of condolence to Muhammad Ali and while doing so, also, informed him of his intention to proceed to the Carnatic to restore law and order in that country[41].

He also addressed a letter to Dupleix to the following effect[42].

"It has been frequently represented that you have seemingly joined that disobedient wretch (Muzaffar Jung) who is arrived in that province. The consideration of your true regard to me makes me it be how it will, I now require you will no more act in conjunction with him and with the other unfortunate wretches and believe that my victorious army will soon arrive in your parts in order to punish the said wretch. If I hear again of your like proceedings (which God forbid) I will write to the several Governors in the Empire to destroy your settlements both in Bengal Provinces and in the Deccan Country. I pass this edict and give you warning".

Nasir Jung sought the help of Raghoji Bhonslay and that of the Peishwa in the Carnatic expedition, and the latter agreed to help him. Murarl Rao Ghorpade was sent at the head of 10,000 Maratha soldiers to the help of Nasir Jung, besides him Janoji Bhonslay the son of Raghoji also came to the help of Nasir Jung with 10,000 horse[43].

Nasir Jung also sent instructions to all the Mughal tributaries and dependents in the Carnatic region to come and join him as he advanced towards the South. So, soon after his arrival in the Carnatic Murari Rao Ghorpade, the Raja of Mysore, the Nabobs of Cuddapah, Kurnool and Savanoor, Muhammad Ali of Arcot and the English at Fort St. David hastened to join him.

The English agreed to be auxiliaries in this struggle after receiving a grant from Muhammad Ali for San Thome, Trivendipuram and Poonamalli countries[44].

Nasir Jung had sent in advance the Pathan Nawabs of Cuddapah and Kurnool along with Syed Lashkar Khan to seize Adoni, and Rayachoti the Subah of Muzffar Jung. Rayachoti was seized by Syed Lashkar Khan and the Nizam's flag was hoisted there.

On hearing of the news of the capture of Rayachoti Muzaffar Jung thought of going to Adoni and seeking his uncle's pardon, but he was dissu-

40. Burhan's Tuzuki Walajahi (Eng. Trns. by Nainar)., Vol. II., p.27.
41. Ibid., p.29.
42. Records of Fort St. George., CC. 1749., p.60., L.No. 192.
43. Grant Duff. History of the Mahrattas. Vol. II., pp. 511, 12, 520.
44. Records of Fort St. George. C.,C., p.3., L.No.6.,1751.

aded by Chanda Sahib from doing so and they both now swore on the Holy Qoran to stand or fall together in the ensuing struggle[45].

After this reaffirmation of faith in each other, they laid siege to Tanjore with the hope of replenishing their depleting treasury. They attacked Tanjore on the pretext of realising the arrears due from that kingdom, to the Nawab of Arcot eversince the days of Safdar Ali, against the wishes of Dupleix, who was anxious that Trichinopoly the stronghold of Muhammad Ali should be reduced first[46].

They wasted their time at Tanjore in long drawn out negotiations. In the meanwhile Nasir Jung arrived on the outskisrts of the Carnatic. He reached Sirpi on the 10th Feb, 1750 and from there sent two emissaries, Moropant and Qaze Dayem, to Muzaffar Jung and Chanda Sahib to negotiate a settlement. The latter two, duly intimated Dupleix of the arrival of Nasirjung's emissaries, and Dupleix instructed them to reply to the effect that[47] "though we have three bodies our life is one, peace cannot be made without me (Dupleix) and if the matter is to be settled satisfactorily, they must come here to Pondicherry".

Nasir Jung reached the Changama pass in March 1750.

Dupleix on hearing the above news, sent instructions to Chanda Sahib to seize either Tanjore or Ginjee and to use it as a strong-hold against Nasir Jung. But Chanda Sahib after concluding a hurried treaty with the Rajah of Tanjore went to Chidambaram[48]. There a short skirmish took place between his forces and those of Nasirjung's sent under Mir Dayem. From there he proceeded to Pondicherry[49].

There Chanda Sahib represented his financial troubles to Dupleix, but the latter was not in a position to help him with money. So, after expressing his helplessness in that respect, he assured Chanda Sahib that he would help him with the necessary arms to enable him to fight Nasir Jung. Chanda Sahib was soon joined by Muzaffar Jung at Pondicherry on the 15th March[50]. The former, in view of their financial stringency and the vastness of Nasir Jung's armies, and the likelihood of his own troops deserting to Nasir Jung, was inclined to prolong his stay in the Carnatic till such time as Nasir Jung would leave the territory. But Dupleix, considering it as a disgrace spoke to Chanda Sahib in the following manner, "if you refuse to attack him, you will dishonour me your ally, put your trust in Him and attack Nasir

45. Ananda Ranga Pillay's Diary , Vol. V., p. 236, 237.
46. Orme.Vol. I., "A History of the Military transactions of the British Nation in Indostan"., p.133.
47. Ananda Ranga Pillay's Diary., II Vol. VI,, p.367.
Tuzuki-Walajahi (Engl. Trans-Nainar) Vol. II., p.28.
48. Sardesai - Selection from the Peishwas Daftar., Vol. 28., L.No. 60.
49. Ananda Ranga Pillays Diary., Vol. VI.,p.369.
50. Ibid., p.364.

Jung. If he falls in battle you shall march to Aurangabad, and I will give you the Subhas of the Deccan, but if it falls out as you fear, it is the will of God[51]".

After speaking to him in the above manner, Duplcix loaned £. 50,000 on the surety of Muzzafar Jung. Dupleix also increased the strength of the French battalion to 2000 Europeans; These armies were placed under the command of d'Auteuil. Then the allies were sent to Villianallur where the armies of Muzaffar Jung lay encamped.

Nasir Jung arrived in the Carnatic in the middle of March and encamped at Valudavur village which was 35 miles from Pondicherry. From Valudavur he sent messages to the English and to Nawab Muhammad Ali to come and join him.

Nasir Jung's army was 300,000strong,besides this he had 800 pieces of cannon and 1300 elephants. His ally, the Maratha leader Murari Rao Gorpade had 10,000 horse. Moreover he was joined by Nawab Muhammad Ali at Villipuram (Belpur) with 6000 horse while the English under the command of Lawrence, sent a contingent of 600 Europeans, Lawrence joined the camp of Nasir Jung on the 22nd March. On his arrival he was appointed to the command of the Mughal troops by Nasir Jung[52].

Lawrence advised Nasir Jung to change the position of his troops and to station them between Villiyanallur and Pondicherry so that supplies to Chanda Sahib and Muzaffar Jung might be cut off. But Nasir Jung seems to have regarded it as beneath his dignity to accept this advice and exclaimed, " What shall the great Nasir Jung, the son of Nizamul-mulk even for an advantage seem to retreat before so despicable an enemy? No he would march and attack them in front[53].

This passage clearly reveals the petty notions of prestige that limited the vision of our Indian Princes in the 18th Century while power was fast slipping from their incapable hands.

The appointment of Lawrence to the command of the Mughal forces shows that Nasir Jung recognised the superiority of the English tactics in fighting, but his obsession with his notions of princely dignity and false prestige prevented him from accepting the advice of Lawrence.

The Mughal forces occupied Gingee on the 18th March 1950[54]. On the 4th April a cannonade took place but it proved ineffective. Meanwhile, the

---

51. Ibid.
52. Orme " A History of the Military transactions of the British Nation in Indostan., Vol. 1., p. 139.
53. Cambridge-"Account of the war in India., p. 6.
 Malcolm-Life of Lord Clive.,p.5.
54. Srinivasa Chari-Ananda Ranga Pillay. The Pepys of French India., pp. 158.

affairs in the French Camp took a serious turn owing to a mutiny among the soldiers led by thirteen disgruntled French-Officers[55]. The French soldiers had borne the brunt of the fighting both at Amboor and Tanjore. The soldiers after returning from the siege of Tanjore demanded that they might be relieved of further field duty.

Dupleix complied with their demand and to placate the replacing soldiers he gave them one month's batta (allowance) in advance[56].

The French officers were not to be placated in the above manner, and they refused to fight. D' Auteuil the French commander considering his position to be untenable, retired to Villiyanallur inspite of Chanda Sahib's remonstrances. Chanda Sahib, finding himself helpless, also retired to Pondicherry after suffering a great deal of harassment at the hands of the Marathas and the troops of Nawab Muhammad Ali.

Muzaffar Jung preferred to stay behind, and to appeal to his uncle's sense of mercy rather than suffer the ignominy of a retreat[57].

Nasir Jung had orginally tried to reach a settlement with his nephew by promising to grant jaghirs both to Muzaffar Jung and Chanda Sahib and also to repay the debts that he might have incurred with the French[58]. Muzaffar Jung refused this offer in the presence of Mons. Bussy, by replying to Nasir Jung's emissaries that no negotiations could take place without the concurrence of Dupleix[59].

Now Muzaffar Jung sent emissaries to Shah Nawaz Khan asking him to intercede on his behalf with his uncle. Thereafter, Shah Nawaz Khan exerted himself on Muzaffar Jung's behalf and extracted a promise from Nasir Jung that he would not harm the person of his nephew and that he would restore the possessions of Muzaffar Jung to him once again.

After getting these assurances, Muzaffar Jung went to pay his respects to his uncle, and the latter, for reasons of security, promptly arrested him and kept him in prison. No sooner did Dupleix hear of Muzaffar Jung's intention to surrender to his uncle than he placed the family of Muzaffar Jung at Pondicherry under strong guard lest they should escape[60].

---

55. Ibid., p. 159.
    Orme–"A History of Military transactions of the British Nation in Indostan.," Vol. I., p. 139.
56. Srinivasachari – Ananda Ranga Pillay the Pepys of French India., p. 160.
    Orme – Vol. I., p. 143., Malleson - p. 253.
57. Srinivasachary – Ananda Ranga Pillay – The pepys of French India., p. 162.
    Orme – "A History of the Military transactions of the British Nation in Indostan., p.141.
58. Ananda Ranga Pillays Diary., Vol. VI., pp. 435; 448.
59. Ibid.
60. Orme - "A History of Military transactions of the British Nation in Indostan.," Vol. I., p. 141.

Muzaffar Jung's imprisonment was not rigorous and he was soon able to establish contacts with Dupleix at Pondicherry and communicate with the latter.

The courtiers and nobles in the camp of Nasir Jung were averse to the idea of inflicting any harm on Muzaffar Jung, the favourite grandson of the late Nizamul-Mulk. As a matter of fact an influential party headed by Syed Lashkar Khan was in favour of conferring the Nawabship of the Carnatic on Muzaffar Jung by way of arriving at a compromise with the French who were dead set against Muhammad Ali, and thus resolving the conflict in the Carnatic once for all. It was obvious that Nasir Jung could not afford to prolong his stay in the Carnatic, far removed from his seat of power. Moreover the Maratha generals like Murari Rao, Janoji Nimbalkar and Chandra Shekar Jhadav were anxious to return to their homes as the rainy season was fast approaching[61]. Even Shah Nawaz Khan, the Diwan, was anxious to return to the Deccan soon, and he tried to persuade his master Nasir Jung, who was demanding the person of Chanda Sahib, to confer Tanjore and Trichinopoly on the latter by way of a speedy settlement and return to the Deccan[62].

The Peshcar, Ramdas Pandit was at heart a keen partisan of Muzaffar Jung and he was quite willing to be won over to the French side[63].

Thus it was clear that almost all the Deccan nobles were anxious to return to their homes and to bring the conflict to an end.

Though the imprisonment of Muzaffar Jung had apparently brought the whole of the Carnatic at the feet of Nasir Jung, the situation was really explosive. The Mughul camp was vacillating and it was divided in its loyalties.

In the midst of these confusing and contradictory advices Nasir Jung spent a full month in complete inaction at Valudavur. During this period he ordered the seizure of the French factories at Masulipatam and Yanam. His army captured Masulipatam in May, and Yanam in July 1750.

On hearing this Dupleix, quite undeterred despatched a strong detachment of 200 Europeans and 300 Sepoys, and cannon to recover Masulipatam. The French succeeded in taking it by surprise[64].

Dupleix also opened negotiations with Nasir Jung and tried to make it appear that d' Auteuil had withdrawn from the field of battle at his express commands. Dupleix also showed his willingness to come to a settlement

---

61. Ananda Ranga Pillay's Diary., Vol. VII.
62. Ibid.
63. Orme - "A History of the Military transactions of the British Nation in Indostan., Vol. I., p.146.
64. Ibid.

with Nasir Jung on two conditions, namely that Chanda Sahib should be confirmed as the Nawab of the Carnatic, and Muzaffar Jung should receive back his hereditary dominions[65]. Dupleix addressed six communications to Nasir Jung in this connection, but finding that the latter disdained to reply he wrote the following letter to Nasir Jung.

[66]"I wrote you two letters, but you have neither answered them nor returned the peons. Two of your chief messengers came here on Thursday and said that you desired peace and that you would return to your country as soon as affairs here had been settled and before the rains set in. I told them that I also desired peace and had written to you but that you had not answered and that I was prepared for peace or war just as you should choose. Though the two messengers were unworthy to stand before me, yet I spoke with them out of respect for you. They excused your delay and departed saying that I and you were of the same mind and that on their return they would desire you to write to me. I have waited till now but no reply arrived. Moreover your troops have plundered my villages and molested my people. Today therefore I have determined to send out my troops as you are resolved on war. Do not suppose that I am fighting now for Muzaffar Jung or Chanda Sahib. You and I are now enemies and they have nothing to do with it. I shall come and you also must make ready".

At this juncture Major Stringer Lawrence offered to negotiate between the French and the Mughals but Dupleix informed Nasir Jung, that he would never accept the English mediation. Thus there was a complete stalemate in the negotiations between the two powers. While these discussions were going on, the country and the people suffered a lot. The country was devastated by the depredations of the troops. Prices of food grains and other articles soared high and even drinking water became scarce. The sufferings of the poor went unheeded.

In the meantime, Dupleix received a letter from Nawab Shah Nawaz Khan, the Diwan of Nasir Jung, informing him that the letters written hitherto by Dupleix to Nasir Jung were not shown to the latter as they were written in an impolite and arrogant tone.

Shah Nawaz Khan wrote to Dupleix [67].

"Your letter to Nasir Jang was not politely written. Even the Sultan of Rum and Ahmed Shah Padshah write politely to Nasir Jung when Nadir Shah invaded the country, seized Muhammed Shah Padshah was still treated with the usual respect.

How great the difference between you, the master of one seaport and Nasir Jung the Padshahs' deputy throughout the Deccan! Should you not

65. Ibid., p. 143.
66. Ananda Ranga Pillays Diary., Vol. VII., p. 33.
67. Ibid., Vol. VII., p. 42.

therefore treat him with due reverence? He has even treated you with respect, but now you have been brought to ruin, by the ill advice of others. We have captured Muzaffar Jung the Nawab's relative who went astray. If you had only sent us his family whom you have treated honourably you would have been more esteemed than ever. As your former letters were not politely written I did not communicate them to Nasir Jung, but your last letter is different; I shall show it to him and send his reply".

To this admonishing letter of Shah Nawaz Khan, Dupleix, sent a flaunting reply saying that he was aware of only two Padshahs, namely the Emperor of Delhi and the King of France, and that if Nasir Jung claimed to be the deputy of the Mughal Emperor, he was his equal in that he was the deputy of the King of France. With regard to the releasing of Muzaffar Jung's family Dupleix wrote, that even the Padshah's army could not secure freedom for them[68].

This letter of Dupleix reveals to us not only his arrogant self-confidence but also the little regard he had for the Native Powers. He seems to have realised the fact that the facade of Native Power was resting on crumbling foundations, and that it would fall to pieces sooner or later.

While this correspondence was going on, the courtiers of Nasir Jung lead by Syed Lashkar Khan tried to persuade the Nawab to receive his nephew, Muzaffar Jung into favour, and bestow the Carnatic on him.

They were averse to make Muhammad Ali the Nawab of the Carnatic, as they felt it would result in bloodshed once their backs were turned from the Carnatic. They impressed on Nasir Jung the inadvisability of staying too long in the Carnatic and exposing the Deccan to the dangers of maladministration.

Owing to their endeavours, Nasir Jung agreed to receive Dupleix's envoys; So, Shah Nawaz Khan once again wrote to Dupleix to send his envoys to the Mughal camp for discussions. He advised Dupleix to go by the wishes of Nasir Jung and wrote to him saying[69];

"You wrote that the Padshah's whole army (were it to come) could not secure even a sight of Muzaffar Jang's family. But what do we want with them? We have him who is useful to us and we need no more. Surely you were unwise to write that we cannot appoint anyone to the Subah of Arcot without your consent. A wise man would not have written so. What have you to do with our countries? Write to me of your welfare and remember that Nasir Jung is the Padshah of the Deccan".

68. Ananda Ranga Pillay's Diary.. Vol. VII., p. 43.
69. Ibid., VII., p. 53.
Orme - "A History of the Military Transactions of the British Nation in Indostan"., Vol. I., p. 1[illegible]

Inspite of his grandiloquent and pompous letters, Dupleix was glad at this opportunity of arriving at a speedy settlement and sent two members of his council M. Du. Bausset and Monsieur Delarche, as envoys to Nasir Jung's camp[70].

The French mission stayed in the Mughal camp for eight days. They demanded that the dominions of Muzaffar Jung should be either restored to him or bestowed on his son, and that Chanda Sahib should be made the Nawab of the Carnatic.

Nasir Jung who insisted that Chanda Sahib should be surrendered to him, did not agree to these proposals, and the French mission was dismissed without achieving any purpose.

Though the Freneh mission apparently proved abortive, they gained immensely by their stay in the Mughal camp. They were able to effectively sow the seeds of disaffection in the Mughal camp. The Mughals were getting impatient of their prolonged stay in the Carnatic and they were only too willing to entertain any proposal that would get them out of the impasse.

Among the prominent Mughal nobles, the French were able to win over to their side the Pathan nobles of Cuddapah, Kurnool and Savanur[71]. These nobles were dissatisfied with Nasir Jung because he was demanding tribute from them.

The French envoys by their stay in the Mughal camp gained a clear insight into the minds of the Mughal nobles and their anxiety to return home.

One is not therefore, surprised to hear that they were even advised by Shah Nawaz Khan and Ramdas Pandit to make a surprise attack on Nasir Jung's camp so that the latter could be induced to leave the Carnatic and confer Arcot on Chanda Sahib and Adoni on Muzaffar Jung[72].

The English Commander Major Stringer Lawrence, scenting the activities of the French in the Mughal camp, tried to warn Nasir Jung in an interview he had with the latter, but the interpreter deliberately failed to convey the actual meaning of Lawrence's words to Nasir Jung, who remained blissfully ignorant of the developments in his own camp[73]. Plots and intrigues began to thicken day by day, and divide the courtiers of Nasir Jung.

Secret correspondence between Dupleix and the Mughal nobles to mention a few, Ramadas Pandit, Murari Rao Ghorpade and the Pathan Nawabs

---

70. Ibid., pp. 143, 145.
71. Ananda Ranga Pillay's Diary., Vol. VII., p. 98.
72. Ibid.
73. Orme. - Vol., I., p. 145.

continued to increase[74]. This was possible because streams of men were allowed to move freely between Pondicherry and Valudavur[75].

Meanwhile Dupleix, gaining confidence from the reports of his envoys sent instructions to the French Generals Mons.Law and d'Auteuil to attack the camp of Nasir Jung. The French attacked the Mughal camp on the night of 12 April 1750 and even succeeded in penetrating a distance of one mile[76]. This made Nasir Jung realise the danger to which his camp was exposed. Already, horses and cattle, were dying in great numbers in his camp for lack of fuel and fodder.

He, therefore, decided to move his camp to Arcot and from there to return to the Deccan as early as possible after settling the question of the Nawabi of Arcot. Before he moved on, to Arcot, Nasir Jung held a Durbar with a view to confer the Nawabi of Arcot on Muhammad Ali, but as this was met with bitter opposition from both Syed Laskhar Khan and Shah Nawaz Khan, the former pleading that it would alienate the French, while the latter spoke in favour of Chanda Sahib, he broke up the camp without coming to any decision and proceeded to Arcot[77].

Prior to his departure, the English Commander Lawrence, had an interview with Nasir Jung on 21st April 1750, and during the course of the interview he requested him to sanction the grant of the Poonamalle country to the English. But Nasir Jung felt, that such a measure might lower the dignity of the Nizam. Morever the Diwan Shah Nawaz Khan, who favoured the French at heart was also against it. So Nasir Jung in order to evade the issue asked Lawrence to accompany him to Arcot, where he said he would think over the matter carefully.

Lawrence did not like the idea of the Mughals moving to Arcot, and he advised Nasir Jung against the imprudence of adopting such a course. He said that the Mughals by remaining at Valudavur could effectively prevent the outbreak of hostilities[78].

But finding that Nasir Jung was neither inclined to accept his advice, nor grant the Poonamalle country to the English, he left the Mughal camp on the 22nd April for Fort St. David[79]. Shortly after his departure Nasir Jung proceeded to Arcot via Wandiwash[80].

74. Ananda Ranga Pillays Diary., Vol. VII., p. 80.
75. Ibid., p. 98.
76. Malleson-'History of French in India'., p. 256.
Orme - 'A History of the Military Transctions of the British Nation in Indostan"., p. 146.
77. Ananda Ranga Pillay's Diary., Vol. VII., p. 98.
78. Orme-"A History of the Military Transactions of the British Nation in Indostan"., Vol., 1., p. 146.
Dodwell - Madras Despatches, (1744-1755)., p. 113.
79. Ibid.
80.. **Ananda Ranga Pillay's Diary., Vol. VII., p. 147.**

After his arrival at Arcot another Durbar was held on the 3rd May, in which Syed Lashkar Khan, and the Pathan Nawabs led by Abdul Nabi Khan of Cuddapah pleaded for the release of Muzaffar Jung. After promising to fulfil their desire, Nasir Jung despatched Syed Lashkar Khan, Syed Sherif and Rajah Ramachandra Jhadav; to Hyderabad to put down the Maratha depredations.

Inspite of his having promised to set Muzaffar Jung free, Nasir Jung did not do so, as he was afraid that his nephew might rebel against him.

Thus Nasir Jung remained in a state of indecision at Arcot sometimes contemplating the release of his nephew and at other times wishing to confer the Carnatic on Chanda Sahib.

As late as the 26th May, Dupleix, received messages from Jayaram Pandit, the agent of Shah Nawaz Khan, that Nasir Jung would confer Trichinopoly and Tanjore on Chanda Sahib, leaving Arcot in the control of Shah Nawaz Khan, who would wait for four months, and if Chanda Sahib's conduct proved satisfactory during that period, would confer Arcot also on him[81]. In the meantime plots began to thicken around the person of Nasir Jung. The French attempted twice to bring about the escape of Muzaffar Jung with the connivance of the guards, but failed[82].

Muzaffar Jung's imprisonment was never rigorous. Every consideration was shown to him as befitted his dignity and rank. A separate tent was allotted to him where he would receive officers. But after reaching Arcot, Nasir Jung, suspecting his nephew, placed him in a fort and made his confinement somewhat stringent. Muzaffar Jung, taking this as a personal insult tried to commit suicide, but was prevented from doing so by the prison guards.

On hearing about this, Nasir Jung sent Shah Nawaz Khan to his nephew to assure him that he would be released soon, and that his jagirs would also be restored to him. Nasir Jung was anxious to depart to the Deccan soon but at the same time he was eager to collect the arrears of tribute from the Carnatic.

Nasir Jung sent away a large number of the Mughal troops to the Deccan under the impression that he would be leaving the Carnatic soon. The troops that remained behind, suffered from disease and pestilence. They were all anxious to depart to their homes as the rainy season was setting in. Countless bullocks, horses and other animals died in the camp daily and one of the vakils in the camp of Nasir Jung wrote; "The place stinks so that none can lie down there[83]"

The camp was full of rumours about Muzaffar Jung being released and set up as a rival to his uncle. Disgusted with the prolonged and indefinite

81. Ibid., p. 192.
82. Ibid., p. 182.
83. Anantaji's Fandit's letter - Ananda Ranga Pillay's Diary., Vol. VII., p. 131.

stay in the Carnatic groups of horsemen secretly began to leave the camp daily.

Nasir Jung was oblivious of the things that were happening in his camp. He spent his time in drunken bouts in the company of the Pathan Nawabs, Abdul Nabi Khan of Cuddapah, Himmat Bahadur Khan of Kurnool, Abdul Karim Khan of Savanur and Bankapur. On hearing about this Dupleix remarked;

"They are behaving like children or drunkards instead of strong and prudent rulers[84]".

Dupleix now ordered the seizure of the forts around Arcot, and the fortresses of Tiruvati, Villipuram and Chidambaram were seized by the French forces. Dupleix also gave orders to the French Troops to seize Valudavur.

Seeing the belligerent activities of the French, Nawab Muhammad Ali, sought Nasir Jung's permission to march against the French. After obtaining his permission he wrote to the English for reinforcements and also sent a sanad to them confirming the grant of the Poonamalle and the Devanampatnam territories. He also despatched a sum of Rs. 20,000 towards the expenses of the English army in lieu of the revenues of the Poonamalle country[85].

Realising that the rise of Chanda Sahib, would spell disaster to their interests the English despatched Capt.Cope with 400 Europeans and 1500 men to help Muhammad Ali; Cope, joined the latter at Tiruvati on the 30th July 1750[86].

The French garrisoned Tiruvati, but they would not take the initiative in opening hostilities; So Muhammad Ali was held up before Tiruvati till August, with his army encamped on the northern bank of the river Pennar.

Capt.Cope, suggested to Muhammad Ali, that the Nawab's troops should make a general assault while the English would batter the walls of the Fort, but the Nawab's army refused to undertake such a perilous task.

Then, it was decided that the combined armies of the Nawab and the English should be arranged within gunshot distance of the Fort. Seeing these manoeuvres, the French commander, La Touche, demanded from the English an explanation for having stationed themselves within firing distance from the Fort, in view of the fact that the English and the French were not at war[87].

84. Ibid., p. 250.
85. Dodwell - Madras Despatches (1744-1755)., p. 114.
86. Malleson - 'History of French in India'., p. 257.
Orme-'A History of the Military Transactions of the British Nation in Indostan'., Vol. 1., p. 148.
Dodwell - Madras Despatches, (1744-1755)., p. 148.
87. Orme - Vol. 1., p. 148.

Capt.Cope, replied that the English had come in the capacity of the allies of Nawab Muhammad Ali, and as such they would fight against all those with whom the Nawab was at war. After this, fire was exchanged between the garrison inside the fort and the battalions outside. Owing to their entrenched position the losses sustained by the French were negligible; the English lost 10 Europeans, and 50 sepoys while Nawab Muhammad Ali lost 200 men.

Feeling discouraged, Muhammad Ali, suggested that their troops should be moved west so that their communications with Arcot might not be impaired, but as Cope's instructions were not to go beyond the outskirts of Fort St. David, he suggested stationing the troops between Tiruvati and Pondicherry so that the French line of communications could be cut off. But his advice was not to the liking of Muhammad Ali. Capt.Cope, also asked for the money due to the English for the services rendered by them to the Nawab, who, now expressed his inability to meet the demands of the English at once.

On hearing this Major Stringer Lawrence, who happened to be acting as the Governor of Fort St. David asked Cope to come back and the latter returned to Fort St. David on the 19th August 1750[88].

Soon after the withdrawal of the English, the French, strengthened, by the arrival of reinforcements from Valudavur, completely routed the troops of Muhammad Ali and the Nawab was forced to fly to Arcot with only two or three attendants[89].

This was a great victory to the French and Dupleix, to commemorate it distributed sugar to the people of Pondicherry, saying to the merchants, that all their troubles would soon be over[90].

Even this defeat of Muhammad Ali did not strike Nasir Jung with the seriousness of the situtien. Once or twice he made disultory efforts to march against the French but the pro - French party in his camp dissuaded him from doing so saying that it was beneath the dignity for a potentate like Nasir Jung to march in person against a mere body of merchants, and that only the Mughal sardars must be sent against the French[91].

Meanwhile the Pathan Nawabs in the Mughal camp maintained an active correspondence with Chanda Sahib to which Dupleix was also privy. Courtiers engaged themselves in active intrigue, and we hear from Ananda Ranga Pillay, that even Shah Nawaz Khan did not hesitate to advise the

---

88. Dodwell - Madras Despatches, (1744-55)., p. 114.
Orme. - 'A History of the Military Transactions of the British Nation in Indostan'., Vol. I., p. 149.
89. Ibid., p. 156.
90. Ananda Ranga Pillay's Diary., Vol. VII., p. 363.
91. Tuzuki - Walajahi, (Eng. Trans. by Nainar)., Vol. II., p. 44.

French to attack Valudavur, in order to impress Nasir Jung, so that he could be induced to leave the Carnatic, after settling its affairs in favour of the French.

Dupleix, taking advantage of Nasir Jung's lethargy instructed his general Monsieur Bussy, to capture the fortress of Gingee, and the latter proceeded to Arcot. The impregnable fortress of Gingee was captured by Bussy on the 11th September with difficulty, which made Dupleix write[92];

" As to the spot from which the Rock was scaled undoubtedly, we were dealing with men willing to allow things to occur because the numbr of those who entered was insufficient to lose his head".

While the conquest of Gingee increased the prestige of the French immensely, it also had the effect of rousing Nasir Jung from his apathetic state. Realising the seriousness of the situation, he made up his mind to march against the French. He instructed Muhammad Ali to march in advance, and also sent word for reinforcements to the English, at Fort St. David[93].

The English Governor Saunders expressed his willingness to help Nasir Jung in the ensuing struggle, in lieu of the Poonamalle and the Devanampatnam territories. He also insisted that the English should be allowed to act as Principals against the French in the ensuing war.

Nasir Jung also recalled some of the troops that were on their way to the Deccan, and after their rejoining him he proceeded towards Gingee and reached the Cheyyar river in the middle of October.

Meanwhile, Dupleix, who was engaged in active correspondence with the Pathan Nawabs, Rajah Ramachander Jhadav and Ramdas Pandit, wrote to them that he would be greatly pleased if Muzzaffar Jung was made the Subedar of the Deccan once Nasir Jung was over thrown, which he proposed to bring about with their connivance[94]. In these letters the monetary benefit to be derived by the conspirators on the consummation of their plot was left deliberatély vague by Dupleix. But they assumed it would be considerable and that the amount would run into several lakhs

In reply, to these letters of Dupleix, the Pathan Nawabs and Rajah Ramdas Pandit sent word that the French should march towards Arcot in order to overthrow Nasir Jung[95].

But the French Commander d'e Auteuil, lost his heart on hearing about the huge hordes of Nasir Jung's army and hastily retreated to Gingee from

92. Versailles Records No. 3751.
93. Dodwell - Madras despatchs, (1744–1857).. p. 117.
94. Ananda Ranga Pillay's Diary., Vol., VII., p.304.
95. Ramdas Pandit was originally inthe employment of Anwar-ud-din when the latter was the Nazim of Chicacole, and gradually came into prominence in the Durbar of Nizamul-Mulk. Later Nasir Jung conferred on him the title of Rajah and made him the Peshkari-Bakshi of the Army - - - Tuzuk -i-Walajahi.

Chetpattu, where he had previously gone after the fall of Gingee; Dupleix tried to console himself with the thought that the French retired not because of lack of confidence but owing to the heavy rains that obstructed smooth communications.

Conditions in the army of Nasir Jung were far from satisfactory. The river Cheyyar was in floods and cattle were dying in great numbers for lack of fodder; The army could make only four miles a day with the greatest difficulty; Nasir Jung himself was forced to march in the rear of the army and not in front. The price of foodstuffs rose steeply and the people were put to great hardships[96]. Seeing the pitiable condition of the army the Mughal Sardars lost heart and advised the Nizam to make peace. Even the Diwan Shah Nawaz Khan advised the Nizam to defer fighting till a favourable opportunity occurred[97].

Dupleix, to induce d'Auteuil to take up the offensive against the Mughals, sent a faithful account of the plight of the Mughal army to the latter, but d' Auteuil pleading sickness retired to Pondicherry on the 22nd October, 1750. There after La Touche was appointed to the command of the French forces.

Nasir Jung, in the last week of October, reached within 16 miles of Gingee and halted there. Though his army was considerably less than what it was, when he first arrived in the Carnatic; he was still able to command 60,000 foot, 45,000 horse, 700 elephants and 360 pieces of cannon[98].

A skirmish took place between the two armies on the evening of the 24th October but owing to heay rain, neither party gained any decisive advantage[99].

On account of heavy rains the communications of the Mughal camp with the nearby neighbouring villages were cut off, and severe sickness began to spread in the camp. Even the French garrison in the fortress of Gingee was short of provisions but Dupleix saw to it that a regular supply of provisions was sent to Gingee.

Conditions in the Mughal camp began to deteriorate day by day and this state of things continued up to the month of December. Seeing the condition of his camp, Nasir Jung grew anxious and wanted to return, to the Deccan soon.

With this object in view, he once again opened negotiations with Dupleix through his agent Qazi Dayem[100]. Qazi Dayem accordingly sent his

96. Ananda Ranga Pilly's Diary., Vol. VII., p. 402.
97. Ibid., pp. 401, 404, 405.
98. Orme.-'A History of the Military Transactions of the British Nation in Indostan'., Vol. I., p. 153.
99. Ananda Ranga Pillay's Diary., Vol. VII., p. 420.
100. Ibid., Vol. VII., p. 423.

emissary Krishnaji, to Dupleix, and conveyed to him in a letter that Nasir Jung was willing to let bygones be bygones and would visit Pondicherry to treat with Dupleix. In spite of his previous intrigues Dupleix also expressed his willingness to come to a settlement with the Nizam, and informed Qazi Dayem of the same, and also assured him that the French would cease fighting while, the negotiations were being carried on. After this understanding, Krishnaji returned to the camp of Nasir Jung.

Though Dupleix expressed his willingness to come to a settlement with Nasir Jung, he also at the same time came to an understanding with the Pathan Nawabs, by which it was agreed that the French were to attack the Mughal camp in case an agreement was not reached, on the receipt of a message from the conspirators. It was decided that the conspirators in the meanwhile should withdraw and station themselves with their armies at a short distance from the main camp, and hoist the French flag at a convenient moment. A French Standard was secretly conveyed into the Mughal camp for this purpose[101].

Dupleix, assured of success in either case, seems to have decided to let chance take its own course. On the one hand he expressed to the agents of Nasir Jung to get the treaty ratified, while on the other, he sent instructions to La Touche to attack the Mughal camp as soon as the signal was received from the conspirators.

Nasir Jung in the end, agreed, to set free Muzaffar Jung, to appoint Chanda Sahib as the Nawab of the Carnatic and to restore the Port of Musulipatam to the French. On receiving the above terms Dupleix sent instructions to La Touche to suspend hostilities but they reached him too late[102].

The Pathan Nawabs, on hearing that an amicable settlement was being arrived at between Nasir Jang and the French became alarmed of their own safety. They wanted to prevent this at any cost, and on the night of Wednesday the 3rd December, they sent word to La Touche to attack the Mughal camp.

La Touche, was ignorant of the latest developments at Pondicherry and so, after consulting Bussy, led an attack against the Mughal camp in the early hours of the dawn of the 4th December with 800 Europeans, 3000 sepoys and 10 field pieces[103].

The guide sent by the conspirators conducted the French, to the Mughal camp that was directly under the command of Nasir Jung. After marching

101. Malleson - 'History of the French in India', p. 266.

102. Ibid., p. 267.

103. Orme - 'A History of the Military Transactions of the British Nation Indostan.,' Vol. I., p. 155.

a distance of 16 miles the French reached the camp of Nasir Jung at about 4'o' Clock in the morning.

The Mughal camp extended over an area of 18 miles, where each noble had his own seperate quarters.

Some cavalry men going on their usual rounds in the night discovered the presence of the French and they opened fire, but they were soon overpowered by the French. The French then came upon the artillery of Nasir Jung, behind which were drawn about 2500 troops. Here the conflict became acute and the sound of the artillery discharges spread the alarm in the whole camp.

The Generals, who were faithful to Nasir Jung, at once ordered their troops to the place of action and no sooner was one body of Mughal troops were repulsed their place was taken by another, and even those who originally mounted to retire now rallied back and formed the rear[104].

The French field pieces proved to be of immense use at this juncture, and the continuous fire maintained by them, prevented the French army from being broken up by the Mughal cavalry. With great difficulty the French were able to make headway and their joy knew no bounds when after penetrating a distance of about 3 miles they espied the white French flag fluttering in the midst of a body of horse and foot. On seeing this LaTouche brought his troops to a halt and awaited news from the Pathan Nawabs.

The day previous to the French attack Mir Dayem, the advance gaurd of Nasir Jung suspecting the evil designs of the Pathan Nawabs warned him of the same but Nasir Jung failed to pay heed to this warning attributing the suspicion of Mir Dayem to his wild imagination[105]. In spite of this Nasir Jung to make sure sent a Chobdar to Janoji, but the latter, having joined the conspirators allayed the fears of Nasir Jung saving that his fears were baseless.

So when he was informed of the French attack Nasir Jung could not at first believe the news, all the more, because on the previous day only he had ratified the treaty with the French[106].

But when he became convinced of the truth he at once ordered the head of Muzaffar Jung to be cut off, declaring the French, action, as "the mad attempt of a parcel of Europeans". But when the executors went to the tent of Muzaffar Jung the latter pretended to be reading the Qoran, and Ramdas

104. Orme - 'A History of the Military Transactions of the British Nation in Indostan'., Vol. I., p. 55.

105. Tuzuk-i-Walajahi (Eng. Trans. by Nainar)., p. 55
Rahvaare Farooqi-Nasir Jung Shaheed.

106. Orme. - 'A History of the Military Transactions of the British Nation in Indostan'., Vol. I., p. 156.

Pandit who was a partisan of Muzaffar Jung bribed the executors to delay the execution[107].

After hearing of the French attack, Nasir Jung, prepared to dress himself, putting on a white tunic without any armour; He is said to have exclaimed a standing before a mirror; "Oh Mir Muhammad, may God preserve you"[108] Then, quite unarmed he mounted on an elephant with his family in the imari and went towards the scene of battle with a few torch bearers in attendance.

In the meanwhile messengers were pouring one after the other to inform Nasir Jung about the Franch advance. On hearing this Nasir Jung asked about the disposition of the various Sardars, upon which, he was informed of the inactivity of the Pathan Nawabs and the general confusion in the Mughal camp due to heavy inundation.

Then in the early hours of the dawn, Nasir Jung sighted the Pathan Nawabs with their troops standing aloof from the scene of battle[109].

On sighting them, Nasir Jung drove towards them and saluted them. The Nawabs on seeing the Nizam, pretended, not to be aware of his presence, but Nasir Jung saluting them a second time appealed to them to go and fight the common enemy as became brethren belonging to the same faith[110].

Abdul Nabi Khan, the Nawab of Cudapah, replied that he was not aware of any enemy; on hearing this Nasir Jung ordered his attendants to fire on the troops of the Pathans.

In the melee that ensued, Himmat Bahadur Khan the Nawab of Kurnool, discharged his musket at Nasir Jung, and the latter fell down dead when the bullet pierced his heart[111].

The body guard of Nasir Jung before they could recover from the shock of this dastardly action were cut down, while a few contrived to escape.

Abdul Nabi Khan after severing the head of Nasir Jung went to announce the news to Muzaffar Jung. The latter ordered his uncle's head to be placed on a pike so that it could be seen by the entire Mughal

---

107. Orme. - 'A History of the Military Transactions of the British Nation in Indostan'., Vol. I., p. 156.
108. Tuzuk-i-Walajahi - (Eng. Trans. by Nainar.,) Vol. II., 57.
Wilks. - 'Historical Sketches of South India'., Vol. I., p. 267.,
Rahvaare Farooqi - Nasir Jung Shaheed.
109. Orme. - 'A History of the Military Transactions of the British Nation in Indostan'., Vol. I., p. 157.
110. Ibid., 156.
111. Sardesai - 'Peshwai Daftars Records., Vol. XXVII., L. No. 93., D/23-12-1750 and L. No. 94., D/ 25-12-1750.
Burhan-ud-din-Tuzuk-i- Walajahi-(Eng. Trans. by Nainar)., Vol. II., p. 57.,
Rahvaare Farooqi - Nasir Jung Shaheed.

army. After raising the French Standard, the conspirators conveyed to La-Touche the news of the recent happenings. On receiving the above news La-Touche sent Mons.Bussy to compliment Muzaffar Jung on his success.

The whole Mughal camp was thrown into utter confusion by the sudden turn of events. Nawab Muhammad Ali and Shah Nawaz Khan on hearing of Nasir Jung's death fled to Chetpattu[112]. The Maratha Generals Janoji Nimbalkar and Râmchandra Jadhav immediately took charge of the three younger brothers of Nasir Jung; Nawab Salabat Jung, Nizam Ali Khan and Basalat Jung, who were in the camp as prisoners, and also of the family of Nasir Jung; but they handed over their charge to the Pathan Nawabs[113], when the latter threatened them, and encamped separately.

By 9 o' clock on the morning of the 4th, all fighting ceased and Muzaffar Jung occupied the state tent as the new Nizam, and was ready to receive homage from the Mughal nobles[114].

The Pathan Nawabs at first tried to surround Muzaffar Jung and seize the treasury of the late Nizam but they were effectively prevented from doing so by the French commander La Touche[115]. The Pathans demanded exorbitant sums from Muzaffar Jung for their assistance, but the latter put them off saying that he would settle the matter after going to Pondicherry[116].

Thereupon the Pathan Nawabs withdrew and encamped about 4 miles distance from the French camp.

Fearing that the Pathan Nawabs who had proved traitors to his uncle might also prove the same towards him, Muzaffar Jung, entrusted himself and his treasury to the care of the French. The Mughal army, whose pay, was in arrears began to clamour for it at this juncture; but Muzaffar Jung, pacified them with promises and decided to go to Pondicherry.

Before starting to Pondicherry he wrote letters to Syed Lashkar Khan and Hyder Quli Khan, the Daroga of Hyderabad, intimating them of his elevation and appealing to them to guard the frontiers of the State against the encroachment of the Marathas.

He also wrote a conciliatory letter to Shah Nawaz Khan on receiving which the latter came to pay his respects and joined Muzaffar Jung at Pondicherry.

---

112. Orme - 'A History of the Military Transactions of the British Nation in Indostan'., Vol. I., p. 156.
113. Sardesai - 'Peshwa's Daftari Record', Vol. XXV., L., No. 100 D/2-1-1751.
114. Orme. - "A History of the Military transactions of the British Nation in Indostan". Vol. I., p. 157.
115. Sardesai - "Peshwa's Daftari Records"., Vol. 25., L. No. 100.
116. Ibid.

Meanwhile, at Pondicherry, as soon as the news of Nasir Jung's death was received, Chanda Sahib, was so overwhelmed with joy that he ran through the streets of Pondicherry to Dupleix, and almost stifled him in his embrace[117].

Dupleix, to celebrate the event held a grand court at Pondicherry and received the compliments of the people; He instructed that special ballads should be composed and sung to commemorate the French victory. He also sent six deputies to compliment Muzaffar Jung, on his success[118].

Muzaffar Jung, amidst great pomp arrived in Pondicherry on the 26th December, 1750[119]. Out of gratitude to the French, he got the French flag also displayed among the emblems of his sovereignty. He was received at the gates of Pondicherry, by Dupleix and Chanda Saheb. Dupleix, triumphantly entered Pondicherry seated in the same palanquin as Muzaffar Jung.

Muzaffar Jung on his arrival at Pondicherry, unburdened his soul to Dupleix, concerning his fears of the Pathan Nawabs.

The Nawabs, themselves, came to Pondicherry the next day and placed their demands before Dupleix. They demanded that they must be exempted from paying the arrears of tribute to the Nizam due from them for the last three years, and that their territories should be increased by the addition of the surrounding areas belonging to the late Nawab Nasir Jung.

Dupliex firmly told them that their demands were exorbitant and it was impossible for Muzaffar Jung to comply with them. Instead, he suggested, that half the treasury of the late Nizam, should be divided among the Pathan Nawabs and other conspirators while the remaining half along with the Jewellery of the late Nizam, should go to Muzaffar Jung[120]. He also promised to see that they acquired some crown lands at low rates.

Finding that Dupleix was determined not to concede anything beyond this, the Nawabs closed in with this proposal, and swore on the Qoran to observe loyalty to the new Subah.

The treasury of Nasir Jung was supposed to contain £ 2 million, while his Jewellery was estimated at £. 500,000. Out of this Muzaffar Jung gave £. 50,000 to the French to be divided among their officers and troops who had fought at Gingee, while another £. 50,000 were given to meet the expenses incurred by the French during the course of the war[121].

117. Tuzuki - Walajahi-(Eng. Trans. by Nainar)., Vol. II., p. 61.

118. Orme - 'A History of the Milirary Transactions of the British Nation in Indostan',, Vol. I., p. 159.

119. Malleson. - 'History of the French in India'., p. 272.

120. Orme. - 'A History of the Military Transactions of the British Nation in Indostan'., Vol. I., p. 162.

121. Ibid.

On the 31st December, 1750, a grand Durbar was held by Muzaffar Jung, wherein Dupleix dressed in the native costume, was the first to render his homage to Muzaffar Jung[122].

Out of gratitude to the French, Muzaffar Jung apart from conferring the title of Zafar Jung on Dupleix, also appointed him as his deputy for the territories that lay to the South of the river Krishna[123]. Besides this he was also appointed the Nawab of the Carnatic and Mysore, while Chanda Sahib who was given the title of the Nawab of Arcot, was made his deputy. The Pondicherry currency was made legal tender throughout the Carnatic country and Dupleix was empowered to collect its revenues. The rank of a Mughal Mansabdar of 7000, and also the honour of the Fish Standard (Mahi maratib) was conferred on him. Apart from the above honours, Jaghirs besides Valudavur, yeilding a revenue of Rs. 10,000 per annum were given to Dupleix. Madame Dupleix, was given the title of Jahan-ara Begam.

The French were also given Masulipatam, Yanam and Karikal, and the country adjoining Pondicherry, territories that Dupleix had originally asked from Nasir Jang[124]. The revenues of these territorial grants were estimated at £. 36,000 sterling[125].

Technically speaking, Muzaffar Jung was only the subedar of the Deccan, and he did not have the right to give away territories without the permission of his liege lord the Mughal Emperor; But the Emperor during this period was only a figure head and his firmans were respected by the people, only, when it suited their purposes.

The treasury of Nasir Jung consisted of 18 chest of Jewels, a crore of Rupees besides bullion. These were divided into six portions among the following people, namely, Muzaffar Jung, Abdul Nabi Khan the Nawab of Cudapah, Himmat Bahadur Khan the Nawab of Kurnool and Abdur Karim Khan the Nawab of Savanur, Dupleix and the Marathas[126].

The Pathan Nawabs were rewarded in a suitable manner, Himmat Bahadur Khan of Kurnool receiving the title of Rustom Jung and the Raichur territories being added to his dominions. Abdul Nabhi Khan of

---

122. Ibid., p. 160.
123. Tuzuk-i-Walajahi-(Eng. Trans. by Nainar)., Vol. II., p. 61.
Malleson.- 'History of the French in India'., p. 273.
124. Peddapura Samsthana Charitramu., p. 88.
Malleson - 'History of the French in India'., p. 273.
125. Orme. - 'A History of the Military Transactions of the British Nation in Indostan'., Vol. I., p. 161.
Karaikal yielded Rs. 10,600, Masulipatnam with its adjoining dependancies. Rs. 14,4000, while territories round about Pondicherry yeilded Rs. 9,6000 - Orme.
126. Tuzuk-i-Walajahi (Eng. Trans. by Nainar)., Vol. II., p. 61.
Sultan Nawaz Khan Miratus Sikander.
Rahvaare Farooqi-Nasir Jung Shaheed.

Cudapah got the Jaghirs of Gandi Kota, Gooty and Gurram Konda while to Savanur was added the Jaghir of Sara.

Ramdas Pandit was given the title of Rajah Raghunath Das while Janoji Nimbalkar received the title of Maharajah Arjun Jaswant[127]. The brothers of Nasir Jung, Salabat Jung, Nizam Ali Khan and Basalat Jung were elevated to the rank of 7000, while, the sons of Nasir Jung were kept as prisoners.

Muzaffar Jung tried to conciliate Nawab Muhammad Ali Khan by sending a friendly letter to him through Janoji. The latter in order to gain time and await the future developments pretended to be friendly towards Muzaffar Jung but at the same time he continued to inform the English of all that was planned between him and the French[128]. He apparently, showed his willingness to agree to the suggestion put forward by Muzaffar Jung that he should be content with the possession of his father's treasures and some other Subah in Deccan instead of Arcot and Trichinopoly which were now to be conferred on Chanda Sahib[129]. Naturally, this behaviour of Muhammad Ali made Muzaffar Jung believe that the affairs of the Carnatic would be settled soon and peace restored there. So he decided to proceed to the Deccan.

But Mazaffar Jung, was feeling far from secure on the throne. His apprehensions about the Pathan Nawabs did not cease. Hence, he requested Dupleix to send along with him a French contingent upto Aurangabad.

Dupleix, was too glad to let go this opportunity. He knew that through the French Contingent he could always influence the Nizam, even though the latter might be in the far off Deccan. So, he agreed to send a French detachment consisting 300 Europeans and 2000 sepoys, 10 field pieces under the command of Mons. Bussy[130].

Muzaffar Jung was greatly elated by this and he granted to the French, Masulipatam and Yanam with the adjoining territories. Previous to this, he had also given to the French, Karikal and the surrounding territories in the Tanjore Country[131].

Thus Dupleix, by his subtle diplomacy, made Pondicherry the political axis of all events in the Deccan and the Carnatic. French influence in the whole of South India became profound and supreme. The sending of the French detachment with the Nizam, ensured against any change in the

---

127. Tuzuk-i-Walajahi-(Eng. Trans. by Nainar)., Vol. I., p. 61.
128. Orme. - "A History of the Military Transactions of the British Nation in Indostan."., Vol. I., p. 163.
129. 'History of the French in India.'., p. 271.
130. Ibid.
Orme. Vol. I., p. 163.
"Bussy in the Deccan"., p. 15.
131. Orme. - Vol. I., p. 161.

Nizam's policy towards the French. Its presence acted as a deterrent against anti - French cliques in the Nizam's court and it made Dupleix the virtual master of the whole of the South India, through the Deccan Subedar who was the representative of the Mughal Emperor.

The growth of French influence and power created great apprehensions in the mind of the English East India Company regarding the security of their trade on the Coromandal Coast. The English decided to defend their interests at the point of the sword. The following letter of Floyer, the Governor of Fort St. David to the Court of Directors, shows the vivid fears of the English at this juncture. He says[131A] "Company's affairs depend on a strong force to curb the French. It might have been better for trade if the country powers had been left to decide their own quarrels, but once the French attempted to surround the English settlements so as to be able to cut off their trade and supplies of provisions it was judged necessary to oppose them to avoid a situation ill in peace and worse in war".

In another despatch he further writes[132]. "Could the country powers settle their own affairs peace might be hoped for, but that is impossible".

Realising that the only way to save their trade interests, in view of the grants made to the French by Muzaffar Jung, was by supporting Nawab Muhammad Ali, the rival candidate, they decided to promote his interests as the Nawab of the Carnatic against Chanda Sahib.

On Muhammad Ali confirming the grant of the Poonamalle, St. Thome and Trivenderipuram territories, the English sent to him a detachment consisting of 280 Europeans and 300 sepoys under Gingens[133]. They also garrisoned the Fort of Trichinopoly under Captain Cope. At the same time they also appealed to the Mughal Emperor and the Dalwai of Mysore against the encroachments of the French and Chanda Sahib[134]. About this time the Rajah of Tanjore appealed to the English for help against the French and Chanda Sahib, and he agreed to give Devikotai to the English in return for their help.

Thus the English formed the spearhead of opposition in the Carnatic, consisting of Nawab Muhammad Ali, the Dalwai of Mysore, the Rajah of Tanjore, against the French and their nominee Chanda Sahib, and they were able to take Arcot from the French finally by the 25th November, 1751.

Muzaffar Jung left Pondicherry for the Deccan on the 7th January 1751[135], while his camp left 5 days later, as Dupleix needed sometime to choose the personnel of the French detachment and select an able commander.

---

131 A. Dodwell - Madras Despatches - (1744-1755) p. 121.

132. Ibid., p. 128.

133. Records of Fort St. George., C. C., 1751., L. No. 6., p. 2.

134. Ibid., p. 54., L. No. 113.

135. Malleson-History of the French in India., p. 272.

Mons. Bussy, was chosen as the commander of the French detachment which consisted of 300 Europeans, 2000 Sepoys, 10 field pieces and a large train of artillery[136]. Along with Bussy, Kerjean the nephew of Dupleix, and Vincens, Dupleix's stepson were sent to the Deccan as the second and third in command of the French detachment. Special care was taken in choosing the personnel of this detachment as its task was two-fold. It was to serve, not only the military needs of the Nizam but had to fulfil the political designs of Dupleix.

Dupleix hoped to control the whole of the Deccan Subedari, by effectively securing the Subedar on the side of the French. It was for this reason, that he did not hesitate to split up the small French army, in spite of the deadly struggle he had to carry on against the English in the Carnatic.

In spite of the support he received from the French, Muzaffar Jung's position on the throne was far from secure. The Mughal officers were greatly perturbed by the sudden turn of events, and in the army itself there were frequent desertions. The desertions of the Mughal soldiers were so frequent that Dupleix was forced to write to Muzaffar Jung that if it did not cease, he would have to recall his French army[137].

The Pathan Nawabs, in spite of the various rewards they received still remained disgruntled, and were always averse to discipline[138]. They tried by every means to create dissensions between the French and the Nizam, Himmat Bahadur Khan going to the extent of trying to entertain a separate and rival company of Europeans in his service. Dupleix on hearing of these intrigues advised Muzaffar Jung to placate these dissentient elements by fair words till a suitable opportunity should occur to crush them.

On reaching the precints of the river Krishna, the Pathan Nawabs sent word to their polygars to be ready to face all eventualities and to strengthen their arms and defences. While, this was the state of affairs in the Mughal camp, in Aurangabad Syed Lashkar Khan who desired to see, a son of Nizamul-Mulk seated on the masnad, preferably the eldest, Ghazi-ud-Din Khan Feroze Jung or even the young son of Nasir Jung, was carrying on active correspondence with Peishwa Balaji Baji Rao[138-A].

The Peishwa showed his willingness to march at the head of 400 troops against Muzaffar Jung, in return for the Subahs of Burhampur and Aurangabad

136. "Bussy in the Deccan"., p. 240.
Orme.—"A History of the Military Transactions of theBritish Nation in Indostan"., Vol. I, p. 16.
137. "Bussy in the Deccan"., (Eng. Trans.)., p. 20.
138. Selections from the Peshwa's Daftari Records., Vol. XXVIII, L. No. 71.
138-A. Rajwade., Vol. III, L. No. 372-A, 373.

with its treasury. Syed Lashkar Khan, agreed to these terms and awaited the arrival of Ghazi-ud-Din Khan Feroze Jung in the Deccan[139].

The Mughal Emperor on hearing of the death of Nasir Jung, conferred the Deccan Subedari, on Gazi-ud-Din Khan Feroze Jung and also instructed the various Qiledars to obey him. Ghazi-ud-Din while informing Nawab Muhammed Ali of the same, also appointed the latter through a letter dated 29th January 1751, as the Nawab of the Carnatic Painghat[140].

The Peishwa was also interested in seeing Ghazi-ud-Din Khan Feroze Jung succeed to the Deccan Subedari and he wrote to his agent Vasudev Pandit, in the Nizam's court to the following effect[141];

" The best course would be to re-instate Feroze Jang. If he does not arrive you should support Nasir Jang's son. If that also is not possible see that my plans succeed. I would not depart from these plans. Syed Lashkar Khan also mentions to carry out the proposals suggested before ". The Peishwa expresses the same sentiments in another letter[142]. "If Feroze Jang comes it is well and good. Otherwise by Gods Grace I am alone strong enough to defeat the enemy. See that the treasury is collected at one place and 25 to 30 lakhs are given to us. You should try to come out. The Pathans have been very arrogant and it is difficult to put them down for a year or so. The disease must be rooted out as long as it is new. Syed Lashkar Khan is a very capable man. Even if Nawab Nasir Jang is dead Syed Lashkar Khan should support Feroze Jang only, so that we may have common interest. Our dues should be paid up to enable me to mobilise my generals. Syed Lashkar Khan should try to meet me on the banks of the Godavary. Help should be taken from Sultanji's son Janaba Nimbalkar. By this the least possible blame would be attached to him (Syed Lashkar Khan). On the other hand his fame would reach as far as Delhi, Lahore and Multan for having preserved the Nawabs Dominions by securing the help of the Peishwa. A brave man should try to attain fame by taking advantage of an opportunity when he would get the least blame, and when it is possible for him to secure his own interests, as well as those of his friends ".

While these plans were being discussed against Muzaffar Jung, the latter along with his army reached the village of Rayachoti near the Lakkireddipalli pass, a village 25 miles to the south of Cudapah[143]. This was on 31st January, 1751. Here some of the Mughal officers, set fire to the neighbouring villages, in spite of Muzaffar Jung's orders to the contrary.

139. Ibid.
140. Records of Fort St. George., C. C. L. No. 30, 31, p. 14.
141. Rajwade., Vol. III, L. No. 374.
142. Ibid., L. No. 399.
143. G. S. Sardesai—"New History of the Mahrattas"., Vol. II, p. 320.
"Bussy in the Deccan"., p. 23.
Selections from the Peishwas Daftar., Vol. XXV, L. No. 109

The Nawab of Cudapah, who was on the look out for such an opportunity to create trouble, seized this opportunity and asked his followers to take revenge on the Nizam's men. The Afghan troops went into action immediately, but instead of attacking the Nizam's troops in the front, they attacked the rear where the Mughal ladies were quartered, which was a great affront. Muzaffar Jung wanted to attack them immediately, but Bussy, pacified him and sent an envoy to negotiate. The Pathan Nawabs conveyed to Bussy through the envoy. their willingness to come to terms, but their message to Muzaffar Jung at the same time was quite provocative. They sent word to him saying that they waited for him, sword in hand[144].

Muzaffar Jung, was stung to the quick by the arrogance of the Pathans, and he at once marched against them in spite of Bussay's remonstrances, leaving the French far behind. But the French soon joined Muzaffar Jung with their artillary and succeeded in putting the army of the rebels to flight.

During the course of the struggle the Nawab of Savanur was killed, while the Nawab of Kurnool, was severely wounded. Finding that the Nawab of Cudapah, was trying to escape from the battlefield Muzaffar Jung went, in pursuit of him leaving his men behind. Perceiving this Himmat Bahadur Khan, the Nawab of Kurnool, closed in, with his men and charged against the elephant of Muzaffar Jung[145]. The latter, greatly enraged, charged against the elephant of Himmat Bahadur Khan and lifted his sword to strike him down. Seeing this Himmat Bahadur Khan fatally struck him on the head with his javelin, while he himself was cut down by the sword of Muzaffar Jung almost at the same instant. Muzaffar Jung was seated in the howdah when the javelin struck him; Ramdas Pandit seeing the sad end of Muzaffar Jung realised, that it would create panic among the troops if they were to know it; So, he conveyed the dead body of Muzaffar Jung, in a sitting position into the camp in such a manner that it gave the impression of the Nawab being alive.

Then he conveyed the news of the Nawab's death, to the courtiers[146]. The news created great panic and confusion among the Mughals who had hardly recovered from the shock of Nasir Jung's death. The pay of the army was greatly in arrears and the nobles feared, that the army might revolt any time.

The party that was greatly affected by this unforseen calamity were the French. The death of Nawab Muzaffar Jung, destroyed all chances of their interfering in the affairs of the Deccan. But the astuteness and courage of Bussy, saved the French interests. He rose to the occasion, and he made all

144. Orme — A History of the Military Transactions of the British Nation in Indostan., Vol. I, p. [illegible]
145. ibid
146. Rajwade, Vol. III, L. No. 377A. dated 12-2-1751.

the Mughal nobles and generals who were in the camp to assemble and accept Salabat Jung, the third son of Nizamul-Mulk, as the Subedar of the Deccan[147].

The smooth manner in which Salabat Jung, was chosen as the Subedar, reveals the extent to which the French gained a hold on the mind of the Indian chiefs, and the awe in which the French Power was held. The two brothers of Salabat Jung also swore their loyalty to their brother, and the claims of Muzaffar Jung's son, were met, by the granting of Adoni, Raichur, Bijapur, Kurnool and Cudapah to him[148]. Thus a situation which contained potential germs for internecine warfare, and which would under ordinary circumstances have entailed an appeal to the far-off Mughal Emperor was brought under control by the strong personality of Mons. Bussy. The French action in getting Salabat Jung chosen as the Nizam, without any reference to the Emperor, was a veritable revolution. In fact it was a challenge to the supremacy of the Emperor.

Salabat Jung, was very mild by disposition, and neither Bussy nor Dupleix rated his intelligence highly. In fact, Dupleix, went to the extent of calling him a "duffer."

But the French preferred to carry out their ambitious designs through Salabat Jung, not only because he happened to be the eldest, among the three brothers who were in the camp, but, also, because he was more pliable than his more efficient younger brother Nizam Ali Khan.

Salabat Jung, was overwhelmed, by his sudden good fortune and he was full of gratitude to the French, the main instruments for his elevation. He not only confirmed all the grants made by Muzaffar Jung to the French but also placed the whole country south of the river Krishna, including Madura and Tinnevelley districts under the French control. He also granted to the French, the territories of Nizampatnam, Alammanar in Krishna Districts and Kondavid and Narsapur in the Godavary district, thus rounding off the French territory, around Masulipatam. He allowed the French, to rebuild their territory at Yanam, that was originally destroyed by the orders of Nasir Jung. Salabat Jung granted to Dupleix, Mahfuz Bandar in Chicacole district and distributed huge sums of money as presents to Bussy and other French officers in his camp.

He also requested Dupleix, to allow Bussy, along with the French detachment to accompany him, to Aurangabad.

Salabat Jung chose Ramdas Pandit as his Diwan and conferred on him the title of Bahadur.

147. Orme.--Vol. I.
"Peddapura Samsthana Charitramu"., p. 88.

148. "Bussy in the Deccan"., p. 24.

Dupleix, was greatly elated at the dextrous manner in which Bussy, procured so many benefits to the French. He advised Bussy, to maintain cordial relations with Raghunath Das and to proceed to Aurangabad. He wrote to Bussy[149]; "Keep it foremost in your mind that you are the law maker in that army; do not abuse but let all things concur to attain the end I desire. Your whole object and mine should be to retain the possessions of the company and increase them whenever possible; this must be your main purpose in whatever circumstances, you may be placed. - - - Once everything is settled affect great cautiousness to everybody and do your utmost to draw yourself the friendship of the people".

Bussy, on the receipt of the above letter replied in the following manner[150]; "I think the movement for us to achieve great things has come. From the highest to the lowest the whole army trusts in you alone and in the French nation. If you but make up your mind the treasures of Golcondah will be ours on our arrival there. I am of opinion that the nation can derive great benefit from the last revolt. It is too late for us to withdraw. All our energies have to be spent extending the glory of the French name and the welfare of the Company. I am sure we shall never meet a better opportunity. I shall do whatever lies in my power to attain the above mentioned ends. My earlier letters could not speak of the advantages but thanks to the genius of Ramdas Pandit, to the fear of French arms, to the veneration in which our nation is held and to the absolute conviction that they can do nothing of themselves if we were to abandon, we are in a position to dictate law and to draw all profits even greater ones than those we had hoped to obtain during Modin Khan's life time".

Yet, in another letter dated 22nd February 1751, Bussy wrote to Dupleix[151]; "My hands are tied for the time being but once I am in possession of your further orders let me act and you will be pleased with my management, while in Pondicherry you will be able to govern Golcondah and its dependencies as if you were there. I foresee too many good things to believe, that you would take any other view but that of supporting the new Nawab. Though we have but a handful of men we hold sway over everybody round about us".

The above correspondence between Dupleix and Bussy, shows the ambitious designs they entertained with regard to the French Policy in the Deccan and the rosy visions they had of French predominence in South India.

After receiving instructions from Dupleix, Bussy, with the French detachment accompanied Salabat Jung to Aurangabad. The army moved slowly from Cudapah and reached Kurnool on the 11th March, and there, after the

---

149. "Bussy in the Deccan"., p. 25.
150. Ibid.
151. Ibid.

French had put down a local rebellion against the Mughals, the army continued its onward journey, but ere long it had to face another menace, in the shape of the Marathas under the command of Peishwa Balaji Baji Rao[152].

We have already seen, that active correspondence took place between the Peishwa Balaji Baji Rao and Syed Lashkar Khan and that they had agreed to oppose Muzaffar Jung and place Ghazi-ud-Din Khan, the eldest son of Nizamul-Mulk on the masnad. But Syed Lashkar Khan, after hearing that Muzaffar Jung was killed and that Salabat Jung, also, a son of Nizamul-Mulk, was chosen as the Nizam, decided to accept the *fait accompli* and he wrote to the Peishwa not to carry on hostilities against Salabat Jung but to return to Poona[153].

But the Peishwa desired to reap the utmost benefit out of the troubled conditions in the Deccan and so he proceeded to the banks of the river Krishna with an army of 20,000. He stationed the Maratha armies at Nizam-Konda near Panagal in the vicinity of the confluence of the rivers Krishna and Tungabhadra[154], while the Nizam, lay encamped 15 miles down south.

The Peishwa though he made it appear that he had come to fight, did not actually like to force matters, and the Nizam's forces were also loth to risk a fresh battle. So, both sides decided to come to an understanding, and an agreement was reached on the 23rd March, through, Janoji Nimbalkar, by which it was decided that the Peishwa should be paid 17 lakhs of rupees to secure his neutrality in the war of succession. But of this sum only two lakhs was actually paid to the Peishwa on the spot, while the rest was guaranteed by the bankers. The Peishwa, further agreed to give up his claims to Khandesh and to the territory that lay between Aurangabad and Burhanpur for consideration of a further sum of 3 lakhs of rupees[155].

Having, bought off, the Maratha menace in the above manner, the army reached Aurangabad on the 29th June 1751[156].

On his arrival at Aurangabad, Bussy, played with consummate skill, on the fears of Salabat Jung, by speaking to him about the imminent French departure from the Deccan.

The timorous Salabat Jung pleaded with Bussy and the French to remain in the Deccan and gave them liberal presents, Bussy himself, receiving a sum of. £. 2,250,000[157]. Ultimately, owing to the importunities of Salabat Jung, Dupleix agreed to maintain a contingent of 2000 strong, at Aurangabad.

---

152. Ibid., p. 28.
153. Selections from the Peshawas Daftari Records., Vol. XXV, "Balaji Baji Rao, Peishwa and the Nizam, (1750-1751)"., L. Nos. 109-110.
154. G. S. Sardesai—"A New History of the Mahrattas"., Vol. II, pp. 308, 321.
155. G. S. Sardesai—"A New History of the Mahrattas"., Vol. II, p. 321.
156. Dodwell—Dupleix and Clive., p. 61.
157. "Bussy in the Deccan"., p. 29.

Bussy, on his arrival in the Deccan, chose a place for his troops which commanded the defences of the city. He was careful to see that he did not in his behaviour give offence to any of the premier nobles of the state, at the same time he saw that nothing escaped his vigilant eye, and by his tactful and firm behaviour, he laid a strong grip on the political life of the country. He also introduced, strict disciplinary rules in his army and saw that the soldiers did not indulge in drunken bouts and provoke the people by their insolent behaviour.

Salabat Jung, issued a firman by which he agreed to pay one lakh of Rupees for the French detachment, and he also empowered Dupleix, to depute any one he liked as the Nawab of the Carnatic[158].

Referring to this grant Dupleix, wrote to the Directors of the French East India Company "You will find in them an event which I had not anticipated and which is altogether the work of M. De. Bussy. It is a question of securing the Arcot Government for the Nation with power of regulating the annual payment to the Royal Treasury. This affair is of the highest importance to the Nation, deserves the closest attention. For it will dispense with the need of sending funds to India for your investment[159].

The above letter reveals to us the extent to which Dupleix's ambitions were fired on seeing the predominant position occupied by the French in the Deccan. No wonder, Mallesor wrote; "What a vista did it not hold out to a patriotic ambition? What dreams of empire, what visions of imperial dominion! Possessing the Karnatik by this policy, gaining the Dakhan...... the minarets of Jami Masjid, and the jewelled ornaments of the Peacock throne seemed near enough to excite the fancy and stimulate to irresistible action[160].

Dupleix, was not satisfied by merely getting a firman from Salabat Jung, he wanted, Bussy, to obtain a firman from the Mughal Emperor confirming the grants of Salabat Jung. The firman from the Mughal Emperor was duly obtained on the 13th September, but the English, at Madras, entertained serious doubts about the authenticity of the document.

Bussy's ego rose to such heights by these events that he even dreamed of sending embassies to the Mughal Emperor and to the King of France, and

---

158. Dodwell—Dupleix and Clive., p. 86.
Though Dupleix was declared as the Nawab of Carnatic on the advice of Bussy he did not openly accept that title. Bussy, asked him not to accept that title till Salabat Jung's position was secure on the throne.
— "Bussy in the Deccan"., p. 72.
159. Dodwell—Dupleix and Clive., p. 87.
160. Malleson.—"History of the French in India"., p. 353.

we find him writing to Dupleix; "I take upon myself to have the whole country up to the river Krishna granted to the French by the Emperor himself but we need European troops"[161].

But these ambitions schemes of Bussy, were, all brought to nought, due to the financial stringency from which the French East India Company always suffered.

The struggle in the Carnatic, between Chanda Sahib with French support on one hand, and Nawab Muhammad Ali with English support on the other, was still going on fiercely. Dupleix, tried to induce Muhammad Ali, to give up the struggle by making Salabat Jung issue a firman on 12th March 1751 granting to Muhammad Ali the Sarkars of Rajahmundry, Chicacole, Ellore, Masulipatam, Mustafanagar, Muzaffarnagar, along with two strong forts, with the arrears of tribute due from Anwar-ud-din Khan written off[161-A]. But, Nawab Muhammad Ali, did not give up the struggle in the Carnatic.

In the meantime Ghazi-ud-Din Khan, along with the Marathas was coming to the Deccan, to claim his fathers masnad. In spite of the understanding that was reached between the Marathas on the banks of the river Krishna, neither the Marathas, nor Salabat Jung, took it seriously. Ramdas Pandit openly violated the agreement by attacking and appropriating Maratha treasure of about 5 lakhs near Aurangabad on the 22nd April[162].

Now, Bussy, wanted to anticipate the Marathas, by advising Salabat Jung to march against Poona, the seat of Maratha power. They also opened secret negotiations with Tara Bai, the enemy of the Peishwa. The Nizam's army left Aurangabad, on the 15th November, crossed the Godavary and continued their onward march towards the north ravaging the Maratha country on the way. The Peishwa, tried to meet the menace from the Nizam, by himself, marching south towards Aurangabad, at the head of 40,000 cavalry, ravaging his own villages on the way, so that the Mughals might not get any provisions[163].

Though the Nizam's forces won some initial victories, two months of desultory fighting, convinced Bussy, that it was difficult to defeat the Peishwa in a decisive battle[164].

---

161. "Bussy in the Deccan"., p. 144.
161-A. Srinivasachari.-Ananda Ranga Pillay—"The Pepy's of French India"., p. 199. Ananda Ranga Pillay's Diary., Vol. III, Appendix I.
162. G. S. Sardesai—" A New History of the Mahrattas"., Vol. II, p. 322.
163. Malleson—" A History of the French in India "., p. 362.
164. G. S. Sardesai.—"New History of the Mahrattas"., Vol. II, p. 323.
"The Nizam won victories at Parnar, Kukadi and plundered Shikarpur and Talegoan but had to retire to Pedgaon on seeing the junction of Raghoji Bhonslay's troops with that of the Peishwa"-Sardesai.
Orme.—"A History of the Military Transactions of the British Nations in Indostan"., p. 252.

The Nizm's officers like Syed Lashkar Khan and Janoji Nimbalkar, were at heart, averse to giving decisive blow to the power of the Peishwa, lest it should increase the power of the French and make them free from all rivals[165]. The Nizam's troops, whose pay was always in arrears and who had undergone great hardships for food and fodder were also anxious to return home.

The Peishwa himself, was willing to come to terms. So, he gave up the Fort of Triambak as a token of his goodwill towards Salabat Jung and the latter retreated to Ahmadnagar[166].

Hostilities, were soon brought to an end by both the sides concluding the agreement of Singwa, on 6th January, 1752[167]. Salabat Jung, returned to Aurangabad. His treasury was almost empty and his troops were clamouring for the arrears of pay that was held over for the last seven months. The troops remained quiet, apparently, owing to their awe of the French. While this was the condition of the Nizam's troops, Dupleix was writing urgent letters to Salabat Jung and Mons. Bussy to come to his help in the Carnatic against Nawab Muhammad Ali and the English[168].

Salabat Jung agreed to this and he decided to send Khwaja Namatullah Khan in advance to the Carnatic while he himself would proceed along with Bussy, to the banks of the Krishna to direct operations against Muhammad Ali from there. But all these plans came to naught by the unexpected and sudden death of Rajah Raghunath Das (Ramadas Pandit) the Divan. Rajah Ragunath Das was murdered on the 17th April, 1752 by some of the disgruntled army officers, near Bhalki about 40 miles from Tuljapur[169].

Salabat Jung sought the advice of Bussy in choosing a successor to Ramdas Pandit, and Bussy, advised him to choose Syed Lashkar Khan as the Diwan, since he happened to be one of the senior-most officers of the State and was also a sincere and zealous servant of the first Nizam[170]. While giving this advice, Bussy knew fully well that Syed Lashkar Khan was inimical towards the French and that he resented, at heart, the manner in which Salabat Jung always tried to please the French; But Bussy did not consider this as serious and we find him writing to Moracin the French Governor, at Masulipatam;

---

165. Malleson—"History of the French in India"., p. 363.
"Bussy in the Deccan"., p. 60.
166. G. S. Sardesai—"New History of the Mahrattas"., Vol. II, p. 323.
167. Ibid.
168. "Bussy in the Deccan"., p. 62.
169. Chronology of Modern Hyderabad (1720-1890).
Ed. by Dr. Yusuf Hussain Central Records Office Publication, Hyderabad., 1960.
G. S. Sardesai, the Maratha Historian gives the date as 7th April 1752 while Martineau's "Bussy and French India" gives the date as 4th May.
170. Malleson—"History of the French in India"., p. 366.
Ananda Ranga Pillay's Diary., Vol. VIII, p. 100.
Briggs.—"The Nizam—His History"., Vol. I, p. 124.

"Now that Salabat Jang governs by himself or rather through us what does it matter whether the new Diwan is a little more, or less devoted to us than his predecessor was?[171]".

Moreover, his advice to Salabat Jung to choose Syed Lashkar Khan as the Diwan was very subtle, and it reveals Bussy, as a shrewd judge of human psychology. Had any other man of a lesser calibre than Syed Lashkar Khan been choosen, he would have felt highly flattered and would have become a servile instrument of the French.

Dupleix, on hearing of th appointment of Syed Lashkar Khan wrote to Bussy, to contrive to win over, the Diwan, to the French interests and he also wrote to Syed Lashkar Khan in the following manner;

" So long as you are Diwan you must bear two things in mind, one is to labour with a single heart in Salabat Jang's affairs, and the other is to be our man and manage our affairs with all fidelity. If you will observe these and behave well, you need fear nothing under our protection and your authority will be maintained. You know how Rajah Raghunath Das managed our affairs. I have written about other secret matters to M. Bussy who will inform you of them. If you will act properly, you and Salabat Jang will prosper"[172].

The patronising manner, in which the above letter was written, shows the arrogant confidence the French entertained of their hold on the Deccan. No wonder, such an attitude was galling to many of the patriotic noblemen like Syed Lashkar Khan in the Nizam's court.

While, he wrote to Syed Lashkar Khan to be always amenable to Bussy's wishes, Dupleix, the subtle diplomat that he was, advised Bussy, to keep the younger brothers of Salabat Jung under restraint or if possible to imprison them because he entertained suspicions of their being at the bottom of all intrigues against the French. He also warned Bussy, to see that Salabat Jung did not come under the influence of Syed Laskhar Khan and the anti-French party at the court. He wrote "What I ceaselessly request of you is as far as possible never to let the Subah realise that he is dependent on us; The stronger you are, the more you should appear to be most obligated to him for all things and the more eager for his safety and the more ready to follow his orders"[173].

The above passage shows what consummate diplomats and statesmen the French leaders Dupleix and Bussy were. It can as well be said, that, it was they, who set the pattern of diplomacy that a foreign power should follow and

171. "Bussy in the Deccan"., p. 65.
172. Ananda Ranga Pillay's Diary., Vol. VIII, p. 104.
173. "Bussy in the Deccan"., p. 67.

which was successfully followed by their successors, the British. The British who were more fortunate than the French in their attempts in establishing their Paramountcy in India, always saw that the Diwans of the Indian States were indirectly chosen by them.

Ever since the time of Mir Alam, the Diwans of Hyderabad, were mere pliable instruments in the hands of the British Resident. and they were usually the nominees of the British. This policy, we can as well say, was a legacy, inherited by the British from the French, as was revealed in the latters attitude towards Ramdas Pandit, Syed Lashkar Khan, Shah Nawaz Khan etc. But of course, the French were not as successful in their policy of appointing the Diwans as the British were, but the reason for their failure lies not so much in the unsoundness of their diplomacy as in the type of men they had to deal with. Both Syed Lashkar Khan and his successor Shah Nawaz Khan had seen the heights of Mughal power under Nizamul-Mulk and they resented the fact that a son of Asaf Jah Nizamul-Mulk should be dictated by a mere body of merchants.

Moreover, the awe that the Indians developed towards the foreign powers like the French and the British in later times, was not yet felt by the Indians during this period.

This was just the beginning of the foreign venture, for supremay in India.

The Deccan nobles who were hitherto, used to receiving, orders directly from the Nizam their Sovereign, began to resent the growing power of the French. Most of them found, Bussy's presence irksome, as the latter made his influence felt in every detail of administration. Confident of his old on the Nizam, Bussy, adopted a pompous and overbearing manner towards the nobles of the court. For this reason both Syed Lashkar Khan and show Nawaz Khan, who was now made the Governor of Aurangabad heartily desired to get rid of the French General; with this object in view Syed Lashkar Khan was eagerly looking forward to the arrival of Ghazi-ud-Din Khan.

Meanwhile, French prospects in the Carnatic were becoming bleak. Their commander, Law, failed to take Trichinopoly and he surrendered to the English in June 1752, while the French nominee, Chanda Sahib, was taken prisoner and put to death by the army of the Rajah of Tanjore, an ally of the English[174].

So Dupleix, once again urged Bussy to come South to his aid[175]. Bussy, was quite willing to go to the Carnatic. But, ere long, he heard of Ghazi-ud-Din's imminent arrival in the Deccan in the vicinity of Aurangabad along with his Maratha allies.

---

174. Ananda Ranga Pillay's Diary, Vol. VIII, p. 113.
'Bussy in the Deccan'., p. 74.

175. Ibid., p. 72.

In view of these circumstances it was not possible for Bussy to leave the Deccan and go to the help of Dupleix. Bussy, in a letter to Dupleix, dated 13th July, suggested to him to come to some understanding with Nawab Muhammad Ali, and not to assume the title of Nawab of Carnatic till Salabat Jung was placed securely on the throne[176]. He also made Salabat Jung write to Dupleix, to the same effect, and send a firman to Nawab Muhammmad Ali, conferring Arcot on him through the French at Pondicherry. Nawab Muhammad Ali, was also willing to come to an understanding on these terms, but as Dupleix insisted that he would not discuss this topic unless all the French prisoners of war were first released, the negotiations fell through[177].

In the mean time, Nawab Ghazi-ud-Din Khan arrived in Aurangabad, on the 28th September, 1752 at the head of a force of 150,000 while the forces of his Maratha allies, consisting of the Peishwa, Holkar and Raghoji Bhonslay, numbered 100,000[178]. Bussy, was in a desparate position in the Deccan. He was faced with accute financial bankruptcy and the troops at his command were also not sufficient. He wrote to Dupleix, expressing his fears that he might have to retire to Masulipatam for safety along with Salabat Jung[179]. The French were also becoming unpopular in the Deccan and rumours were afloat among the sepoys that the French had stolen the accumulated wealth of the Nizam. Under such conditions, Bussy, could rely little on their fidelity.

But Dupleix, advised Bussy, to relax by no means his hold on Salabat Jung, because the fortunes of the French in India depended on their position in the Deccan. So he promised to send to Bussy, an additional detachment of 300 Europeans, 50 East Indians and 300 sepoys[180]. But these additional French forces reached the Deccan much too late.

[181]Dupleix, further advised Bussy, to adopt any of the three following courses of action as the conditions dictated; Ghazi-ud-Din should be paid a subsidy while Salabat Jung remained the Subedar; If this proposal was not accepted by Ghazi-ud-Din, to see if Salabat Jung could not be appointed as the deputy of his elder brother; If Ghazi-ud-Din was not prepared to accept the above proposals and forced a battle, and if Salabat Jung happened to be killed in battle, then the French should offer their services either to Ghazi-ud-Din or to the Peishwa, according to the terms they offered to the French.

---

176. 'Bussy in the Deccan'., p. 72.
177. Ananda Ranga Pillay's Diary., Vol. III, p. 194, 201.
178. Orme.—'A History of the Military Transactions of the British Nation in Indostan', Vol. I., p. 27.
Malleson—'History of the French in India'., p. 366.
179. Dodwell—'Dupleix and Clive'., p. 87.
180. 'Bussy in the Deccan'., p. 67.
181. Ibid., p. 75.
Dodwell-Dupleix and Clive., p. 87.

On hearing of the approach of Ghazi-ud-Din, Bussy, along with Salabat Jung retired to Hyderabad. Bussy's, apprehensions that the Mughal officers might become recalcitrant on hearing of Ghazi-ud-Din's approach, proved correct. The Qiledar of Hyderabad at first refused to throw open the gates of Golconda to foreigners, but he was surprised by Salabat Jung and Bussy. From Hyderabad, Salabat Jung and Bussy went to Bidar and from there they sent Syed Lashkar Khan to open negotiations with Ghazi-ud-Din and the Marathas[182]. Syed Lashkar Khan advised Salabat Jung to come to some compromise with his elder brother, but Salabat Jung did not heed his advice[183]. Then Syed Lashkar Khan, went to the camp of Ghazi-ud-Din, on the pretext that he had incurred the displeasure of Salabat Jung. Ghazi-ud-Din proposed to give Bidar, to Salabat Jung, but this offer was turned down by the latter. Syed Lashkar Khan who at heart was a partisan of Ghazi-ud-Din tried to whip up anti-French feelings in the camp of the latter While the negotiations with Ghazi-ud-Din Khan were still going on, the worries of Salabt Jung and Bussy, were put to an end by the sudden death of Ghazi-ud-Din Khan. Nawab Ghazi-ud-Din Khan Feroze Jung was poisoned by his step mother, the mother of Salabat Jung, on the 16th October, 1752[184].

This sudden removal of Ghazi-ud-Din from the scene, brought the struggle to an end. Bussy, on being appraised of Ghazi-ud-Din Khan's death, started towards Hyderabad, with Salabat Jung from Bidar; the Marathas who had accompanied Ghazi-ud-Din started harassing the Nizam's army a great deal, and at Bhalki, they completely surrounded the Mughal army and harassed Salabat Jung to such an extent that he opened negotiations with them through Bussy[185]. Peishwa, Balaji Baji Rao, conveyed his willingness to open negotiations if Salabat Jung was prepared to give him the same grants as were promised by Ghazi-ud-Din Khan. Nawab Salabat Jung agreed to these terms and the treaty of Bhalki was concluded between the Nizam and the Marathas on 22nd November, 1752[186].

[187]By this treaty, the Nizam, ceded to the Marathas, the western half of Berar, between the rivers Godavari and the Tapti. This included the whole of

182. Malleson—'History of the French in India'., p. 367.
183. According to Masir-ul-Umara Syed Lashkar Khan's original name was Mir Ismail Khan. Nizam-ul-Mulk gave him the title of Syed Lashkar Khan. After the accession of Salabat Jung he was given a mansab of 6000 Infantry, 6000 cavalry and the title of Rukn-ud-Dowla.
184. Orme—'A History of the Military Transactions of the British Nation in Indostan.', Vol. II, p. 214.
'Chronology of Modern Hyderabad'., (1720-1890), p. 11.
Dodwell—Dupleix and Clive, p. 81.
185. Sardesai—"Selections from the Peshwa's Daftari Records"., Vol. XX, "The Bhonslas of Nagpur", L. No. 148.
186. G. S. Sardesai—A New History of the Mahrattas., Vol. II, p. 325.
Dodwell—Dupleix and Clive., p. 88.
187. Records of Fort St. George, C. C. 1753., L. No. 2.
Ananda Ranga Pillay's Diary., Vol. VIII, p. 261.
Dodwell—Dupleix and Clive., p. 88.

Baglana and the Khandesh regions: It was also agreed that the Marathas should lead an expedition into the Carnatic, to punish the Dalwai of Mysore. The Maratha right of levying Chouth and Sardeshmukhi in the South was also recognised.

Syed Laskhar Khan, after the death of Ghazi-ud-Din Khan Feroze Jung, fled to Bhalki and shut himself up in that fortress. Salabat Jung now sent for him and reinstated him as the Divan once again.

Bussy, in return for having brought the issue with the Marathas to a successful termination requested Salabat Jung, to grant Kondavid and territories adjacent to Masulipatam, to the French. Salabat Jung, willingly agreed to this and granted Kondavid for life, to Bussy. Afterwards, Salabat Jung, along with his army and Bussy, returned to Hyderabad in January 1753.

Thus by 1753 the French position for all outward appearances was firmly established in the Deccan. They not only made themselves predominent but also made the position of Salabat Jung apparently secure. The masterly and sound diplomacy of Dupleix and Bussy was vindicated by the successful turn of events. To Dupleix, it was a matter of great pride and he could show to the Indian powers at large, that in spite of the severe reverses, that the French had suffered in the Carnatic, their position and power in the Deccan was still strong and something to be reckoned with.

Dupleix, foresaw in the recognition of Maratha rights of Chouth and Sardeshmukhi, in the Carnatic by the treaty of Bhalki, a fresh source of strength to the French. He hoped not only to get the help of the Nizam, but also of the Marathas in putting down the Dalwai of Mysore who was instrumental in bringing about the death of Chanda Sahib.

Fired by this vision, Dupleix, impressed upon Bussy, the absolute necessity of Salabat Jung coming to Mysore, as its overlord to vindicate his rights over that Kingdom.

In spite of the financial difficulties and the loss of political prestige the French suffered in the Carnatic, their prestige in the Deccan, was unsullied. But in the Deccan, the growing power of the French was resented by the nobles, in whose eyes the Freneh were mere upstarts. So within five years the French were made to come down from their pinnacle of glory and realise how untenable their position was in the Deccan.

CHAPTER III

Anglo-French Rivalry in the Deccan

Soon after his arrival in Hyderabad, Bussy, fell ill and he was advised to go to the coastal town of Musulipatam, to recoupe his health. He left Hyderabad, on the 23 January 1753, leaving Mons. Goupil, in charge of the French detachment[1].

By disposition Mons. Goupil, was a mild man and he lacked the grit and intelligence to cope with the forces he had to contend against, in the Deccan.

The Diwan Syed Lashkar Khan, was at heart bitterly opposed to the French predominance in Salabat Jung's court and he was on the look out for allies with whose aid he could bring about the downfall of the French power in the Deccan. With this intention, ever since he was appointed to the office of the Diwan, he was carrying on secret correspondence with the English at Fort St. George.

The temporary absence of Bussy from the capital gave him the eagerly awaited opportunity to undermine the French Power.

Mons. Goupil failed to evoke the qualities of discipline and implicit obedience that were so characteristic of Bussy's relations with his soldiers. Under Goupil, the indiscipline in the French regiment increased, and the irresponsible and arrogant behaviour of the soldiers, served, only to increase the peoples disgust with them.

The quick manner, in which the French officers became rich soon after their coming to the Deccan, and the huge salaries that were drawn by them, made the people regard them as mercenaries and exploiters.

Syed Lashkar Khan, tried by every means to intensify the people's dislike for the French, and in this he found the general economic distress in the State, a helpful factor.

The treasury of the Nizam, was almost empty and the Nizam's troops had not been paid for six months. Salabat Jung found it still more difficult to pay the French detachment, and their pay was in arrears for two months.

---

1. 'Bussy in the Deccan'., p. 101.
   Orme.—'A History of the Military Transactions of the British Nation in Indostan'., Vol. I, p. 330.
   Najmul Ghani Khan of Rampur–'Tarikhi Riyasat Hyderabad-Deccan'., p. 239.

The French sepoys, threatened to rebel, if their arrears were not paid, and Salabat Jung was forced to pay their salaries by raising a loan of 150,000 Rupees from the local soucars and from the revenues of Hyderabad.

But the troops of the Nizam, had to go without their pay. So, these soldiers, started clamouring for the payment of their arrears and refused to go on the proposed Carnatic expedition unless their arrears were cleared. The general discontent was so great in the Nizam's army that even the nagar-beaters and camel drivers took a solemn oath not to proceed to the Carnatic until their salaries were paid[2]. The Mughal soldires, openly went about saying, that the French were robbing the Nizam of his riches, which the family had accumulated for the past sixty years, while the subjects of the Nizam, were starving. Their discontent was so great, that they went to the extent of threatening the life of Rumi Khan. the agent of the French[3].

It was this economic distress of the Nizam and the general discontent among the soldiery, that made Bussy and Salabat Jung, drop the idea of going to the Carnatic has had been previously decided at Bhalki.

Bussy, realised that the French had become unpopular in the Deccan, and that the leading nobles at the Nizam's court were plotting against them. Hence, after the death of Ghazi-ud-Din Khan, Bussy, suggested to Dupleix, the advisability of the French withdrawing from the Deccan, now that Salabat Jung was placed securely on the throne[4]. But Dupleix, who was far removed from the scene, could not fully comprehend the situation and he advised, Bussy, to stay on and carry on the project that he "so well began".

He also, advised Bussy, to raise funds for the French at Pondicherry by asking for a loan from the firm of the bankers, Kasi Das Bukkanji at Hyderabad. He further advised Bussy to ask Salabat Jung for the grant of the four Northern Sarkars, namely Ellore, Mustafanagar, Rajahmundry and Chicaole, towards the maintenance of the French detachment. Bussy, moved the matter with Salabat Jung, but Syed Lashkar Khan, saw, that the consideration of the matter was postponed for the time being and before Bussy could further move in the matter, he had to go to Masulipatam on account of his illness[5].

Taking advantage of the financial distress of the Nizam and the general indiscipline that had crept into the French forces, Syed Lashkar Khan, used all his ingenuity to make the French unpopular and their stay, untenable in the Deccan. He started exploring his moorings in a very cautious manner.

2. Records of Fort St. George., C. C. (1753), L. No. 12, p. 134, 135
3. 'Bussy in the Deccan'., pp. 86, 87.
4. Ibid.
5. 'Bussy in the Deccan'., p. 103.
Orme.-'A History of the Military Transactions of the British Nation in Indostan'., Vol. I, p. 330.
6. Malleson.—'History of the French in India'., p. 814.

Early in April 1753[6] he appealed to the English, "to leave no stone unturned and to assist him to expel the French". The letter of Syed Lashkar Khan, was intercepted by the spies of Dupleix, but Syed Lashkar Khan, even after knowing it, did not desist from intriguing against the French. On the contrary, he wrote another letter to the English in July 1753 to the following effect;

[7]"I was extremely glad tc receive your agreeable letter of congratulations concerning my being appointed an absolute agent by His Excellency and which letter gave me an account of proper schemes in regard to settling the country and also the bad proceeding of the wicked. I wish that God may grant joy on account of the favour bestowed on me by His Excellency as above and that he may conclude the event with happiness. By the blessings of God His Excellency's entire resolutions to settle the affairs of the country and wealth as also to extirpate the wicked enemy. My thoughts are bent upon the same because of my duty to him who was pardoned, (supposed to be the deceased Nizam) and my attachment to the interests of my Excellency, and therefore I always exert myself in regulating the affairs of the country and in procuring happiness to the people. I suppose you have heard of the scheme (which has been executed lately) by the other hands.

There are some other schemes in my mind to be executed in future, which by the blessings of God shall be done in a short time and the enemies will meet with their desert, you gave me an hint concerning the assistance to be given to the lawful person, which indeed is very right. His Excellency has the same act in view, but as soon as the above schemes are executed the country in those parts shall be settled as desired. As you are giving instances of your duties to His Excellency and have a perfect regard to him in your hearts. It is my wish that God may grant you a good reward, continue your attachmant to His Excellency's interests in the same manner, exert yourself and show yourself to be his well-wisher. What can I say more".

Though the plans of Syed Lashkar Khan against the French were welcome to the English, they could not send him any material help owing to their preoccupations in the Carnatic.

[8]Syed Laskhar Khan tried to harass the French by with-holding their salaries. To the original detachment of 300 Europeans and 2000 sepoys, Bussy added further a battalion of 5000 sepoys, and all these were entirely under the personal command of Bussy. All together, their salaries amounted to, two and a half lakhs of Rupees, per month or nearly 29 lakhs per year[9].

6. Malleson - 'History of French in India', p. 814.
7. Records of Fort St. George, C. C. (1753), L. No. 140, p. 87.
8. Orme.--"A History of the Military Transactions of the British Nation in Indostan", Vol. I, p. 331.
"Bussy in the Deccan", p. 103.
9. Dodwell.--Dupleix and Clive. Beginnings of the Empire, p. 91.

The French troops, finding their salaries withheld, clamoured for payment and their hardship at this juncture, was all the more, augmented by an attack of the small-pox epidemic that took a heavy toll. Unable to face these hardships many of the troopers deserted their ranks.

[10]The French Commander, Goupil, tried to raise the issue of granting the Northern Sarkars to the French as a way out of the financial stalemate after consulting Moracin, but the latter refused to give his assent to this step without consulting Bussy, who was too ill to consider the matter. So the matter was postponed, while, the financial crisis began to deepen daily.

Salabat Jung was in a position to pay only Rs. 20,00,000 towards the arrears of the French detachment's salary, out of which Rs. 70,000 were to paid to the Europen troops, while 130,000 was to be paid to the French sepoys. But it still left a deficit of Rs. 70,000/-

Syed Lashkar Khan, suggested a novel method to the French, to tide over the difficulty. He told Mons. Goupil, that all these financial troubles of the Nizam, arose out of the reluctance of the polygars to pay their tribute in the proper manner, and he suggested to Goupil, to send the French soldiers to collect the revenues of the State from the polygars. By doing so, they would not only be helping their friend the Nizam but would also be able to meet their own monetary requirement.

The task of revenue collection in the countryside was no easy one and the collectors very often during the process of realising the revenue came to a clash with the polygars. Syed Lashkar Khan's only object in suggesting this novel plan was to make the French unpopular with the people. He also hoped, that many French soldiers would desert their ranks in disgust, once, they realised the difficulties of their task.

Goupil, easily fell into the trap set by the shrewd Diwan and he sent small detachments of soldiers under European officers in different directions to collect the revenues.

This involved scattering of the French forces in different parts of the State, which was a potentially dangerous thing to happen in an alien country.

As expected, many soldiers deserted while the European officers misused their powers and exacted money in an arbitrary manner. This roused the people against them and they demanded justice from the Nizam against the French[11].

10. According to Martineau the Sarkars yielded an annual revenue of 40 lakhs, while according to Orme and Dodwell, the four Sarkars exclusively yielded 3,100,000 and Masulipatam alone yielded an annual revenue Rs. 42,87,000.

11. Ibid., p. 250.

Syed Lashkar Khan tried to separate Salabat Jung from his French friends, by suggesting to him at this juncture, that he should proceed to Aurangabad, which was in danger of being attacked by Raghoji Bhonslay and the Rajah of Nirmal. He also told Salabat Jung to take with him only a small detachment. The Nizam assented to this proposal, and so Syed Lashkar Khan went to Goupil, and conveyed the Nizam's intentions and asked him if he would accompany the Nizam to Aurangabad at the head of the French detachment[12].

Goupil, though he hesitated, at first to divide his forces, consented in the end to send M.de. Mainville, to Aurangabad at the head of 100 Europeans and 100 sepoys. He instructed Mainville, to guard the person of the Subedar always, but in no circumstances to agree to go on an expedition, on account of the smallness of the French forces[13]. Goupil further advised Mainville, that if any miship were to overtake Salabat Jung, he should acknowledge as Subedar, who ever happened to be nominated to that office. The entrusting of such a responsible job to a junior officer like Mainville and his agreeing to divide the small French detachment shows nothing but imprudence.

After this Syed Lashkar Khan instructed Mir Mahmmud Hussain the Qiledar of Golconda Fort to harass the French in every possible manner, short of declaring war, and the latter carried out these instructions so zealously, that the French were reduced to sore straits. Syed Lashkar Khan, also sent secret instructions that the fortresses of Kondavid, Guntur and Khambhammeta, which were given as Jaghirs to Bussy, should be seized[14]. After making all these arrangements, the Diwan, awaited further developments. He hoped that the French, unable to put up with the harassment, would ultimately leave the Deccan in disgust. He was also secretly corresponding with the Marathas inciting them to attack the French. He was so confident of his sucess that he wrote to Saunders, the English Governor, that he would succeed in his plans before the rainy season was over[15].

Dupleix, who had intercepted some of Syed Lashkar Khan's letters to the English, realised the seriousness of the developments in the Deccan. He not only recalled all the French soldiers who were noted for indiscipline but also vested Bussy with special powers, so that if there was any serious crisis, he could act immediately without waiting for instructions from Dupleix[16]. He also drew the attention of Bussy, to the urgency of his going to Hyderabad as early as possible.

---

12. Malleson-"History of the French in India", p. 378.
13. "Bussy in the Deccan". p. 106.
    Records of Fort St. George, C. C. L. No. 142, p. 88.
14. Ananda Ranga Pillay's Diary, Vol. VIII, p. 290.
15. Malleson—"History of the French in India", p. 375.
    'Bussy in the Deccan', p. 109.
16. Ibid.

Bussy, accordingly started from Masulipatam on the 25th June 1753, and reached Hyderabad on the 15th July 1753[17].

He arrived in Hyderabad with the firm resolve not to leave the Deccan unless the financial condition of the Subedar warranted such a step.

On his arrival he found that the French commandant Goupil, was busy elsewhere, collecting the revenues, and that great confusion and disorder prevailed in the French ranks.

He soon restored order and discipline among the 500 Europeans and 4000 sepoys who were in Hyderabad and opened negotiations with the Qiledar, Mahammud Hussain. The latter, realising that Bussy was not the man to mince matters, arranged the necessary money for the payment of the French troops. Bussy, cleared the arrears of pay of the troops partly by raising money from the Bankers and partly by advancing from his own private funds.

Bussy, then called upon Goupil and Mainville to submit accounts of the money, so for, collected by the French troops. He found on a careful scrutiny of the accounts submitted that the French had over-reached themselves in collecting taxes, and that they exorted gratuities from the nawabs and polygars and oppressed the people in general.

When Dupleix was informed of this he sent the following letter of admonition to the French officers;

[18]" I have been informed that several of you have worried and tried the Nawab and other lords by the irksome demands for gratuities, almost always ill-founded. As such a procedure can be nothing else than extremely harmful to the transactions of the Company as also to the glory of the King and the nation, as it tends to bring disgust even to the very ones who much need our protection. It is absolutely essential to prohibit in the future all endeavours which have the slightest appearance of a solicitation and to forbid visits to the lords except after receiving the sanction of the commander. Moreover, you are warned, that you are all bound to consider yourself as being directly in the service of the king and the Company that you must deem yourself very fortunate to draw the higher salaries which you receive and that on no account you should think of gratuties except in so far as circumstances may allow and that they shall be freely granted by those who have the power to do so. The King, the Company and I will it so, and whosoever does not submit shall be a rebel ".

Bussy realised that the irresponsible and arrogant manner of the French soldiers had alienated the people from them and that intrigues were afoot in the court against the French.

17. Ibid.
18. Ibid, p. 117.

Syed Lashkar Khan, the Marathas, especially Janoji Nimbalkar and Rajah Ramchander, and the English at Fort St. George were interested in ousting, the French power from the Deccan.

Syed Lashkar Khan, even after the arrival of Bussy, did not desist from plotting against the French. He induced Salabat Jung to write to Dupleix, that the arrears, due to the French troops must be deducted from the 50 lakhs of Rupees, that Dupleix owed to the Nizam, as his deputy in the Carnatic[19]. He also proposed that during the rainy season the French troops should be stationed at Masulipatam so that they could collect the revenues with greater ease[20]. Syed Lashkar Khan, though he advised the French in the above manner, at the same time sent secret instructions to the zamindars on the East Coast not to pay taxes to the French and to attack the French Jaghirs in the various districts. Encouraged by such messages, Rajah Ramachandra of Ongole, seized Bandurti, with the help of the English[21].

Syed Lashkar Khan also put the two younger brothers of Salabat Jung, Nizam Ali and Basalat Jung into prison in the Fort of Doulatabad on the plea that the latter were intriguing with Mons. Mainville and ordered the French Commandant to return forthwith to Hyderabad[22].

He also made Salabat Jung to write to Bussy, suggesting that the French should stay, during the monsoons in Masulipatam and that the Subah would call them whenever he required their assistance[23]. Apart from this, no sooner did he hear that Mahammud Hussain, the Qiledar of Hyderabad, had assisted Bussy in arranging the loans for the payment of the French troops, than he got him replaced by a new Governor[24]. Seeing these manoeuvres, Bussy, decided to deal with Syed Lashkar Khan, in a very drastic manner. He decided to adopt one of the following three courses[25]; namely; to demand from the Subah fresh territories to maintain the French forces and if the Subah refused to grant them, to seize certain territories and attach them to Masulipatam which was under Mons. Moracin, and inform Salabat Jung that those territories would be safe guarded by the French for the Nizam. But, if either of

19. Ananda Ranga Pillay's Diary, Vol. VIII. p. 357.
20. Ibid.
21. Ibid, pp. 374, 375.
22. Ibid.
Records of Fort St. George, C. C. 1753-9, L. No. 172, pp. 103-104.
23. Ibid.
24. Bussy in the Deccan p. 135.
25. Ibid p. 136.
The maintenance of the French corps cost more than 2 lakhs of Rupees per month of which the maintenance of the sepoys alone came to 141, 568 Rs.
While the strength of the European soldiers was 400, their salaries amounted to 72,700/- Rs. per month.
'Bussy in the Deccan', p. 136

these plans failed, Bussy, even decided to get the help of the Peishwa, against the Nizam in exchange for Surat being ceded to the Marathas. On being informed of these plans, Dupleix fully concurred with them and he sent to Bussy, an additional force of 350 men. Of these, Bussy, despatched 150 men to Masulipatam, under the command of the Marquis of Conflans.

Feeling himself sufficiently strong, Bussy, now decided to march against Aurangabad. Prior to this, he sent a letter to Salabat Jung, in which he reminded the Subah that if he became the Deccan Subedar, it was mainly due to the efforts of the French.

He wrote;[26] "Besides my usual straight-forwardness well known to you I am entitled to write to you as I am doing because everybody in the Deccan is aware that I call you my son and that you consider me as father. Whence is it that you no longer hold the same language? Who could have changed your mind? Despite the change in your feelings and words I shall be near you in a couple of days. It is nothing but proper that you should expect my arrival in order that we might together arrange a campaign which may honour and bring you profit, whereas you are aware that your last campaign was neither honourable nor profitable to you.

You followed the advice of your enemies rather than mine - - - your behaviour is so irregular that I believe you are anxious to ruin your country. You have just knocked off Mir Muhammad of whom you told me all sorts of good. Probably this too is the work of my enemies who are also yours as well, and who being jealous of seeing the perfect understanding between Mir Muhammad and myself and of the settlement we had reached for the regular payment of our troops have set up to dismiss him. I warn you that if you continue blindly trusting those people you will lose yourself and you will infalliably lose the Deccan. I shall be beside you in a few days. I hope you will be cured from your blindness which may lead you to your downfall".

The above letter of Bussy fully reveals the canker that had begun to infect Indian politics and the imbecilty to which the Indian princes were reduced during this period. No doubt, Saunders, the English Governor, remarked; "The weakness of the Moors is now known and it is certain any European nation resolved to wage war on them with a tolerable force may overrun the whole country".

After writing the above letter to Salabat Jung, Bussy, started to Aurangadad, towards the end of October, and arrived there in November, 1753. His journey to Aurangabad was full of obstacles and he had to meet the silent opposition of the people, inspired by the manoeuvres of Syed Lashkar Khan.

26. 'Bussy in the Deccan', p. 136.

Seeing this, Bussy decided to enter Aurangabad in full battle array; Syed Lashkar Khan seeing the preparations made by Bussy. decided to yield and opened negotiations with the latter.

On Bussy's arrival, Syed Lashkar Khan at the head of 21 nobles mounted on elephants, went to receive him. Bussy, when he met them, contrived to arrange their order of arrival in such a manner that they had to dismount first as though doing obeisance to the French General[27].

On approaching Bussy, the Diwan, Syed Lashkar Khan dimounted from his elephant and bowed to the French General, seeing which, the other Deccan nobles followed suit; Bussy, getting down from his elephant embraced the Diwan. The latter then offered to surrender his official seals as a token of his resignation[28]. Bussy, was shrewed enough to perceive that Syed Lashkar Khan was popular with the people, and whatever intrigues he had carried on against the French he had done for the noble purpose of ridding his country and his ruler of foreign domination. So Bussy, realised, that however much he desired to get rid of the minister, making him to resign openly was not the proper method. Hence he refused to accept the seals. and mildly hinted to the Diwan, that he would be satisfied with the cession of the Northern Sarkars to the French.

The Northern Sarkars, constituted the most fertile coastal strip of the Nizam's Dominions. They were watered by the three important rivers of the Deccan, the Krishna, the Godavari and the Gundlakamma. Syed Lashkar Khan was loth to part with those fertile regions and he sounded Bussy, whether he would not be satisfied with territorial grants in the interior ; but on finding that Bussy had set his heart on the acquisition of the Northern Sarkars alone, he gave way.

On the 23rd November, a grand Durbar was held at Aurangabad, and the treaty of Aurangabad, was signed between Salabat Jung and the French. By this treaty the four Northern Sarkars, Ellore, Mustafanagar (Kondapalli) Rajahmundry and Chicacole were granted to the French[29].

The Sarkars were personally conferred on Bussy towards the maintenance of the Franch troops.

It was also decided that the revenues of the Sarkars should be spent exclusively for disbursing the pay of the Franch troops. At this period a

27. Orme - "A History of the Military Transactions of the British Nation in Indostan" Vol. I, p. 331, "Bussy in the Deccan". p. 141.
28. Ananda Ranga Pillay's Diary. Vol. VIII, p. 357
29. Central Records Office (Hyderabad) Daftari Diwani Section (unpublished)
Acc. Reg. No. 5053: 5054: 1167
Letters to Fort St. George 1754. Vol. XXXI, L. No. 8.
Letters from Fort St. George 1754, Vol. XXX, L. No. 5, 6, 7.
Mackenzie Ms. Kondavidu Kaifiyat O. Ms. Library, Madras.

Mughal Governor, Jaffar Ali, was in charge of the revenue adminstration of the Sarkars. So it was settled that if Jaffar Ali, failed to remit the revenues of the sarkars to Bussy within the stipulated time, the sum should be made good from the treasury of the Nizam.

Secondly, the safety of the person of the Subah was entrusted to the care of the French, and further, it was agreed that the Nizam should not interfere in the administration of the Subah of Arcot. It was also mutually agreed, that in matters of general administration also, the Nizam should govern the country in accordance with the wishes of Bussy. Bussy in his turn agreed to support and befriend Syed Lashkar Khan[30].

Soon after receiving the patent for the Sarkars, Bussy, instructed the French agent at Masulipatam to take charge of those territories, and he despatched 150 Europeans and 2500 sepoys to Moracin, at Masulipatam, to bring those territories under the French control[31].

The acquisition of the Northern Sarkars is an important landmark in the history of the French Nation in India[32].

---

30. Orme—'A History of the Military Transactions of the British Nation in Indostan', Vol. I, pp. 333, 334.

31. Malleson—"History of the French in India", p. 381.

32. The Northern Sarkars constituted a part of the Vijaynagar Empire, till the year 1565. But the Vijaynagar Empire was dismembered by the Bahamani Sultans in 1565 in the battle of Tallikota. Then these territories passed under the control of the Qutb Shah rulers of Golgonda. When Golconda was conquerred by Aurangazeb in 1687, these territories became an integral part of the Mughal Empire and were governed by the Subedar of the Deccan. After the death of Aurangazeb great disorder was created in the Mughal Empire, and the zamindars on the East Coast also tried to take advantage of the situation, and usurp the power of the Mughal Collectors. The leading zamindars on the East Coast were the Rajahs of Vizanagaram, Bobbili, Peddapur, Pithapuram, Mogaliturru and Nuzvid.

    When Nizamul-Mulk became the Subedar, he tried to establish order in this region; He divided his kingdom into 24 parghanas of which Rajahmundry was one; He appointed Nawabs to rule over the parghanas. At the time of granting of the Sarkars to the French, Jaffar Ali Khan was the Governor of the Rajahmundry and Chicacole Sarkars.

    Peddapura Charitramu, pp. 64, 65, 72.
    Samalkot Kaifiyat, Mackenzie Mss.
    East Godavari District Manual.
    Mogali Turru Kaifiyat Mackenie Mss.

    When the English East India Company, took over the Sarkars in 1766 from the Nizam they yielded a revenue of Rs. 5,40,000 or Rs. 1,60,000 varahas but according to the unpublished records (Daftar-i-Diwani Section) in the Central Records Office, Hyderabad, they yielded a revenue of 24 lakhs at the time of their being granted to the French.

It placed at their disposal a contiguous territory of 470 miles of sea coast stretching from Orissa to the Coramandal Coast. These territories were also noted for their economic wealth; Masulipatam was noted at this period for its dyeing and printing industry, while Rajahmundry abounded in rich teak forests. Chicacole was a rice producing area. The presence of the Eastern Ghats made this region unvulnerable to outside attack. The Eastern Ghats abounded in thick bamboo forests, and in those days of infantry and cavalry warfare, it was difficult for the enemy to penetrate through them.

The English were filled with jealousy on hearing of the grant of the Sarkaras to the French and they started intriguing with the zamindars in that region who also did not relish the idea of the French dominating over them.

While intrigues were afoot in the Sarkars against the French, the Deccan also became a hot-bed of intrigues.

Bussy, though he had solemnly affirmed to treat Syed Lashkar Khan as a friend, was soon able to create an anti-Diwan Party in the court by his adroitness. One of the most important persons to join this party was Shah-Nawaz Khan. By their intrigues this clique made it impossible for Syed Lashker Khan to carry on the administration. The treasury was almost empty, coupled with this Syed Lashkar Khan found it hard to put up with this intrigues set up by Bussy. So he offered to resign, but Bussy in keeping with his protestations of friendship refused to accept the resignation, but when the Diwan offered to resign a second time he induced Salabat Jung to aceept the resignation without much ado[34]. On the advice of Bussy, Salabat Jung appointed Shah Nawaz Khan as the Diwan[35].

On hearing of the resignation of Syed Lashkar Khan, Dupleix wanted him to be sent as a prisoner to Masulipatam, but Bussy was shrewd enough to guess that such a step would not be liked by the peoole in the Deccan and that it would make the French unpopular. He deliberately advised Salabat Jung to confer the Subah of Berar on Syed Lashkar Khan[36].

Berar, at this time was occupied by Raghoji Bhonslay the Maratha leader, and if Syed Lashkar Khan was to wrench it from him he had to raise an army of at least seven to eight thousand troops to fight with the Marathas. Thus the conferring of Berar on Syed Lashkar Khan was nothing but a deliberate step taken to keep the ex-Diwan engaged.

During his Diwanship, Syed Lashkar Khan had interned Nizam Ali and Basalat Jung in the fort of Doulatabad[37]. The Deccani courtiers realising

33. 'Bussy in the Deccan', pp. 160, 161, 162, 163.
34. Ibid.
35. Records of Fort St. George, C. C. (1754), p. 77–78.
Robert Sewell and S. K. Aiyangar –'Historical Inscriptions of South India', p. 299.
36. 'Bussy in the Deccan', p. 162.
37. Ibid, p. 162.
Muh. Siraj-ud-Din Talib—Nizam Ali Khan, Sawale, Zindagi, p. 19.

that Syed Lashkar Khan could not have adopted such a bold step unless he had the tacit approval of the French, held the latter responsible for this. Bussy, in order to make the French cause popular in the Deccan, ordered the Qiledar of Doulatabad to set those princes free, but the latter refused to do so, unless he was paid a gratuity of Rs. 50,000[38].

The Peishwa, realising the potential importance of the princess, in his diplomatic dealings with the Nizam made overtures to the Qiledar and offered to pay him three lakhs if the Princes were handed over to him[39]. The Qiledar was hesitating between the two offers. Bussy, on hearing of the proposal of the Marathas, realised that matters were going too far; so he quickly apprised Salabat Jung of the dangerous turn of events and he made the latter issue a warrant for the release of the princes. The son of Qalandar Khan was sent at the head of 200 French soldiers to Doulatabad. On seeing them the Qiledar gave way and the princes were released in early January 1754, and they were duly escorted to Aurangabad.

Salabat Jung's financial position was far from satisfactory, and when he told Bussy of his bankruptcy, the latter hit upon a novel plan to tide over the difficulty. He suggested, that Government posts in the State should be given to the highest bidder[40]. This novel device of Bussy served two purpose. It not only replenished the treasury with 19 lakhs of Rupees but also brought into the various offices only those men who were favourably disposed towards the French and who were willing to promote the French interests in the Deccan. Thus Bussy, exploited to his advantage, the clauses of the treaty of Aurangabad, and succeeded in establishing French influence and power in all matters of administration.

Shah Nawaz Khan, who had hoped that Bussy would be prudent enough to observe restraint in interfering in the internal affairs of the State, soon found himself disillusioned. Naturally, the Minister found the French interference galling and resented it. While the resentment of the Minister was mounting up slowly Bussy's ego was increasing daily. He wrote in one of his letters to the Director of the French East India Company[41].

"The French are the protectors, friends, arbitrators and mediators at one the same time. I am highly pleased to note that my ceaseless toil for the last 4 years during which the most singular events which occurred and all my deeds crowned by the most beneficial results have secured to the Company some wealthy settlements and have guaranteed the throne of his father to Salābat Jang".

---

38. Ibid, p. 162.
39. Ibid.
40. Ibid, p. 131.
    A. C. C. 284, (pp. 138-151)., Letter addressed to Roth the future Director of the French East India Company.
41. Ibid.

Shah Nawaz Khan, finding that the country was being ruined by the incessant wars of the French, suggested to them the advisibility of bringing the conflict in the Carnatic to an end by recognising Nawab Muhammad Ali as the Nawab of the Carnatic[42]. He persuabed Salabat Jung to send a Firman to Muhammud Ali conferring the Carnatic on him and also made Salabat Jung to write to the Mysore Ruler to desist from fighting.

Thus Shah Nawaz Khan exerted himself to restore peace in his master's dominions. Whenever, the French demanded money he replied to Bussy firmly, that all the expenses of the French army should be met from the revenues of the Northern Sarkars[43].

The main hurdle that faced the Diwan was finance. The chronic bankruptcy of the Nizam made Shah Nawaz Khan to dissuade the Nizam from going on an expedition to the South along with the Marathas, at Bussy's instigation. The Diwan also realised that the country was being ruined by the Nizam getting himself entangled with the French. He hoped to relieve the Nizam of his financial embarrassments by borrowing from Dupelix, the French Governor. In this connection he wrote to Dupleix[44]; "I consider you to be unique in sympathy and benevolence. We are sure that you what improvement and tranquillity in our affairs just as we want in yours. During the time that the Mughal Emperor has lain low at the hands of the Marathas the latter's pride has increased hundredfold. So far as our administration is concerned we do not find ourselves in a position to undertake conquest or realise tribute form others owing to lack of resources and excess of expenditure on salaried persons of which the details may be known later. Now it seems impossible to realise the tribute from Seringapatam on which our prosperity is dependent. Unless a tour is undertaken after the rainy season, the country cannot remain in a state of tranquillity and the opposition crushed.

"As there prevails complete friendship and harmony between us it should be feasible to advance us a loan of ten or fifteen lakhs of rupees so that we could conciliate the soldiery and undertake expeditions. Otherwise, there is danger of the country shrinking and the resources getting attenuated beyond recovery. As you know. we on our part paid the contributions, promised by Muzaffar Jung which was not a small sum I should like to assure you that after completing the general organisation of the administration there will not be any negligence or delay towards the payment of the loan. Your fame will spread far and wide for helping with an army under Monsieur Bussy and also for offering us monetary help at such a critical moment. This will be taken as the tribute of the Carnatic by some people. But if the loan is advanced the soldiery will find a basis for hope, the enemy will be overawed and the Government shall regain its lost confidence.

42. Records of Fort St. George, C. C. 165, pp. 77, 78, 82, 83, L. No. 146.
43. "Bussy in the Deccan", p. 181.
44. "Dr. Yusuf Hussain".—Some unpublished letters of Shah Nawaz Khan, "Proceedings of the Deccan History Conference, 1945, Hyderabad Session".

You might realise this injustice that we have foregone for your sake thirty two lakhs of rupees annually which would be one crore and thirty lakhs in four years. It was in consideration of your interests that that we even refused to receive fifteen lakhs from Mumammad Ali of Arcot, and twenty lakhs from the English in the form of cash or draft cheques, It is against reason and expediency to give away portion of the state which is like a mole on the fair face of the Deccan. In this connection let us know whatever you consider to bo right and proper. As a true friend it would be in the fitness of things to give us full authority as a free agent to do what is expedient in the circumstances. Hope that you will give us the benefit of your valuable advice in detail which will be a means of comforting us a great deal"—

But this will reasoned appeal of the Minister was of little avail; Dupleix, himself during this period was faced with acute financial difficulties. Finding that the French were in no way in a position to relieve the Nizam of his difficulties, but on the contrary were a source of vexation owing to the frequent interference of Bussy in the admiristration, Shah Nawaz Khan decided to do away with the Franch.

He orgainsed an anti-French Party in the Court with the help of the Nizam's Brothers, Nawab Nizam Ali Khan and Basalat Jung. He also persuaded Salabat Jung to open negotiations with the English at Madras.

The acquisition of the Northern Sarkars was the crowning achievment of Bussy's three year stay in the Deccan. These territories gave to the French a contiguous coast line on the East coast where the French had already two factories namely that of Masulipatam and Yanam. To these were added the factories at the Divi Islands on the 18th February 1752.

The English also possessed several flourishing factories in this region, namely at Masulipatam, Narsapur, Ingeram and Vizagapatam. The Dutch also possessed a factory at Bhimilipatam.

On account of their clashing commercial interests the English, viewed with dismay and jealousy the granting of the Northern Sarkars to the French. They tried to instigate the various Qiledars and Chiefs in that region to oppose the French occupation of those lands. No sooner did the English Resident at Ingeram, Westcott, hear of the transfer of the Sarkars to the French than he wanted to challenge it, but, Thomas Saunders the Governor of Madras, advised him against taking such a step in view of the English struggle in the Carnatic, lest it should lead to further complications[45].

Nevertheless, the Madras Government, procured additional battalions of artillery of about 428 men, and they also advised the Bombay Government to maintain cordial relations with the Peishwa so that at an opportune time they

45, Records of Fort St. George Pub. Cons. Feb. 14, 1754.
"Bussy in the Deccan", p. 178.

might both attack Salabat Jung under the cover of attacking the Angrias, a naval power of considerable interest in Maharastra[46]. They also decided to wrest the Divi Islands from the French. To achieve their objective they started intriguing with Jaffar Ali the Governor of Rajahmundry and Chicacole Sarkars and with the Rajah of Vizianagaram, the subtenant of the Chicacole Sarkar.

Bussy, was shrewd enough to foresee that the acquisition of the Sarkars would rouse the ire of the other Europen rivals of the French. So, he was careful to see, that the Sarkars were personally granted to him to meet the expenses of the French troops.

He also made it known that the French troops would stay in the Deccan only, as long as the Nizam required them. This news was spread apparently to lull the suspicions and jealously of the Indian Princes.

However much, Dupleix, disliked this arrangement he had to acquiesce in this view of the French interests. At the time of the granting of the Sarkars, Dupleix was negotiating a truce with the English at Sadras. He did not like the idea of the Sarkars being dragged into the discussions at Sadras. So, he made it appear, that the Sarkars were granted to Bussy in his personal capacity towards the maintenance of the French detachment and that the French East India Company had nothing to do with it. So in consonance with this attitude he deliberately refrained from observing any jubilations at Pondicherry. He wrote to Bussy[47]; "You should use this title only when dealing with the French, whereas with foreigners you must behave as acting according to the powers, granted to you by the Suba or the Mughal Emperor and that the Indian or European troops you command were directly dependent on the Nawab just as you yourself seem to be. It would even not be wise to inform the Muhammedans of the patent conferred on you but merely to tell them that I had sanctioned all that the Nawab had done through you for the sustenance of our troops and that you had been appointed by me to collect revenues while the commander at Masulipatam would be entrusted with the same duties in your absence; In such circumstances he would be your procurator. At all events it would be suitable that foreigners should be under the impression that we have no other interests in possessing that territory except in so far as the pay of our troops is concerned and that you are collecting the revenues only on behalf of the Nawab".

Even after acquiring the Sarkars the French could not make good their financial position sound in the Deccan. They found the revenues of the Sarkars insufficient to meet their growing expenses. Once the Sarkars were given away, Shah Nawaz Khan, refused to entertain any further demands for money from the French.

46. Dodwell.—'Madras Despatches' (1754-1765), pp. 15, 1720.

47. 'Bussy in the Deccan', p. 174.

Jaffar Ali Khan, the Governor of Rajahmundry and Chicacole Sarkars found himself reduced now to the anomalous position of a tenant of the French. So he wanted to get the grant of the Sarkars to the French nullified. Moreover, he had also heard, that, Dupliex, wanted to replace him by appointing his own favourite Qalandar Khan as the Governor of the Rajahmundry Sarkars. So, no sooner, did Jaffar Ali, hear of the grant to the French, than he sent his family to the English factory at Vizagapatam and also requested the English to send him a garrison so that he could fortify Rajahmundry[48]. But the English could not comply with this request on account of their preoccupations in the Carnatic. Jaffar Ali also induced the Chiefs of Vizianagaram and Bobbili to join him in a league against the French[49]. Jaffar Ali had to pay Rs. 500,000 to Salabat Jung instead of remitting the amount directly in cash, he assigned a portion of the debit to every tenant zamindar, knowing fully well that they would be able to pay the amount[50]. This, increased the financial difficulties of the French, all the more, and Bussy wrote to Pondicherry repeatedly asking for some relief.

But conditions in Pondicherry were far from happy. The French, had lost heavily in their wars in the Carnatic and the Directors of the French East India Company were thinking of recalling Dupleix.

To carry on the wars in the Carnatic, Dupleix was forced to borrow heavily from the local sowcars in his own name and he was definitely, not in a position to relieve Bussy owing to his financial straits.

So, in order to extricate himself from his financial difficulties, Bussy, thought of going personally to the Sarkars and collecting its revenues. But he was prevented from doing so, as he had to accompany Salabat Jung on a campaign against Raghoji Bhonslay, of Nagpur. Raghoji, resented the granting of Berar to Syed Lashkar Khan. So hostilities broke out between him and Salabat Jung. The latter returned from this campaign to Hyderabad in May 1754[51].

In the meanwhile, Bussy, had sent Ibrahim Khan, one of the commanders of his detachment, at the head of 2186 sepoys, 674 cavaliers and a European Commander Dugrez, at the head of 150 Europeans, to the assistance of Moracin, the French Governor at Masulipatam.

Ibrahim Khan was instructed to bring the recalcitrant polygars in the Sarkars to book, while collecting the revenues without resorting to the help of the European troops as far as possible, so that it might not rouse the jealousy of the English.

48. Records of Fort St. George, Pub. Consultation, Feb. 14, 1754.
49. Peddapura Samsthana Charitramu, pp. 90-91.
50. "Bussy in the Deccan", p. 176.
51. Orme.—"Military Transactions of the British Nation in Indostan", Vol. I, p. 372.
52. "Bussy in the Deccan", p. 176.

The European troops were retained at Masulipatam, as a reserve force while Ibrahim Khan, with some additional reinforcements from Moracin, marched at the head of his troops against the rebellious polygars in the Sarkars.

On hearing the news about the arrival of Ibrahim Khan, Jaffar Ali, made preparations to defend himself. He collected an army of 4000 cavalry and 30,000 infantry. Seeing him, almost every petty zamindar on the East Coast tried to follow his example and become independent, and they withheld paying tribute. As a result of this, the whole of the Sarkars area was thrown into confusion.

Meanwhile, Bussy, was sending desperate letters to Moracin and Dupleix asking for financial relief. As a matter of fact, the troops which had accompanied him to Nagpur against Raghoji Bhonslay, refused to march back unless their arrears were paid. The Sepoys deserted in great numbers while some of them sold their rifles to buy food. Bussy, to pay off their arrears, was reduced to the extremity of borrowing from the firm of Kasi Das Bukkanji and even from petty merchants like chilly sellers[53]. The French became, the laughing-stock of the whole of the Deccan. Fortunately, for Bussy, at this juncture, Moracin, sent a lakh of Rupees which was just enough to tide over the difficulty. Moracin, finding that almost all the zamindars in the Sarkars had lined up with Jaffar Ali in opposing the French, tried to detach some of them by his diplomatic exertions. One of the most powerful zamindars whom he was able to wean away from Jaffar Ali was Rajah Vijaya Rama Raju Gajapati of Vizianagaram[54].

Moracin, persuaded Vijaya Rama Raju to visit Masulipatam and there, an understanding was reached to the effect, that Rajahmundry and Chicacole Sarkars should be rented to Vijaya Rama Raju for 16 lakhs of Rupees per annum, a rate that was lower than that paid by Jaffar Ali[55]. It was also decided that of these 16 lakhs four lakhs were to be exempted, for, Jaffar Ali had already collected that amount. Of the balance, Vijaya Rama Raju, paid on the spot 3 lakhs of Rupees. It was out of this amount that, Moracin, despatched Re. 1 lakh to Bussy, to relieve him of his immediate financial difficulties. It was settled, that the balance of 9 lakh of Rupees, should be paid by Vijaya Rama Raju in three equal instalments every Second month, the last instalment to be paid in September.

After this agreement was drawn up, Dugrez, at the head of 80 Europeans and 400 sepoys was sent along with Vijaya Rama Raju, to assist him in bringing the Sarkars under his control. Vijaya Rama Raju left Masulipatam with the French troops on the 2nd April.

---

53. "Bussy in the Deccan", p. 197.
    Records of Fort St. George, C. C. 1754, pp. 96–120.
54. Records of Fort St. George, C. C. 1754, pp. 5–54.
    Peddapura Samsthana Charitramu, p. 91.
    Dodwell. Dupleix and Clive, p. 93.
55. Ibid.

Jaffar Ali, on hearing of the adove transaction, decided to seek the help of the Marathas against the French and VijayaRama Raju. Jaffar Ali, left the Sarkars to procure the aid of Raghoji Bhonslay, of Nagpur. On his way to Raghoji's court, Jaffar Ali met Janoji, the son of Raghoji. Janoji was going on an expedition to Bengal, at the head of 2000 Maratha troops. However, he was soon persuaded by Jaffar Ali, to change his course and to lead an expedition into the Sarkars instead of to far off Bengal.

The Marathas entered Chicacole and after plundering the country side attacked the Dutch factory at Bhimlipatam and ravaged it. From there, they proceeded to Rajahmundry and carried on great depredations in the country and collected much booty. In the beginning Vijaya Rama Raju and Dugrez tried to oppose the Maratha inroads in the Sarkars, but their forces received an initial set back at Vizianagaram, at the hands of the Marathas.

Finding the strength of their troops inadequate, to oppose the Marathas, they, applied to Moracin for reinforcements. The Marathas, anxious to preserve their booty, never allowed the main part of their troops to come into conflict with the French troops. Nevertheless, on the 4th May 1754, a skirmish took place at Tumpala between the Marathas and Moracin, in which the former were forced to give way, before the French artillery[56]. Fearing that their position might become precarious if fresh reinforcements were to arrive from Masulipatam, the Marathas suddently decamped from the Sarkars fording the river Godavary at Ellore[57].

Seeing his allies desert him so suddenly, Jaffar Ali went to Aurangabad and tendered his submission to Salabat Jung[58]. Vijaya Rama Raju was at heart favourably disposed towards the English and he also secretly corresponded with them.

The Maratha depredations affected the Sarkars very badly. Finding the Sarkars, ruined. by the Martha incursion, Vijaya Rama Raju, now expressed his inability to pay the stipulated 3 lakhs of Rupees that were due in May, to the French. His refusal had the effect of totally paralysing, the French trade on the East Coast and Moracin could not remit any money to Bussy, at Aurangabad.

Moreover, Moracin, yielding to local intrigues, had replaced, Ibrahim Khan, who was made the Governor of Ellore after the flight of Jaffar Ali, to the Marathas by Hassan Ali Beg. This made Ibrahim Khan the French

---

56. Vizagapatam District Gazetteer, p. 31.
    Orme"—A History of the Military Transactions of the British Nation in Indostan", Vol. I, p. 374.
    "Bussy in the Deccan", p. 192.
57. Orme.—"A History of the Military Transactions of the British Nation in Indostan", Vol. I, p. 374.
58. Ibid.

commander powerless and increased the confusion in the Sarkars all the more.

Realising, that he alone could set matters right, Bussy, decided to go to the Sarkars and he wrote to Dupleix, depicting the plight of the French army, in the Deccan, and stating that he was reduced to the extremity of selling his personal jewels for procuring money for the payment of his troops.

He also sought, the permission, of Dupleix, to proceed to the Sarkars. Dupleix, was afraid, that Bussy's absence might lead to some fresh intrigues againt Salabat Jung and the French. He was afraid that some harm might befall Salabat Jung. But, Bussy, the hardened diplomat wrote to Dupleix to the following effect[59]. "We ought not to cling merely to his person but whomsoever happend to be the lord of the country, even if the latter held his rank merely through the strange fancy of luck. The real way to lose all would be to follow the erroneous doctrine of clinging steadfastly to the person of Salabat Jung".

Dupleix, had to give way before the repeated and reasonable request of Bussy, and he permitted him to proceed to the Sarkars.

So after solemnly assuring Nawab Salabat Jung and his nobles that he would return to Hyderabad, as early as possible. Bussy left Aurangabad, on the 9th June, 1754 for Masulipatnam[60]. He left behind a major portion of the French army for the protection of Salabat Jung and allayed the latter's fears by assuring him that he would return to Hyderabad as soon as he settled the affairs of the Sarkars.

Bussy, met Moracin, on the 5th July at Bezwada; and learnt from him the deterioration that had set in the administration of the Sarkars and the pecuniary difficulties of the French.

Vijaya Rama Raju had neither the inclination nor the means to pay the arrears to the French; All the while the energy and resources of the French troops under Dugrez were dissipated in an aimless manner in putting down the rebellious polygars.

Bussy, decided to take matters into his own hands and restore the administration of the Sarkars. The news of his arrival itself, had a salutary effect. Many, of the hitherto recalcitrant zamindars now decided to tender their submission to the French.

Bussy, in the company of Moracin, now left Bezwada for Rajahmundry, via Ellore, and after arriving at Rajahmundry, he held a Durbar there. Many of the zamindars on the East Coast hastened to offer their allegiance to him.

59. "Bussy in the Deccan", p. 170
60. Malleson-'History of the French in India', p. 383.
"Bussy in the Deccan". p. 198.

Bussy, settled the administration of the Northern Sarkars on the following lines[61].

The Rajahmundry Sarkar was rented to Vijaya Rama Raju for Rs. 13 lakhs while Chicacole was given for 9 lakhs to Ibrahim Khan Gardi.

Ellore and Mustafanagar were given to Hussain Ali Beg for a rent of 9 lakhs of Rupees. It was expected that the four districts would yield a revenue of Rs. 31 lakhs and that it would leave a surplus after defraying the expenses of the French detachment in the Deccan.

Vijaya Rama Raju, was made a mansabdar of 2000 and the title of Munna Sultan Mirza was conferred on him, while the Rajahs of Bobbili and Peddapur were made mansabdars of 1000 each. Referring to these arrangements Vijaya Rama Raju wrote to the English Governor at Madras[62];

" I write this to acquaint you that Hayedar Jang was come to Satavaram in order to finish affairs with me. I thereupon went there and paid a visit to him, and delivered the account of revenues received from the two Circars and then resigned the employment thereof. I have finished the affairs of the Zamadary of Vizianagaram and Pedapore and intended to take my leave to return to Vizianagaram, but the said Hayedar Jang entreated me very much and told me that if I did not go to Monsr. Bussy he then said Monsieur Bussy's credit would be lessened at court and as this gentleman was Governor of the Circars I thought fit to go to Rajahmundrum in company with Hayedar Jang where I paid a visit to Monsieur Bussy who was pleased to send for the Mensel and C' from Nabab Salabat Jang's court on my account and others and gave as follows ". Here Vijaya Rama Raju narrated the above details of administrative matters as settled by Bussy. This letter of Raju clearly proves that he was not genuinely attached to the French but that he submitted to Bussy more for reasons of expediency, than because of his actual desire to acknowledge the French authority.

While Bussy was engaged in bringing about a settlement in the Sarkars, matters of grave importance were taking place in the Carnatic. The French failed to take Trichinopoly and a greater portion of the Carnatic fell into the hands of the English. Dupleix, tried to retreive matters by entering into an alliance with the Mysoreans and Murari Rao Ghorpade, the Maratha leader, but all his effects proved in vain. This resulted in a great loss to the French commercial interests. The French Government, anxious to put an end to this ruinious war, sent one Mons. Godeheu, to India to replace Dupleix, and to negotiate with the English. Godeheu, arrived in Pondicheery in August 1754, and he took over charge from Dupleix, and the latter left Pondicheery, on the 14th October.

61. Records of Fort St. George., C. C. (1755)., p. 4., L. No. 9., D/ 12th May 1754.

62. Ibid.

63. Orme - ' History of the Military Transactions of the British Nation in Indostan., Vol. I., p. 376.

Malleson.- 'History of the French in India'., p. 436.

Bussy heard of these events while he was at Masulipatam.

Soon after his arrival, Godeheu, entered into a truce with the English, called the Convention of Sadras which was to last from 11th October 1754 to 11th January 1755. According to the agreement both the English and the French East India Companies agreed not to enter into alliances with or intervene in the internal disputes of the Native Powers in India. They also agreed to give up all those territories that were not mentioned in the new treaty signed at Sadras.

According to this treaty, the English were to have Devi Kotah and the French, Karaikal in the Tanjore country. On the Coramandal Coast it was decided that the English should retain Madras and Fort St. David and the French should retain Pondicherry and other districts equivalent in value to those held by the English. If the French felt, that the English possessions were of more value, than those held by them, they could then take territories between Nizampatnam and the Gundlakamma river thus equalising their possessions with that of the English. Divi Island and the districts around Masulipatam were to be partitioned equally between the two Companies.

[63]As regards the Northern Sarkars it was decided that both the Companies should have subordinate factories at Rajahmundry and Chicacole, without any claim to the territorial revenues of the country.

The Powers also decided that in the event of either of the two Companies entering into hostilities, the matter should be referred for arbitration and in the event of the Indian Powers committing hostilities, to unite together in putting down the Indian Powers.

This truce arranged by Godeheu, clearly shows that the English were the victors. Though the English till now did not directly interfere in the Deccan, yet by making themselves supreme in the Carnatic they were able to dictate terms to the French in the Deccan; the terms of the above agreement were sent to the respective Home Governments of both the Companies, and if it were to be ratified, it clearly meant that the French were to give up their position of pre-eminence in the Deccan, a position for which Bussy, had monoeuvred so painstakingly, and a position, due to which, both Bussy and Dupleix dreamed of dictating terms not only to the Deccan Subedar but even to the Mughal Emperor.

By being a party to this truce, the French violated the trust reposed in them by the Nizam. Not only was this truce concluded without the knowledge of Salabat Jung, but even the allies of the French, the Mysoreans and the Maratha leader, Murari Rao Ghorpade, were not consulted.

63. Orme. - 'A History of the Military Transactions of the British Nation in Indostan., Vol. I., p. 376.
Malleson—"History of the French in India", p. 436.

Naturally the news of the agreement was received with a great deal of surprise and perturbation in Hyderabad. Salabat Jung, on hearing about the treaty, wrote to Bussy, urging him to return to the Deccan. Dupleix's recall from India was a great shock to Salabat Jung and his nobles. On receiving the report of Dupleix's recall, Shah Nawaz Khan, the Diwan wrote to Mahammud Hussain the Qiledar of Hyderabad in the following manner[64].

"I cannot recover from the surprise which the news of the recall of the Governor Bahadur has caused me. I cannot imagine what the French are at, but by that act they will lose their honour and territories. I cannot conceal from you that we can arrange nothing with the new Governor, who has not the least knowledge of our affairs. Besides it appears that the French are neither so powerful nor so generous as they would have us believe, and that the English have the absolute mastery over them. I will not hide from you then that I am about to negotiate with the English and Muhammad Ali".

The above letter clearly shows, the amount of damage done to the French prestige in the Deccan; the nobles in the Nizam's court now began to praise the steadfastness of the English who supported Nawab Muhammad Ali even under adverse circumstances.

Shah Nawaz Khan and Jaffar Ali, the ex-Foujdar of the Sarkars, now exerted themselves to wean Salabat Jung away from the French influence. They also opened correspondence with the English with a view to undermine French influence in the Nizam's Court.

Instigated by Shah Nawaz Khan, Salabat Jung now wrote to Bussy, who was still in the Sarkars to hasten to the Deccan and assist him in a campaign against the Rajah of Mysore who had neglected to pay the tribute due to the Nizam after the death of Nizamul-Mulk.

Salabat Jung had also not received any tribute from Arcot, ever since those territories were given to Dupleix by Muzaffar Jung. So with even, the revenues of the Northern Sarkars taken away from him, Salabat Jung found it very difficult to pay his own troops. Hence, he now decided to go on a campaign to Mysore to realise the arrears of tribute from there.

Moreover, the arbitrary manner in which the English and the French tried to appropriate territories by the Convention of Sadras in 1754, territories, that technically and legally belonged to the Nizam, made the Nizam and his courtiers disconsolate. They now decided to test the bona-fides of the French and their protestations of friendship and good faith towards the Nizam.

Bussy, on receiving Salabat Jung's letter asking him to come back to the Deccan, wrote to Godeheu for instructions. The latter was of the opinion

64 Malleson. - 'History of the French in India', p. 476.

that the truce applied only to Anglo-French relations in the Carnatic and therefore, it did not affect the French position in the Deccan. Moreover, the treaty was yet to be ratified by the respective Home Governments and as long as it was not ratified, Godeheu, saw no harm in the French maintaining normal relations with their Indian allies. So he permitted, Bussy, to proceed to the Deccan and the latter arrived in Aurangabad in January 1755[65].

On his arrival, Bussy, found the atmosphere in the court hostile towards the French. Even Salabat Jung was alienated from him. The Subah and his Ministers had heard that according to the clauses of the agreement drawn up at Sadras, the French had provisionally recognised Muhammad Ali as the Nawab of Arcot.

The Nizam had incurred a heavy loss by not recognising Muhammad Ali as the Nawab of Arcot and leaving the Carnatic affairs in the hands of Dupleix. Now, the Subah and his Minister were indignant to hear that an agreement was reached regarding the Carnatic without any reference to its liege-lord, the Subedar of the Deccan.

Salabat Jung inveighed Bussy, in the following manner[66]; "Your Sovereign promised to support me against my enemies, to establish my authority, and to make it respected. Of this you yourself had given me assurance on which I have always depended, yet I now hear everywhere it is the King of England who specially concerns himself with the affairs of India even with those which affect me --- You have put me in the balance against Muhammed Ali, you have allowed to be placed at the head of one of my tributory provinces a man whom I have never employed, who has always rebelled against my authority. Nay more, if I were to proceed to the Karnatic to drive him out of it, the English would support him, and you on account of this truce would hold back, you, who are engaged to support me on all occassions, would aid me neither against the English nor against Muhammed Ali --- you know that the state of my affairs necessarily demands the support of a European Power, on this condition I am able to govern, either you remain here or I must enlist the English in my interest. Are you disposed to render me the service which you have rendered hitherto ?

I must do you the justice to say that I am grateful for them; but it would appear now that you have neither the power nor the inclination" ---.

Bussy, assured the Nizam that the French attitude towards the latter had not changed. Thereupon Salabat Jung asked Bussy, to accompany him, on his campaign against Mysore, impressing upon Bussy, the necessity of undertaking the campaign in view of his not having received any tribute from the Carnatic, ever since, that region was left to the management of Dupleix.

65. Orme.—"A History of the Military Transactions of the British Nation in Indostan"., Vol. I.
Malleson —'History of the French in India'.
66. Malleson—'History of the French in India., p. 478.

Here Bussy was thrown into a quandary. The French, were the allies of the Rajah of Mysore. Now if Bussy were to support Salabat Jung against the Rajah of Mysore, it would mean that he was helping the Nizam against an avowed ally of the French. At the same time Bussy could not refuse Salabat Jung's request as it would be violating the treaty of Aurangabad according to which Bussy, had promised to assist Salabat Jung whenever the latter required his help.

There was also a further complication. According to the Convention of Sadras the French and the English agreed not to assist the Indian Princess in their wars and, if, Bussy, were to assist Salabat Jung it would imply a direct violation of the Convention of Sadras.

So Bussy wrote to Godeheu for advice, but before his letter could reach Pondicherry, the latter had already left for France, on the 16th February 1755[67].

Seeing, that, he alone had to decide the issue, Bussy, determined to accompany Salabat Jung with a contingent of 500 French soldiers. At the same time he wished, not to put the Rajah of Mysore to undue harassment. Hence in his letters he urged the Dalwai of Mysore to come to an understanding with the Nizam. However much he desired to avoid it, Bussy could not but help the Nizam in reducing minor forts in the Mysore country, while on their way to Srirangapatam. The Mughal armies laid siege to Srirangapatam in March 1755.

The Dalwai of Mysore at first sent a letter of protest to the new French Governor, De'Leyrit, against Bussy helping the Nizam in the war against Mysore.

De'Leyrit, on his arrival at Pondicherry, became cognisant of the course of events on the Coramandal Coast. He realised that the truce agreed at Sadras would not last long, and that in spite of the truce, the English had already occupied Madura and Tinnevelly. So, he, quite agreed with the stand taken by Bussy, the only course that could be adopted if the French were to remain in the Deccan. Hence De'Leyrit tried to pacify the Dalwai of Mysore, by telling him that Bussy had accompanied the Nizam, in the capacity of a servant of the Subedar of the Northern Sarkars and not as a representative of the French East India Company.

However he also wrote to the Dalwai saying that he would write to Bussy, to help the Rajah of Mysore by bringing about an amicable settlement between the Nizam and the Mysoreans.

The Rajah of Mysore in the beginning was prepared to withstand a long siege at the hands of the Nizam, but on hearing that the Peishwa was

67. Malleson - 'History of the French in India', p. 436.

also approaching their country to levy Chouth he lost heart and agreed to Bussy's proposals for peace[68].

He allowed Salabat Jung to encamp under the walls of Srirangapatam thereby recognising the Nizam's supremacy over Mysore. Bussy settled the matters between Salabat Jung and Mysore for 56 lakhs of Rupees[69]. The Mysoreans found it hard to make up the amount even after requisitioning the plates and jewellery of the Rajah's family. He prevailed upon the Soucars in the country to send their gumasthas as hostages. However they were able to pay, Rs. 27 lakhs as cash, while it was agreed that the balance should be paid in the form of bills[70]. Bussy by his exertions was also able to ward off a further devastation of the Mysore country at the hands of the Peishwa and his Maratha troops who came to Srirangapatam at this juncture[71]. Salabat Jung, highly pleased with the successful termination of his campaign, returned to Hyderabad on the 13th July, 1755[72]. But the campaign in no way solved his financial problems. He required 76 lakhs of Rupees to pay the troops. So, Shah Nawaz Khan still remained disgruntled, and his annoyance towards Bussy, increased all the more, when he perceived the latters anxiety to protect Mysore, the ally of the French, against the Nizam and the Marathas. Bussy, saw to it that the Mysore French alliance was not strained to a breaking point. Shah Nawaz Khan tried to convince Salabat Jung that Bussy's apparent devotion to Salabat Jung during the Mysore campaign was not actuated by sincere motives, and that throughout the Mysore campaign he tried to serve the French interests rather than the interests of the Nizam.

The Mysore campaign, had widespread repercussions on the course of the Anglo-French struggle in the Carnatic. Seeing Bussy's intervention in the Mysore campaign on behalf of the Nizam, the English helped Nawab Muhammad Ali to occupy Vellore and the surrounding countries. When, the French Governor De'Leyrit, protested against this action of the English, their Governor Pigot, replied saying, that they were doing for thier ally what Bussy, was doing for the Nizam[73].

Thus, in spite of the truce, both the Companies actively helped their Indian allies in local wars and acquired territories in the name of their allies. The French, not only seized the English factories at Ingeram and Bandarlanka but also planned to attack their factories at Vizagapatam[74].

---

68. Ananda Ranga Pillay's Diary, Vol. IX, p. 156.
Orme.–'A History of the Military Transactions of the British Nation in Indostan', Vol. I, p. 404.
69. Wilks–-'Historical Sketches of South India', Vol. I, p. 348.
70. Records of Fort St. George.–-'Military consultations', (1755), p. 92.
71. Kincaid and Parasnis–-'A History of the Maratha People', Vol. VIII, p. 34.
72. 'Bussy in the Deccan', p. 219.
73. Ananda Ranga Pillay's Diary, Vol. IX, p. 229.
74. Dodwell–-Madras Despatches, (1754 1765), p. 97.

The Nizam's army which had arrived in Hyderabad in July, remained there till the end of 1755. In the meanwhile, Bussy got a letter from the Mughal Emperor asking for French help[75].

The Mughal Emperor was anxious to put down the Marathas. Hence, he wrote to Bussy, asking, whether, it would be possible for him to send a French contingent of 1000 strong, to Delhi. In return for the French help, the Emperor promised to confirm all settlements that the French had acquired in the Carnatic and in the Sarkars and to settle the Arcot issue, in their favour, by placing it under the control of Salabat Jung, after paying some compensation to the English for the loss they might sustain by the taking away of Arcot[76]. The Emperor also conveyed his willingness to pay Rs. 3 lakhs per month for the maintenance of the French troops.

Bussy, received these proposals from the Emperor in the month of October, 1755. He knew, that, in the event of an outbreak of hostilities between the French and the English, East India Companies, the French would require all the forces they could muster.

Hence after consulting De'Leyrit, he decided to gain time and not to commit himself in any definite manner. In the meanwhile the Seven Years War broke out in Europe on the 17th May, 1756.

In this war England and France fought on opposite sides. This war spread not only in Europe but on all fronts, where, the English and the French possessed colonies and commercial settlements.

The news of the outbreak of war reached India by the 12th November, 1756[77]. This naturally made it possible for the French to accede to the Mughal Emperor's proposals. Commmenting about this, Bussy wrote to De'Leyrit[78] ; " By making the English realise the sacrifice we have made, we might make what is happening now seem a plausible retreat. Our stay of six years besides the Suba has not in any way helped us in the Arcot affair where the English and Muhammed Ali did as they pleased without worrying about our rights. Under these circumstances we can hope for no help whatsoever from the Moghal Nation; even our alliance with them will be burdensome. We have no more need of the Moghals, to retain what we have in the North than the English needed then for what they own in the South. I know the weak points of that nation. We have nothing to be afraid of them nor have we anything to expect from them. If we intend continuing taking part in their affairs then the expedition to Delhi (that is to sign an agreement with the Moghal Emperor) would be very useful to us.

75. Dodwell—'Dupleix and Clive', p. 94.
76. Dodwell—Madras Despatches, (1754-1765), p. 122.
Dodwell—'Dupleix and Clive', p. 94.
"Bussy in the Deccan", p. 226.
77. Ananda Ranga Piliay's Diary, Vol. IX, p. 170.
78. "Bussy in the Deccan", p. 226.

Otherwise I think we should keep within our own territory and await developments in Asia and in Europe ''.

This letter amply reveals that Bussy had realised how ineffective was the power of the Indian Princes, and that the real contest for supremacy in the South lay between the English and the French.

The English were also in the meanwhile actively engaged in carrying on intrigues against the French. [79] The Madras Governor, Pigot and his council suggested to the Bombay Government, that, they, should enter into an alliance with the Peishwa ostensibly against the Angrias, a naval power, but actually with the intention of making a surprise attack on Salabat Jung and the French. To justify such an attack, Pigot, suggested, that the English should first demand from Salabat Jung the restoration of the Divi Island and the English factories at Masulipatam. The Madras Council also proposed sending an English squadron of ships to lie off the Divi Island, on the coast to give weight to this demand.

This scheme also received the approval of the Home Government and the Secret Committee of the English East India Company sent instructions to both the Bombay and the Madras Governments to carry out this plan[80]. The Madras Government, being of the opinion that the truce of Sadras, applied only to the Coramandal Coast suggested that the English should also make an attack from Masulipatam drawing into an alliance all those zamindars on the East Coast who were inimical towards the French.

But the Bombay Government did not approve of the plan. They were of the opinion that the Marathas might not be quite amenable to a scheme that would surely result in the increase of English power. The Home Government, later on started thinking on the same lines, so it instructed the Madras and the Bombay Governments to drop the scheme, and to offer to assist the Marathas if they asked for it and also agreed to defray the expenses of the campaigns.

But in the meanwhile, the English East India Company according to its original plan had sent Robert Clive to India, with reinforcements and appointed him as the Deputy Governor of Bombay[81].

Clive, on his arrival wanted to execute the original plan but he was prevented from doing so, by the Bombay Government. Nevertheless, the Bombay Government sent Clive at the head of a naval squadron to assist the Marathas against Tulaji Angria and the latter was defeated. But very soon differences arose over the division of the spoils between the English and the Marathas and the English withdrew from the contest.

---

79. Dodwell--Madras Despatches, (1754-1765), p. 20.
80. Dodwell-Dupleix and Clive, pp. 98-99.
81. Orme.--'A History of the Military Transactions of the British Nation in Indostan', Vol. I, p. 406.

As a matter of fact the Peishwa, Balaji Baji Rao, had first approached, Bussy, for help against the Angria. Bussy, was not in a position to spare any troops and so he replied, to the Peishwa, that he did not want to bring disgrace to the French by sending small ineffective detachments. So the Peishwa turned to the English for help and the English sent a naval squadron under Clive[82].

Early in 1756, Salabat Jung, proposed to Bussy an expedition against the Nawab of Savanur, Abdul Hakim Khan Afghani[83], who had withheld paying tribute to the Nizam, for sometime and aspired to defy the Nizam with the help of Murari Rao Ghorpade the Maratha Sardar of Gooty. He had also given asylum to one Muzaffar Khan Gardi, a former employee of the Peishwa, and neglected to pay the customary Chouth to the Peishwa. So, the Peishwa, was alo dissatisfied with the Nawab of Savanur and with Murari Rao who had refused to pay his tribute to the Peiṣhwa saying he owed his powers directly to the Chatrapati and not to the Peishwa Balaji[84]. Seeing that both the Peishwa as well as the Nizam had grounds to be dissatisfied with these feudatories, Shah Nawaz Khan decided to make common cause with the Peishwa to punish these recalcitrant chiefs.

Murari Rao Ghorpade entered into an agreement with the Nawab of Savanur and agreed to garrison and defend the fortress of Savanur against the combined forces of the Peishwa Balaji Baji Rao and the Nizam.

The Peishwa along with his Maratha forces and that of the forces of Maratha Chiefs like Malhar Rao Holkar and Mudhoji Holkar arrived at Savanur in the beginning of March 1756[85].

Though the Nizam's army started early in 1756 from Bidar it arrived at Savanur much later than the Marathas. Shah Nawaz Khan seized this opportunity to prejudice the Peishwa against the French, by telling him that the French were responsible for the tardy manner in which the Mughals arrived at Savanur.

Shah Nawaz Khan had sufficient grounds to assume that the French were unwilling to fight with Murari Rao Ghorpade, a former ally of the French. Murari Rao had helped the French during the siege of Trichinopoly and the French owed him a sum of Rs. 14 lakhs. The French, owing to their vicissitudes of fortune in the Carnatic and the subsequent loss of their trade, found themselves unable to pay that amount to Murari Rao[86]. So, when the dispute between the Peishwa and Murari Rao Ghorpade was first

---

82. 'Bussy in the Deccan', p. 229.
83. Muhammad Siraj-ud-Din Talib—Nizam Ali Khan Sawale Zindagi, Part I, p. 23.
84. G. S. Sardesai—'New History of the Mahrattas', Vol. II, p. 328.
85. Sanpuri Bhakkar.
86. 'Bussy in the Deccan', p. 230.

referred to Bussy, the latter in consultation with De'Leyrit decided to support Murari Rao, in the hope that he could get the debts to the Maratha chief written off[86]. But when Murari Rao allied himself with the Nawab of Savanur, a rebel against the authority of the Nizam, Bussy, found it impossible to side with Murari Rao against the Peishwa, lest the latter should prejudice Salabat Jung against the French. Hence, Bussy, decided to go with Salabat Jung in his campaign against Savanur and Murari Rao, but to conduct the campaign in such a manner as to provide some means by which Murari Rao could come to terms through French mediation.

The Fort of Savanur was ably defended by Murari Rao and, therefore, its siege dragged on throughout the month of April. Opinion in the camps of the Nizam as well as the Peishwa was divided regarding the attitude they should adopt towards the besieged. Mulhar Rao Holkar wanted to save Murari Rao at any cost, while, the Pathan nobles in the camp of the Nizam were inclined to sympathise with the Nawab of Savanur.

Sensing this general feeling in the camp, Bussy, tried to negotiate with Balaji on behalf of Murari Rao. Meanwhile, the siege dragged on, seeing which Shah Nawaz Khan and Jaffar Ali blamed Bussy, saying that he was deliberately prolonging the siege because he wanted to favour Murari Rao. Seeing this attitude of the Diwan, Bussy, in order to clear himself of these charges, directed his artillery to capture the fortress and Savanur surrendered on the 25th April 1756.

A peace was arranged between the hitherto combating powers, through Bussy's mediation[87].

The Nawab of Savanur agreed to recongnise Salabat Jung as his overlord once again, while Murari Rao agreed to pay the Customary Chouth to the Peishwa, and he was again taken into the Peishwa's service. Out of gratitude for Bussy's exertion on his behalf, Murari Rao wrote off, the money that was due to him from the French East India Company[88].

The only gain that the Nizam got out of this Savanur expedition was the nominal recognition of his sovereignity by the Nawab of Savanur. Naturally many of the Mughal nobles felt, that Bussy, preferred the interests of his own nation to that of the Nizam in the Savanur transactions.

Shah Nawaz Khan impressed upon the mind of Salabat Jung the selfish conduct of Bussy and advised him to dismiss Bussy from his service. He also reminded Salabat Jung that, so far, the French had not paid any tribute for holding the Government of Arcot and if the same were to be conferred on

86. Ibid.
87. Sardesai--'Selection from the Peshwas Daftar', Vol. XXVIII, L. No. 140.
    Sewell & Aiyangar-'Historical Inscriptions of South India', p. 300.
88. "Bussy in the Deccan", p. 232.
    Orme. - 'A History of the Military Transactions of the British Nation in Indostan', Vol. I., p. 427.

Nawab Muhammad Ali, the latter had offerred to pay a tribute of 32 lakhs of Rupees, which would benefit the Nizam a great deal.

Jaffar Ali, further told, Salabat Jung that if he considered the presence of a foreign contingent essential, he could get the French detachment substituted by an English contingent, by entering into an agreement with the English.

Shah Nawaz Khan further sought to win over the Peishwa on his side in his anti-French activities, and to get rid of, Bussy, if necessary by poison. But the Peishwa, was greatly impressed by the ability and the energetic manner of Bussy, and he was even willing to entertain Bussy in his service, in case of a rupture between the French and the Nizam. Yet he represented to Salabat Jung the danger of the various concessions he made to the French[89]. The Peishwa further offered to the Nizam to supply him with an auxiliary Maratha force to replace the French troops, and advised him to take his brother Nawab Nizam Ali Khan Bahadur into his confidence and administer the State in consultation with him.

Shah Nawaz Khan realised that the sharing of power with Nizam Ali might endanger the position of Salabat Jung, yet such was his anxiety to be rid of the French, that he approved the plan of the Peishwa. He persuaded Salabat Jung, to write to the English at Madras, to send a battalion of English troops to replace the French. He hoped to recover the Northern Sarkars with the help of the Peishwa, while he aspired to assert the Nizam's authority over Arcot and realise its revenues with the help of the English.

Salabat Jung decided to act in accordance with the advice of the Peishwa and Shah Nawaz Khan. He accordingly released his brothers and conferred honours on them. He conferred the title of Nizam-ud-Dowla on Nizam Ali Khan and entrusted to him the administration of the Northern districts with Berar as the capital, while Basalat Jung was given the title of Basalat-dowla and the Subhas of Bijapur and Adoni. The later made Adoni his capital[90]. He also conferred on the youngest brother Mir Mughal Ali a Khillat for Aurangabad.

Bussy, saw that all these transactions were made by Salabat Jung without any reference to him, and before he could adjust himself to the new set up, he received orders of dismissal from Shaw Nawaz Khan asking him to leave the Nizam's service and retire to the French territories. The Diwan, assured him, in his letter that the Nizam's troops would not molest the French while the latter were retreating[91].

89. Cambridge–Account of the war in India, p. 100.
Dodwell–Madras Despatches, (1754–1765).
Malleson.—'History of the French in India'., p. 485.
Orme - Vol. I., p. 428.

90. Muh. Siraj-ud-Din Talib—Nizam Ali Khan, Sawale Zindagi, Part I.
Sanpuri Bhakkar.
Malleson.—"History of the French in India"., p. 435.

91. Ibid.

The English received Salabat Jung's letter asking for the loan of an English contingent in the Deccan on 14th January, 1756[92]. Previous to this the Peishwa while laying seige to Savanur had written to them for help and they decided to send a body of English troops to the assistance of the Peishwa in return for Gheria, but before they could do so, Savanur, was already educed by Bussy's artillery. So when the English received Salabat Jung's letter requesting for an English batallion they were very glad to help the Nizam.

The English Governor, Pigot, at Madras, declared such an alliance would secure the company "all the advantages desired"[93]. The English happily dreamt of the various territorial grants they could obtain from the Nizam.

The English thought of sending a battalion of 400 European troops and artillery, but before they could do so, they received, on the 13th July, news of the out break of war between the Nawab of Bengal and the English East India Company and of the capture of Kasimbazar and Calcutta by the former. This made them abandon their ambitious plans in the Deccan, and send Sir Robert Clive and Kirkpatrick at the head of the English forces to Bengal. The Madras Committee referring to this matter said, "It was most unfortunate that the Committee should have been prevented by affairs in Bengal from availing themselves of so good an opportunity to supplant the French at Golcondah but the Committee are not without hopes of breaking a connection based merely on force"[94].

Thus the English, for the time being, were forced to remain content, with the hope of replacing the French, in the Deccan, at some future date.

Bussy, on receipt of his orders of dismissal realised that Shah Nawaz Khan was behind all these anti-French plots and that it was he who had influenced the Nawab Salabat Jung to issue the orders of dismissal. Bussy, did not have sufficient men with him to oppose the Subah. So, on receipt of the orders he prudently moved away and encamped at a distance from Salabat Jung's camp, giving out, that he intended to proceed to Masulipatam, after a few days stay at Hyderabad, in order, to collect all his effects.

In the meanwhile he sent urgent letters to Pondicherry asking for help[95]. At this juncture Balaji Baji Rao, the Peishwa, offered to take Bussy into his service, but the latter, realising that it would be difficult to play the role of an auxiliary to such a shrewd person as the Peishwa, politely refused the offer saying that he could not decide anything, until he got instructions from

92. Dodwell - Madras Despatches, (1754-1765)., p. 68.
93. Ibid.
94. Ibid, p.p. 68-69.
95. 'Bussy in the Deccan', p. 245.

Pondicheery. At the same time the subtle diplomat that he was, Bussy by his behaviour made everyone remain under the impression that an alliance between the French and the Marathas was imminent.

Finding the Peishwa, averse, to the idea of removing Bussy, by poison, or in some such subtle manner, Shah Nawaz Khan suggested that the Maratha troops should fall on the French troops which were small in number and destroy them. But the Peishwa did not like this suggestion. He was anxious to impress Bussy, a possible ally in the future, favourably. So he instructed Malhar Rao Holkar to go at the head of 6000 Maratha horse and accompany Bussy on his way to the Deccan, till he was out of danger[96].

After marching for about a week, finding, that the Mughals were not giving him any trouble, Bussy, dismissed his Maratha escort with grateful acknowledgement. Bussy had with him 600 Europeans, a battallion of 5,000 sepoys, 200 European cavalry and 2000 Hussars, and an efficient train of artillery[97].

But no sooner did the Marathas withdraw the Mughals started harassing the French.

Shah Nawaz Khan, refrained hitherto, from troubling Bussy, lest he should embroil himself with the Marathas. Now, that Bussy, had sent away Malhar Rao Holkar, Shah Nawaz Khan sent Jaffar Ali at the head of 25,000 troops in pursuit of the departing Bussy. He also sent instructions to the various qiledars and polygars in the countryside to harass the detachment under Bussy and not to supply any provisions to the French soldiers[98]. Insructions were also sent to the zamindars in the Northern Sarkars to withhold the payment of the revenues to the French as the latter were no longer in the employment of the Nizam.

When, Bussy, reached, the banks of the river Krishna, he was there opposed by the forces of Maladi Rao, a polygar, and in the skirmish that ensued some French soldiers were killed. In spite of this, Bussy, was able to cross the river Krishna; But, Jaffar Ali, who was closely pursueing the French could not do so as the Krishna rose in spate immediately after the French had crossed the river[99]. So, he was held up on the banks of the Krishna for fifteen days. During this period, Bussy's forces made headway towards Hyderabad.

---

96. Orme.—'A History of the Military Transactions of the British Nation in Indostan'., Vol. I, p. 429.
'Bussy in the Decan'., p. 245.
97. Ibid.
98. Orme.—'A History of the Military Transactions of the British Nation in Indostan', Vol. I., p. 429.
99. Malleson—'History of the French in India'., p. 488.

The French army on their way to Hyderabad had to undergo many privations. The whole countryside turned hostile and harassed them by not supplying them with food and provisions.

The French also ran short of ammunition. Unable to bear these hardships the sepoys started deserting their ranks. Bussy realised that the only way to surmount all these difficulties was by reaching Hyderabad as early as possible. So he directed his march towards that city and arrived on its outskirts on the 14th June, 1756, and encamped outside the city walls[100]. The people of Hyderabad were naturally terrified on the approach of the French, but Bussy, quieted their fears by assuring them that they would not be molested in any manner. Later, he sent for City Bankers and asked them to advance money on his personal credit, to enable him to discharge the arrears of his troops.

With, the money advanced by the soucars, Bussy, paid the salaries of his troops, but the sepoys were not satisfied. They demanded a month's salary in advance. Apart from the vexatious conditions in the army, Bussy had to undergo great vexatious at the hands of the Mughals who were bent upon harassing the French out of the Deccan.

Bussy, sent urgent messages to Moracin and De'Leyrit for assistance. The latter sent 150 men under the command of Monsr. Law to Masulipatam, so that they could go to the help of Bussy.

Salabat Jung, who had started for Aurangabad, a few days after Bussy had left, decided to proceed to Hyderabad instead, in order to meet Bussy. He sent his Maratha Vanguard in advance to oppose Bussy.

The Maratha cavalry, above 12,000 strong reached Hyderabad on the 26th June and encamped at a distance of about six miles from the French. They demanded that Bussy should surrender all the artillery, except the six guns he had brought from Pondicherry. They also wanted him to give up all titles and dignities that he had received at the hands of Salabat Jung. Bussy, refused to do so saying that he received those honours from the Mughal Emperor and not from Salabat Jung - - -

Bussy did not like to provoke the Marathas unnecessarily. He also knew that they were none too friendly with the Nizam. Realising that he was living in a hostile country where the people disliked him as an alien, he tried to make overtures to the Marathas. But he was prevented from doing so by an incident that took place on the 30th June.

Mons. Mayers the French Lieutenant of the Hussars while reconnoitering his French troops was ambushed by the Marathas. The Hussars tried to disperse in different directions but could not do so. Seeing their plight the remaining body of the Hussars tried to go to their rescue. But they commit-

100. Ibid.

ted a tactical blunder in going singly to attack the Marathas. The Marathas who were past masters in the guerilla type of warfare had the advantage in this contest. Seeing the Hussars in difficulty the French dragoons were sent to cover their retreat. On the approach of the dragoons the Marathas dispersed.

In the skimish, Mayer, the Lieutenant of the Hussars, and two other Hussars lost their lives and twenty eight men were disabled on the French side.

The Marathas took six horses and they sent six French hats as a trophy of their victory to Salabat Jung[101].

This incident created panic among the French troops and the sepoys started deserting the French camp. The servants and cartmen on the French side also fled leaving the artillery and the provisions which were in their charge.

The French troops were encamped near the gardens of the Char Mahal by the Musi River, while 400 yards from there stood the Gosha Mahal, the gardens of which were situated in a walled enclosure. The gardens of the Gosha Mahal contained many buildings which were capable of accommodating the troops[102].

Bussy's position at this juncture was singular. He knew that his cavalry was defective and so it would be impossible for the infantry and artillery to protect the long train of carriages containing the sick, ammunition and provisions. The expected help from De'Leyrit or Moracin had not come yet. To march to Masulipatam under such adverse conditions, braving the hostility of the coastal zamindars and the Mughal soldiery, would mean a complete annihilation of the small French army under him.

So he decided to entrench himself strongly in the Gosha Mahal and await the arrival of reinforcements from Masulipatam. He moved into the gardens of the Gosha Mahal on the 5th July.

Bussy, had come to the Deccan at the head of the mercenary troops that the Nizam had entertained in his service. Now, that the Nizam, no longer desired to keep them, Bussy had no legitimate reason to remain in the Deccan. But Bussy decided to stay on, in the Deccan. He knew that the orders of his dismissal were more due to the instigation of Shah Nawaz Khan than due to an actual desire on the part of Salabat Jung.

Bussy had also heard that Jaffar Ali and Muzaffar Khan, who was sent by Murari Rao, were marching towards Hvderabad to attack the French[103].

---

101. 'Bussy in the Deccan', p. 249.
102. Ibid.
103. Ananda Ranga Pillay's Diary, Vol. IX.

There were also daily rumours of Nawab Muhammad Ali in the Carnatic sending troops to the assistance of Salabat Jung. So Bussy in order to play on the good feelings of the Nizam, wrote a letter to Salabat Jung, asking him to allow him to proceed to the Coast peacefully.

At the same time, he wrote urgent letters to De'Leyrit to send him 300 Europeans and a good battalion of sepoys. He also despatched Mons. Guyounet to Masulipatam, to impress on Moracin, the precarious condition in which the French were placed in Hyderabad, and to expedite the sending of reinforcements.

Bussy, apart from occupying the Char Mahal and Gosha Mahal, also stationed his troops at Daud Mahal, a building that was situated on a hillock on the western side of the Char Mahal. It was a two storeyed building with arched masonry roofed by a terrace, and it was strong enough to withstand cannon fire. Bussy, mounted the twelve pounders on the terrace and effectively barricaded the adjoining streets and avenues; He also placed 500 sepoys in charge of the defences. He assured, the local people at the same time that no harm would be done to them.

After making all these arrangements Bussy awaited the further course of events.

On the evening of the 6th July the Marathas attacked the French but they were repulsed, and the French took possession of all the magazines in the city and also of the cannon of the Marathas. The place between the French ranges and the building and tank in Char Mahal was planted with Palmyra and coconut trees; With these the stations for the musketry were built.

On the 8th July, the French under the command of Du'Passage attacked and cannonaded the Maratha camp and forced them to quit their positions.

The Marathas under their General Lakshman Cadagula retreated to Golconda and took their positions under the walls of the Fortress. Bussy, sent his German troops under Brandt to harass them but they could do little damage to the Marathas owing to the setting in of rains[104].

The various foujdars and qiledars to whom Shah Nawaz Khan sent letters urging them to come to the help of the Subah began to arrive only in July[105].

The Nawabs of Kurnool and Kondanur arrived with 3,000 Pathan troops to help the Nizam. But these chieftains at the same time were perifidious enough to send word to Bussy to the effect that they would not fight seriously on the side of Salabat Jung.

104. Malleson - 'History of the French in India', p. 490.
105. Ibid.

Jaffar Ali arrived on the 10th July at the head of 3000 horse, 3,000 foot and 20 pieces of cannon followed closely in his wake, by Salabat Jung and Shah Nawaz Khan[106].

Jaffar Ali, at once, decided to launch hostilities against the French, and with that intention he tried to occupy all the important strategic places, the Char Minar being one of them. But Bussy forestalled him by sending a detachment to occupy the Char Minar and placed his artillery on the top of the Tower.

He made dispositions of his artillery in such a manner that they faced the city and then sent word to Jaffar Ali saying that if the Mughal troops came to oppose him, he would destroy the whole city of Hyderabad. This deterred Jaffar Ali from commencing hostilities immediately.

On the 20th July, Bussy, received news of Janoji Nimbalkar attacking near Aurangabad a body of 600 Arabs and Abyssinians who were sent from Pondicherry to the assistance of Bussy. Of these 50 were killed, 150 absconded, while the remaining 400 were confined in the fortress of Golconda by Janoji Nimbalkar[107]. Inspite of this the French sallied forth on the 26th night, but the attack remained indecisive owing to certain tactical blunders on the part of the French.

Muzaffar Khan, arrived from the Carnatic at the head of 4000 troops on the 27th July, and on the next day the Mughal forces marched against Char Mahal taking with them 20 pieces of cannon, but they were repulsed by the French artillery. Skirmishes between the French and the Mughals continued to take place intermittently. Meanwhile, Salabat Jung arrived with his main army on the 1st August, 1756 [108].

Muzaffar Khan after his arrival started intriguing with the sepoys in the French camp with the result, that they deserted to the Mughals in great numbers. Seeing this, Bussy refrained from making any fresh sallies.

On the night of 30th August, a pitched battle took place between the French and the Nizam's forces. In this battle the French forces under the command of Du'Passage and Reboux, inflicted a severe defeat on the Mughals [109].

Apart from sending about 150 men under Mons. Law on the 5th July, De'Leyrit further sent on the 19th July, a battalion of 500 Europeans and 200 sepoys under the command of Saubinet [110]. Moracin, sent Law on the 16th

---

106. 'Bussy in the Deccan', p. 249.
107. Orme—'History of the Military Transactions of the British Nation in Indostan.', Vol. II, p. 91.
108. Ibid, Vol. II, p. 94.
Malleson—"History of the French in India"., p. 492
109. 'Bussy in the Deccan', p. 250.
110. Ibid.

July from Masulipatam at the head of 160 Europeans and 700 sepoys and a few field pieces. Law, reached Bezawada on the 20th July and there he stopped till the 3rd August, awaiting the arrival of fresh reinforcements from Pondicherry.

The troops under Saubinct, reached Bezwada on the 3rd August and there Law, after assuming command of the whole army proceeded towards Hyderabad. On the 10th August they arrived at the village of Magnapura about 50 miles from Hyderabad"[111].

Shah Nawaz Khan who was finding it difficult to dislodge Bussy, from his entrenched position at Char Mahal was perturbed on hearing of the arrival of these reinforcements. He sent his Maratha forces to intercept the arrival of the French reinforcements. This was a brilliant stroke of strategy on the part of Shah Nawaz Khan. The French were marching through dense forests in an unfamiliar country, and nothing would have been easier than to cut them off, and force Bussy to surrender. For Bussy, finding himself encircled by the hostile Mughal armies on all sides would have had no option but to surrender to Shah Nawaz Khan.

But all these plans of the Diwan came to nought owing to the tactics of the Maratha forces.

Bussy, had always striven to placate the Marathas in various ways. Now his policy bore fruit. Owing to the existence of various rival cliques in the Mughal camp, Bussy always managed to keep himself well informed of the various developments in the Nizam's camp. In the usual manner now also, he was informed in advance that the Maratha generals Janoji Nimbalkar, Ramachandra Jadhav, Lakshman Cadagula, Bala Rao and Muzaffar Khan of Savanur were being sent by Shah Nawaz Khan to intercept the arrival of the French reinforcements[112].

Bussy now contrived to come to an understanding in a secret conference, at Gosha Mahal with the Maratha leaders, Janoji Nimbalkar and Ramachendra Jadhav. The Marathas assured Bussy, that they would only feign to fight against the French forces. Bussy in return promised them that he would grant high favours to them if he was restored to power, once again in the Deccan. After this successful negotiation Bussy sent a secret message to Law, conveying to him the understanding that was reached between him and the Marathas. He also sent to Law, the banners of the Maratha leaders in advance, so that, on the battlefield, Law might easily identify them as the friends of the French.

111. Ibid.
112. Orme - "History of the Military Transactions of the British Nation in Indostan", Vol. II, p. 95.

The French troops, under Law were marching four abreast through thick woods, while the vanguard of about 4000 sepoys was under the command of one Muhammad Khan, who was enticed by promises of money by Muzaffar Khan, to betray the French. Muhammad Khan, pretending as through he was anxious to attack the Mughal troops, marched in advance and went over to the side of Muzaffar Khan quietly. Then, he sent a message to the French grenadiers, saying, that he was encircled by Muzaffar Khan and that they should come to his rescue. But the captain of the grenadiers, suspecting treacherry, sent four scouts in advance, who on reconnoitreing discovered that Muhammad Khan had deliberately went over to the side of Muzaffar Khan [113].

Then the Mughals made an attack on the French but, the latter, under the able command of Saubinet not only repulsed them but also compelled them to retire to Gurrampalli, a neighbouring village[114]. The next morning, the Mughals once again made an attack but had to suffer a set back owing to the feigned fight put up by Janoji Nimbalkar and Ramachendra Jadhav against the the French. After this victory the French reached Meliapore, a village 15 miles from Gurrampalli and 17 miles from Hyderabad, with only a part of their baggage lost on the morning of the 13th August[115]. Law decided to halt at Meliapore village till he got some definite information. He was pleasantly intrigued by the behaviour of the Maratha troops who under the command of Lakshman Cadagula, now pretended to fight.

The condition of the troops, who were with Law was most distressing. They suffered from lack of victuals, exhaustion and fatigue. The sepoys were daily deserting their ranks. In order to stave off hunger they had to kill the draught bullocks of the artillery. Under such disheartening conditions Law wrote to Bussy to send some troops for their relief.

The Mughals on the other hand were greatly encouraged by the defection of Muhammad Khan and they decided to send troops against Law.

Bussy, realising the gravity of the situation, did not hesitate to divide his troops. On the night of 12th August he sent a strong detachment of Europeans for the relief of Law, while, he remained behind, with only 150 Europeans and 300 sepoys at Char Mahal to face the battery of the Mughals.

Bussy also sent instructions to Law to march forthwith to Hyderabad in the name of the French King.

On receiving this message, Law, at once set out for Hiatnagar on the 15th August. The path between Meliapore to Singavaram river which was about

113. "Bussy in the Deccan", p. 252.

114. Orme - 'History of the Military Transactions of the British Nation in Indostan., Vol. II, p. 95.
'Bussy in the Deccan', p. 252.

115. Ibid.
Malleson—" A History of the French in India "., p. 496.

10 Coss from Golconda was full of thick jungle defiles, and the French were quite unfamiliar with the country. Taking advantage of this the Maratha General, Lakhsman Cadagula, harassed the French and retarded the progress of their march by cutting down the trees and placing the logs in the way.

Though many French troopers fell on their way, fortunately, for them they had no baggage to carry, which facilitated quick movement. Moreover, the French artillery proved very effective in keeping the enemy at a distance. Lakshman Cadagula, tried, to obstruct the French advance in the night by harassing them a great deal, with the result that the French could cover only 3 miles by the time, dawn broke. Now there remained only one mile between them and the river Singavaram that they had to cross in order to reach Hiatnagar.

With daybreak the Mughal attack was intensified. The French vanguard came face to face with the Mughal cannon, behind which appeared the Mughal cavalry.

But the Mughal artillery was quite ineffective, and it could not prevent the French army from emerging from the forest defiles and forming themselves into battle array.

After arranging themselves, in battle array, the French awaited the Marathas who now came out of the forest defiles. Then the French opened fire against them and dispersed the Mughal cavalry. But the Mughals now decided to take their stand on the banks of the Singavaram river and prevent the fording of the river by the French.

[116]"The Singavaram river flowed into a deep ravine. The Mughal forces awaited the arrival of the French on the opposite bank. So it became necessary, that if Law along with his French troops was to cross the river, the rear of the French should be protected against a possible Mughal attack. So he made D'Harambure, another French Commandant, to cover the rear with the cannons while the French effected their crossing. Once Law crossed the river, Harambure, sent his cannon one by one, at the same time maintaining a constant fire against the Mughals. This tactics of the French greatly discouraged the Mughal soldiery. Once the river was forded, Hiatnagar was just six miles of plain country from the Singavaram River. The French arrived at Hiatnagar on the 16th evening at 5 p. m., without further incident. This was made possible by the conduct of Janoji Nimbalkar and Ramachendra Jadhav. Law, offered a bribe of 10,000 Pagodas to the son of Janoji and the latter allowed him to enter the town without any further trouble from the Mughals"[117].

---

116. "Bussy in the Deccan", p. 255.
Malleson-"History of the French in India", p. 496.
117. Records of Fort St. George, C. C. (Military Department), 1756.

During the encounter the French lost altogether 25 Europeans while 65 were wounded; The losses on the Mughal side were estimated at nearly 2000 men and 800 horses[118].

On hearing of the arrival of these reinforcements Bussy sent 140 Europeans and 1000 sepoys with provisions and carriages to bring the sick and wounded[119].

At the same time he led a vigorous attack on the camp of Salabat Jung so that the Mughals might be kept engaged, in such a way they would not interrupt the arrival of Law and his forces. Law along with his troops reached Hyderabad at 10 A. M., on the 17th. The Mughals who had set all their hopes in preventing the French from fording the river Singavaram and isolating Bussy, now lost heart and decided to sue for peace.

Salabat Jung sent a camel rider to the French camp, sueing for peace. Bussy demanded that if Salabat Jung desired peace he should send Mughal chieftains to the French camp as a surety for the Subah's good faith. At last through the good offices of Muhammad Hussain, a Diwan of the Mughal Emperor, a conference was arranged between Bussy, Salabat Jung and Shah Nawaz Khan.

Bussy by his conduct made it appear that peace or war was the same to him. He attended the conference fully armed. The Subah and the Diwan finding themselves helpless before the superior military tactics of Bussy, now, appealed to Bussy to forget the recent events and behave as though nothing had happened to rupture the friendship that existed between the two.

Bussy, demanded that Muzaffar Khan and Muhammad Khan should be handed over to the French. But Salabat Jung nobly refused to do so since these two Mughal officers had fought loyally on the side of the Subah. Jaffar Ali came and formally expressed regret to Bussy for his past conduct towards the French. The Abyssinians and Arabs who were imprisoned in the Golconda Fort by Janoji were now set free. Bussy knew that the position of Shah Nawaz Khan was still strong and so he could not demand the dismissal of the Diwan; therefore, he pretended to be reconciled to the Diwan. Muhammad Hussain along with some of the leading nobles in the Nizam's Court visited Bussy on the 20th August 1756 and once again reinstated him in his former position and restored all his former titles and honours. The Sarkar of Kondavid which was originally conferred on Bussy, was now ceded to the French in perpetuity.

---

118. Orme.—"History of the Military Transactions of the British Nation in Indostan., Vol. II, p. 101.
119. Orme.—"History of the Military Transactions of the British Nation in Indostan", Vol. II, p. 101.

The stand taken by Bussy, at Char Mahal, in an alien country, surrounded by hostile people, and his braving the Mughals in the name of the French King cannot but excite one's admiration for the courage displayed by him and also for the superiority of the Western technique of warfare in the 18th century. In contrast the Nizam and his courtiers torn by internecine strife and jealousy, present, a sad picture. On account of their disunity and lack of a national ideal, the Mughals in spite of their numerical strength and a overwhelming desire, to be rid, of the foreigners, could not achieve their object. The Mughal princes and their followers, nay even the Indian people in general during the 18th century seem to have forgotten what it is to rise above self and fight in the name of their country.

Though the victor, Bussy, was really glad to have made peace with Salabat Jung. He had practically no money to pay his troops. At first he raised money on credit, later on, he gave receipts to the bankers on the revenues of the Northern Sarkars. But the zamindars in the Sarkars encouraged by the letters of Shah Nawaz Khan had withheld the sending of the revenues to Bussy. Of all the zamindars on the East Coast only Vijaya Rama Raju continued to remit the revenues regularly[120]. Seeing this, Bussy decided to go personally to the Sarkars and bring them under the French hegemony once again. So he started for the Sarkars on the 16th November taking with him 500 Europeans and 4000 sepoys[121]. He left behind 200 Europeans and 500 sepoys to guard the person of Salabat Jung. Salabat Jung left for Aurangabad towards the end of November.

De'Leyrit had by now became completely disgusted and disillusioned by the various intrigues against the French at the Nizam's court. He realised that in spite of the French victory and the respect and fear in which Bussy, was held in the Nizam's court, it was impossible to remain long in security in the Deccan in a hostile atmosphere. He advised Bussy to go to the Sarkars and restore order there. Commenting on Bussy's position at the court of the Nizam, he wrote to the Controller General, of the French East India Company, Moras, on the 19th October 1756 in the following manner[122]: "Since the rupture of our entente with Salabat Jang. I do not think that it is any longer necessary for Mons. Bussy to reside beside the Subah. I am told that, Bussy, still continues to be dreaded there, but he is no longer loved and that the people long for his departure. I am anxiously awaiting for the reply to the letter I wrote to him to return to our provinces. This arrangement is in accordance with the wishes of the Nawab who desires that we should remain Jaghirdars that is to say we shall be obliged to send him troops and go to his help if he calls. Mr. Bussy, has sufficiently drained us, for the upkeep of the Nawab's Army, of arms, munitions and money without much profit to us".

---

120. Orme—"History of the Military Transactions of the British Nation in Indostan". Vol. II, p. 105.
121. 'Bussy in the Deccan', p. 262.
122. Ibid.

This letter of De'Leyrit reveals to us that on account of their basic weakness in the Carnatic, the French were finding their position in the far off Deccan quite untenable. The animosity of the Deccan nobles and the coastal zamindars made their position all the more difficult.

Conditions in the Sarkars had also deteriorated to a great extent. Bussy, while going to Hyderabad, on the eve of the Mysore expedition, had placed Moracin in charge of Masulipatam and the districts south of Masulipatam, while Mons. De'La Selle was placed in charge of the Northern Sarkars. Finding De'La Selle inefficient, De'Leyrit recalled him and appointed Duplant Laval in his place in November 1755. Laval, discharged his duties efficiently, and saw that Vijaya Rama Raju remitted the revenues punctiliously. But very soon troubles broke out in early 1756, on account of the instructions sent to the zamindars by Shah Nawaz Khan.

An insurrection broke out in the fortress of Rajahmundry. The sepoys there rose in rebellion and demanded from Laval, the surrender of the keys of the fortress. Laval who had under him only 12 soldiers whom he could trust, prudently complied with their request, but he secretly sent word to Moracin for reinforcements.

This rebellion of the Rajahmundry sepoys, was instigated by Ibrahim Khan, the Foujdar of Chicacole; He now demanded the remission of payments, that were, hitherto, made to the French.

Of all the zamindars in the Sarkars, Vijaya Rama Raju alone sent help to Moracin. By this time Bussy who had already started for the Sarkars from Hyderabad now reached Rajahmundry on the 19th December. He went via Bezwada and Ellore to Rajahmundry[123].

On hearing of Bussy's approach Ibrahim Khan fled to the Rajah of Bobbili. Vijaya Rama Raju collecting 10,000 men under him along with some local chieftains went and joined Bussy at Rajahmundry[124]. Besides him almost all the zamindars in the Sarkars, except, the Rajah of Bobbili, hastened to pay their homage to Bussy[125].

Taking advantage of this omission on the part of the Rajah of Bobbili, Vijaya Rama Raju who had some ancient enmity with the Rajah over the canal waters between Bobbili and Vizianagaram, represented matters in such a way, to Bussy, that an impression was created in the latter's mind that the Rajah was inimical towards the French[126]. Vijaya Rama Raju suggested that the Rajah should be deprived of Bobbili his ancestral place and given some other zamindari in its place.

123. Raya Gajapati Varma—"Peddapura Samasthana Charitramu", p. 95.
124. Ibid, p. 65.
Pusapati Vari Kaifiyat, Mackenzie, Mss. O. M. S. Library.
Orme.—"History of the Military Transactions of the British Nation in Indostan", Vol. I, p. 253.
125. Ditta Kavi Narayana Kavi—"Ranga Raya Charitramu".
126. Andhra Kavula Charitramu, Kaifiyat Bobbili-Mackenzie, Mss.

Rajah Ranga Rao of Bobbili, on hearing of this proposal refused to leave Bobbili; while these negotiations were still going on, a body of 30 French soldiers who were passing through the territories of the Rajah were attacked by some sepoys and killed.

Bussy, was already, displeased with the Rajah, for having given asylum to Ibrahim Khan. This incident infuriated him all the more. Vijaya Rama Raju found in this, a suitable opportunity to wreak his own vengeance on the Rajah. He instigated, Bussy, to march against Rajah Ranga Rao. So Bussy accompanied by Vijaya Rama Raju and his Diwan Hyder Jung[127] and the local zamindars like the Rajah of Peddapurm, went to Bobbili and laid siege to that fortress on the 24th January, 1757[128].

It was here that the battle of Bobbili, the popular theme, of many a ballad in Andhra, took place. Prior, to attacking Bobbili, Vijaya Rama Raju sent a secret message to Ibrahim Khan to dissociate himself from the Rajah. The chivalrous Rajah, true to the ideals of Indian hospitality, himself, advised Ibrahim Khan to leave Bobbili lest he might not be able to safeguard him.

After seeing that Ibrahim was safely escorted out of Bobbili the Rajah put up a brave defence, but the numerical strength of the enemy and the efficacy of the French artillery went against the Rajah. When it was found that victory was not possible, all the women folk in the fortress were put to death by the Rajah's orders lest their honour should be sullied at the hands of the enemy. They set fire to all the habitations in the fort, and inspired by despair, stabbed without remorse all those women who attempted to escape from the flames.

Then the garrison in the fortress decided to defend it to the last man. Even, though, they knew that death was certain not a singleman left the ramparts nor did they seek quarter from the enemy. Ranga Rao himself was killed in the course of the battle by a musket-ball, but the garrison held on, to the last man, the ditch, that surrounded the fortress becoming a veritable pool of blood.

---

127. Hyder Jung was the son of Qalandar Khan who was originally in the employment of Nasir Jung, but was able to win the goodwill of Dupleix by his pro-French activities. Bussy made Hyder Jung his confidant and conferred on him high titles. Later, on the recommendation of Bussy he was appointed as the Diwan of Salabat Jung.

—"Bussy in the Deccan".

Kaifiyat Bobbili Paraghana., Book 7, Mackenzie Mss.

128. Raya Gajapati Varma—"Peddapura Samasthana Charitramu", p. 100.
Orme—Vol. II, p. 250.
Sewell and Aiyangar—"Historical Inscriptions in South India", p. 300.

When the French troops entered the fortress Bussy was horrified to see fire and desolation on all sides. Yet, to be on the safe side a general massacre of the population was ordered. Fortunately, the young son of the Rajah was saved by the devotion of the maid servant Lakshmi. On him Bussy conferred all those territories that he had offered to give to the Rajah in place of Bobbili[130]. On the 3rd night after the battle of Bobbili, Vijaya Rama Raju was surprised and killed while sleeping in his tent, by Tandra Papaiah the sardar of the Rajah, and two of his followers who could not come in time to participate in the battle of Bobbili. Bussy got 2 lakhs of Rupees from the revenues of the Bobbili Zamindari. With the fall of Bobbili, all rebellion on the East Coast ceased. All the polygars excepting the polygar of Gumser went to pay tribute to Bussy. But he was soon brought to book.

Feeling that the French authority was sufficiently restored in the Sarkars, Bussy now thought of going to the assistance of the Nawab of Bengal Siraj-ud-Doula, againt the English East India Company. Bussy had received letters from Siraj-ud-Doula asking him to come to his assistance. Siraj-ud-Doula wrote[131]: "Surajah Doula to the Exalted in station great test amoung great officers, the support of friendship. Monsieur Bussy, Bahadre; (No. 5)". "These disturbers of my country, the Admiral and Colonel Clive, Sabut Jung, whom bad fortune attends without any reason whatever are waving againt Zubdat-ool-Joo Jah, Monsieur Rinnault, the Governor of Chandernagore, this you will learn from his letters, I who in all things seek the good of mankind assist him in every respect, and have sent him the best of my troops, that he may join with them and fight the English who are unfortunate will be punished for the disturbance they have raised. Be confident, look on my forces as your own, I have wrote you before for 2000 soldiers, and musqueteers under the command of one or two trusty chiefs. I persuade myself you have already sent them immediately, further particulars you will learn from Monsieur Rinnault-Oblige me with frequent news of your health".

On receipt of these letters of appeal from Siraj-ud-Doula, Bussy despatched Law in advance with 61 men to Bengal. Law, reached Rajamahal[132]. But, before Bussy himself could proceed to Bengal, he received news of the defeat of Sirajud-Doula at the hands of the English. As it was futile, to go to Bengal, Bussy tried to retaliate against the English by attempting to capture the English factories on the East Coast. The English had factories at

---

129. Orme.—"History of the Military Transactions of the British Nation in Indostan", Vol. II, p. 256.
"Bussy in the Deccan", p. 266.
130. Dittakavi Narayana Kavi—"Ranga Raya Charitrakamu", p. 164.
Kaifiyat Bobbili, Pusapativari Kaifiyat.
Mackenzie Mss. O.M.S. Library Madras Book 7.
131. Forrest—"Madras and Bengal Papers", Vol. III, (1757 1785).
Imperial Records Department Calcutta, L. No. 1 of Feb. 1757.
132. Ibid, L. No. 2, Middle of March 1757 & L. No. 5 of April 1957.

Madapollam, Banderlanka and Ingeram. By this time the Seven Years' War between the English and the French had already broken in Europe. So De'Leyrit encouraged Bussy to launch hositilics against the English in India by capturing their factory at Vizagapatam. Bussy, went from Chicacole to Vizagapatam collecting taxes on the way. He reached Vizagapatam on the 24th June 1757[133]. The English garrison at Vizagapatam, consisted of 150 Europeans and 300 sepoys. It's commandent Capt. Charles Campbell realised that it was futile to think of resistance with such a small force. So he decided to capitulate but before doing so he wanted to send all the Europeans aboard the Marlborough, an English ship that had just arrived.

But very soon the English found that it was not so easy to send the European soldiers aboard, as the fishermen and boatmen had deserted.

Perceval, the Governor, of the Vizagapatam factory offered to surrender on condition of the garrison being allowed to leave the factory with their baggage, and the inhabitants of the town allowed to go unmolested[134]. Bussy agreed to this conditions. Thereupon Perceval and his Council surrendered and the garrison was disarmed. The French then taken took possession of Vizagapatam formally, and that factory remained in French hands till October 1758. Perceval, and his staff were subsequently allowed to depart for Bimlipatam. While, Bussy was busy establishing the French power on the East Coast plots were once again thickening at the Nizam's court against the French power due to the active machinations of Shah Nawaz Khan. On hearing of these development, Bussy, hastened to the Deccan early in January 1758[135].

After the departure of Bussy, to the Sarkars, Salabat Jung left Hyderabad on the 17th December and reached Auraugabad on the 8th May 1757. Shah-Nawaz Khan was at heart very angry at the treacherous conduct of Chandrasen Jadhav, during the recent war, against Bussy, by the Mughals. He wanted to wreak vengeance on him. Hence in order to accomplish his designs he asked, Basalat Jung, who was at Adoni to come and join him.

At this juncture Syed Lashkar Khan, the old Diwan, died in the fort of Doulatabad.

Shah Nawaz Khan had for a long time coveted the treasures of Doulatabad. So soon after hearing of the death of Syed Lashker Khan he seized the Treasury of Doulatabad and appointed his own son as the Qiledar of Doulatabad, against the wishes of Salabat Jung[136].

---

133. Orme—"History of the Military Transactions of the British Nation in Indostan", Vol. II, p. 256.
134. "Bussy in the Deccan", p. 271.
135. Ibid.
136. Records of Fort St. George, C. C. (1753), L. No. 134, p. 280.

Shah Nawaz Khan became so overweening and arrogant in his behaviour that it was said that sometimes he even refused to grant an interview to Salabat Jung when the latter visited him[137].

Shah Nawaz Khan also intensely disliked the proclivity of Salabat Jung towards the French. He also did not at heart like the granting of Berar, to Nizam Ali, and Adoni and Bijapur to Basalat Jung though at the time when these changes were made, he had acquiesced in the plan partly because he coveted the Peishwa's help against Bussy, and also partly because he felt that the princes would be useful as a curb on the growing French influence[138]. At this juncture the Marathas under the command of Viswas Rao, the son of the Peishwa, came to attack Aurangabad. They demanded the cession of all the districts to the north of the river Godavari[139].

While matters were in such a state, the Mughal troops who had not received their pay for the past 22 months, rose in revolt. They attacked the residence of the Diwan and demanded the dismissal of Shah Nawaz Khan and the appointment of Basalat Jung as the Diwan. Shah Nawaz Khan took fright at this unexpected turn of events. He now decided to take refuge in the fortress of Doulatabad, where he took along with him all his possessions, baggage and the ladies of his family[140]. Shah Nawaz Khan from Doulatabad appealed to the Marathas to help him against Salabat Jung[141].

Salabat Jung on the other hand demanded that Shah Nawaz Khan must tender his submission and he sent word to his brother Nizam Ali to come to his assistance[142].

---

137. A. N. Ghani Khan Sahib of Rampur—"Tarikhi Riyasat, Hyderabad Deccan", p. 270.
138. Martineau, Malleson and other historians are of the opinion that Shah Nawaz Khan favoured Nizam Ali and that in order to procure that prince's interests he wanted to imprison Salabat Jung in the Fort of Doulatabad. But the contemporary authority Rahat-e-Afza, does not support this view.
139. According to Orme, Malleson, Grant Duff and even Lakshmi Narayan Shafiq the author of Masire.—Asafia, Shah Nawaz Khan was responsible for the Maratha invasion. He incited the Marathas to invade Aurangabad in order to decrease the power of Salabat Jung and the French party. The English historians further think that the motive of Shah Nawaz Khan in inviting the Maratha forces was to find a pretext to muster all the forces, including the forces under Nizam Ali, and proclaim the latter Subedar, but the Masir-e-Asafia says, it was Salabat Jung who summoned Nizam Ali on the approach of the Maratha Forces.
140. "Bussy in the Deccan", p. 279.
Muh. Siraj-ud-din Talib—"Nizam Ali Khan Sawale Zindagi", Part I, p. 42.

NOTE:—The Maisar-e-Asafia, says that Salabat Jung must have had an hand in the revolt of the Mughal troops against Shah Nawaz Khan.

141. "Bussy in the Deccan", p. 279.
Records of Fort St. George, C. C. L. No. 207, p. 441.
142. "Bussy in the Deccan", p. 274.

At this time it was not only the Maratha forces which plundered the country, but so great was the indiscipline among the Mughal troops that they also started looting and plundering in the countryside. These depradations made food grains scarce in the country.

At this critical juncture Nizam Ali arrived from Berar. He assured his elder brother that he would soon restore law and order. But before doing so, he demanded from Salabat Jung, the surrender of the Diwan's Seal to him. Salabat Jung did not like to do this, yet, he had no option but to comply with the demand of Nizam Ali if he were to see peace once again re- stored in the country[143]. So he duly surrendered the Seal.

The transference of the Seal actually vested real power in the hands of Nizam Ali, but the latter affected indifference to the office and entrusted the Seal to the care of his younger brother Basalat Jung.

After, obtaining the Seal from his brother, Nizam Ali, paid the arrears of pay to the troops. He also induced Shah Nawaz Khan to come out of the Doulatabad fort and tender his submission to Salabat Jung, and the latter once again received the Diwan into his favour.

Nizam Ali, also came to a settlement with the Peishwa at Sindkhed. By this agreement apart from ceding the fort of Naldrug he also gave to the Marathas 25 lakhs of rupees[144].

In the meanwhile, Bussy who had started from the Sarkars on hearing of the Maratha advance reached Aurangabad in February. Soon after his arrival he paid a ceremonial visit to Salabat Jung. Then, the next day with the permission of Salabat Jung he visited the Peishwa who was in command of the Maratha troops[145].

On Bussy's arrival, Shah Nawaz Khan hastened to wait on him and clear himself of the general charge that he was responsible for the Maratha incursion. But Bussy, knew what importance he should attach to the Diwan's protestations of innocence. So, he deputed his own Diwan, Hyder Jung, to listen to the explanation of Shah Nawaz Khan. Nevertheless, he decided to enlist the co-operation of Shah Nawaz Khan in discharging his responsibilities. Bussy, next went to visit Nizam Ali, at the head of a small force. Nizam Ali, insisted that Bussy, accompanied by the Diwan alone, should come and see him. In this interview, Bussy, demanded of Nizam Ali the surrender of the State Seal. But the latter, refused to surrender the Seal ou the plea that he took it by the consent of all in the State, and that it would be unjust to deprive him

---

143. Muh. Saraj-ud-din Talib—"Nizam Ali Khan Sawale Zindagi", Part I.
144. G. S. Sardesai—"A New History of the Marathas", Vol. II, p. 334.
A. N. Ghani Khan—"Tarikhi-Riyasat, Hyderabad Deccan", p. 275.
145. Records of Fort St. George, C. C. No. (1758), L. No. 107, p. 65.

of the only means by which he could reimburse the salary of the troops. Bussy, thought it prudent, not to interfere in the arrangement and to agree to Nizam Ali Khan being the Diwan and Basalat Jung being the Naib. Salabat Jung also, now asked for the return of the Seal. But his two younger brothers refused to surrender it saying that the army had empowered them, and if he desired the Seal back, he should take it from the army[146]. Nizam Ali Khan, also reproached Shah Nawaz Khan for having joined the French so soon after his being restored to favour by the efforts of Nizam Ali.

[147]But Shah Nawaz Khan who greatly desired that he should be reinstated as the Diwan, onee again entered into a conspiracy with Hyder Jung. They both resolved to request Salabat Jung to tell his brothers to return to their respective dominions. They, also decided to ask Salabat Jung to reinstate Shah Nawaz Khan as the Diwan.

Nizam Ali, refused to leave Aurangabad and demanded from Shah Nawaz Khan accounts for the sum of 40 lakhs of Rupees which the latter had taken from the Marathas.

Finding themselves thwarted in their designs, Shah Nawaz Khan and Hyder Jung now decided to assassinate Basalat Jung, whom they found too clever and a real obstruction in their path[148]. Moreover they knew that the Diwan's Seal was in the custody of Basalat Jung.

They paid Rs. 5,000 to a sepoy and engaged him to shoot Basalat Jung while the latter was going to pay his usual respects to Salabat Jung. On the 14th February, Basalat Jung, mounted on an elephant was going towards the palace of Salabat Jung to pay his respects to the latter. Then the sepoy fired at him but fortunately the shot missed and the sepoy was caught and he confessed the whole plot.

Nizam Ali Khan on hearing of the attack on Basalat Jung hastened to go to his brother's assistance but on hearing that he was safe returned to his quarters. The next day in order to show the disgust that the brothers felt at this base attack, Basalat Jung went to the Durbar, and throwing down the seal of Diwanship on the ground, came back to his quarters.

Salabat Jung to placate his brother ordered the Seal to be sent to Nizam Ali Khan but the latter refused to accept it. Bussy knew that the odium would fall on the French for the plot against Basalat Jung. So, in order to wipe away the blame that might fall on the French, Bussy had the Seal sent back to Basalat Jung, but, at the same time he contrived to see that the actual custody of the seal would be in the hands of the French.

---

146. Records of Fort St. George, C. C. No. (1758), p. 65.
147. Records of Fort St. George, C. C. L. No. 109 (1758), p. 66.
A. N. Ghani Khan of Rampur—"Tarikhi-Riyasat, Hyderabad-Dn.", p. 275.
148. Records of Fort St. George, C. C. (1758), L. No. 109.

[149]"He appointed an officer under Hyder Jung to keep the Seal in a special bag always at hand, and to give it to Basalat Jung whenever the latter required it. This was a very shrewd arrangement on the part of Bussy. It indirectly prevented Basalat Jung from entering into any secret agreement against the French or Salabat Jung without the French coming to know of it.

Bussy also advised Salabat Jung to order Nizam Ali Khan to proceed to Berar, and to receive a pension of Rs. 20,000. But Nizam Ali Khan refused to be hastened out of Aurangabad. His troops on hearing the orders of Salabat Jung also grew indignant at the insult offered to Nizam Ali a son of Nizamul-Mulk.

Bussy realising that it was not so easy to dislodge Nizam Ali Khan, tried to win over the nobles, by offers of money. They now agreed to a new scheme, namely that Nizam Ali should be given some other territories instead of Berar.

In the meantime ill feelings become rife between Shah Nawaz Khan and Hyder Jung. Shah Nawaz Khan for reasons of security started fortifying Doulatabad, this time with the secret connivance of Nizam Ali and Basalat Jung[150].

Bussy, sensing new danger in the movements of Shah Nawaz Khan, decided to take the fortress of Doulatabad by strategem. Bussy's Diwan, Hyder Jung, conspired with the Qiledar of Doulatabad and the letter agreed to surrender the fortress for money[151]. Bussy on the pretext of viewing the beautiful scenery atop the fortress went therewith a body of 300 Europeans[152]. The qiledar invited Bussy for breakfast inside the fort. He also contrived to send the garrision away to the lower ramparts of the fortress. Bussy without sitting at the breakfast table informed the Qiledar that he had come to arrest him. The latter pretended to be surprised but surrendered quietly. The Mughal garrison was caught unawares and it could do nothing against this *fait accompli* ; The French soldiers entered the fortress and occupied it.

Prior to his going to Doulatabad, Bussy saw that the tents of Shah-Nawaz Khan, Muhammad Khan the representative of the Mughal Emperor and a partisan of Shah Nawaz Khan, and those of Nizam Ali Khan and Basalat Jung were surrounded by French troops.

Thus was Shah Nawaz Khan the main leader of the opposition against foreign influences in the Deccan, made a prisoner even before he knew of the capture of the Doulatabad fort.

---

149. "Bussy in the Deccan", p. 278.
150. Ibid, pp. 279-80.
151. Orme—"History of the Military Transactions of the British Nation in Indostan", Vol. II, p. 348.
J. S. Mill—"History of British India", Vol. III, p. 152.
152. "Bussy in the Deccan", p. 280.

The Peishwa who had long coveted the strong fort of Doulatabad asked Bussy to hand over the fort to him but the latter refused to do so, saying that Doulatabad was taken by him to safeguard Salabat Jung from danger.

Nizam Ali saw that Bussy by one master-stroke of diplomacy had made the French once again supreme in the Deccan. He resented the manner in which Shah Nawaz Khan and Muhammad Khan were removed from power[153]. But he was careful to conceal his feelings. Then he sent a secrct message to the Peishwa saying that he would give Doulatabad to the Marathas if they helped him against the French. But Balaji was not inclined to accept the offer, so he expressed his inability to be of any help to Nizam Ali Khan.

Though disappointed in this quarter, Nizam Ali, concealed his feelings and pretended to be completely satisfied with the new developments in the court of Salabat Jung.

Now Hyder Jung advised Salabat Jung to confer, instead of Berar, the Subah of Hyderabad, on Nizam Ali Khan, so that Salabat Jung, who resided at Aurangabad, could keep a vigilant watch on the movements of his younger brother.

On hearing of this proposal Nizam Ali expressed his willingness to go to Hyderabad and the 11th of May 1758 was fixed as the day of his departure[154].

On the morning of his departure, Nizam Ali Khan, held a public Durbar, to take leave of the principle nobles of the court. Hyder Jung also went to pay his respects to the departing Nizam Ali. After the Durbar was over, Nizam Ali Khan asked Hyder Jung to come into an inner tent with him to discuss some state matters especially pertaining to the treasury of Shah Nawaz Khan. On Hyder Jung entering the tent, Nizam Ali Khan left the tent making a sign to Hyder Jung to remain there. No sooner did Nizam Ali leave the tent, than two officers of the Nawab, who were hitherto standing there seized him by the shoulders and stabbed him to death[155].

The murder of Hyder Jung created great tumult. On receiving news of Hyder Jung's murder Bussy got his troops ready for battle. Suspecting that Shah Nawaz Khan and Muhammad Hussain Khan also, might have had a hand in bringing about the death of Hyder Jung, he sent a strong French detachment to bring them over to his tent so that he could throw them in prison in the fort of Doulatabad. But, when the French troops went to seize the

153. Orme—"History of the Military Transactions of the British Nation in Indostan", Vol. II, p. 347.
Records of Fort St. George., C. C. (1758), L. No. 109.
154. Orme—"History of the Military Transactions of the British Nation in Indostan", Vol. II, p. 347.
155. Records of Fort St. George, C. C. L. No. 109.

persons of Shah Nawaz Khan and Muhammad Hussain, they found the residences of these two nobles strongly guarded by the Mughal soldiers.

Shah Nawaz Khan encouraged his soldiers to resist the French and in the resultant tumult the Diwan along with his son was killed by a French Dubash, thus putting an end to the life-long enmity of Shah Nawaz Khan against the French and what they stood for. Throughout his life Shah Nawaz Khan tried to drive away the foreigners from his country, but so great were the squabbles among the Deccan nobles that the foreigners became bold enough to attempt the arrest of Shah Nawaz Khan in his own house.

Nizam Ali Khan on hearing of the sudden death of Shah Nawaz Khan and his son lost his nerve and fled to Burhanpur[156].

The next day when the Durbar was held the nobles of Salabat Jung's court wanted Bussy, to lead an army against Nizam Ali Khan. Bussy, was dubious about the sincerity of the nobles in giving such an advice. Bussy, knew that if he were to take any steps against Nizam Ali Khan, a son of Nizamul-Mulk Asafjah, it would surely make the French very unpopular.

Salabat Jung was bent upon pursuing his fugitive brother and Bussy had to fall in with his wishes. But after marching for three days, Bussy, convinced Salabat Jung of the futility of pursuing Nizam Ali Khan who would be always on the move trying to escape from his brother. Salabat Jung saw the truth in Bussy's arguments and returned to Hyderabad via Berar.

Bussy, in the meantime won over Basalat Jung to his side by promising to make him the Diwan. He also promised to give the Subah of Hyderabad to Basalat Jung[157].

Bussy, reached Hyderabad on the 15th July, 1758; On his arrival there he found a letter from Lally, the French general, asking him, to come over to Pondicherry, along with Moracin, so that they might lead an attack against the English at Madras[158].

While asking Bussy to proceed to Pondicherry, Lally, never for a moment considered the obligation and duties the French owed towards the Nizam.

Lally, was inclined to view with total disfavour the French entanglements in the Deccan. Bussy, who had no option in the matter, decided to leave the Deccan in obedience to the orders of Lally.

---

156. Ibid.
J. S. Mill—"History of British India", Vol. III, p. 153.
157. Orme—"History of the Military Transactions of the British Nation in Indostan", Vol. II, p. 355.
158. Malleson—"History of the French in India", p. 505.
Dodwell—"Dupleix and Clive", p. 100.

He decided to leave behind him 100 men to guard the person of Salabat Jung. He left Hyderabad on the 18th July 1758, with a heavy heart, assuring Salabat Jung that he would return soon, but that was not to be. Bussy never set foot on the Deccan soil again. On the 3rd August 1758, he met De'Conflans, at Bezwada and handed over the charge of the Sarkars to him. From there he set forth for Pondicherry via Ongole[159]. With the departure of Bussy from the Deccan the power and glory of the French also departed from the Deccan.

Events in the Northern Sarkars were also taking a serious turn. Vijaya Rama Raju was succeeded by his nephew Ananda Gajapati who was a keen partisan of the English. Soon after his inheriting the Vizianagaram Zamindari, Ananda Gajapati seceded from the French, and opened negotiations with the English at Madras. He wrote incessant letters to the English at Fort St. David to send troops and occupy the Sarkars. The Peishwa also at this juncture promised to help the English against the French[160].

Ananda Gajapati wrote pressing letters to Clive. in Bengal and also to the Madras Government to send troops and free the Sarkars from the French control. He wrote to the Madras Governor on 17th May 1758[161].

"In consideration of the old friendship between us, I wish for the Company's good and benefit and yours in every respect. I maintained a correspondence of letters with Mr. Percival and advised him to remain with firmness in his place promising to assist the Company, besides which at the time of Mons. Bussy's return from Eachepur I sent Appa Raw to Mr. Percival and settled the matter. But on Mons.Bussys taking possession of Vizagapatam it was discovered to him and I have been informed that Mr. Percival has acquainted you with the same. My sincere friendship and union with the English Company enraged Mons. Bussy against me and he extorted a large sum of money and has still a hatred against me. Sometime ago, I advised you that he had left Anwar Ali Khan with a small number of troops in Chicacole and marched to Court (meaning that of Salabat Jang's) and that it was a proper opportunity for us. I have now received letters from certain persons at the court advising me that Mons. Bussy proceeded to Aurangabad and waited upon Salabat Jang, that Ibrahim Khan has a greater influence at court than Mons.Bussy and that a difference subsists between Salabat Jang and Nizam Ali.

Your Honour will see in a few days what will be the fate of Mons. Bussy. Anwar Ali Khan undertook an expedition against Naraindev Jimidar of Purla but by the blessings of God he punished him so hard, that he was obliged to run away, from the Zamindar's country to Eachepur. Now the

159. Records of Fort St. George, C. C. L. No. 178, p. 84.
160. Ibid, C. C. L. No. 6, p. 4.
161. Ibid, L. No. 97.

country is clear of the enemy's people. I have gathered together all the zamindars of Eachepur, Yellore and Rajahmundry - - I am in expectation of the arrival of your assistance. If you send a detachment of 400 soldiers it will be well. Otherwise please send 200 soon that I may take Vizagapatam and all these Sarkars to remain in your possession. Then both your affairs and mine will be finished. If it was not for my friendship with Mr. Percival which I maintained agreeable to your advice, Mons.Bussy would not have been enraged against me. In short I meet with ruin in your friendship.

You should therefore be mindful of me above all things. It may be in your thoughts that the affairs of Bengal and Arcot are to be considered. I must tell you that there is no occasion for a large force in these parts. 200 soldiers are enough. Only just the name. By the blessings of God as soon as soldiers arrive I shall easily settle this country in your name. The sooner you do this the better".

From the above letter it is amply evident that Ananda Gajapati during this period was actively engaged in inciting the local chieftains of Ellore Rajahmundry and Ichapur against the French.

The English were fully engaged in fighting the French in the Carnatic and therefore they could not send any material help to Ananda Gajapati, except to write encouraging letters.

But Clive who had the foresight to see the advantages that might befall the English by helping the Rajah of Vizianagaram sent Col. Forde from Bengal at the head of 500 Europeans, 2000 sepoys and 100 shipmen. Col. Forde was instructed to seize the French factories on the East Coast. He was asked to work in association with Andrews, the Governor of Vizagapatam, and to carry on the operations in the Sarkars in close co-operation with Ananda Gajapati[162].

The English Governor, Pigot, at Madras, at this juncture wrote a letter to Salabat Jung intimating him of the English success in Bengal and of their intention to seize the French possessions on the East Coast. The Governor, also expressed his regret at his inability to send any troops to Salabat Jung when the latter asked for them at Savanur[163].

In the meanwhile, even before the arrival of Forde, Ananda Gajapati marched against Vizagapatam, imprisoned the French commandant and hoisted the English flag. On hearing this, Mons. Conflans, marched against

162. Records of Fort St. George, (1759), C. C. L. No. 204, p. 93.
Forrest—"Bengal and Madras Papers", (1757-1785), Vol. III.
"Madras Papers"—Military Consultations for (1758), Vol. IX.

163. Records of Fort St. George, (1759), C. C. L. No. 203, p. 93.

164. Cambridge—"Account of the war in India".
Letters to Fort St. George, (1758-59), Vol. XXXVIII, L. No. 67.

the Rajah[163]. Seeing this, Ananda Gajapati, wrote an urgent appeal to Clive, for assistance and the latter placed the Rajah's letter before the Bengal Council, and persuaded them to send Col. Forde to the Sarkars.

On hearing of the capture of Vizagapatam the Madras Government, sent Andrews, to take charge of that factory. Col. Forde, arrived at Vizagapatam on the 20th October; There, he was joined by Andrews and Captain Calliaud[164].

The combined English forces joined Ananda Gajapati at Kasim Kotah[165]. There on the 2nd November, 1758 an agreement was reached with the Rajah, through the efforts of Andrews[166]. According to this agreement it was decided, to divide the plunder equally between both the parties. The revenues of those areas that were not seaports or were not situated at the mouth of navigable rivers were to be enjoyed by the Rajah, while the revenues of all sea ports and those situated at the mouths of the navigable rivers were to be enjoyed by the English East India Company. The Rajah agreed to pay a sum of Rs. 50,000 per month for the English troops, during the time they were in action. He agreed to pay the first instalment after the fortress of Rajahmundry was given to him and the subsequent payments on a monthly basis[167].

This agreement was a very bold one on the part of the English East India Company. As a matter of fact it aimed at the acquisition of all strategic territories in the Sarkars leaving to the Rajah only the name of being supreme in the Sarkars. The English who were not yet thinking in terms of territorial aggrandisement did not approve of this ambitious measure. They were content to be the auxiliaries of the Rajah. As a matter of fact the council at Fort William showed its disapproval by resolving as follows[168];

"On pursuing the above letters of Andrews, the Council at Fort William deplores his tendency to acquire more territories in the name of the Company which according to them was against the Company's interest because it entails the maintenance of a large force, the revenues of the country will not be sufficient to defray their maintenance and that it is inconsistent with the general plan of assisting the gentleman on the coast in driving away the French entirely out of India."

164. Cambridge—"Account of the war in India".
J. S. Mill—"History of British India", Vol. III, p. 192.
165. V. Rava Jagapati Varma—"Peddapura Samasthana Charitramu", p. 102.
Mackenzie Mss. O. M. Library, Madras, Pusapativari Kaifiyat.
166. Letter to Fort St. George, (1758-59), Vol. XXXVIII, L. No. 72.
167. Ibid.
168. Forrest—"Bengal and Madras Papers", Vol. III, (1757-1785), Fort William Select Committee.

This resolution makes it clear, that the English East India Company, at this juncture regarded themselves as the auxiliaries of the Rajah and in keeping with this spirit they asked Forde, to destroy the fortifications of the Masulipatam fortress in the event of his capturing it[169].

After concluding this agreement the Rajah and the English, marched against the French forces, that were under the command of De'Conflan's. They sighted the French forces at Gollaprolu, on the 3rd December 1758[170].

De'Conflans, had under him 500 Europeans, 6.000 sepoys and 500 cavalry.

The English forces consisted of 470 Europeans, 1,900 sepoys. Their ally, the Rajah, had with him 500 infantry and 500 cavalry. He had also some of the local tribes with him.

At first the English, occupied, the village of Chebrolu. But subsequently, in order, that they might be between the French encampment and Rajahmundry, a fortress of strategic importance, they moved over to the village of Chandurti[171]. The distance between Chandurti and the French camp was only 4 miles, and it also gave a vantage point to the English.

The French now started cannonading the English; Ananda Gajapati who was directly under fire sent word to Col. Forde to come to his assistance. Realising that the English might encircle him, Conflans, himself marched forward and occupied Vodula Penta which gave a vantage point to the French. But, Forde, did not leave Chandurti. De'Conflans mistaking this to be hesitancy on the part of Forde, made a sally on the English. Forde, took the fullest advantage of this and opened fire on the moving French army and routed them completely. Many French, soldiers were taken prisoners and their baggage also was captured. The battle of Chandurti had very far reaching effects. It established the English supremacy in that region and enabled the English later on, to separate the Sarkars from the Hyderabad State and tag them on to the Madras Presidency. These areas and the Nizam's territories, after centuries of separation, could only be joined together in November 1956, when the State of Andhra Pradesh was formed in an Independent India.

This battle of Chandurti, took place on the 7th December 1758[170].

But the Rajah Ananda Gajapati was not fully conscious of the victory gained. He was more anxious to win glory against the local zamindars[171].

169. Ibid.

170. Letters to Fort St. George, Vol. XXXVIII, (1758-59), L. No. 72.
V. Raya Jagapati Varma—"Peddapura Samasthna Charitra", p. 103.
Forrest—"Bengal and Madras State Papers", Vol. III, (1757-1785), L. No. 159.
Records of Fort St. George, Sundry Book, Public Dept., (1758-1759), L. No. 62.

171. Orme—"History of the Military Transactions of the British Nation in Indostan", Vol. II, p. 377
Samalkot Kaifiyat, Mackenzie, Mss., O. M. Library, Madras.

The defeated French army dispersed in many directions lest they should go to Rajahmundry, their stronghold. Forde, despatched 1,500 sepoys under Capt.Knox and Macleans to go in advance and occupy that fortress.

The small French garrison, that was at Rajahmundry, mistook the army under Capt. Knox, to be the main army of the English and it vacated the fortress in panic and crossed over to the other bank of the river Godavari. The English after occupying Rajahmundry, connonaded the departing French.

They were able to capture 15 French soldiers, 4 guns and the bullocks and baggage of the French[172].

Rajahmundry was of great strategtic importance to the French possessions on the East Coast. With its capture, we can say, that the whole of the Northern Sarkar regions came under the English control.

According to the agreement reached, on the 2nd November, Rajahmundry was handed over to Ananda Gajapati. The latter appointed Capt. Bristol as the Governor of the fortress.

From there the English and the Rajah, decided to proceed to Masulipatam. But very soon differences arose between the Rajah and Forde, over the question of payment, but these differences were patched up and a fresh agreement was drawn up between the English and the Rajah[173]. According to this new agreement, it was agreed that whatever sums Ananda Gajapati had hitherto advanced, were to be regarded as a loan to the English and the territories that belonged to the French on either side of the Godavary River, were to be equally divided between the English and the Rajah[174]. This treaty raised the status of the English considerably. From being mere auxiliaries of the Rajah, they became his equal partners asserting equal rights to the Sarkars.

After, the conclusion of the above agreement, the English and the Rajah marched against Masulipatam, capturing on their way the French factory at Narsapur.

In the meanwhile, De'Conflans, reached Masulipatam and from there sent word to Salabat Jung, to come to his aid in driving away the English. Salabat Jung, started with his army, to Masulipatam, but his progress was greatly retarded by the recalcitrance of the Qiledar of Udgir[175]. However,

172. Forrest--"Bengal and Madras State Papers", Vol. III, (1757-85), L. No. 160, From Col. Forde to Andrew's.

173. Letters to Fort St. George, Vol. XXXIX, L. No. 9.

174. Forrest—"Bengal and Madras Papers", Vol. III, Fort Willam.

175. Hollingbery—"Nizam Ali Khan".
Forrest—"Bengal and Madras Papers", Vol. III, (1757-1785), Madras Consultations.

Salabat Jung before starting to Masulipatam had sent instructions to the various zamindars in the sarkars to rise against the English. On hearing this Ananda Gajapati, hastily left the Sarkars, leaving the field to the English[176].

Forde, after laying siege to Masulipatam, for more than one month, stormed that fortress on the 8th April, 1759[177].

The reinforcements, that were sent to the besieged French garrison, arrived too late and Moracin who was in command of them made a hasty retreat.

Salabat Jung, on his arrival at Ibrahampatnam, learnt of the English victory over the French, and realised that he had arrived too late. He was also anxious to return to Hyderabad, since, he had heard that Nizam Ali Khan was harbouring hostile intentions[178].

The English, on their part, were also, anxious to come to terms with Salabat Jung. The Madras Council advised Forde, to win over Salabat Jung to their side and make Ananda Gajapati acknowledge Salabat Jung as the Subedar. They wrote; "After the final blow you have given to the power of French in the Deccan, Salabat Jung will be willing to be friends with us upon terms you can reasonably propose. We doubt not you will make use of the opportunities of securing for the Company such beneficial grants and privileges, as will make ample amends for the expenses of the expedition"[179].

Nizam Ali Khan, also wrote a letter, of congratulations to the English, on their success against the French[180]. As a matter of fact, he had at one time written a letter to Clive, in Bengal, asking for English assistance but the English, on account of their pre-occupations in the Carnatic and Bengal could not send him any help[181].

As both Salabat Jung, and the English were anxious for an accommodation, a treaty was concluded between both the Powers, on 14th May 1759[182].

By this treaty, Salabat Jung, ceded to the Company as free gift, the eight districts of the Sarkars of Masulipatam, the Sarkar of Nizampatnam and the district of Kondavid, and Akulamannadu[183]. It was also agreed that the

---

176. Dr. Lanka Sundaram—"Revenue Administration of the Northern Sarkars". J. A H. R. S. Vol. VI, (1931-32).
177. Forrest—"Bengal and Madras Papers", Vol. III, Fort William.
178. Dr. Lanka Sundaram—"Revenue Administration of the Northern Sarkars", J. A. H. R. S. Vol. VI.
179. Forrest—"Bengal and Madras Papers", Vol. III, (1757-85).
180. Calender of Persian Correspondence, Vol. I, (1759-1761).
181. Malcolm—"Life of Robert Clive", Vol. II, p. 18.
182. Aitchison, Vol. IX, p. 20.
Forrest—"Bengal and Madras Papers", Vol. III, (1757-85).
183. Bandar Kaifiyat Mackenzie, Mss. O.M.S. Library, Madras.

Nizam should not entertain the French in his service, and, should see that they did not acquire any settlements in the Sarkars.

Salabat Jung, also agreed not to demand more than the customary tribute from Ananda Gajapati and also, the money, that the latter had collected on his way from Chicacole to Masulipatam. The English on their part promised not to give protection, or assist the enemies of Salabat Jung. Referring to the terms of this treaty, the Madras Council wrote[184]; "The Board cannot but regard it as a most favourable circumstance, that Col. Forde has succeeded in making a friend of Salabat Jung, as whilst he continues in our interests, there can be little reason to apprehend that the French will be able to regain their Northward possessions".

After the conclusion of the treaty, Salabat Jung conferred high titles and a Mansab on Col. Forde, and asked him to accompany him to the Deccan, so that the English presence might act as a deterrent on Nizam Ali. But, Forde, was not in a position to comply with this request because the Madras Government was already pressing him to send troops for their assistance[185]. So, Forde, expressed his inability to comply with the Nizam's request, upon which Salabat Jung revoked the honours he had conferred on Forde and hastily departed to Hyderabad[186].

The treaty of 1759, is an important landmark in the history of the erstwhile Hyderabad State. It was the first political agreement between the English and the Nizams of Hyderabad and marks the beginning of the British ascendancy in Hyderabad.

---

184. Forrest—"Bengal and Madras Papers", Vol. III, (1757–85).
185. Ibid—"Forde to Fort William".
186. Ibid.

CHAPTER IV

Nizam Ali Khan And The Cession Of The Northern Sarkars To The English East India Company

Soon after his arrival in Hyderabad, Salabat Jung was reconciled to his brother Nizam Ali Khan and they decided, to fight with the Marathas who had occupied the fort of Ahmednagar[1]. They now, proceeded to Udgir, where the Marathas were assembled under the command of the Peishwa, Balaji Baji Rao[2]. In the battle that ensued between the two powers, the forces of Salabat Jung suffered a reverse and he was forced to conclude a treaty with the Marathas in 1760[3]. By this treaty, Salabat Jung promised to cede to the Marathas the fortresses of Doulatabad, Sewnerce, Asirghar, Bijapur, a part of Bidar and also the Subah of Aurangabad, excepting the city and two of its parghanas, Sittara and Harolc. The territories which were to be ceded yielded an annual revenue of more than 62 lakhs of Rupees. But soon after the conclusion of the Treaty of Udgir, the Marathas, suffered a severe defeat in the battle of Panipat, at the hands of Ahmed Shah Abdali, and the Peishwa, Balaji Baji Rao, unable to bear the shock of the disaster, died in June 1761[3].

The territories, that Nizam Ali, promised to cede to the Peishwa under the treaty of Udgir, were under the nominal control of the Peishwa. Nizam Ali, could not get over the humiliation he had suffered at Udgir. It rankled in his heart and he was waiting for an opportunity to turn the tables against the Marathas.

The eclipse, in the fortunes of the Marathas on the field of Panipat and the subsequent death of the Peishwa, Balaji Baji Rao, and the dissensions that ensued between Peishwa Madhava Rao and his uncle, Raghunath Rao, gave him the much awaited opportunity. He also opened secret negotiations with the English, and Maratha chiefs like Murrari Rao Ghorpade and Hanumantha Rao Nimbalkar against the Marathas[4].

Though holding the office of the Diwan, Nizam Ali was the real power at Hyderabad. He had usurped almost all sovereign powers, and was exercising them, keeping Salabat Jung as the nominal ruler.

---

1. Briggs—"The Nizam", Vol. I, p. 60.
2. W. Hollingbery—"Nizam Ali Khan", Chapter II, p. 29.
3. G. S. Sardesai—"New History of the Mahrattas", Vol. II, p. 447.
4. "Selections from the Peshwa's Dafter", Vol. XXXVIII, L. No. 10.

Seeing the Maratha power, stricken and weakened, Nizam Ali Khan despatched a large army under one of his generals, Lal Brijdas, to devastate the Maratha territories [5].

Nizam Ali and Salabat Jung, were at Bidar when they first heard of the news, of the Peishwa's death. Apart, from sending Lal Brijdas to devastate the Maratha country, Nizam Ali, tried to cripple the Maratha power by striking at Poona, the nerve centre of the Maratha State. So he marched towards Poona, at the head of a huge army, in alliance with Ramachandra Jhadav. On his way to Poona, he not only captured Naldurg but also destroyed Toka and Pravara Sangam, two Hindu religious centres, to the great chargin of the Hindu generals. Nizam Ali also dug up the Scindias palace at Shrigonda for hidden treasures [6].

Nizam Ali Khan's, march to Poona, was one of destruction and devastation. Seeing the fury of his forces, the general populace of Poona including the Peishwa's family fled to Lohgad, Purandar, Sinhagad and other places for safety [7].

Madhava Rao, who had just succeeded to the Peishwaship became nervous on hearing of the menacing approach of the Mughal army under Nizam Ali Khan. He, along with his uncle Raghunath Rao, appealed to the English East India Company, in Bombay, for assistance [8].

On receiving this letter of appeal, from Madhava Rao, the Government of Fort William, resolved; "The president is desired to acquaint him, we shall interfere no further in the affairs than to protect the family from entire ruin, and make up their disputes with Nizam Ali nor even so far unless they will resign over to the Hon.Company some of their territories adjacent to us in consideration thereof [9]".

The territory which the English desired in return, for their help, to the Marathas was the island of Salsette, but the Marathas were reluctant to cede Salsette. Instead they proposed to cede territories in Jambosur, which would yield a revenue of 150,000 Rupees [10].

However, the Bombay Government, insisted on the cession of the island of Salsette and the Maratha agent, Gangadhar Pant, agreed to the proposal [11]. But when these proposals were sent to the Bengal and Madras Governments for approval the latter two Governments came forth with conflicting advice.

5. K. Sajun Lal—"Studies in Deccan History", p. 4.
6. G. S. Sardesai—"New History of the Mahrattas", Vol. II, p. 466.
7. "Selections from the Peshwa's Daftar", Vol. XXXVIII, L. No. 38.
8. Records of Fort William (Bombay)—"Public Department Diary", Vol. XXXVII, (1761), p. 672.
9. Ibid—"Fort William, Consultations", D/3 November, 1761.
10. Ibid—"Public Department Diary", Vol. XXXVII, (1761), pp. 720–721.
11. Bombay Castle—"Secret & Political Department Diary", Vol. VII, pp. 117, 119.

The Madras Government, turned down the proposal altogether, giving as excuse its own preoccupation in the Carnatic, on the other hand the Bengal Government, was in favour of assisting the Nizam against the Marathas. Faced with such conflicting opinions the Bombay Government, decided to drop the scheme altogether[12].

In the meanwhile Nizam Ali, who had started from Aurangabad, was rapidly marching towards Poona. His wanton destruction of Hindu piligrimage centres, on the banks of the Godavary and the looting of Shadeshwar, alienated some of the Hindu chiefs who had accompanied him. Prominent among them was Ramachandra Jhadav, who along with Mir Moghal Ali now left the camp and joined the Marathas[12-A].

In spite of this, Nizam Ali Khan continued his march towards Poona. The Maratha forces under the command of Janoji Bhonslay and Raghunath Rao met the Moghuls at Shrigonda and a battle ensued between the two forces on the 15th, December 1761[13].

Finding himself hemmed in by the Marathas on all sides, Nizam Ali Khan left all his equipment behind at Shrigonda, and continued his march to Poona in an undaunted manner and reached Dumergaon, a place about 3 *coss* distance from Poona, on the 21st December[14].

Here he received the news of the death of Tarabai, his chief partisan among the Marathas[15]. From Dumergaon Nizam Ali proceeded to Urali about 14 miles' distance from Poona.

The Maratha camp was full of dissensions and the Peishwa often received contradictory advice from his friends. However, Raghunath Rao, the uncle of the Peishwa sent overtures for peace to Nizam Ali, and the latter, agreed to bring about a cessation of hostilities, if the Marathas ceded territories yielding an annual revenue of 27 lakhs of Rupees[16]. According to Naro Shankar the Marathas did not cede any territory to Nizam Ali; But the Peishwa, Madhava Rao, in a letter to his mother wrote, that the Nizam had agreed to conclude peace with the Marathas for a cession of territory yielding an annual revenue of 40 lakhs of Rupees[17]. Grant Duff, and Briggs disagree with this statement and they say that territories yielding an annual revenue of 27 lakhs of Rupees were ceded to the Nizam. This treaty was concluded in January, 1762.

12. Ibid, Vol. VIII, (1762), D/16th February, p. 5.

12-A. Records of Fort William, Bombay Castle--"Public Department Diary", Vol. XXXVII, p. 672.

13. K. Sajun Lal—"Studies in Deccan History", p. 8.

14. Ibid, p. 9.

15. Records of Fort William—"Secret & Political Department Diary", Vol. VIII, p. 7.

16. Briggs--"The Nizam", Vol. I, p. 64.

17. G. S. Sardesai--"New History of the Mahrattas", Vol. II, p. 468.

The Marathas after the conclusion of the above treaty engaged themselves in making preparations for an expedition to the Carnatic in order to check the rising power of Hyder Ali of Mysore[18].

In the meanwhile, Nizam Ali Khan returned to Bidar[19]. There he was received with great honour by his brother Salabat Jung. It was solemnly agreed between the two brothers that while Salabat Jung continued to remain the Subedar, the actual administration of the state would be looked after by Nizam Ali Khan[20].

In spite of these solemn assurances, Nizam Ali, contrived to throw Salabat Jung into prison on the 6th July, 1762, and also got him murdered fifteen months later, and proclaimed himself as the Nizam of Hyderabad. Nizam Ali Khan, was the first ruler of Hyderabad, to have used the title of Nizam, and henceforth, this title, was adopted by all the subsequent rulers of the State.

It is of interest to note that the English East India Company, during the late war wanted to take the side of the Nizam and not that of the Marathas. The English realising the weak position of the Nizam, seemed to have realised as early as 1762, that he was their natural ally against the powerful Maratha State if they wanted to build up their political and commercial power in India.

As a matter of fact the Government of Bengal not only advised the Bombay Government, to co-operate with the Nizam, in the Nizam-Maratha struggle, but it also intimated the Home Government, as well as Salabat Jung and Nizam Ali of their intentions[21].

We find the Bengal Government, writing to the President and Council of Fort William[22] as follows; "The execution we believe will not be very difficult nor do we apprehend it can be attended with any bad consequences but on the contrary will be a step towards giving a check to the overgrown and dangerous power of the Marattas for which the commotions in their Government by the death of Ballajee offer a fair opportunity, and we wish that it suited the situation of your affairs as well as those on the coast to render this attempt more complete by joining the Moghul Government in attacking the Marattas on all sides.

The President, has wrote to the King as well as to Salabat Jung and Nizam Ally to acquaint them of our intentions, and represent to them the benefits that will accrue to them from this division in their favour". But

18. Ibid, p. 470.
19. Briggs--"The Nizam", Vol. I, p. 64.
20. "Selections from the Peshwa's Daftar, Vol. XXXVIII, L. No.
21. Records of Fort William--"Political Department Diary", Vol. VIII, (Secret), p. 4.
22. Ibid.

this suggestion, was rejected by the Madras Government on account of its pre-occupations in the Carnatic.

Referring to this the Government of Fort William wrote to the Secret Committee[23];

"Your Honours have likewise been advised of the proposal made to us by your servants at Bengal for driving the Morattas out of the province of Cuttack, by joining the Moghull Government and attacking them on all sides, from which they are of opinion no bad consequences can ensue, but on the contrary that it would be a means of checking the overgrown power of the Morattas for which the civil commotions in their Government by the death of Ballajee or Nannah offered a fair opportunity but as your servants at Madras have declined the same on account of their being themselves engaged in troubles and as in the present situation of your affairs, we are of opinion on marching all force in land would only serve to involve your Honours in troubles on this side likewise without having any good effect upon the operation of your servants at Bengal, as we have the greatest reason to think the Morattas in that Province act in a great measure independent of the Government at Poonah, we have thought it most prudent to decline interfering at present, though should it hereafter appear to us that any solid advantages will accrue to your Honours by our entering into any engagements with the Moghulls you may rest assured we shall pursue every measure necessary for promoting that desirable end and shall never fail to co-operate with your servants at your other Presidencies in everything which may be convinced tends thereto".

Conditions in the Northern Sarkars, meanwhile, had deteriorated considerably owing to the internecine quarrels among the local zamindars.

Ananda Gajapati, the Rajah of Vizianagaram died in the year 1760[24].

So, shortly after the conclusion of the treaty of Udgir, Nizam Ali Khan visited these parts to settle the administrative matters in the Sarkars[25]. Taking advantage of Nizam Ali's, visit to these parts, James Alexander, the Chief of Masulipatam, tried to get a Sanad from him confirming the grants which were originally made to Col. Forde by Salabat Jung[26].

Nizam Ali was averse to conferring this grant on the English East India Company. So he informed the Chief of Masulipatam that he would grant them the Sanad if they assisted him against the Marathas, so that he might recover the territories he had lost under the treaty of Udgir[26]. So great was the

23. Ibid, Vol. VIII, pp. 11, 14 & 25.
24. Samalkot Kaifiyat--"Mackenzie, Mss. O. M. S. Library, Madras".
25. Ibid.
—"Kondavidu Kaifiyat", Pusapativari Kaifiyat.
26. Dr. Lanka Sundaram -"Revenue Administration of the Northern Sarkars", J. A. H. R. S., Vol. VI, (1931-32).

anxiety of Nizam Ali to wipe off the disgrace he had suffered at Udgir that he promised to pay the English not only 1 lakh of Rupees for their help but also to cede the middle Sarkars[27].

But this proposal was not accepted by the Madras Government. Hence Nizam Ali left for Hyderabad appointing Hussain Ali Khan as the Foujdar of Ellore, Rajahmundry and Mustafanagar. He also entrusted to the infant Rajah of Vizianagaram the work of collecting the revenues of the Chicacole Sarkars[28].

Though loth to part with the Sarkars, Nizam Ali's eagerness to avenge his defeat at Udgir, was so great that he once again deputed Hussain Ali Khan, to Madras, to procure English assistance against the Marathas, in return for the Nizam granting to them the five Northern Sarkars[29]. His eagerness for obtaining English assistance was so great that he, even, sent the Sanads granting the Sarkars to Madras through Hussain Ali, in anticipation of English help[30].

The Madras Government, did not send any help to the Nizam since its full attention was required to make the English position in the Carnatic impregnable. Yet it was loth to let go so fine an opportunity of acquiring the Northern Sarkars. But it was clearly not possible for it to obtain the Sarkars from the Nizam without sending any assistance to him. So the Madras Government, tried to circumvent this difficulty by entering into an agreement with Hussain Ali Khan, without any reference to the Nizam.

According to this agreement the Madras Government, agreed to supply Hussain Ali Khan, with a body of 1000 troops, to assist him in realising the revenues of the Sarkars. The unique feature of this agreement was, that Hussain Ali Khan, was not to have any control, in the internal administration of the Northern Sarkars, but was to be consulted only in matters of revenue administration[31]. This was a subtle agreement on the part of the English. In fact the English aimed at the peaceful penetration of the Northern Sarkars, in the guise of being Hussain Ali Khan's friends.

Nizam Ali, was highly incensed on hearing of this agreement which had been concluded behind his back and he promptly dismissed Hussain Ali Khan from Office and appointed Sultan Muhammad Khan as the Foujdar of

27. Ibid.
28. "Pusapativari Kaifiyat".
Mogali Turru Kaifiyat. } "Mackenzie Mss. O. M. S. Library, Madras".
Bandar Kaifiyat. }
Hollingberry--"Nizam Ali Khan".
29. "Selections from the Peshwa's Daftar", Vol. XXXVIII, L. No, 40.
30. Ibid.
31. Records of Fort St. George, Madras Military Consulations, (1762), Vol. XXXVIII, pp. 248-52.

Rajahmundry, Ellore and Mustafanagar[32]. In spite of his being dimissed, Hussain Ali continued to collect the revenues of the Sarkars by force.

The Madras Government also adhered to their original intention of sending troops to the Sarkars as they were of the opinion that they "never intended that Hussain Ally Caun should have any power or direction of the Sarkars".

The Madras Government also instructed the Chief of Masulipatam to "depend chiefly on the voluntary submission of the zamindars, but should the greater part of the most powerful of them prove disobedient, it would not by any means be advisable to attempt to reduce them[33].

The above letter reveals to us that the Madras Government were anxious to retain the Northern Sarkars at any cost short of declaring war against the local chiefs.

Nizam Ali, now demanded from the English the return of the Sanads which had been sent to the Madras Government through Hussain Ali Khan, since the conditions, in which the Sanads would have become operative were not fulfilled by the English[34]. The Madras Government complied with these orders but retained the fort of Rajahmundry under its control till the expenses of the troops lent by it to Hussain Ali were made good[35].

The Company had also rented, the Vinnakota Parghana, in the Guntur District to one Mangu Appana. Nizam Ali Khan questioned the propriety of the Madras Government's action and he deputed one Abdul Rahman Khan, a former Bakshi, of Hussain Ali Khan, as the manager of the three Sarkars of Rajahmudry, Ellore, and Mustafanagar[36]. The Madras Government, demanded from Abdul Rahman Khan, the payment for the troops which were lent to Hussain Ali Khan, but he refused to be accountable for it. Hussain Ali himself, unable to control his undisciplined troops of nearly 20,000 gave a lot of trouble to the English. In their anxiety to collect as much as they could, he and his officers, committed many acts of tyranny, that told on the prosperity of the country[37]. Hussain Ali Khan, ultimately fled to Masulipatam and from there to Hyderabad, to ingratiate himself into the Nizam's favour once again[38].

In the meanwhile, an accommodation was reached between the English and Abdul Rahman Khan through the exertions of one Jogi Pantulu. By

32. "Selections from the Peshwa's Daftar", Vol. XXXVIII, L. No. 151.
Bandar (Masulipatam) Kaifiyat, Mackenzie Mss., O. M. S. Library.
33. Records of Fort St George—"Military Consulation", Vol. XXXVIII, (1762). (Madras to Masulipatam, pp. 343-47).
34. Records of St. George—C. C. (1762), L. No. 165, 166, 167.
Military Consultations, Vol. XLVIII, 15th Nov., pp. 115-19,
35. Ibid, pp. 111-21, 22.
36. Ibid, Vol. XLIX, 3rd Jan. 1763, pp. 1-3.
37. Ibid, Vol. XLVIII, (1762), pp. 111-125.
38. Ibid, Vol. XLIX, Consultation D/21st, 28th Feb., pp. 99, 103.

this agreement. John Pybus, the Chief of Masulipatam, promised not to assist any local zamindar in the Sarkars against Abdul Rahman Khan and also agreed to evacuate the fort of Rajahmundry. In return, Abdul Rahman, promised to bear the expenses of the English troops that were sent to the Sarkars.

Abdul Rahman, paid off, the expenses of the troops on 21st June 1763, and the Company's troops withdrew from the Sarkars. With the withdrawal of the English these areas were once again thrown into anarchy and confusion. The disturbances, in the Sarkars were accentuated all the more by the malevolent activities of Sitaramaraju, the elder brother of the Raja of Vizianagaram.

Basalat Jung, the younger brother of Nizam Ali, who resented the usurpation of power by the latter also sought to take advantage of the general confusion that prevailed in the Sarkars.

He compelled the English Chief of Masulipatam, John Pybus, to send him boats to cross the Krishna river as he was intending to join Sitaramaraju and undermine the power of Nizam Ali Khan in those areas. The Nizam, who was pre-occupied with the Maratha affairs once again wrote to the Madras Government, for assistance[39]. The main anxiety of the English was, that these areas should not revert to the French. But they were clearly not in a position to help the Nizam. So the Madras Governor Palk and his Council resolved; "Although it is not in our power to afford Nizam Ally any assistance he required (Sic) yet as the Company have earnestly recommended to us to procure grants for the Circars to the northward, it may possibly in some measure facilitate our obtaining them were we to enter into a correspondence with Nizam Ally and amuse him with promises of our assistance as soon as we are able, as he may by that means be induced to decline in engaging in any connection with the French[40].

The Nizam, in the meanwhile, suffered a severe defeat at the hands of the Marathas in 1763 in the battle of Rakshasbhavan, and was forced to conclude a dis-advantageous treaty with the Marathas. Hussain Ali Khan, the former Foujdar of the Sarkars, succeeded, by this time in winning the favour of the Nizam, and was once again restored to office[41]. The Nizam, who was thirsting for revenge against the Marathas, once again made, overtures to the English for assistance.

The Madras Government, was anxious to become the renter of the Northern Sarkars, with the power to interfere in the internal matters of the various zamindaries[42]. With this object in view, it deputed Kandregula Jogi

39. Records of Fort St. George—C. C. (1763), L. No. 184, 185, 186.
40. Records of Fort St. George—'Military Consultations', Vol. XLIX (1763), 2nd Nov.
41. Selections from the "Pashwas Daftar", Vol. XXXVIII, L. No. 51.
42. Dr. Lanka Sundaram, "Revenue Administration of the Northern Sarkars" J.A.H.R.S., Vol. VI, (1931-32)

Pantulu to Hyderabad to negotiate with the Nizam. Jogi Pantulu was not successful in his mission but he entered into an agreement with Hussain Ali Khan, to assist him with troops whenever the latter required it, and the latter, agreed, to defray the expenses of the troops[43]. The English were anxious to get a footing in the Sarkars and so they were very happy to make this agreement with Hussain Ali Khan.

At this juncture the English also received letters from Hyder Ali Khan of Mysore, proposing an alliance between him, the Nizam and the English against the Marathas[44]. Though the Nizam, did dally with the idea of entering into an alliance with Hyder Ali and the English, against the Marathas, he soon gave up the project, and joined the Peishwa, Madhava Rao, in reducing Janoji Bhonslay the Chief of Berar, who had proved treacherous to both the Peishwa and the Nizam during the recent Nizam-Maratha wars[45].

The English, by this time became very anxious to come to some understanding with regard to the Northern Sarkars. the more so, after the arrival of Mons.Law and the renewal of aggressive activities on the part of the French in India.

Both the Madras and the Bombay Governments, impressed upon the Home Government the necessity of procuring a contiguous territory, from Bengal to Madras, which would be possible, only, by the acquisition of the Sarkars and Orissa by the English East India Company. With the object of gaining Orissa, the English East India Company opened negotiations with Janoji Bhonslay[46].

Discussing this, the Select Committee of Fort William recorded[47]; "The Select Committee being of opinion that, opening a communication between the Northern Circars and Bengal would prove mutually advantageous to the Presidencies of Fort St. George, and Bengal, they determined to embrace the favourable opportunity, which the feeble condition of the Mahrattas afforded, to carry the measure into execution, for which purpose they set on foot a negotiation with this Chief proposing that he should cede to the Company the Northern parts of Orissa, now in his possession, upon our paying a certain stipulated annual revenue. But whatever his determination might be, it was resolved not to attempt gaining the advantage by violence or force of arms".

43. Records of Fort St. George—"Military Consultations", Vol. 52, pp. 133, 153-154., dated 20th and 25th February.
44. Records of Fort William -"Political Department Diary", (1764), pp. 592-594 and pp. 733-735.
45. K. Sajun Lal—"Studies in Deccan History", 46.
46. India Records Series-"Fort William and India House Correspondence", Vol. V., (1767-1769), L. No. 19.
47. Auber-"Rise and Progress of the British Power", Vol, I., p p. 153.

The Court of Directors, approving of the above suggestion wrote[48]; we have paid much attention to your negotiation- - - -and much approve of it, if it can be done on the terms you mention of ceding their possessions in Orissa, which would join our Bengal Possessions to the Circars, and would afford the means of preventing any hostile attempts of any European enemy who might land in that part".

[49]About this time, Clive arrived in Madras, and the President of Fort St. George, pressed him to obtain a grant for the Northern Sarkars from the Mughal Emperor, which was duly obtained by him in 1765[50].

The Company was jubilant over the grant, but it prudently refrained from publishing it, lest it should rouse the ire of Nizam Ali Khan.

The next year, in 1766, when the Nizam was pre-occupied in fighting the Bhonslay, the Madras Government saw in it an opportune moment to publish the Sanads, and to occupy the Northern Sarkars[51].

Copies of the Sanads, were sent to Basalat Jung, the Nawabs of Cudapah, Kurnool and to the other polygars with the message that if they wanted to remain on friendly terms with the English they should obey the Emperor's firman[52].

The Madras Government deputed General Caillaud, to take possession of the Sarkars; and this general, after successfully accomplishing his task, occupied the Fort of Kondapally to prevent any possible aggression on the part of the Nizam[53].

Notwithstanding, their occupying the Sarkars without the Nizam's permission, the Madras Government were anxious to win his goodwill. So it deputed one Mutabir Khan to the Nizam's court to get the Sanad of the Emperor, confirmed by the Nizam, in return for their military support to the Nizam.

The publication of the Sanads and the consequent occupation of Kondapally, created great panic in Hyderabad. The Qiledar of Hyderabad, after taking the necessary precautions, wrote to the Nizam who was at Berar to come to Hyderabad soon[54].

The Nizam, after defeating Janoji Bhonslay, was busy drawing up plans with the Peishwa, for an invasion of Mysore. However, on hearing of

48. Ibid.
49. Auber – " Rise and Progress of the British Power", Vol. I., p. 125.
50. Records of Fort St. George, C. C. (1765), L. No. 235, p. 209.
51. Auber–"Rise and Progress of the British Power", Vol. I, p. 208.
52. "Selections from the Peshwas Daftar" Vol., XXXVIII, L. No. 181.
53. Ibid.
54. Ibid.

the publication of the Sanads he hastened to Hyderabad[55]. On his arrival at Hyderabad he sent a note of protest to the English through his Minister Rukun-ud-Doula[56]. He even thought of making war on the English but financial embarrassments came in his way[57]. Hence, he decided to give ear to the English proposals only, if they were sent through any one, other than Mutabir Khan.

The English Government deputed General Caillaud and General Smith, to negotiate with the Nizam and they concluded a treaty with the Nizam on the 12th November, 1766.

[58]By this treaty, the Sarkars of Rajahmundry, Ellore, Mustafanagar, Murtizanagar and Chicacole were given as free gift to the English East India Company, and the Company had to pay a rent of nine lakhs of Rupees per annum for the above Sarkars at the rate of 4 lakhs for the Sarkars of Rajahmundry, Ellore and Mustafanagar and 2 lakhs each as rent for Murtizanagar and Chicacole.

Since Murtizanagar was given as a Jaghir in 1761 to Basalat Jung, the younger brother of the Nizam, it was decided that the Company should take possession of it either after the demise of Basalat Jung or in the event of the latter proving disloyal to the Nizam, the rent for the above Sarkar being payable from the date of its resumption by the Company.

The Company agreed to assist the Nizam with troops in anything that was right and proper provided their commitments in the Carnatic did not come in the way. The expenditure of the Company's troops was to be met from the rent of nine lakhs which the Company, was to pay to the Nizam. If the expenditure on the troops exceeded nine lakhs, the Nizam was to bear the extra expenditure.

Another important feature of this treaty of 1766 was that the East India Company agreed to place an indefinite number of troops at the Nizam's disposal, which he could use against any power.

Shortly, after the conclusion of the above treaty, the Nizam, requisitioned English help against Hyder Ali. The English, who were greatly displeased with Hyder's policy on the Malabar Coast, did not require a great deal of persuasion to join the Nizam. As a matter of fact, they hoped to completely demolish Hyder's power in the Carnatic, by forming this alliance.

But the Court of Directors did not approve of this alliance. They wrote[60]; "The exclusion of the French from the Circars has been our principal view

55. Ibid.
56. Records of Fort St. George C. C. (1766)., L. No. 77.
57. "Selections from the Peshwa's Dafter", Vol.38 , L. No. 172.
58. Aitchison–Vol. IX, pp. 22, 25.
60. Auber–"Rise and Progress of the British Power", Vol. I, pp. 213, 17.

in obtaining them, but we have ever shown a repugnance to holding them on terms of assisting the Subah with our troops.- - - -The growing greatness of Hyder Ally was but a weak pretence for a junction with the Subah. - - - - - The Mahrattas instead of being reduced are like to be aggrandised by this conquest of the Mysore dominions, which brings them so much nearer the Carnatic".

The Court of Directors, also disapproved of the vagueness of the clause which placed an indefinite number of troops at the Nizam's disposal.

But Clive, who had a greater insight into Indian affairs, wrote; "Whatever power may be added to the Morattas by lessening that of Hyder Ally may be recovered hereafter by an alliance with the Subah of Deccan, who will soon begin to think coolly of his own interests"[61].

The fact was, that the English at this juncture were clearly conscious of their strength and were thinking in terms of being the umpires in India between the various Indian Powers which were struggling for power.

The Bengal Government, wrote to the Court of Directors;[62] " The first and great cause of our security is the general indigence of the Moghul Empire. The invasion of Nadirshah gave the first stroke to its power and populence - - - The irruption of the Mahrattas ensured; their wide extended ravages laid desolate almost everything on the south side of the Ganges from near the frontiers of *Behar on the East to Sarhind on the North and West.* The expeditions of the Shah Abdally succeeded which - - - conduced greatly to exhaust the declining State.

The natural consequence of these circumstances had been that the different powers find their finances narrow and their treasures unequal to the maintenance of a respectable army or the prosecution of a war of any duration. Whenever therefore they are urged by ambition or necessity to enter on an expedition, they assemble new levies for the purpose with most unreflecting precipitancy they risk everything on one campaign because they have seldom resources for a second. - - - - - - -

These circumstances, I apprehend gentleman, have been very principal sources of our repeated victories over these immense Asiatic armies which have fled before a handful of our troops - - - - and these will I trust either deter others in future or ensure success against any who may be desperate enough to brave a force like ours, so strengthened by discipline and rendered formidable by uninterrupted success.

---

61. Records of Fort William - (Bombay Castle) - "Secret Political Department Diary", Vol. IX, (1767) - Dated 28th September, p. 13.
62. Fort William - "Indian House Correspondence" Vol. V, (1767-69). Letters from the Bengal Government to the Court of Directors., L. No. 17., pp. 398-400.

A second and no less powerful reason for our resting perfectly easy as to our situation is the discordancy of the principle, views and interests of the neighbouring Powers; and which must ever defeat any project of accomplishing by an association what the wealth or power of a single one must prove unequal to - - - - - - - - - - - - - - -.

Thus circumstanced it will always be easy for a watchful and active administration on one side to hold the general balance of Hindustan and crush every combination in the bud by spiriting up some neighbouring power who may be either ill disposed or at least not favourable to the Confederates. A very little acquaintance with the disposition of the natives will shew their arder for change where they have a prospect of support and the situation of Allahabad and the station of a Brigade there renders the plan still more practicable. Its situation makes it in some measure the key of the surrounding territories, and its vicinity to the several countries Shuja Doulah, the Rohillas, the Jats and Mahrattas enables us to penetrate their views with more certainity. And in case of necessity to enter any part with an army in ten or fifteen days where we can have either an Ally to support or any enemy to punish. It is for these reasons we have been obliged to retain a Brigade out of the Provinces. - - - - - - - - -

Such gentlemen seem to be the causes of our present security here but they receive additional strength from the particular characters and situations of the several potentates themselves".

The Nizam's and the English troops went to Srirangapatnam in March 1767; the Peishwa, who was also a party to this alliance, preceded them and was already carrying on operations against Hyder Ali.

Hyder Ali, realising that the odds were against him, sued for peace, by agreeing to pay thirty one lakhs of rupees as tribute to the Peishwa[63]. At the Peishwa's intercession, he also agreed, to pay Rs. 18 lakhs as peishcush to the Nizam[64], though later on this peishcush was reduced to twelve and a half lakhs.[65]

The Nizam, who at heart disliked the treaty of 1766, was soon persuaded by those of his courtiers who were friendly with Hyder, to come to an amicable understanding with the latter. Ere long, an agreement was concluded between the Nizam and Hyder Ali by which the former agreed to recognise Tippu, the son of Hyder Ali, as the Nawab of Arcot in place of Nawab Muhammad Ali, the protege of the English.

The Nizam and Hyder now resolved to put an end to the growing power of the English. The complete reversal of policy on the part of the Nizam

63. "Selections from the Peshwa's Dafter", Vol. 36. L. No. 15.
64. Ibid., L. No. 163.
65. News letters (un published); Central Records Office, Hyderabad-Dn.

showed, that he entered into the treaty of 1766 more because of financial exigency, than any willingness on his part. He resented that he, the over-lord of the Carnatic, should be set aside by the English in matters pertaining to the Carnatic. Hence, he wanted to strike at the English power at the very first opportunity that came in his way.

The Nizam, now dismissed the English troops which accompanied him to Mysore[66], despite the remonstrances of the English General Colonel Smith and Mr. Bourchier.

But any project to be successful requires firmness and good faith. The Nizam and Hyder could not entirely get over their distrust for each other though each tried to hide it by assumed cordiality. Hyder's distrust of the Nizam, was so great, that he posted spies in the Nizam's camp and every movement of the Nizam's troops was jealously watched and restricted.

The English in the meanwhile were so disgusted with the Nizam's behaviour that the Bengal Government, applied for a blank firman from the Mughal Emperor so that they might confer the Subedari of the Deccan on a candidate of their own choice, and also instructed the English troops in the Sarkars, to march towards the borders of Hyderabad[67].

The Nizam, on receiving news that the English forces had occupied the strategic fortress of Khammam, became nervous[68]. So, informing Hyder, that he would send troops from Hyderabad, to drive the English out of the Sarkars, he hastily returned to Cudapah from where he sent overtures of peace to the English at Madras through his Diwan, Rukun-ud-Doula[69].

The English, in spite of the Nizam's dislike for them, were eager to win his friendship since they realised that he could be their ally against the Marathas about whose growing power they were jealous. As a matter of fact, the Peishwa's vakeel at Arcot on the eve of the campaign against Hyder had sounded the English, on ousting the Nizam from the Deccan, but the English did not respond to these overtures. We find the President and Council of Fort St. George, writing to the Bombay Government regarding this in the following manner;

"The Vackeel of Madhavrow now at Arcot has made some proposals of this kind to our Nabob, and has been alleged that his master would be

66. Records of Fort William - (Bombay Castle)-"Political Department Diary", Vol. IX, p. 13, d/ 28th 1767.
67. Fort William - "India House Correspondence", Vol. V, (1767 68). Letter from the Court of Directors to the Bengal Government, Vol. 88, L. No. 181. p. 146.
68. "Selections from the Peshwa's Daftar", Vol.38 . L. No. 181., p. 146.
69. M.M.D.L.T. - "History of Hyder Ali Khan.", Vol. II, p. 143.
70. Records of Fort William--(Bombay-Castle) - "Secret and Political Department Diary", Vol. IX, p. 3, d/ 28th September, 1767.

very glad to see Nizam Ally and all the family of Nizam-ul-mulk expelled from the Deccan Government, and one of the King Shah Allam's sons established in their room but this would be extending our view too far for the present. The Principal point is to root out Hyder Ally and then consider in whose person the balance against the Morattas shall be kept up, for it is our incontestible maxim that the Government of the Deccan should be preserved, if possible entire, otherwise it must fall to the Morattas, and increase their power and make them our neighbours both in the Carnatick and Circars to avoid which has been the ground object of all our operations".

Since the object of the English was to preserve the Nizam and use him as an ally against the Marathas whose power they really dreaded, the English readily responded to the overtures of peace from the Nizam and a treaty was concluded at Madras on the 23rd February 1768.

The Nawab of Arcot was also made a party to this treaty by the English, thus giving him the status of an independent Power.

[71]By this treaty of 1768, Muhammad Ali Khan, the Nawab of Arcot, was recognised as the rightful ruler of the Carnatic, and he was released from all dependence on the Subedar of the Deccan. The English were given the "Diwani rights" over the Carnatic Balaghat for which they promised to pay the Nizam a sum of Rs. 7 lakhs per annum and also the necessary Chouth to the Marathas. The five Northern Sarkars of Rajahmundry, Ellore, Mustafanagar, Chicacole and Murtizanagar were ceded to the Company. The English as a gesture of goodwill agreed to to take possession of the Murtizanagar Sarkar, only after the demise of Basalat Jung provided ofcourse he did not carry on any anti-British activities.

The annual tribute of the Sarkars, was reduced from the original 9 lakhs to 7 lakhs per annum and the Madras Government wrote; "We have also taken care to have the treaty so worded that the payment of this sum does not appear to be by virtue of our holding the Sarkars from the Subah but only in consideration of the friendship subsisting between us[72]".

The above letter gives a sufficient insight into the mind of the English. It shows that they did not like to recognise the Nizam's authority over the Sarkars at all, and that they were only too eager to throw it off at the earliest opportunity.

The English further agreed to assist the Nizam with two battalions of sepoys and six pieces of artillery manned by Europeans, whenever he required

71. Aitchison, Vol. IV. pp.25–27.

72. Forrest —"Bombay and Madras Papers", (1757–1790). Madras Letter.

it. The Nizam, was expected to pay for the troops whenever he employed them.

The Nizam in his turn undertook to direct all the zamindars in the Sarkars to obey the English henceforth, as their lawful masters.

Thus by the treaty of 1768, the Nizam had to give up all claims to the Carnatic and to surrender the Sarkars to the English.

He was naturally displeased, with this agreement and he sought to nullify it by entering into a fresh agreement with the Marathas and Hyder Ali against the English[73]. But this project did not materialise owing to the pre-occupation of the Peishwa's Court with the intrigues of Raghunath Rao.

Yet, we know how great was his dislike of the treaty of 1763 from the following letter of the Bombay Government[74]; "Nizam Ally Khan, since his return to Haiderabad, and recovery from the apprehensions he was undergoing---, begins to show evident signs of an intention to keep the late peace as ill as he did the former. His brother Bazalat Jang is already active in raising troops for Hyder, and Nizam Ally has discovered his dislike to his Diwan Ruccun-ud-Doulah, who made the peace with us, and whom he suspects to be in our interest, by attempting to cut him off and surrounding him with troops in his house, where the Duan endeavours to defend himself from these circumstances we conclude, notwithstanding the most scrupulous exactness on our part in observing the treaty, that Nizam Ally will pay little or no regard to his engagement if any opportunity offers to give us trouble".

The English, no doubt, had agreed to the retention of the Murtizanagar (Guntur) Sarkar by Basalat Jung during the lifetime of the latter. But that agreement, was not entirely to their satisfaction, more so, after Basalat Jung had started employing the French troops dismissed by his brother, in his service.

Guntur, formed a contiguous link with the other four Sarkars, and its retention by Basalat Jung broke the continuity of the line of communication from Madras to Ganjam. Hence the Company became anxious to take the Guntur Sarkar, into its own hands. With this object in view, the Madras Government, opened negotiations with Basalat Jung in 1772, but the talks proved abortive.

---

73. "Selections from the Peshwa,s Daftar", Vol. 37.
   Poona Akbhars.
   Records of the Fort William - (Bombay Castle) "Public Department Diray., Vol. 52, pp. 441-42.
74. Records of Fort William-(Bombay Castle)- "Public Deptartment Diary", Vol. 52, pp. 324-25, d/17th September, 1768.

[75]In the beginning of 1775, the Chief of Masulipatam, drew the attention of the Madras Government to the danger to the English possessions due to the presence of the French troops under Basalat Jung.

The Madras Government, sought the opinion of the Bengal Government, with regard to this matter. The Bengal Government, advised the Madras Government to inform Basalat Jung "That they would take possession of his country, and negotiate with the Nizam even by an entire renunciation of the revenues, for the cession of it to the Company"[76].

The Madras Government, also moved this matter with the Nizam and solicited the latters assistance to induce Basalat Jung to hand over the defence of the French from his service.

The Nizam replied in a friendly manner to the Madras Governor saying[77]; "As regards Murtizanagar, it is laid down in the treaty that the Company will not take possession of it, till the death of his brother Basalat Jang and on his demise it would be ceded to the Company. If in spite of the assurance the Company wants that, owing to some special purposes it would be restored and the French driven out of it." The Nizam appealed to the English to adhere to the terms of the treaty of 1768. He also sent messages to Basalat Jung asking him not to employ the French in his service but his advise went unheeded[77].

The question of the Guntur Sarkar, was shelved for another three years, owing to disputes within the Council of Fort St. George.

While the English were engaged in making their interests secure in the South, the Nizam was engaged in a war against Mudhoji Bhonslay[78].

According to the treaty of 1768, the Nizam was entitled to seek English help against the Marathas. Hence, the Nizam asked the English, to assist him aginst Mudhoji, suggesting that they could occupy Cuttack which was under Mudhoji, and secure a contiguous coast-line from Bengal to Madras[79].

But the Madras Government was against this proposed alliance as it was of the opinion that "Our affairs will not allow of our engaging in such distant operations, and it would be our constant endeavour to avoid all connections

75. "Calender of Indian State Papers"-(Secret Series), Vol. V, p. 2, (Masulipatam to Madras)
"Foreign Department Series III" -(Secret)- Vol. I., (1763-75).
Fort William to Fort St. George, Masulipatam to Madras.
76. Dr. Yusuf Hussain-"Anglo-Hyderabad Relations", (1772-1818), Islamic Culture, January 1953. Vol. XXVII.
77. "Khairitas" -(Unpublished), Darul-Inshah Section, Central Records Office, Hyderabad.
78. Hollingbery "Nizam Ali Khan", Chap. III, p. 44.
79. "Calendar of Indian State Papers", Vol. I, (Foreign Department Secrecy.)

with the country power which can only involve us in endless expense and difficulties[80]".

So now, the Supreme Government of Bengal, came out with altogether a novel interpretation[81]. It maintained that the treaty of 1768 was purely defensive, and that the English were entitled to send help, only, when the common interests of the Nizam and the Company were affected. Taking their stand in the above manner they forbade the Madras Government to send help to the Nizam.

The Nizam, was angry because the English let him down so badly in the hour of his need. His feelings were all the more aggravated to find that the English had also withheld the tribute due to him from the Sarkars. In a letter to Sir Eyre Coote, he clearly expressed his feelings by saying that while he strove not to violate the terms of the treaty of 1768, by which it was agreed[82]", to render mutual help and assistance, to esteem the enemies of one, the enemies of both, and the friends of one, the friends of both", the English had flagrantly violated it by refusing to come to his assistance, and also by withholding the tribute due from the Sarkars.

The problem of the Guntur Sarkar became more acute with the outbreak of hostilies between the French and the English once again. The English were anxious to secure it at any cost. The Madras Governor, Sir Thomas Rumbold, was anxious to raise the issue once again.

Basalat Jung, at this juncture, becoming apprehensive of Hyder Ali's aggression, sent vakils to negotiate for the rent of the Guntur Sarkar[83].

The Madras Government, seized this opportunity eagerly and they decided to come to an understanding with Basalat Jung even without any reference to the Nizam, the overlord. The Bengal Government, gave a free hand to the Madras Government, in these negotiations[84].

[85]An agreement was reached between the English and Basalat Jung on the 27th January, 1779, by which the latter agreed to dismiss the French, and to lease the Guntur Sarkar to the English for a specific rent. The English, promised to assist him with troops and defend his territories.

---

80. Records of Fort William-(Bombay), "Secret and Political Department Diary"., Vol. X, p. 101.
81. "Calender of Indian State Papers"- (Fort William).,Vol. V, p. 32, p. 273.
82. Dr. Yusuf Hussain-Some unpublished Documents in the Imperial Record Department of the Government of India having a bearing on Anglo-Nizam Relations Islamic Culture, Vol. XXIII -(1949).
"Kharitas" (unpublished)-Darul-Insha-Central Records Office, Hyderabad.
83. Forrest-"State Papers" Vol. II (Foreign Department), Fort William., Secret Department.
84. Forrest-"Selections from State Papers"-(Foreign Department)., Vol. II., Fort William.
Ibid.,
85. Briggs, Vol. I., p. 248.

After obtaining the Guntur Sarkar from Basalat Jung in the above manner, the Madras Government, leased the Guntur Sarkar to the Nawab of Carnatic for a period of ten years, without consulting the Bengal Government.

The Nizam, on hearing of this treaty was greatly incensed against the English. He promptly started engaging, the French soldiers dismissed by his brother. Fearing the antogonism of the Nizam, the Madras Government deputed Mr. Holland to the Nizam's Court to conciliate and convince him of English friendship and sincerity towards him. Holland, was further instructed to request the Nizam, for the total remission of the tribute from the Sarkars, the levying of which, the Madras Government, felt was unjustified in view of the fact that the Sarkars were originally granted by the Mughal Emperor to the East India Company [85-A].

Holland, reached Hyderabad, in April 1779. He explained that the English were forced to conclude the treaty with Basalat Jung without intimating the Nizam because of the emergency arising out of Hyder Ali's activities on the Southern Coast.

The Nizam was apprehensive of Basalat Jung asserting his independence with the aid of the English. He complained that by treating separately with his brother, the English had violated the treaty of 1768. He now forbade, the English to send assistance to Basalat Jung. He also firmly refused to remit the tribute of the Sarkars. His annoyance with the English was so great, that he sent instructions to his various generals and Qiledars to be prepared for war[86]. He even contemplated entering into an alliance with Hyder Ali Khan of Mysore, and the Marathas against the English[87].

Holland, communicated the aggrieved feelings of the Nizam, directly, to the Bengal Government. The English, on account of their hostilities with Hyder Ali, needed the Nizam's support and friendship. Hence Warren Hastings, the British Governor General, wrote a friendly letter placating the Nizam and assuring him of the Company's friendship and good faith[88].

He also, severely condemned, the action of the Madras Government, in concluding a greaty with Basalat Jung and the measures they adopted regarding the Guntur Sarkar. He now passed orders for the immediate restitution of the Guntur Sarkar[89].

85-A. Dr. Yusuf Hussain -"Anglo Hyderabad Relations" -(1772-1818).
"Islamic Culture", Vol. XXVII.
Second Report of the Committee of Secrecy -(1781).

86. "Kharitas" -(unpublished)- Central Records Office, Hyderabad.

87. Ibid.—(News-letters,) M. M. D. L. T-"History of Hyder Ali Khan." Vol., II.. p. 195.

88. Forrest-"State Papers", (Foreign Secret Department), (Fort William), Vol. II.,

89. Ibid.

The Nizam, was highly satisfied, with the stand taken by the Bengal Government, while the Madras Governor, Rumbold, grew indignant at the attitude of the Governor General and his Council. Rumbold, protested saying that the Bengal Government, was trying to appropriate undue authority. Rumbold, even deprived Holland, of his office for having communicated directly with the Bengal Government; but he was restored once again to his former position by the Government of Bengal[90].

In the meanwhile, Rumbold, was succeeded by Whitehill, as the Governor of Madras. He was instructed by the Supreme Government of Bengal, to restore the Guntur Sarkar to Basalat Jung. The latter, embarrassed by the anger of his brother and the jealousy of Hyder Ali, had also requested the Madras Government, to withdraw their troops from his frontiers, and to restore the Guntur Sarkar to him[91].

But Whitehill, was neither willing to comply with the orders of the Supreme Government nor anxious to accede to the request of Basalat Jung. He tried, on the other hand to delay matters as long as possible.

The Bengal Government, which disapproved of the leasing of the Guntur Sarkar, found the behaviour of Whitehill, objectionable and so it removed him from his office. It now sent Sir Eyre Coote, to Madras to take charge of the operations againt Hyder Ali[92].

Warren Hastings justified the stand taken by the Bengal Government, in the following manner[93]; "The first intimation conveyed to us of the business relative to the Guntur Circar was in a letter from the Select Committee, 31st December 1778, in which after acquainting us "That they were thoroughly convinced of the necessity of removing the French troops from the service of Bazalat Jang, and that they had received certain proposals from him relative to the Guntur Circar, to which they had returned such an answer as they thought proper and necessary on the occasion". They refer us to the letter from the Presidency dated 5th July and 11th December 1775 in which they say, "they find ample authority from us to the then Government to proceed in effecting the dismission of the French troops by treaty or in any other manner they might think proper." What the ample authority was, in what manner and in what terms it was conveyed, the letters themselves are the only proofs to establish, and if from these letters and from other references it shall appear that not only the spirit but even the letter of our instructions made the consent of the Nawab Nizam Ally Cawn indispensably necessary to the conclusion of any treaty with Bazalat Jung, the terms of general approval in which he replied to the letter from the Select Committee of the 31st December 1778 cannot be understood to commit us for the sanction of any

90. Ibid., (Fort William)—Secrtet Committee Consultation.
91. Ibid., Embodied in the Consultations.
92. Ibid.
93. Ibid.

treaty afterwards ratified with Bazalat Jung without the knowledge, or privity of the Nizam his superior- - - -To accomplish the treaty with Bazalat Jang,and by that means to secure the Guntoor Circar to Mahomed Ally they violated another treaty in actual existence between the Company and the Nizam. When the knowledge of the business reached the Nizam and when Bazalat Jang, too late convinced of the jealousy it had excited on the part of his brother and Hyder Ally, and finding himself surrounded with difficulties, the continuance of which portended everything dangerous to his affairs, desired to be released from the treaty, declaring at the same time his inability to fulfil it, they accept just as much of his request as it suited them to accept it, they give orders for stopping the march of the detachment but they retain the possession of the Circar. Whereas from the moment that Bazalat Jung proclaimed his inability to fulfil the conditions of the treaty and desired not only that the march of the detachment should be stopped, but that the circar should be given back to him from that moment the treaty was *ipso-facto* void, and the Circar ought to have been restored, or it was binding in every part of it. In the second instant therefore they broke the treaty entered into with Bazalat Jung."

The firm action taken by Warren Hastings, came at an opportune time. It prevented an open rupture between the English and the Nizam, for we learn from Holland's letter to Fort William, that the Nizam had thought of forming an alliance with the Marathas against the English, and to deprive them of their possessions in Bengal and in the Sarkars[94]. He even went to the extent of conferring a Khilat on Chimnaji Bhonslay who was to lead the Nizam's armies[95].

But the directions given by Warren Hastings to the Madras Government regarding the Guntur Sarkar made the Nizam give up his contemplated offensive against the English[96].

Had he joined the Marathas and Hyder Ali, the English position in India would have become precarious. But the Nizam, could never get over his inhibition that the Marathas were his natural enemies and the greater the dislike he had, for the Marathas, the more he tended to look towards the English for assistance. We find Holland writing; "I am greatly of opinion that he holds a disposition to court our friendship and alliance- - - - - on the principle of reciprocation of benefits[96]".

In July 1781, Warren Hastings, went to the extent of recommending the restitution of the Sarkars to the Nizam, the Company retaining only the seaports and factories on condition of the Nizam always co-operating with the Company and foregoing the tribute of the Sarkars.

---

94. Forrest - "State Papers." Vol. III., (Fort William - Secret Consultations)
95. Ibid.
96. Ibid., Holland to Fort William.
    Poona Akhbars.-(1781-1796)-Letter of Haibat Rao to his son, dated 7th January, 1782.

But this proposal was disapproved by Lord Macartney, the Govenor of Madras, and latter's views prevailed ultimately.

Basalat Jung died in the year 1782. The Nizam ordered his officers to seize the Guntur Sarkar because the English had not yet settled the arrears of tribute due to him from the Sarkars. The English representative at the court of the Nizam, Mr. Grant did not feel that he would be justified in protesting at the Nizam's action. Hence he resigned his post in 1784. Then the Company deputed Mr. Johnson to the Nizam's court with the instructions to demand the restoration of the Guntur Sarkar as per the treaty of 1768, and also to reach an agreement with him regarding the arrears of tribute from the Sarkars[97].

Johnson found the Nizam greatly dissatisfied with his English allies; writing about the Nizam, Johnson says:[98] "The Nizam ------would have remained as I found him fearfully polite and hearty inimical ------ who alleged (TheEnglish policy) it to have been unjust, though successful through force. He stood deprived of his rights."

[99] The Nizam proposed to Johnson the restoration of the Guntur Sarkar to him on the condition of his foregoing all the arrears due to him from the Company and further presenting the Company with a crore of rupees.

The Nizam also desired, that the Carnatic should be returned to him on condition of his discharging the debts, owed by the Nawab of the Carnatic, Muhammad Ali, to the English East India Company and its servants.

These proposals were forwarded by Johnson with a strong note of recommendation to the Government of Bengal, who forwarded them to the Court of Directors[100]; But the Court of Directors, did not approve of the above proposals and Johnson was recalled from Hyderabad. After the recall of Johnson the negotiations concerning the Sarkars were suspended. The Madras Government, also withheld the tribute due to the Nizam from the Carnatic Balaghat, on the plea that the Carnatic Balaghat was under the occupation of Tippu Sultan of Mysore.

In the meanwhile Warren Hastings left India, and he was succeeded by Lord Cornwallis as the Governor General of India.

At the time of sending Cornwallis to India, the Court of Directors, instructed him to take up the question of the Guntur Sarkar, after he reached

97. Records of Fort William—"Secret & Political Department Diary", Vol. 32, p. 109. Bombay Castle-Consultation dated 21st June 1784.
98. Bengal and Madras Papers., Vol. III, (1757–1790), Johnson to Fort William–(Secret Department.)
99. Ibid.,
100. "Kharitas"-(unpublished)-Darul-Insha Section–Central Records Office, Hyderabad.

India. The Court of Directors, were anxious to acquire the Guntur Sarkar on account of its strategic importance, and its nearness to the Port of Motupalli.

But Cornwallis did not deem it advisable to take up this issue immediately after his arrival in India. He was apprehensive of the likelihood of outbreak of hostilities between the French and the English. He was expecting the French to go to the assistance of Tippu against the English. So he was afraid, that if he ruffled the Nizam's feelings, the latter might also join Tippu, against the English. So, we find him writing to Dundas in 1787[101], "The business of the Guntur Circar is very delicate one, and requires the most mature reflection --- Our demand of the Circar from the Nizam in the hour of his distress, would not only appear ungenerous but would undoubtedly hurt him in the negotiation for a peace with Tippu".

Cornwallis found the next year more favourable to broach the subject; peace prevailed between the Courts of Versailles and London. The Marathas and the Nizam had forced Tippu, to conclude the treaty of Gajendragaon with them, and Tippu was not in a position to enter into hostilities so soon after the conclusion of that treaty. All these factors made Cornwallis, bold enough to take up the question of the Guntur Sarkar.

He sent Captain Kennaway, "a gentleman well acquainted with the country, languages and customs", to the Nizam's Court in July 1788, to demand the cession of the Guntur Sarkar[102]. While making this demand, Cornwallis, also took care to see that his demand had sufficient force behind it, by taking care to make the necessary military preparations.

He wrote to the Secret Committee[103]; "I considered myself as called upon by public duty to take every precaution of your Government against the disgrace of disappointment, and I thought it therefore equally prudent and necessary to leave him but a very short time after making the requisitions, for consulting with any of his neighours on the means of opposition, and to direct that a good body of troops should be assembled near the Circar under other pretexts, to be ready to act if necessary in support of our demand of his performance of the terms of the treaty".

The Nizam was helpless against the aggressive attitude assumed by Lord Cornwallis. Unable to withstand the English demand, he ceded the Guntur Sarkar to the Company, and sent Mir Alam, to Calcutta to negotiate the settlement of the arrears due to him[104]. Cornwallis, after

101. Ross -"Cornwallis", Vol. I., p. 252.
102. "Kharitas" -(unpublished)., Central Records Office., Hyderabad-Dn.
103. Ross-"Cornwallis". Vol. I, pp. 537-38.
104. "Kharitas" -(unpublished), Central Records Office, Hyderabad-Dn.

settling the arrears question, addressed his famous letter to the Nizam dated 7th July, 1789. In this letter, Cornwallis, gave a new interpretation to Article VI of the Treaty of 1768, that empowered the Nizam to receive the English assistance, the assistance that he failed to procure against Mudhoji Bhonsle.

Cornwallis, now interpreted the clause as meaning, that the English military assistance would be given to the Nizam, only against those powers who did not happen to be the allies of the English. The Nizam, perforce had to remain content with this interpretation.

The suggestion of the Nizam, that a portion of the Sarkars should be mortgaged to ensure the regular payment of tribute was turned down. Cornwallis also expressed the inability of the Company to pay the tribute of the Carnatic Balaghat, according to the treaty of 1768, as that territory was under the occupation of Tippu. He promised, however, to fulfil that part of the treaty of 1768, at a future date, when conditions might change in the Carnatic. Finding that the odds were against him, the Nizam, acquiesced in the English demands and accepted this new interpretation of the treaty of 1768.

CHAPTER V

The Subsidiary Alliance

The Nizam, while sending Mir Alam[1], to Calcutta, to negotiate about the peishcush of the Northern Sarkars, also instructed him to conclude with the English an offensive and defensive treaty.

After a few conferences the Governor General Lord Cornwallis, fixed the balance of the peishcush due to the Nizam at Rs. 916,665; After settling the issue of the peishcush Mir Alam desired the English East India Company to conclude an offensive and defensive treaty with the Nizam, saying that the latter was surprised and pained at the English not helping him and the Marathas in their late war with Tippu[2]. He also drew the attention of the Governor General to article 9 of the Treaty of 1768, and pointed out that just as the English had forced the Nizam to abide by the Treaty of 1768 by demanding the cession of the Guntur Sarkar, they must also adhere to the other terms of the treaty of 1768[3].

Article 9 of the Treaty of 1768 unequivocally declared Hyder Ali to be an usurper, and asserted the intention of the Nizam and the English to exterminate his power and free the Carnatic Balaghat[4]. In spite of this, the English had concluded the Treaty of Madras in 1729, with Hyder and the Treaty of Mangalore in 1784, with Tippu, by which they recognised the right of these two rulers to the territories of the Carnatic Balaghat.

---

1. Mir Alam, by birth was a Persian nobleman. His talents were first noticed by Azim-ul-Umara the Diwan, of the Nizam and on his recommendation the Nizam deputed Mir Alam to Calcutta to negotiate with the English about the Peishcush from the Northern Sarkars. He accompained the Nizam's forces to Mysore and played a considerable part in negotiating the terms of the treaty of Srirangapatam on behalf of his master. In 1794 he was sent to Poona, but could not bring about amicability between the courts of Poona and Hyderabad. On the advise of Azim-ul-Umara he was appointed by the Nizam as the Minister for English affairs, and in that capacity he negotiated the subsidiary treaty of 1798. He soon won the English favour and friendship by his conduct, much to the chargin of Azim-ul-Umara, who contrived to get him banished to his Jaghir in 1800. He lived in disgrace there till 1803 and was allowed to return to Hyderabad on grounds of health and the recommendation of the Resident. On the death of Azim-ul-Umara the Resident contrived to get him appointed as the Diwan, which office he held till his death in 1808.

   Briggs—Vol. I, p. 140-41.
2. Kharitas (unpublished)—Daftari Darul Insha, No. 34, Central Records Office, Hyderabad.
3. Forrest—Selections from the State Papers of the Governor General of India, Cornwallis, Vol. I, p. 37.
4. Aitchison, Vol. IX, p. 33.

Even though these treaties were concluded with the Mysore rulers, the English were at heart not actually reconciled to Hyder Ali and Tippu, because they were their potential rivals for power in the Carnatic country. Hence it is not surprising to note, that Cornwallis, the Governor General, believed that the treaty of 1768 with the Nizam was still in existenee and therefore enforceable in spite of the treaties of Madras and Mangalore.

Yet, Cornwallis, found clause No. 34 of the Pitts India Act a great obstacle, in his desire to form an unequivocal alliance with the Nizam. Clause No. 34 of the Pitts India Act had forbidden the formation of any military alliances on the part of the English East India Company. It declared. "And Whereas to pursue schemes of conquest and extension of dominion in India, are measures repugnant to the wish, the honour and policy of this nation. Be it therefore be further enacted that it shall not be lawful for the Governor General and Council without the express command of the Court of Directors, or of the Secret Committee, in any case (except where hostilities have actually been commenced or preparations actually made for the commencement of hostilities against the British Nation in India, or against some of the Princes, or States, whose territories the Company shall be engaged by any subsisting treaty to defend or guarantee) either to declare war or commence hostilities, or enter into any treaty for making war, against any of the country provinces, or States in India or any treaty for guaranteeing the possession of any country, princes of States".

Though Cornwallis, had been unwilling to commit himself to hostilities the previous year; he now fully realised that a war against Tippu, was inevitable, and he was anxious to secure the alliance of the Nizam and the Marathas in such an event.

The previous year, he had been willing to follow a policy of masterly inactivity, and even rejected a request for an alliance with the Nizam, against Tippu, on the plea that the treaty of 1768 did not warrant it mainly because he felt that the finances of the Company would be put to a great strain. We find him writing : "Considering the state of our finances and the uncertainity of all negotiations with the country states the line of this Government was clear before them. It was to avoid war and every connection or engagement that might involve us in war, and to devote our labour and attention to regulate our finances to reduce our expenses within salutory bounds, to restore the Company's credits at home and their investments without heavy drafts upon their credit and above all to adopt such regulation as would in the event of war, enable as to carry it on upon a system of regular disbursements of check and economy in accounts. Mr. Macpherson, the Governer-General was the first to initiate the system of masterly inactivity and he thought that the best policy would be not to rouse the jealousy of any of the Indian powers by negotiations or by views hostile to their particular interests but "to endeavour to obtain perfect intelligence of their designs and to let them severally and unitedly feel that though we wish not to be parties in their own disputes we are determined to maintain a decisive influence in whatever scale we may think it just and political to throw the force of our aid"[5].

Now Cornwallis, felt the time had come for him to take a decisive step in making allies in the inevitable war against Tippu; so he now tried to resort to a clever ruse by which he could circumvent the hindrances placed in his path by clause 34 of the Pitts India Act. Instead of entering into a regular political treaty with the Nizam, he concieved the idea of writing a letter to him, in which, he reinterpreted the treaty of 1768, and gave the necessary assurances to the Nizam, fully confident that the Home Government would support him, once it was convinced of the sagacity and desirability of his policy and methods. He wrote a letter to the Nizam, dated 7th July 1789, by which, according to Forrest, "he aimed to lay a foundation of permanent and powerful co-operation."

In this he explained the stand of the English East India Company regarding the treaty of 1768. He wrote----"[6] In proof of the sincerity of my intentions that the treaty should be carried into effect, I agree that, in the 6th Article of the Treaty, the words "whenever the situation of affairs will allow such a body of troops to march into the Deccan" shall be understood to mean that the force engaged for by this Article *viz.*. two battalions of Sepoys and six pieces of Cannon, manned by Europeans-shall be granted whenever your Highness shall apply for it, making only one exception, that it is not to be employed against any power in alliance with the Company *viz.* Pandit Pirdhun Peishwa, Raghoji Bhoosla, Madajee Sindia, and the other Mahratta Chiefs, the Nawab of Arcot, the Nawab Vazier, the Rajahs of Tanjore and Travancore. That the battalions at present not defined in number shall not consist of less than eight hundred men each. That the six field pieces shall be manned with number of Europeans which is usual in time of war." He further wrote "In regard to the Article relative to the Dewanny of the Carnatic Ballaghat Your Highness must be well convinced that circumstances have totally prevented the execution of these Articles and the Company are in the full employment of peace with all the world, but should it hereafter happen that the Company should obtain possession of the country mentioned in these Articles with your Highness's assistance they will strictly perform the stipulations in favour of your Highness and the Mahrattas."

Thus Cornwallis, by deliberately omitting the name of Tippu, with whom the Company was still at peace, among the list of allies he had enumerated in his letter and by promising the Nizam that the Peishcush of the Carnatic Balaghat would be paid to him on the event of that country being freed with the assistance of the Nizam, in a very subtle manner indicated to the Nizam the possibility of the Nizam, the Marathas and the English East India

5. Forrest-State Papers-Cornwallis, Vol. II.
6. Aitchison, Vol. IX, p. 44.
Ibid.

Company, forming an alliance and carrying on operations against Tippu Sultan in the near future. By hinting that the p ..sh of the Carnatic Balaghat would be paid to the Nizam once those territories were freed from the control of Tippu, he shrewdly tried to raise hopes in the heart of the Nizam, about the way things might develop in the future. To create confidence in the Nizam, he assured him in the following manner[7]. "Although I have not agreed to enter into a new treaty with your Highness, in consideration of the authority vested in me by the King and Parliament of England, will consider my letter, though merely purporting a clear explanation of the several articles in the Treaty of 1768, strong and efficient upon the English Government in India equally so as a treaty in due form could be, since the members of the Council have given their cheerful acquiescence to its contents".

The Directors of the East India Company were also anxious to retain the friendship of the Nizam and we find Dundas, writing to Cornwallis[8]: "It is so very essential to our interest to detach him from all other Indian connexions and to unite him in the closest connexion and dependance upon our protection, that there is no alliance formed upon that basis to which you may not expect our concurrence".

Since Pitt, the Prime Minister of England at this time and Dundas, were close friends it was not surprising that the House of Commons, approved of the action of Cornwallis and passed a resolution by which they placed the letter written by Cornwallis to the Nizam in the category of a regularly transacted treaty[9].

Thus Cornwallis byepassed the spirit of the Parliamentary Act of 1784, and indirectly concluded an offensive alliance against Tippu. Commenting about this Thoronton observes: "It is highly instructive to observe a statesman, justly extolled for moderate and pacific disposition thus indirectly violating a law enacted for the enforcement of these virtues, by entering into a very intelligent offensive alliance[10].

The shrewd man that he was, Nawab Nizam Ali Khan, while these negotiations were going on with the English, also opened negotiations with Tippu's court. The manner in which the Guntur Sarkar was taken away from the Nizam, left a bad taste behind. The Nizam, was very bitter for having lost a strategic place, and the manner in which Guntur was taken created apprehensions in the mind of every Indian Prince. Col. Read says: "I believe, it is the received opinion among the Princes of India that we have a desire to enfeeble every power in connection with us and consequently every one who is tenacious of his dependency is wary in trusting our support"[11].

7. Ibid.
8. Forrest–State Papers Cornwaillis, Vol. II.
9. Mill—History of British India, Vol. IV. Appendix-A.
10. Thoronton--Vol. II. p. 395--96.
11. Mackenzie Mss. 58, Vol. LXVI.

The Nizam, on account of his resentment against the English, even opened correspondence with the French Governor Mons. De Cossigny, at Pondicherry [12]. He wrote to Mons. De Cossingny [13]:" I have heard with much surprise and concern that you are at present closely connected with my servant and enemy Tippoo Fatty Aly Caun. What can this mean ? You are not ignorant of my being the immediate representative of the Great King and the villian is only a vassal of mine, but not withstanding this he has presumed to enter my country to destroy it ; my reason now in writing you this is to offer you my alliance and former friendship if you will accept it. Be assured you will become of more consequence than ever you were, even in the time of Bussy ; the English and myself are at present friends but I set greater value upon you". He again wrote [14], "I have well understood the contents of your last and am perfectly convinced of your friendship, without your support and advice I see no remedy, I will in future abide by your directions in everything. I, therefore, request that on mature deliberation you will give me your opinion and state what part I ought to pursue." To this the French replied saying, [15]"Your Highness has done us too much honour, but since you order, it is our part to obey, as the necessary step to the accomplishment of all your plans and indeed for your present security and quiet, you must contrive to cultivate and cement an alliance with Tippu Sultan, (he is a firm friend and a dangerous enemy). This point once gained you may look forward with a prosperous hope".

To this advice the Nizam replied, saying, that as it would be below his dignity to court the friendship of Tippu Sultan whom he considered as his vassal, he would be glad if the French would exert themselves to bring about the establishment of cordial relations between the courts of Hyderabad and Mysore.

These manoeuvers of the French to bring about an understanding between the Nizam, the Marathas and Tippu created the greatest apprehension in the mind of the English, and the Bengal Government wrote to Malet, the Resident at Poona, in this connection[16]: "I have now to communicate to you a piece of information that has been transmitted to me through different channels, which if true, requires the whole address of the English Government in India to counteract and defeat.

It is no less than a plan said to be formed for an alliance between the Mahrattas, the Nizam and Tippoo".

The Bengal Government, in view of these developments, pressed the Resident Malet, to induce Nana Farnavis, the Maratha Chief, to enter into an alliance with the English, against Tippu.

12. Poona Residency Correspondence, Vol. 3. L. No. 12.
13. Ibid. p. 9.
14. Ibid. pp. 9-10.
15. Ibid. p. 10
16. Ibid. pp. 16 and 17.

In the meanwhile the Nizam sent two emissaries to the court of Tippu, in August 1787. These were Imtiaz-ud-Doula and his brother-in-law, Shums-ul-Umara, the commander of his household troops. They were sent to discuss the possibility of an alliance between the Courts of Hyderabad and Mysore. Later on the Nizam sent more agents, Farid-ud-din and Bahadur Khan[17], who reached Srirangapatam in November, 1787.

Tippu was glad to receive these envoys. He expressed his readiness to enter into an alliance with the Nizam, and to return the territories that legally belonged to him. He further proposed, a matrimonial alliance, between Tippu's son and one of the nieces of the Nizam in order to cement this political alliance[18].

But nothing came out of this mission. The Nizam, once again despatched Hafiz Farid-ud-din and one Ramachandra, to Tippu in November, 1788, with a message that they should patch up their differences and as a proof of his sincerity, he sent a copy of the Holy Qoran along with his envoys[19].

Tippu was at Coimbatore when the envoys arrived and he once again conveyed his willingness to form an alliance with the Nizam and proposed the same terms as before[20]. But the Nizam, a descendant of the Asaf Jahi dynasty, thought it would be degrading if he were to enter into a matrimonial alliance with Tippu, a man of humble origin, and so he turned down the proposed alliance ; He now eagerly, turned to accept the bait that Cornwallis, offered him in his letter, namely the resuming of the peishcush of the Carnatic Balaghat, once those territories were freed from Tippu's control.

Apart from this hitch over the matrimonial alliance, the Nizam, was at heart never sincere towards Tippu. He regarded him as an usurper and was glad to embrace the English alliance, againist him. The Nizam sought Tippu's alliance mainly because he did not like to be isolated. Once, he became convinced, of the eagerness of the English, for his friendship, he forthwith turned down Tippu's alliance; He even did not pay any heed to Tippu's request that in the event of a struggle between Tippu and the English East India Company the Nizam should remain neutral[21]. Had the Nizam and the Marathas formed an alliance with Tippu Sultan rather than with the English, perhaps the course of history in India would have been different. But unfortunately the Nizam did not choose to side Tippu.

After the breakdown of the negotiations with the Nizam, Tippu, launched hostilities against the Rajah of Travancore, an ally of the English[22].

17. Mackenzie Mss. pp. 53-54, Vol. LXVI. pp. 55.
18. Ibid.,
Forrest-State Papers-Cornwallis. Vol. I, p. 37.
19. Mackenzie Mss, p. p. 86, Vol. LXVI.
20. Ibid.
21. Poona Residency Correspondence, Vol. III. No. 31. pp. 31-32.
22. Ibid.

He demanded the demolition of the Travancore defence lines on the plea that they were constructed in the territories of the Rajah of Cochin, a tributory of Tippu[23]. The Raja of Travancore, refused to comply with this demand, and his refusal led to the outbreak of hostilities between him and Tippu.

Cornwillis, was anxiously waiting for such an opportunity to form a confederacy against Tippu. Tippu's aggression against Travancore, enabled him to circumvent the restrictions that were imposed upon him, by the Pitt's India Act. He now instructed Malet, the Resident at Poona, to redouble his efforts to draw the tardy Nana Farnavis, into an alliance with the English against Tippu[24]. He also wrote to Capt. Kennaway, the Resident at the Hyderabad court, to persuade the Nizam to enter into an alliance with the English against Tippu[25].

The Hyderabad Court, and the Resident Kennaway, looked upon the proposed defensive alliance, as a furtherance of the Treaty of 1768, as interpreted in the letter of Cornwallis. Under the new alliance, the Nizam aspired, to get his rights recompensed over the Carnatic Balaghat[26]. But this was not liked bythe Peishwa's Government, which felt that such an operation of the treaty might result in the loss of tribute that the Poona Court was receiving form Tippu[27].

The Marathas on their part made the following proposals[28]. They demanded, the restoration of all those territories that once belonged to the Peishwa. The reinstatement of the zamindars and the equal distribution among the allies of the *nazarana* that might be colleced from the zamindars.

The Marathas also demanded their right to exact tribute from the zamindars. They wanted an equal division among the allies of the territories that might be conquered from Tippu, and equal military commitments on the part of the allies. They also insisted, that peace should be concluded with Tippu, only, with the mutual consent of all the allies. They further proposed a defensive pact, to prevent future possible attacks from Tippu.

The proposals from the Peishwa's Court led to a lot of dispute between the Poona Court, the Hyderabad Government and the Bengal Government[29].

The English Resident, Malet, questioned the right of the Poona Government to treat for the Nizam[30]. Apart from this, disputes also arose over the number of troops that each party was expected to provide, and the definition

23. Gleig-History of the British Empire in India, Vol. III. p. 102.
    Poona Residency Correspondence, Vol. III. No. 52, pp. 49-50.
24. Ibid.
25. Ibid.
26. Ibid. No. 80.
27. Ibid., L. No. 104.
28. Secret Proceedings Foreign Department (Secret Branch 1780-90).
29. P. R. C. Vol. III. No. 69.—p. 77
30. Ibid.

of the words Zamindar, Polygar and a District. A great deal of acrimony also arose, over the question as to who should bear the expenses of the British contingent attached to the Maratha army and about the general plan of attack on Tippu.

Malet, the Resident at Poona, objected to the Maratha courts claim, that the ancient territories which had once belonged to the Peishwa should be restored to the Poona Government, because, these territories were undefined and the jurisdiction of the Marathas over them was vague [31]. Cornwallis, did not like the demand made by the Poona Government, that they should be allowed to levy tribute from the zamindars as it would amount to, not only giving a share to the Marathas from Tippu's territories, but also giving them an extra tribute of twelve lakhs from the zamindars. But finding, that Nana Farnavis was adamant over this issue, he gave way, to the demand of the Marathas.

As regards, the bearing of the expenses of the British detachment, which would accompany the Maratha forces, Malet persuaded the Poona Government to bear its expenses [32].

A compromise was also reached over the definition of the words, Pargana, Circar and District. Nana Farnavis was inclined to give different meanings to these different words but Malet, at last, made him agree, to the definition that the word 'district' is synonym of the words, Circar, Samsthanam and Parganah. But Nana Farnavis did not like to accept this interpretation. As, a matter of fact, he wanted, to regain the former possessions of the Peishwa in the Carnatic country north of the Tungabhadra region, over and above, the territories he might get after the partition of Tippu's territories.

According to Nana, the revenues yielded by these ancient territories would not exceed more than 15 lakhs, and he wanted the Company to give up, its one third share in this territory saying that it would not be actually more than 15 lakhs in value. But Malet, was of the opinion that the territories might be worth 60 lakhs and he was afraid, that, if the English were to yield on this point to the Marathas, they might also have to yield to a similar demand on the part of the Nizam, who might claim exclusive rights over Cudapah, a territory that yielded a revenue of 40 lakhs of rupees. So, at last, it was agreed that the word 'district' must be interpreted as a territory yielding not more than 15 lakhs and not less than ten lakhs of rupees annually.

To avoid, any difficulties that might arise, over the imterpretation of the proposed alliance *Vis-a-vis* the treaty of 1768, two separate treaties were envisaged, one with the Marathas and the other with the Nizam.

---

31. Ibid. No. 73. pp.79-82.
32. Ibid. No. 93. Vol. III. pp. 108-112.
    Ibid. No. No. 82, 83, 99, 90 : 91 ; 92-95.

The preliminary treaty was signed by the Poona Court on the 29th March 1790. Parasuram Baho, was placed in charge of the Maratha forces, as the Peishwa, was too young to personally, lead his armies into the field.

The main features of the treaty were as follows: It admitted the right of the Company to all those territories that it might have conquered before the formation of the alliance. It was now decided to divide equally all those conquests that the allied forces might make during the course of the war. The Marathas also agreed to bear the expenses of the Company's detachment and to entertain a vakil on behalf of the English forces. They also agreed to send a vakil on their behalf, to the English, along with their respective forces. The allies also agreed, to invade Tippu's territories, soon after the English made their attack on his dominions. It was also agreed that peace should be concluded after mutual consultations among the allies and that they should also contribute the maximum force they could spare. The Nizam and the Marathas agreed to invade Tippu's territories with a force, each, of not less than 25,000 and if necessary to furnish an additional force of 10,000 cavalry, if the Company was prepared to bear its expenses[33].

In spite of their approving the above treaty, the Marathas still persisted, in raising objections regarding the order of precedence, in which the names of the allies should be mentioned in the proposed defensive treaty. They also raised objection at Capt. Kennaway, the Resident at Hyderabad, promising the Nizam an additional detachment, under Col. Cockrell, apart from the battalions promised in the treaty of 1768.

Cornwallis, who was anxious to obtain the Maratha help even by making some concessions to them, wrote[34]: "I felt, a very serious concern at receiving Mr. Malet's letters of the 7th and 10th ultimo for without the co-operation of the Mahrattas I could not flatter myself with a certain prospect of the speedy conclusion as well as the decided success of war, two events which are absolutely necessary to save this Government and indeed the English Company's affairs from the greatest possible distress; besides that, if they had not taken part with us there would always have been reason to apprehend that their jealousy of our getting the Nizam out of their hands might in the course of the contest have even inclined them to take their part against us".

However, Cornwallis, succeeded in pacifying the Marathas and it was finally decided that all conquests should be equally divided among the allies, with due respect to frontiers and the convenience of the parties. It was also agreed, to restore certain zamindars and to divide equally among them the *nazarana* offered by them. If any one of the allies were to receive overtures of peace from Tippu, he was expected to communicate them to the other two. If Tippu attacked any one of the allies after the conclusion of peace, the other

33. Foreign Department. Secret Proceedings—Cornwallis to Malet, D/17th April, 1790.
34. Poona Residency Correspondence, Vol. III, p. 121.
Cornwallis to Kennaway, pp. 156–57.

two were expected to go to the help of the attacked party and punish Tippu. Thus, the defensive treaty alliance was mainly concluded to reduce the power of Tippu.

After having succeeded in bringing the Marathas into the alliance in the above manner, Cornwallis wrote[35]: "The alarm is now happily over, and I trust that everything will go according to our wishes but I must desire you to keep it for ever uppermost in your mind that the great objects to which I with so much anxiety and indeed almost solely look forward, are not the same with those which principally occupy the thoughts of the Nizam or at least of His Minister and Meer Abul Kasim. My views are at present entirely confined to the reduction of Tippoo Saib's power and to the speedy termination of the war, but I suspect the first and favourite point of the others to be the emancipation of His Highness from the power of the Mahrattas, and that they are such short-sighted politicians, that for the chance of obtaining it they would even now he glad to see coldness between us and the Poona Government without considering that such an event might possibly so raise our affairs as to put it out of our power to effect what they desire". This letter of Cornwallis amply reveals to us that though he took so much pains to win over the Marathas against Tippu, he never for one moment forgot that they would be the potential rivals of the English, ultimately.

While, the negotiations with the Poona Court passed through so many critical phases, the negotiations with the Nizam's Court, were relatively smooth. Cornwallis' tried to win over the Nizam by appealing to his desire for territorial aggrandisement. He wrote to Kennaway, the Resident at Hyderabad[36]: "I am the more sanguine in my hopes that your endeavours will be successful, as you can point out to them that Tippo will be obliged to employ the flower of his forces against our main army which will be in readiness to march from Trichinopoly by the middle of next month and consequently that they will not only find easy consequents at present in the northern parts of his dominions but that by the agreement which has been concluded between Mr. Malet and the Poona Government, a larger proportion of these acquisitions will fall to His Highness's share, if they can be obtained before the Mahrattas shall actually commence hostilities".

The renewal of Article 6, of the Treaty of 1768 prepared the general background for an alliance between the Nizam and the English in 1790. The Nizam and his Minister, Azim-ul-Umara, were quite willing to join the confederacy and if necessary to enter into a separate treaty agreement with the English[37]. Cornwallis was highly pleased with their conduct. He gave to the Nizam the option to enter either into separate but similar treaties with the English and the Marathas or to enter into a single joint treaty. The Mara-

35. Ibid.
36. Ibid, No. 89, p. 99.
37. Foreign Department. Secret Proceedings, April 12, 1790—Cornwallis to Malet.

thas raised objection to the Nizam forming separate treaty agreements, with the English.

The Nizam in his turn objected to the method by which the tribute levied from the zamindars would be divided among the allies. His contention was that under the scheme the share of the Marathas would be far larger than his own. He also claimed that in the absence of the Peishwa he must be allowed to command the Maratha troops, but this contention of the Nizam was not appreciated by Cornwallis.

The Nizam, who had had bitter experiences at the hands of the Marathas, wanted a specific assurance from the English that they would even assist him against them He insisted that a defensive agreement should be included in the treaty of 1790, and that Art 6, of the treaty of 1768, must be interpreted as meaning that the Nizam was entitled to receive English help not only against Tippu but against any power that might threaten his dominions.

Kennaway, wanted to introduce such a clause. As a matter of fact the insertion of such a clause would have reduced the position of the Nizam to that of a subservient ally But the Marathas, who realised that the clause was, actually aimed against them, objected to its inclusion. So, Lord Cornwallis by way of a compromise, proposed that the British would exert their good offices in the event of differences between the Nizam and the Marathas to bring about an amicable settlement[38]. He further assured the Nizam, by writing to him, "You will always find me in the best disposition to endeavour to save His Highness from the necessity of submitting to mortification or injury[39].

The Nizam, apart from the help of the British detachment to which he was entitled, wanted an additional force to accompany him on the battlefield and the Governer-General was prepared to send him additional forces under Col. Cockrell, but this was dropped on the Marathas raising objection[40].

After settling all the disputes in the above manner, the treaty was finally signed by the Nizam at Paungal on the 4th July 1790. The clauses of the Treaty of Paungal, were similar to those of the Treaty between the English and the Marathas. Thus the Tripartite Treaty of 1790 finally came into existence in July 1790.

When we examine the exertions of the English, to bring the Marathas and the Nizam into this tripartite alliance we cannot but draw certain conclusions. The English regarded the Treaty of Mangalore, with Tippu, as a humilating pacification and they wanted to reduce the power of Tippu at all costs.

They also realised that if they were to realise their object they should have the co-operation of the Marathas and the Nizam, the only two great

38. Secret Proceedings—Foreign Department. (Secret). Cornwallis to Kennaway, d/12-4-1790.
39. Ibid.
40. Ibid. Kennaway to Cornwallis, d/May 28th, 1790.

Indian powers, and both these powers had claims over certain territories in the dominions of Tippu. If the English did not solicit their help, there was every possibility of there joining Tippu and thus upsetting the balance of power, or causing embarrassment to the English. So the English used all their subtle diplomacy to bring about this Tripartite Treaty.

The Nizam, who looked upon Tippu as a vassal, but was sometimes inclined to maintain friendly relations with him as becomes a fellow Muslim prince, was really prompted to join this alliance, not only to get back the peishcush of the Carnatic Balaghat and to regain his lost territories in the Carnatic but also as a security against Maratha aggression. The Marathas tended to look upon the Nizam as their dependent, while the Nizam never acknowledged this, and also ceased paying the Chouth which the Marathas demanded from him.

The alliance offered by Cornwallis and his assurance that he would never allow the Nizam to suffer any humiliation was a sufficient bait for the Nizam to join the Tripartite Alliance. He looked upon the treaty of 1790 as a protective one against the Marathas[41].

The Marathas regarded the Tripartive Treaty, as a convenient means of recovering their lost territories in the Carnatic. Though, they were anxious to recover their former territories in the Carnatic they were not willing to reduce the power of Tippu so as to facilitate the growth of the supremacy of the British, in India.

Tippu, realising that he would be hemmed in by all these powers, tried to wean away the Nizam and the Marathas from the alliance but all his efforts were in vain.

Major Meadows, who was placed in charge of operations against Tippu, did not prove equal to the task. So Cornwallis replaced him and conducted the operations against Tippu in person. He arrived in Madras on the 12th December, 1790, and invaded Mysore *via* Vellore and Amboor[42].

The Nizam, in the meanwhile moved at the head of a large force of cavalry, artillery and infantry and encamped at Paungal. He was accompanied by the Resident, Captain Kennaway. Lord Cornwallis, complained to Kennaway about the slowness of the Nizam's movements. Thereupon, the Nizam sent Rajah Tejewant in advance at the head of a large force of cavalry, to join the Company's troops in Tippu's Dominions[43].

At this juncture Tippu made overtures for peace to Cornwallis in May, 1791. True to the treaty agreement, Lord Cornwallis asked the Nizam and the Peishwa, to send their representatives to discuss the peace proposals.

41. Foreign Department. See Proc. Const. June 7, 1790.
42. Fort William—India House Correspondence, Vol. VII, (1792–95).
43. Fraser--Our Faithfully ally the Nizam, p. 42.

The Nizam, deputed Mir Alam who arrived in Bangalore in 1791. The Marathas sent Hari Pant Tantia as their representatives. But these peace negotiations failed and war was once again renewed. So in view of the continued hostilities, the Nizam, sent his second son Sikandar Jah and his Minister Azim-ul-Umara at the head of reinforecments, to the assistance of Cornwallis[44]. In spite of this apparent eagerness of the Nizam to go to the assistance of Cornwallis, the Mughal forces were tardy in their march. Prince Sikandar Jah and Azim-ul-Umara in spite of several requests from Cornwallis to march more quickly, followed very dilatory methods ;[45] Nor, were the Marathas, any better in rendering assistance to the English. The attitude of these Indian allies, and especially of the Nizam, appeared to be one of passivity, nay even of reluctance[46]. Commenting on the attitude of the allies, Malet wrote to Cornwallis[47] ; "From the tenor of Your Lordship's letter to Sir John Kennaway, I am apprehensive that you will experience a strong tendency on the part of the allies to evasion and delay in commencing the operations of the ensuring campaign, on the idea of drawing Your Lordship into a greater dependance on them than hitherto and than I hope they will ever experience. But should your Lordship's preparations be such as to convince them that their delays will be attended with evil consequences only to themselves, I think it probable that they may quicken their motions, whereas should they see a prospect of retarding your Lordship's operations by their delay they will, in my humble opinion, have recourse thereto as the mode exactly suited to their genius, to their desire of drawing your Lordship into their views, and to their object of reducing rather by holding up in terror, than by striking the dreaded blow, the enemy to their terms, and this, my Lord, do I humbly conceive, has been their plan from the first and which has only been corrected by the successful vigour and decision of Your Lordship's measures ".

In the meanwhile, the English forces under Cornwallis carried on vigorous warfare, and Tippu once again made overtures for peace in January, 1792,

Prince Sikandarjah accompanied by the Minister Azim-ul-Umara arrived near Ouscota by this time. Capt. Kennaway, also accompanied the Prince's army. The Prince joined the allied army on the 25th January and on the 26th proceeded to lay seige to Srirangapatam the capital of Tippu[48].

The Maratha army arrived under Parasuram Bahu, on the 30th January and joined the confederate army in laying seige to Srirangapatam.

The seige of Srirangapatam commenced on the 15th February, and Tippu finding that the odds were against him, signed the preliminary Treaty

44. Fraser—Ibid, p. 47, P. R. C. Vol. III, No. 346, Cornwallis to Kennaway.
45. Ibid. No. 369, 366.
46. Ibid. No. 378, pp. 507-510, No. 382, pp. 513-534, No. 384, p. 515.
47. Ibid. No. 379, p. 511,
48. Ibid. No. 440 p. 579.

of Srirangapatam on the 24th February. This was immediately followed by a cessation of hostilities.

At the peace conference that brought about the Treaty of Srirangapatam, the Nizam was represented by Mir Alam, while Govinda Rao Kale and Bachaji Pandi represented the Peishwa. Cornwallis, represented the Company. Capt. Kennaway, was also present at the conference.

[49]By the Treaty of Srirangapatam that was finally ratified on the 13th March 1792, Tippu agreed to surrender to the allies, over half of his dominions and to pay an indemnity of three crores and thirty lakhs of Sicca Rupees, half to be paid immediately, while the rest was to be paid in three instalments, the interval between two instalments was not to exceed four months.

By this treaty, the Nizam, got as his share the territories of Gurramkonda, Cudapah, Ganjikotah, Khambham, Bellary and the districts between the Rivers Tungabhadra and Krishna[51]. The Nizam gave up his claims to Gutty, on the intercession of Lord Cornwallis.

The Marathas acquired the Northern Districts of Basavapatam, Chitaldoorg, Raidoorg and Haripanhalli thus extending their frontiers upto the River Tungabhadra.

The English got for their share the territories of Baramahal, Salem, Dindigal, Calicut, Karur, Dharapuram and Coorg.

The Treaty of Srirangapatam was based on the total revenue yield of Tippu's dominions rather than on the total area of his dominions. Therefore the shares of the Nizam and the Marathas was much less in size, than the share of the English, who on the plea that their share consisted of barren and mountainous lands secured greater areas. The Marathas and the Nizam got highly fertile regions. The English acquisitions though less fertile were far more important from the point of view of strategy and were potentially capable of development.

Even after the conclusion of this treaty many disputes arose between the allies and Tippu over the question of frontier arrangements, payment of indemnity, and the release of the prisoners of war. One of the most controversial disputes took place between Tippu and the Nizam over Kurnool. Kurnool was of great strategic importance to the Nizam as well as to Tippu. The Nawabs of Kurnool had always acknowledged the Nizam of Hyderabad as their liege lord. But in 1765, Kurnool, was subdued by Hyder Ali, who forced the Nawab of Kurnool to pay him tribute; From that time onwards the rulers of Kurnool paid tribute to Mysore[50-A]. During the negotiations that preceded the treaty of Srirangapatam, Tippu included Kurnool in the schedule of his dominions in spite of the Nizam's objection. So Ranmast Khan, the

49. Aitchison, Vol. IX, p. 232.

50. Fort Willam—India House Correspondence, Vol. XVII, p. 90, D/ June 1795.

50-A. Fort William--India House Correspondence, Vol. XVII.
Pol. Letter to Court, dated 3rd September, 1792, Para 10-11.

Nawab of Kurnool, continued to pay tribute to Tippu. After the treaty of Srirangapatam was concluded, the Nizam once again revived his claims to Kurnool, and he even proposed to exchange those parts of his State that bordered on Tippu's dominions for Kurnool[51].

After the death of Ranmas Khan, the Nizam tried to interfere with the succession to the Nawabi of Kurnool, at which Tippu protested strongly. But on being informed by Cornwallis through the Resident, Capt. Kennaway, that "the Company was not bound to come to his help if his ill-founded claims upon Kurnool led to a war with Tippu" the Nizam gave up further attempts to regain Kurnool[52].

Even after the conclusion of the Mysore war the Nizam desired that the two battalions of the British detachment should reman with him. The Court of Directors did not raise any objection to this, and the Nizam was allowed to retain these troops at his own expense[53].

Prince Sikandar Jah, along with Azim-ul-Umara arrived at Hyderabad on the 4th of May[54].

The different campaigns of the Nizam against the Marathas, Hyder Ali and Tippu during the course of the last several years told upon the economy and general prosperity of the country. Hyderabad, during this period was passing through a period of scarcity and famine. Rice, was sold at the rate of 2 seers per rupee, and there were frequent riots among the people. On the 15th June, the people continued their riots up to the limits of Golconda, plundered the bazaars, burnt the gates of Golconda and even surrounded the Nizam's palace. They ultimately retired when armed force was used against them[55]. But the Nizam had little time to look into the economic distress of the people.

The 18th century in the history of India is very bleak. It is a period that presents a picture of petty jealousies and intrigues among the Indian Princes; added to this the active power politics of the English and the French East India Companies made the political condition in the country very fluid.

No sooner did the Nizam return to Hyderabad, than he was once again faced with the problem of countering any possible menace at the hands of Mahadaji Scindia who came to Poona from Delhi during the period. Mahadaji Scindia wanted to confer Painghat and Berar on one of the Mughal Princes, and he wanted the Nizam to cede those provinces to the Mughal Prince. So the Nizam expected war once again and instructed Raymond, his

---

51. Ibid.
52. Fort Willam-India House Correspondence. Political letter to Court 13th August, 1793, Para 32–53. Letter from Court, D/5th June 1795, D/25th June, 1795, p. 27.
53. Ibid, D/25th June 1795, para 42.
54. Pol. letter to the Court, D/3rd September, 1792,
55. P.R.C., Vol. III, Raymond's letter to General (Count De Convay), D/13 July 1792.

French General, to raise the necessary troops[56]. Raymond, had 3000 men under him, and he was instructed to raise an additional corps of 5000.

In the meanwhile, Lord Cornwallis came out with a new proposal. He wanted to prevent the possibility of Tippu ever asserting himself, by strengthening the recently concluded Tripartity Treaty by a further treaty of guarantee among the allies. According to this treaty of guarantee proposed by Lord Cornwallis, the allies were to assist one another in the event of an unprovoked attack on any one of them by Tippu. The aggrieved ally was also expected to communicate with his allies all the details of his dispute with Tippu. Cornwallis wrote to Malet, the Resident at Poona[57]: "Although there seems, at present, to be no reason to apprehend that Tippoo will, for a considerable period, be disposed to come to a rupture with any of the members of the late confederacy, yet as it is of great importance, for preserving our reputation for good faith as well as for the general interests of the British nation, that the grounds should be clearly explained on which the Allies can, in consequence of the 13 and 10 Articles of the treaties of alliance that were formed at the commencement of the war, demand assistance and support from each other against any hostile attempt of their late common enemy. I look upon it as proper and desirable that the Treaty of Guarantee which they were bound to enter into, should with all convenient despatch, be put into a distinct form; and I, therefore, wish that you should take an early opportunity to confer fully with the Minister upon this subject -----.

The allies are bound to guarantee against Tippoo the territories that each of them might possess at the conclusion of the war; but it must always be adverted to that the stipulation is merely defensive, and cannot operate unless Tippoo should attack either of them without just provocation.

It must therefore be clearly expressed in the Treaty of Guarantee that in case any difference should arise between one of the latter and Tippoo, the other Allies are to have a right to expect that the nature and circumstances of such difference shall be fully communicated to them, in order that they may give their opinion and advice and endeavour to settle it by a temperate negotiation, and that they shall not be considered as bound to take up arms in his favour untill that they are convinced that he has justice on his side and all means of conciliation shall have proved fruitless".

When the terms of this Treaty of Guarantee were conveyed to the two courts of Hyderabad and Poona respectively, the Hyderabad Government conveyed its willingness to conclude the Treaty of Guarantee. The Nizam, who apprehended a revival of the claims of the Marathas for Chouth and Sardeshmukhi over the Nizam's territories looked upon this Treaty of Guarantee as a security against the Maratha aggression and was willing, even

56. Ibid.
57. Ibid. pp. 197-198.

to conclude this treaty separately, if the Marathas were not willing to enter into this alliance[58].

The Marathas, who viewed with jealousy the increasing tendency on the part of the Nizam to lean more and more on his English allies for support, looked upon this proposed "Treaty of Guarantee as a shield held between it and its dependent the Nizam".

So when the proposal for a Treaty of Guarantee was broached with the Maratha Court, the Maratha General, Mahadaji Scindia, denounced it and on his advice the Minister Nana Farnavis, informed the Resident, Malet, that, as he felt that the tripartite defensive agreement of 1790, was quite an adequate guarantee against any possible revival of hostilities on the part of Tippu, there was no need to enter into a fresh Treaty of Guarantee[59].

Sir John Kennaway, the Resident at Hyderabad, wrote to the Governor General that if the Marathas refused to enter into a treaty of guarantee a separate treaty should be concluded between the Nizam and the English. But such a step was not approved by Malet and he wrote to Kennaway that if such a treaty was concluded between the English and the Nizam, it might lead to the growth of ill-feelings between the Poona Court and the English. He wrote to Kennaway[60]: "The Sovereignties of our two States, I mean the British and the Maratta, have already a strong tendency to rivalship in many parts, and our power is now become the object of its most anxious jealousy. It will of course scan with singular caution every step, that involving the Nizam in a general defensive arrangement may emancipate him in some degree from its present influence and its views of further subjugation.

By a parity of reasoning it is obvious that the Nizam's Minister will be as anxious to promote as this court to avoid arrangement that may be expected more or less conducive to giving him a security which his own power is inadequate......should this Government decline any more specific engagements or further explanations of those already subsisting, I am of opinion that (besides ascertaining the nature of his connection with this Government mentioned in the former paragraph) it would be expedient to ascertain the Nizam's power of acting defensively with us, either actually against this State or "Which would be tantamount" against Tippoo contrary to the inclination of this State, and in the event of those points being satisfactorily cleared up, I presume, no further objection would rest to a separate defensive arrangement with him and vice-versa, should the nature of his territorial possessions, the State of his family, the genius of his Government and the force of his army be found such as to disqualify or his heir from the effectual discharge of such an independent connexion, the agitation of which would excite this courts keenest jealousy".

58. P. R. C., Vol. IV., L. No. 2, 8, 50.
59. P. R. C., Vol. IV., L. No. 23-A.
60. Ibid., L. 2. p. 2, dated 29th October 1792.

He further wrote[61]: "It will, I conceive, be clearly understood that the Court (Poona) could support defensive engagements with us independent of the Nizam, yet the Nizam could not do the same independent of this Court and contrary to its will mixed with and in a great measure subject to the indigenous influence of this state from which however desirous we may be of extricating him, good faith and the most deliberate investigation of consequences deemed that we should be extremely guarded and attentive to opportunity in that pursuit".

Malet's remonstrance against concluding a separate Treaty of Guarantee with the Nizam ultimately prevailed with Cornwallis.

[62] Moreover, the dissensions that prevailed in the Maratha court during this period between Mahadaji Scindia and Nana Farnavis, made Cornwallis to go slow, in bringing about the treaty.

However, he decided to remain in India, till August 1793 and put the treaty clauses in a clearer light and in a specific manner for the benefit of his successor, Sir John Shore[63].

The Nizam while showing his eagerness for concluding a separate Treaty of Guarantee, wanted his claims over Kurnool recognised in that treaty[64]. But finding that the British were determined not to include such a clause, he ultimately gave way and expressed his willingness to enter into the treaty without the clause pertaining to Kurnool. But the British thought that such a treaty exclusively with the Nizam might go against their professions of following a strict policy of non-intervention. So they gave up the idea of concluding the treaty with the Nizam separately[65].

In the meanwhile, Nana Farnavis, the Minister of the Peishwa, revived the claims of the Poona Court, for Chouth and Sardeshmukh over the Nizam's territories and he sent two of his vakeels in 1791, Govind Rao Kale and Govind Rao Pingle, to the Nizam's Court to put forth the claims of the Marathas.

The English were ignorant of the real points of dispute between the Poona and the Hyderabad Courts.

Azim-ul-Umara, the Minister of the Nizam, was maintaining close contacts with Mahadaji Scindia, the Maratha General in the North. His objects in maintaining close contacts with Scindia was to promote dissensions in the Poona Court between the Minister Nana Farnavis and Scindia, so that the Maratha State might be weakened and thus be of less danger to the

61. P. R. C., Vol. IV., L. No. 50., Malet to Kennaway, d/20-12-1792.
62. Political Letter to Court., No. 17, dated 14th December 1792.
63. Ibid., d/5-5-1793.
64. P. R. C., Vol. IV., L. No. 19. Kennaway to Malet, d/1st June 1793. Political Letter to Court., L. No. 22, d/13th August 1793. Para 56.
65. Ibid., L. No. 9, dated 28th January 1793. Para 24., p. 300.

Nizam. The intrigues of Azim-ul-Umara with Mahadaji increased all the more, ever since the latter arrived in Poona in 1791[66]. Capt. Kennaway, the Resident at Hyderabad, perceiving this tendency on the part of Azim-ul-Umara to interfere in the affairs of Poona, tried to warn him mildly about the consequences of his action[67]. But these remonstrances had no effect on the Minister. On the contrary, The Minister contemplated going to Poona, saying that Scindia had invited him and asked the British Resident Kennaway, if he could take the British detachment with him in the capacity of a private guard and if the Resident would accompany him[68]. The British, who were loth to provoke Nana Farnavis, informed Azim-ul-Umara that Kennaway and the British detachment would accompany him, if the Nizam were to inform the Peishwa that the British were accompanying, the minister at his request and obtain the Peishwa's approval for the same.

The British through Sir John Kennaway, expressed their attitude in the following manner; The Government of Fort William wrote to the Court of Directors saying,[69] "Sir John Kennaway was instructed by us to declare that we considered it as totally unjustifiable in any member of the alliance to interfere in the internal disputes and dissensions that might unfortunately prevail either at the Durbars, or amongst the Chiefs of the other States, unless explicitly requested by all the contending parties to endeavour to compromise their differences by a friendly mediation, that, such being our sentiments, we could not suffer any part of the detachment of your troops to accompany him, and that neither Sir John Kennaway, nor any gentelman belonging, to the Residency, could enter the Mahratta territories, without receiving a specific invitation from the Peshwah and his Ministers".

After receiving this downright reply from the English, Azim-ul-Umara tried to obtain a direct invitation from Scindia, to the Nizam asking him to come to Poona. But in this also he did not succeed. Then he proposed to Nana Farnavis that the Nizam wanted to visit Poona on the occasion of the Peishwa's nuptials.

The Poona Minister, politely evaded the issue by saying that the nuptials were already over and the stars were not auspicious to repeat the ceremony a second time[70].

All these attempts of Azim-ul-Umara show his anxiety to fish in the troubled waters of Poona. He wanted to derive the utmost advantage by promoting the dissensions that existed in the Poona Government.

Finding his attempts to go to Poona foiled, he requested the Nizam to march with his tropps to Bidar[71]. The actual motive of Azim-ul-Umara

66. Political Letter to Court. No. 20., dated 18th May 1793.
67. Ibid. Para 56.
68. Ibid., L. No. 17, d/14-12-1792., para 87.
69. Ibid., Para 90., L. No. 19, dated 18th May 1793.
70. Ibid. Para 55.
71. Ibid. Para 54.

in asking the Nizam to go to Bidar, was, that he wanted the Mughal troops to be ready for any eventuality in Poona. But the apparent reason given for the Nizam going to Bidar, was, that the Nizam was going there for a change of air.

The Nizam in accordance with the Minister's wishes moved with his troops to Bidar. This move of the Nizam was looked upon by Nana Farnavis with jealousy, as he interpreted it, as a hostile move against himself[72]. Azim-ul-Umara was not satisfied by merely moving the Mughal troops to Bidar. He also supplied Mahadaji Scindia, with thirty lakhs of rupees in the hope that the latter would succeed in removing Nana Farnavis from his office and promised to pay much more, if Scindia succeeded in his attempts[73].

All these actions of Azim-ul-Umara met with the disapproval of the British. Sir John Shore, who had succeeded Lord Cornwallis as Governor General in October 1793, sent a letter disapproving of the Nizam's march to Bidar[74].

The Resident, Kennaway, warned the Minister that his actions might provoke a war with the Marathas. But the Minister, quite undeterred, followed his policy of intriguing against Nana Farnavis. At this juncture the Nizam and the Minister also asked the help of the British detachment against Raghoji Bhonslay, who, they alleged, had plundered some of the villages belonging to the Nizam at the instigation of Nana[75]. But the English refused to lend the services of the detachment saying that they were at peace with Raghoji Bhonslay, and therefore they could not help the Nizam against him[76].

Contrary to the expectations of Azim-ul-Umara, a reconciliation took place between Nana Farnavis and Mahadaji Scindia. The Minister and the great Maratha General at last decided to patch up their differences and work for the common good of the State. After the reconciliation, Scindia revealed to Nana the various intrigues of the minister Azim-ul-Umara. This roused the Nana, and he redoubled his demands for the long-standing arrears of Chouth and Sardeshmukhi from the Nizam.

Nana Farnavis had been demanding from the Nizam the arrears of Chouth and Sardeshmukhi, ever since the termination of the hostilities against Tippu. Even the attention of Lord Cornwallis was drawn to the Maratha claims on the Nizam's Court, with particular reference to Adoni, and the latter promised to instruct Kennaway to ask the Nizam to discharge the claims of the Marathas[77].

72. Idid., L. No. 23, dated 13th August 1793, para 43.
73. Ibid., Para 43, 45.
P. R. C., Vol. IV., L. No. 16.
74. Ibid.
75. Political Letter to Court., No. 23, dated 13th August 1793, para 46.
76. Ibid., Para 48.
77. Ibid., L. No. 15, D/3rd September 1792.

The Nizam countered these claims of the Nana by presenting his own demands under thirty-four heads[78]; and these vexatious discussions were dragging on for many years; Azim-ul-Umara hoped that the Marathas would be prevented from taking any effective action owing to the differences that existed between Nana Farnavis and Scindia. But now finding that these two Maratha leaders had become reconciled, Azim-ul-Umara realised that events might take a serious turn, and he sounded Sir John Kennaway the Resident, whether the British would come to the assistance of the Nizam in the event of the out-break of hostilities between the Nizam and the Scindia[79].

On Kennaway, informing the Government of Fort William, about this, they resolved that their treaty connections with the Scindia would prevent them from assisting the Nizam. But they also at the same time resolved not to communicate this to the Nizam's Government, unless they renewed their request for assistance once again through the Resident at Hyderabad[80].

In the meanwhile, Mahadaji Scindia died on the 12th February 1794[81]; But this event did not have any effect on the attitude of Nana Farnavis.

The right of Chouth and Sardeshmukhi over the Deccan technically speaking, was gained by the Marathas in the year 1714 from the Syed Brothers, who enjoyed the position of kingmakers in those days. Later on Nizamul-Mulk Asaf Jah I had to tardily recognise it after his defeat at the hands of Baji Rao at Mungi Shevgaon in 1728[82]. But though the right of Chouth and Sardeshmukhi of the Marathas over the six Subhas of the Deccan was technically recognised, in actual practice it was never properly implemented. The Nizam always tried to evade the payment of the Chouth and Sardeshmukhi and the Marathas also allowed things to lapse.

They usually revived the claim, only, when a favourable opportunity occurred, in order, to take advantage of some internal troubles in the Nizam's Dominions.

Apart from the general claim for Chouth and Sardeshmukhi for several years, Nana Farnavis now revived his claims for Chouth and Sardeshmukhi particularly on the basis of the Treaty of Edgheree concluded between the Nizam and Marathas in 1784 on the eve of their war against Tippu in 1786[83].

While the Marathas recognised, the Nizam's claims over Kurnool in this treaty, the Nizam recognised the Maratha rights of Chouth and Sardeshmukhi not only over Adonee and Kurnool but also over all these territories he might acquire beyond the Tungabhadra in the course of their war with

78. Grant Duff.- "History of the Mahrattas", Vol. II, p. 240.
79. Political Letter to Court., L. No. 27., d/27th January, 1794., para 22.
80. Ibid., Para 23, 24.
81. Ibid., L. No. 31, D/10th March 1794, para 1.
82. Dr. Yusuf Hussain.-"Nizamul-Mulk Asaf Jahi", p. 189.
83. P. R. C., Vol. IV.

Tippu. The Marathas also recognised the Nizam's right to Peishcush from these lands. Article 13 of the treaty of Edgheree also recognised the Nizam's right to the Peishcush from the Northern Sarkars and the right of the Marathas to the Nachawar Taluk. Any further acquisitions they proposed to divide equally.

Article 17 of the Treaty of Edgheree also spoke of the probability of a war either against the English or Tippu. It declared that " the partition of any territory which may be acquired in war with the English and Futteh Alli Khan shall be made in conformity to the 3rd and 13th articles of the treaty but any other territory which shall be acquired either by negotiation, intimidation or other means shall in conformity to these articles be equally divided ".

Thus the Treaty of Edgheree was not only formed against Tippu but it was also directed against the English. The Nizam at the time of the treaty of Edgheree was exasperated with the English, over the Guntur Sarkar, and he willingly concluded this treaty. But now the situation was entirely changed. After the triple alliance of 1790, the Nizam looked more and more towards the English for help. When the dispute over the question of Chouth and Sardeshmukhi arose between the Poona and the Hyderabad Governments, he naturally did not reveal to the English the full details of the treaty of Edgheree, because he was anxious to obtain their help against the Marathas.

The Bengal Government wrote to the Resident at Hyderabad to the following effect:[84] "The annihilation of the independency of the Nizam, whether by the power of the Peishwa or Tippoo Sultan, cannot be effected without danger to the Company's possessions in India, and it is therefore an interest to afford him support with respect to Tippoo Sultan, the Nizam derives a security from the confederacy which he does not possess in himself with respect to the Mahrattas, he has no such protection, and they have every advantage over him, both from the wisdom of their councils and the superiority of actual force".

The Bengal Government, asked its Residents at Poona and Hyderabad to express its deep concern over the deterioration of relations between the courts of Poona and Hyderabad.

The English realised that the bellicose attitude of Azim-ul-Umara emanated from his reliance on English support and hoped that Azim-ul-Umara would come to an understanding with the Poona Court, once he realised that English help would not be forthcoming, and that the English were not even prepared to play the part of umpires in the dispute between the two courts.[85]

In the meanwhile the Nizam deputed Mir Alam to Poona, to bring about an amicable settlement between the two Powers.[86]

84. Political Letter to Court., L. No. 34, D/18th August 1794., para 26.

85. Ibid.

86. Ibid. News Letters, dated 18th September 1794.

The Nizam deputed Mir Alam and Sham Raj Bahadur on his behalf[87]. The Marathas claimed arrears of Chouth and Sardeshmukhi for Adoni and other places from 1773 onwards[88]. The Maratha claims for arrears ran into crores and Mir Alam failed, to come to an understanding with the Poona Government and returned to Hyderabad.

While these negotiations were still going on, the British adhered to their policy of strict neutrality hoping that the Nizam would acquiesce in the Poona Government's demands in order to save his prestige.

They wrote to the Court of Directors : "convinced as we are, the Minister must ultimately yield to the claims of the Court of Poona, the dignity of the Nizam would be better consulted by a timely acquiescence in all reasonable claims than by evasion or protraction which might only tend to render them more exorbitant, and at all events to augment the difficulties of adjustment. At the same time, that our advice may not prove detriment to the Nizam in restraining him from taking measure to guard against the possible views of the Mahrattas beyond an equitable settlement of their avowed claims, we have signified to the Resident that under the uncertainity of the real views and intentions of the Mahratta Government it would be unreasonable to expect the Nizam should supinely await the event of negotiations without taking precautions to provide against the most unfavourable result, and that such preparations would probably furnish the most effectual means of securing the object of the negotiation"[89].

The Nizam based all his hopes on the letters that Cornwallis had written to him on the eve of the war with Tippu saying that the British would support the Nizam against any power, and that they would see to it that he was not subjected to any insult or loss of prestige. Azim-ul-Umara was so confident of the English support that he dared to insult the Peishwa and Nana Farnavis in open Durbar by demanding that Nana Farnavis should personally come to Hyderabad to explain the Maratha demands, and by bringing on effigy of the Poona Minister to the Durbar[90].

When he realised to his bitter mortification that the British were not coming to the Nizam's assistance, Azim-ul-Umara proposed a fresh alliance against the English consisting of the Marathas, Tippu and the Nizam[91].

These proceedings of Azim-ul-Umara were secretly conveyed by Mir Alam, who was still at Poona, to the Resident, Malet[92].

But the Marathas turned down the proposal. Then Azim-ul-Umara vainly appealed to Parasuram Bahu to bring about an accommodation

87. Ibid., dated 10th September 1794.
88. Ibid., dated 21st September 1794.
89. Political Letter to Court., L. No. 34. D/18th August. 1794. Para 27.
90. Grant Duff.-"History of the Mahrattas"., p. 243., Vol. II.
Khare.- O. C. P., pp. 4000-4001.
91. P. R. C., Vol. IV. L. No. 132, Matet to Kennaway, d/28th November 1794., p. p. 190-92.
92. Political Letter to Court., L. No. 36, d/30th December 1794, para 79.

between the two courts[93]. But by this time, matters reached such a stage that it was not possible to bring about an accommodation and a war was declared between the Marathas and the Nizam.

The Marathas who were rather cynical about the British professions of neutrality, and suspected that the latter sympathised with the Nizam, made sure that the British were definitely not interceding in the war on behalf of the Nizam.

Prior, to the declaration of the war the Maratha representative at the Nizam's Court, Govind Kishen, cryptically asked the Resident, William Kirkpatrick, if the subsidiary troops stationed at Hyderabad, would be used against the Pindaris in the service of the Poona Government, if they attacked Hyderabad[94].

Kirkpatrick assured him that the British would adhere to their policy of neutrality and would not participate in the ensuing war under any circumstances. The British carried their fetish of neutrality to such an extent that Capt. Kirkpatrick, refused to give advice even about the stationing of the Nizam's forces at strategic places[95].

In the meanwhile Nana Farnavis entered the tents on the 7th December 1794, while the Peishwa entered the tents on the 14th[96]. The Maratha forces in all amounted to 84,000 cavalry and 38,000 Infantry and 192 guns[97].

Azim-ul-Umara, though he had asked the Nizam to proceed to Bidar, failed to concentrate all his troops at Bidar. Now he appealed to the several Jaghirdars under the Nizam to join the banner of the Nizam with their troops. Azim-ul-Umara also asked the Nawab of Kurnool as the polygar of the Nizam to come forward and assist the Nizam with his quota of troops. Tippu was greatly annoyed on hearing this.

The Nizam's army altogether consisted of 45,000 cavalry, 44,000 infantry and 108 guns. The Maratha troops had a European detachment under the Command of M. D. Boigne, while the Nizam had a European detachment under the command of M. Raymond.

The Nizam advanced from Bidar along the banks of the Manjira River towards the Maratha frontiers towards Parinda. On the 14th of February, 1795, he arrived at Paijori and on the 16th, he reviewed his advance army. Raymond's Corps which consisted of 28 battalions was within *2 cos* of the rear of Moorighat, and it constituted the advance guard of the Nizam's forces.

93. P. R. C., Vol. IV., L. No. 149, 157, pp. 205, 206.
94. P. R. C., Vol. IV., L. No. 198., p. 264.
95. Ibid. L. No. 164, Kirkpatrick to Shore, d/10th February 1795.
96. Political Letter to Court., L. No. 37, d/4-2-1795, para 3.
97. Fraser., p. 425.

The Marathas sent their advance troops towards the Nizam's camp about *17 Cos* from the river Sena, north-east of Poona about 85 miles in an Easterly direction. The *Nizam* descending from the Moorighat marched towards Parinda. But the Nizam's forces were prevented from marching by an attack from the Scindia's forces and the Nizam retreated in panic towards Kharda[98].

There on the 11th March, 1795, an action took place between the Marathas and the Mughals, and the Mughals were routed. Nizam Ali in panic took shelter in the small fortress of Kharda and after suffering further harassment at the hands of the Marathas, sued for peace on the 15th March 1795[99]. The battle which was fought between the Mughals and the Marathas was called the battle of Kharda and the Nizam in order to buy peace was forced to conclude a very humilitating treaty with the Marathas. By this Treaty, the Nizam agreed to cede to the Marathas, the fortresses of Daulatabad, Ahmednagar, and Sholapur, territories yielding an annual revenue of 34,50,000 rupees, and also to pay an indemnity of 3 crores[100].

Almost all the sources including the reports of the respective Residents who accompanied the Nizam and the Marathas agree that the defeat of the Nizam was brought about by his pusillanimity.

As it was usual for the Mughals, the Nizam was accompanied by his *harem* to the battlefield. Beveridge, gives an interesting reason for the Nizam retreating to the Fort of Kharda. According to Beveridge, the Nizam's favourite wife, Bakshi Begam was frightened by the booming of the cannon and at the sight of men falling down dead. So, she called the Nizam and threatened him saving that she would expose herself to public gaze, unless he retired to Kharda[101].

The Nizam accordingly retired to the small fort of Kharda lest Bakshi Begam should carry out her threat. If this incident narrated by Beveridge is true, and if the reason for the Nizam's retreat to Kharda was more his anxiety to preserve the honour of his ladies by preserving them from public gaze than[102] pusillanimity brought about by nervous and mental strain, in old age and lack of proper advice, it throws indeed a lurid light on the Nizam's character.

The Nizam should not have allowed his feelings for Bakshi Begam to interfere with the State affairs to the extent of bringing dishonour to his name and his State. If the Nizam had been firm with her, Bakshi Begam would not have carried our her threat at all.

---

98. Briggs.- Vol. I., p. 75.
99. Political Letter to Court., d/12th May 1795, p. 419.
100. Fraser., p. 450. Appendix.
This treaty was based on the treaty of Edgheree except that the stipulations pertaining to the conquests from Tippu, and the Article pertaining to the Northern Sarkars was omitted.
101. News Letter-Central Records Office, Hyderabad.
102. K. Sajjanlal-"Studies in the[Deccan History" Chap. VIII., p. 87.

The reason for the Nizam retreating to Kharda which was a suicidal step must have been taken at a time, when the Nizam was panic-stricken and he must have acted on the advice given to him by his courtiers, without properly weighing the pros and cons of the situation.

It is said that not more than 150 men were actually killed on the battle field of Kharda, which gave the Marathas such a resounding victory. Taking all these facts into consideration we have to come to the conclusion that the defeat of the Mughals on the field of Kharda was due to the bad morale that had set in the Mughal ranks.

According to Grant Duff, the young Peishwa Madhav Rao Narayan, was sad on seeing Azim-ul-Umara arrive at the Poona Court as a hostage. On Nana Farnavees asking the young Peishwa the reason for his sadness, the Peishwa is said to have exclaimed:

"I grieve to observe such degeneracy as there must be on both sides, when such a disgraceful submission has been made by the Moghuls, and our soldiers are vaunting of a victory obtained without an effort"[103].

After concluding the above peace with the Marathas the Nizam started from Poona to Hyderabad on the 3rd April and reached the capital on the 7th May. The Nizam keenly felt the humiliation of surrendering his minister, as a hostage and he felt that the English were responsible for bringing about this calamity. He had till the last moment hoped that the English would exert themselves on his behalf. He now reproached the English for their conduct and told the Resident Capt. Kirkpatrick that had the English told the Marathas emphatically that the declaration of war against the Nizam would terminate the Tripartite alliance, and the friendship that existed between the Company and the Marathas, the latter would not have cared to commit hostilities against him[105].

There was an element of truth in what the Nizam felt. Had the English been more firm in their attitude, in safeguarding the interests of the Nizam, the Marathas perhaps would have hesitated to wage war against the Nizam. But the British decided to adhere to their policy of strict non-intervention.

Sir John Shore, the successor of Lord Cornwallis, was simply paralysed by fear, of complications with the Marathas and of violating the Parliamentary Act of 1784. He said : " Although I foresee great embarrassments and the possibility of serious evils from the subversion of the power of the Nizam, I see still greater in an union which would impose upon us the prevention of it" [106].

103. Grant Duff.—"History of the Marattas"., Vol. II., p. 248.
104. Political Letter to the Court., L. No. 40., dated 12-5-1759., p. 420.
105. Ibid.
106. Life of Lord Teignmouth., Vol. I., p. 467.
Dr. Yusuf Hussain-"Anglo-Hyderabad Relations", (1772-82)., Islamic Culture., Vol. XXVII.

The Nizam was so greatly put out with the English, for not allowing him to use even the two regular battalions which were stipulated under the treaty of 1768, that on his arrival he informed Capt. Kirkpatrick that as he saw no point in maintaining the English battalions at such a heavy cost when they could not serve him in need, they should be withdrawn from his territories. Capt. Kirkpatrick accordingly ordered the British battalions to depart from Hyderabad, towards the British territories.

After dismissing the English troops in the above manner, the Nizam, now began to view with favour the corps under Mons. Raymond. Taking advantage of the Nizam's feelings towards the English, Mon. Raymond, began to impress upon the Nizam the good qualities of the French. Raymond, along with the battalions that he commanded had accompanied the Nizam to Kharda; and during the course of the campaign had lost about 3000 men[107]. The Nizam now wanted to increase the strength of the crops under Raymond and to use them as his auxiliaries. So he wanted to confer on Raymond, additional territories and restore his crops to their original strength of 15,000. The subsidy for Raymond's crops was fixed at 1,30,000 rupees per month.

Mons. Raymond regarded his troops as a French body of troops employed and subsidised by the Nizam. So he named his regiments as "Corps Francois de Raymond". Taking advantage of the Nizam's favourable attitude Raymond tried to acquire from the Nizam, Cudapah and other districts which were in the vicinity of the British territories, for the maintenance of his corps. He also wrote to the Pondicherry Government for equipment and recruited many Frenchmen from Pondicherry in his corps[108]. The rapid advancement of Raymond in the Nizam's favour and his endeavours to get an establishment at Cudapah created great apprehensions in the mind of Kirkpatrick. Cudapah is adjacent to the Northern Sarkars which were then under the control of the English. Naturally, they did not relish the idea of their having a French battalion in their neighbourhood; Yet Kirkpatrick, could not openly raise any objection to the Nizam patronising Raymond.

While matters were in such a state, Mir Alam informed Kirkpatrick on the 17th May, 1795, that Raymond was being sent by the Nizam to Cudapah to maintain law and order there, and that the Nawab of Cudapah Muhammad Ameen Khan Arab, would be deprived of his office and prince Sikandar Jah placed in charge of Cudapah[109].

Taking advantage of this communication, Kirkpatrick, conveyed his feelings to Mir Alam by saying that the conditions in Cudapah did not warrant

107. Fraser., p. 144.
108. Fraser., p., 147.
Raymond entered the Nizam Service originally in the year 1785.- P. R. C., Vol. III, Raymonds Letter to Count De Convay, p. 673.
109. Political Letter to Court., L. No. 41, d/18th August 1795.

the sending of such a large force and that the English would view with great apprehension, the stationing of such a large number of French forces on their border [110].

Apart from expressing his feelings to Mir Alam, Kirkpatrick also conveyed his views to the Nizam's Government in a letter. This resulted in Mir Alam coming to the Resident for a second time with alternative proposals, namely, that Prince Sikandar Jah would remain the nominal Governor of Cudapah, while Mohammed Ameen Khan Arab would remain looking after the administration, and he was to be accompanied by 4000 men of Raymond's corps under the command of Mons. Peron, Raymond's second in command. It was also proposed that Prince Sulaiman Jah should hold Khammam as his Jaghir but that the actual administration of Khammam would be looked after by a vakil of the Peishwa, assisted by a detachment of 1000 belonging to Raymond's corps [111].

The apparent reason given by the Nizam's Court for sending Raymond's detachment to Cudapah was that the Maratha vakeel wanted to take action against Assud Ally Khan, the Talookdar of Cudapah and a friend of Azim-ul-Umara. But while these discussions were still going on, Assud Ally Khan, came to Hyderabad and tendered his submission.

On seeing this, Kirkpatrick, represented to Mir Alam saying, now that Assud Ally Khan had submitted, there was no necessity for the Nizam to send troops to Cudapah.

The Bengal Government, also sent instructions to Kirkpatrick to the effect that if the Nizam did not consent to recall the troops of Raymond, he should be informed that the British intended to move their troops towards their frontiers as a measure of security [112].

But before these instructions reached Kirkpatrick, the latter had already come to an understanding with the Nizam's Government[113]. On hearing the views of Kirkpatrick regarding the despatching of Raymond's detachmentt o Cudapah, the Nizam's Government proposed through Mir Alam, that if the British did not like the idea of the French corps being sent to Cudapah the English detachment could be sent instead to restore law and order in Cudapah [114]. But while making this request, Mir Alam said that the English troops must give their assistance gratuitously. Capt. Kirkpatrick, the Resident, seized this opportunity and informed Mir Alam that he would supply the Nizam with the usual detachment, stipulated under the treaty of 1768, and as a gesture of good will, would waive one month's subsidy, that would have ordinarily been due to the Company's troops, had they continued to remain in the Nizam's service [115].

---

110. Ibid., p. 43.
111. Fraser.– p. 146.
112. Political Letter to Court., L. No. 41., d/18-8-1793, p. 431., para 21.
113. Ibid.
114. Fraser.. p. 150.
115. Ibid., p. 151.

But Mir Alam informed the Resident that the Nizam's Government did not like to incur such a huge expenditure, unless they found that the Nizam's troops were unequal to the task of restoring law and order. At last a compromise was reached, by which it was agreed that only two regiments of Raymond's corps should be sent to Cudapah, and if it was found they were not able to cope with the situation, to employ the Company's troops [116].

The Resident, perforce had to remain content with this. He now requested the Nizam's Government to allow him to employ a news writer in the camp of Ameen Khan, so that he could get first hand knowledge of the day to day events in Cudapah. The reason given by Kirkpatrick for making this demand was that since Cudapah touched the borders of the Company's and Tippu's territories he wanted to have first hand knowledge of developments in Cudapah so that, he might ward off any danger, that might arise, by taking the necessary precautions. But the actual reason that prompted Kirkpatrick, to make this request, was his great distrust for Raymond, who was a French man. He suspected that Raymond, might take full advantage of the situation and carry on anti-British activities. He also suspected that the Nizam, who was greatly dissatisfied with the British for their neutral and unhelpful attitude at Kharda, might have commissioned Muhammed Ameen Khan to re-open negotiations with Tippu. There was a strong party headed by the Rai Rayan in the Nizam's Court, who were in favour of an alliance with Tippu. Capt. Kirkpatricks suspicions were all the more strengthened by the warmth with which Mir Alam who was attached to the British interests, supported his idea of employing a news reporter, saying that it would be of great benefit to the English.

The Nizam's Court during this period was torn by dissensions and faction. While the party headed by the Rai Rayan was in favour of an alliance with Tippu, the rival party headed by Govind Kishen, the Vakeel of the Marathas, was trying with the help of the Paighas to build up the influence of the Marathas by choosing a Minister in place of Azim-ul-Umara, who would be more favourably inclined towards the Poona Government [117].

A third group, represented by Mir Alam, were of the opinion that an alliance with the English would be able to preserve the integrity of the State.

While matters were in such a state the Nizam's eldest son Prince Ali Jah accompanied by Nizam-ool-Moolk the Subah of Hyderabad and the son-in-law of the Nizam and Sadashiv Reddy, the Zamindar of Medak, rose in rebellion and escaped to Bidar. The Fort and the garrison in the Fort of Bidar surrendered to Prince Ali Jah.

The Nizam was greatly perturbed at the news of his son's rebellion and he appealed to the English to furnish him with the regular detachment of the Company's troops to which he was entitled under the treaty of 1768 [118].

116. Political Letter to Court, L. No. 141., d/16th August, 1795.

117. Fraser., p. 160.

118. Political Letter to Court., d/18 August, 1795., P. L. No. 41.

The Resident, who for a long time was awaiting an opportunity to remove the French corps from Cudapah, informed the Nizam that as it would take some time for the Company's troops to march to Hyderabad it would be advisable to order the French corps which were at Cudapah to pursue the prince, while the English contingent of troops would go to Cudapah. But the Nizam did not agree to this proposal, saying that he could not spare the French corps under M. Baptiste to depart from Cudapah.

Thereupon Capt. Kirkpatrick informed the Nizam that apart from the regular battalion of troops to which the Nizam was entitled, additional troops would also be sent to Cudapah to maintain law and order[119]. The Nizam agreed to this proposal. Sir John Shore, the Governor General, also addressed a letter to the Nizam confirming the Residents' proposals.

The Bengal Government were of the opinion, "[120]That the preservation of the Nizam's power is of importance to the Company cannot be doubted, and it is therefore our interest to support his Government as far as it can be done with a probability of success, and without much inconvenience or the risk of involving ourselves in the consequences of its subversion, an event, which, however probable, it is essentially for our advantage to protract without calculating the possible consequences of it.

If the values and importance of our friendship and assistance are to be estimated by the exigency for them, there is no period in which the grant of them could be made with more favourable impression and effect than under the present circumstances of loss and grace sustained by the Nizam in his late contest with the Mahrattas, the disappointment of his expectations of our interposition, the embarrassments in his Government by the insurrection of his subjects, the defection of his son, and even the fears of the Nizam for his own personal safety.

If the commotions excited by Suddasheo Reddy and in Cudapah should be speedily quelled, they might lead to disturbances in other parts of his dominions, and if, by the moderate assistance proposed to be given to the Nizam in addition and disaffection in his dominions should be stopped, we establish a claim upon the attachment of our ally by rendering him an important service at the expense of little exertion".

Though the Bengal Government, was anxious to send additional troops to Cudapah, it left the matter to the discretion of the Madras Government. The Madras Government was not in a position to spare any troops and so it did not agree to this proposal[121]. Thereupon the Bengal Government ordered the two regular battalion of troops which were now under the command of Major Roberts to proceed to Hyderabad so that they might be at hand, to quell any disturbances that might arise, in view of the

119. Ibid. Para 24, 2S.
120. Ibid. Para 29, 30, 31.
121. Ibid, para 21. L. No. 42. Dated 31st October, 1795.

fact that Mons. Raymond with his corps had gone in pursuit of the rebel prince. Major Roberts arrived near Hyderabad on the 31st August 1795 and took his position between that City and Golconda. In the meanwhile Mons. Raymond went in pursuit of the rebel prince. His advance party was defeated by Sadashiv Reddy, but Raymond soon laid siege to Bidar. Finding that Raymond's position was rather critical M. Baptiste went to his aid with reinforcements.

While the siege was still going on, the Nizam sent vakeels to his son. The latter refused to entertain any proposals, unless they were sent through either the Maratha vakeel Govind Kishen or through the English Resident. On hearing this, Sir John Shore, anxious to adhere to the policy of non-interference, asked the Resident to undertake the role of a negotiator.

Finding that the siege of Bidar was likely to be prolonged the Nizam requested that the English battalions should march to Bidar. In accordance with these instructions Major Roberts, left Hyderabad on the 23rd September[122]. The insistence of the Prince that he would not entertain any peace proposals unless they were sent through Govind Kishen, the Maratha envoy, or the Resident, made the Nizam suspect that the Marathas might have instigated the prince to rebellion. But an assurance from the Peishwa's Government that if necessary they would join the Nizam in reducing Prince Alijah, to obedience made the Nizam dismiss all such suspicions from his mind.

The English troops which were sent towards Bidar under Major Roberts were instructed to receive their orders from Mir Alam.

In the meanwhile Prince Ali Jah, sent the following proposals to the Nizam, namely that the Prince should be made the Diwan, while Sadashiv Reddy and the other Chiefs who had joined his ranks should be reinstated in their Jaghirs.

The Prince also suggested that the Nizam should retire from the administration of the country.

Naturally these proposals were turned down by the Nizam, and the latter now decided to proceed in person against his son.

Prince Ali Jah, at this juncture evacuated the fort of Bidar and proceeded towards Turkul about 19 *Cos* from Nanded. There he decided to await the result of the fresh proposals he had sent to his father. The gist of these fresh proposals sent by the prince was that a Jaghir worth 12 lakhs of Rupees should be conferred on him in the vicinity of Berar, while Sadashiv Reddy should be restored to his zamindary of Medak and the surrounding places.

The Nizam in reply guaranteed his son's personal safety and promised to restore Sadashiv Reddy to his original Jaghir.

Finding that Prince Ali Jah, had evacuated Bidar, the English troops were halted at Patancheruvu, while Mir Alam with the Nizam's troops lay

122. Ibid.

encamped at Chickwun. There Sadashiv Reddy, arrived from Shahgoor at the head of 2000 Rohillas, 900 cavalry and 400 infantry and surrendered. Prince Ali Jah, finding himself deserted, proceeded towards Aurangabad, and sent word through Mir Alam, his willingness to surrender.

But Prince Ali Jah shortly after his voluntary surrender committed suicide on the 22nd November.1795 at Khair on his way to Hyderabad lest he should be insulted and disgraced by the Nizam for his rebellion[123]. Thus the rebellion of Prince Ali Jah, which made the Nizam entertain once again, the English battalions which he had dismissed, was put down without the English playing any ostensible part.

No sooner was the news of the prince's death received than the English troops that had proceeded as far as Patancheruvu returned to Hyderabad on the 29th November; from there, they were sent later to Raichur to restore law and order.

In the meanwhile the Nizam's Minister, Azim-ul-Umara, who had gone to Poona as a hostage after the battle of Kharda, returned to Hyderabad and was reinstated as the Diwan in July 1797.

The Minister by his astuteness and shrewd diplomacy brought favourable terms for his master.

The Peishwa, Madhav Rao Narayan, having suddenly died, Azim-ul-Umara took advantage of the confusion in the Poona Court and contrived to obtain from the new Peishwa an agreement known as the treaty of Mahad[124]. The main features of this agreement were that the Peishwa promised to restore not only the fortress of Doulatabad to the Nizam, but also three fourth's of the territories taken and three fourth of the Chouth collected from the Nizam after the battle of Kharda.

During the absence of Azim-ul-Umara, the anti-English faction in the Court of Hyderabad headed by Tippu's vakeels were exerting themselves to get the English dismissed once again. The Nizam acting on their advice informed the acting Resident, Lt. Kirkpatrick, that he wanted to dispense with the services of the English troops, in view of the fact that the English required their services against the French[125].

Azim-ul-Umara, who realised the importance of the English alliance to the Nizam against the Marathas as well as Tippu, heard of the dismissal of the English while he was on his way to Hyderabad. So from there he once again wrote a letter to the Nizam remonstrating against their dismissal.

While matters were in such a condition Mons. Raymond, died on the 25th of March 1798, and he was succeeded by his second in command,

123. Ibid., L. No. 43., dated 15th December. 1795., Para 3.
124. Khare., pp. 5145, 5160.
125. Fraser, p. 215.

M. Perron. His death was a great blow to the French supporters at the Nizam's court. In the meanwhile Lord Wellesley succeeded Sir John Shore as the Governor General in India on the 17th May 1798. Lord Wellesley, an imperialist at heart, had scant respect for the policy of non-intervention so scrupulously followed by his predecessor.

While on his way to India, Lord Wellesley met Capt. Kirkpatrick who had left Hyderabad for reasons of health, at the Cape of Good Hope[127]. He opened the letters which were sent from India to the Court of Directors and also learnt, from Capt. Kirkpatrick, about the various developments in the courts of Hyderabad, Poona and Mysore.

Wellesley, after gaining a first hand knowledge of the various events in the courts of the Indian Princes, was filled with dismay at the growing intrigues of Tippu Sultan, who was actively engaged in carrying on intrigues against the British, in the courts of Persia, Constantinople, Kabul, Poona, Hyderabad and Mauritius.

He now addressed a letter from the Cape, to the President of the Board of Control about the absolute necessity of breaking the power of Tippu Sultan[128]. He also viewed with dismay the influence wielded by Mons. Raymond in the court of Hyderabad and wrote to the President of the Board of Control in the following manner[129]:

" It appears that the Nizam had recently at different periods retained in his service, exclusive of our detachment three distinct corps of Sepoys under the command of European or American officers-----One commanded by a Frenchman named Raymond, another by an American of the name of Boyd, and a third by an Irishman of the name of Finglass.

The corps of Boyd and Finglass were taken into the service of the Nizam during the residence of the Azim-ul-Omara at Poonah, at the suggestion of our Resident at that court, acting under the sanction of Government of Bengal. This measure was taken by our Resident and by that Government principally with a view of forming a counterpoise to the corps of Raymond.

The corps of Raymond had been in the service of the Nizam before the last war with Tippoo Sultan------.

The pay of the corps is now secured by the assignment of a large district of country, part of which borders the Carnatic, at the particular station is a fortified post and constant communication is maintained between it and the post of Narpilly, as well as Ongole and other parts of the

126. Ibid, p. 217.
127. "Memoirs and Correspondence of the Most Noble Richard Marquess Wellesley", Vol. I, p. 136.
128. Ibid.
129. Ibid. pp. 141 to 146.

territories of the Company and the Nabob of Arcot. The Corps is recruited in the proportion of one third of its total numbers, from our territories, and from those of the territories, of the Nabab of Arcot, and partly from deserters abandoning our service.

The Chief Officers are Frenchmen of the most virulent and notorious principles of jacobinism, and the whole corps constitutes an armed French party, of great zeal, diligence and activity. The efforts of this party are continually directed to the object of magnifying the power, resources and success of France in the eyes of the court of Hyderabad and of depreciating the character, force and credit of Great Britian by every possible means.

In this corps consists the main strength of the army of our ally, and it possesses the influence which usually belongs to an army in the councils of the native princes of India ------.

Such is the state of the leading facts communicated by Major Kirkpatrick. The result in my mind is a decided opinion that the continuance, and still more the further growth of the corps of Raymond ought to be prevented by every means within our power, consistent with the respect due to the court of Hyderabad, and with the general principles of moderation and justice, which ought to form the rule of our conduct in India.

I consider it as the basis of a French party in India, on which according to the opportunities of fortune and the variation of events, the activity of the enemy may find a strength of the most formidable kind either in peace or war -----.

I have no doubt that the natural effect of a unchecked and rapid growth of such a party at the court of one of our Principal allies must be in a very short period to detach the Court entirely from our interests and finally to fix it in those of our enemies, to subject its councils to their control, and its military establishments to their discretion.

However, despicable the corps of Raymond may now be in point of discipline or effect in the field, would it be wise to leave such a large body of men in readiness to receive whatever improvement, the ability assiduity and zeal of the French Officers, sent from Europe for that express purpose, might introduce into the constitution of a crops, so prepared by correspondent principles and objects to meet the most sanguine expectation of their new leaders".

After expressing himself in such a decided manner about the presence of the French corps in the service of the Nizam, Wellesley who had already conceived in his mind the nucleus of the subsidiary alliance, further wrote to the President of the Board of Control in the following manner[130] :

130. Ibid., p p. 146, 147.

"The fourth proposition contained in Major Kirkpatrick's paper is that to which I wish to call your most particular, attention. The desire of the court of Hyderabad to obtain from us an increase of our detachment now serving the Nizam, and also an extension of the power of employing the force furnished by us, has appeared on several occasions and you will find allusions to this disposition in the last secret dispatches from Bengal.

There seems to be no objection to the first part of this proposition, provided our consent to it shall secure to us equivalent concessions on the part of the Nizam. In another letter, which I shall forward to you, on the general subject of the political state of India in the present moment, you will find my reasons for entertaining an opinion that it would be a wise policy for us to check by timely aid the rapid declension of the Nizam's weight among the powers of Hindustan. This could be done in no manner so effectual or unobjectionable as by furnishing him with a large increase of our force now in his pay; the pay of the augmented force to be secured in the manner best calculated to prevent future discussion and embarassment. In granting this force to the Nizam, we ought not only to stipulate for the disbanding of Raymond's corps but we ought to take care that the officers should be immediately sent out of India. There are perhaps, other points which, on this occasion, might be obtained from the Court of Hyderabad".

Having reached India with such decided opinions, one is not surprised to note that soon after his arrival Wellesley, instructed the Resident at Hyderabad to negotiate a new treaty alliance, with the Court of Hyderabad. The Nizam was for a long time anxious to enter into a defensive alliance with the English. By forming such an alliance, he hoped to free himself from the clutches of the Marathas.

During the absence of Azim-ul-Umara from Hyderabad, the Nizam sounded the Resident Kirkpatrick, about forming a triple alliance consisting of the Nizam, the English and Tippu against the Marathas[131].

Mir Alam, time and again impressed on the Resident the benefits of a mutual defensive alliance between the English and the Nizam. When the Resident pointed out that the preponderant influence wielded by the French at the Nizam's court might come in the way of such an alliance, Mir Alam pointed out that the surest way of reducing the power of the French would be by the formation of an alliance. He also assured the Resident that if the English were amenable to such an alliance he would "engage to procure the dismissal of every Frenchman in His Highness' country within a very short period after the conclusion of such a treaty as he had metioned"[132].

Naturally when the Resident broached the subject of a fresh treaty the Nizam's Government greatly welcomed the idea. The English insisted on

131. Political Letter to Court., L. No. 42, dated 31st October, 1795.

132. Fraser, p. 206.

the dismissal of the French from the Nizam's service as the primary condition of their concluding this treaty.

The English also proposed by this treaty to increase the quota of troops that they hitherto supplied, to the Nizam, by six battalions, and these were called the Subsidiary Troops. They also agreed to arbitrate between the courts of Hyderabad and Poona in case of any disputes.

The Nizam agreed to these conditions and a new treaty was concluded on the 1st September 1798. By this Treaty the Nizam agreed to pay annually for the six battalions of the English a sum of Rs. 24,17,100/-. If there was any delay or difficulty in paying the said amount, it was agreed that an equivalent amount could be either deducted from the Peishcush of the Northern Sarkars or collected from the revenues of districts that might be specified by the Nizam's Government.

The Nizam also agreed to carry on any correspondence with the Poona Court, only with the full knowledge of the English.

Azim-ul-Umara and the Nizam, anxious for an alliance with the English, agreed to all these conditions. Yet, when it came to implementing them, they hesitated to dismiss the French and said that the French army could be disbanded after the arrival of the additional four battalions of the English. So the Resident J. A. Kirkpatrick demanded the immediate dismissal of the French as soon as the additional battalions arrived in Hyderabad in October. Finding the Nizam still hesitating, the Resident, informed him that in order to fulfil the treaty conditions, he might be forced to attack the French lines. Seeing this aggressive attitude of the Resident the Nizam issued orders for the dismissal of the French[133].

The promulgamation of this order led to the out break of a mutiny among the French soldiery. They confined their officers and refused to surrender their arms and ammunition. But when the Resident ordered Col. Roberts and Hyndman to take up their position in the front and in the rear of the French lines, the French soldiers lost heart, released their officers and surrendered to the English[134].

The drastic action taken by the English against the French, created great discontent among the nobles of the Nizam's court, the chief among them being Rajah Raghotam Rao and Prince Sikandar Jah, the heir apparent to the throne. It was said that Prince Sikandar Jah had so great an admiration for Mons. Raymond that he always swore" by the head of M. Raymond[135]. Besides these the Paigah party, was also greatly dissatisfied with the

133. Fraser., p. 219.
134. Ibid.
135. Ibid., p. 192.

treaty. Mir Alam, who had always sympathised with the English, informed the Resident about the general discontent in the Nizam's court at the loss of their political power. The Treaty of 1798 reduced Hyderabad to the position at a British protected State. Mir Alam suggested to Kirkpatrick that he should prevail on the Nizam to dismiss Rajah Raghotam Rao.

On the Resident informing the Governor General about the conditions at the Nizam's court, Lord Wellesley addressed a letter to Capt. J. A. Kirkpatrick in the following manner ;

[135-A] "It would however he imprudent to urge the removal of Raghotim Rao in the manner suggested by Meer Allum.

You must be particularly careful to abstain from all interference in the nominations of the counsellors of His Highness and of Azim-ul-Umrah. The benefit to be expected from the removal of Raghotim Rao could be greatly overbalanced by the impressions of jealousy and suspicion which would naturally attend your interposition in the private councils of the court of Hyderabad. The power which we recently acquired will be confirmed and extended by a moderate and cautious use of our influence and we may safely rely on the natural operation of the evident advantages secured to the Nizam by the late treaty and on the effects of the discretion and prudence of our troops, contrasted with the ambition of the French Party, to disappoint the efforts of every enemy to the British interests in the councils of High Highness.

I have already recommended the principle of these opinions to your attentive observation, and I am persuaded that the same judgement which enabled you to bring my instructions of the 8th July to so prosperous an issue will now direct you to avoid all invidious display of our power and to mitigate its appearance whenever it must be employed. If however consistently with these principles of caution and reserve, a favourable opportunity should occur for effecting the removal of Raghotim Rao without offence or distrust, your address will not suffer such an occasion to pass away unimproved."

The above letter of Lord Wellesley, shows what a shrewd and farsighted statesman he was. He was prepared to bide his time and strike at a favourable opportunity, to increase the British power in India.

Lord Wellesley, suggested a similar treaty to the Marathas on the same lines as he had concluded with the Nizam, but the Maratha court under the influence of Doulat Rao Scindia refused to conclude this fresh treaty[136].

135-A. Forrest.-"Selections from State Papers."
Maratha Series., Vol. I.
Letters from the Earl of Morrington, L. No. 5, p. 613.

136. Fraser-Appendix- H. H. Wellesley's letter to Kirkpatrick.

In the meanwhile Tippu fearing that the British might once again revive the Triple Alliance against him, sent one Syed Mohammed Madani and Khadir Hussain Khan to the Nizam's court suggesting a triple alliance consisting of the Marathas, Tippu and the Nizam, or suggesting as an alternative that the Nizam should at least remain neutral in the event of hostilities between the English and Tippu. [137]But the Nizam who at this juncture had no reason to fear the Marathas gave no encouragement to these overtures. Lord Wellesley, after concluding the above treaty with the Nizam, also asked Colonel Palmer, who was the Resident at Poonah, to convey to the Peishwa's Government that the Governor General wanted the Poona Court, which was a party to the Triple Alliance of 1790, to once again remonstrate against Tippu Sultan, in conjunction with the English and the Nizam. The Governor-General also conveyed through Col. Palmer that the British Government was willing to assist the Peishwa's Government with additional troops to protect the person of the Peishwa and to enable him to carry on the war against Tippu, provided the Peishwa agreed to enter into a subsidiary treaty similar to that of the Nizam's treaty with the English.

The Governor-General, also wanted the Poona court to submit itself to the arbitration of the British East India Company in case of disputes between itself and the Nizam[138].

Wellesley further informed the Poona court that while he was willing to arbitrate between the two courts, he also felt it his bounden duty as an ally of the Nizam, to see that the Peishwa's-Government observed all the stipulations of the previous treaties concluded between it and the Nizam's Government [139].

Seeing this attitude of the Governor-General, the Peishwa refused to enter the subsidiary alliance. Azim-ul-Umara, soon after the conclusion of this treaty, began to press the Governor-General, to act as a mediator and to settle the disputes between the Nizam and the Peishwa and also between the the Nizam and Doulat Rao Scindia.

The Governor-General, assured the minister saying that the best period for arbitration would be after settling the affair of Tippu [140].

Wellesley, declared war against Tippu in 1799. The Nizam joined the British in the declaration of war against Tippu. In this war not only

---

137. Record of Fort William-Bombay Castle-Secret Department Diary., Vol. 58., p. 719.

138. Poona Residency Papers and Letters. L. No. 125.

139. Poona Residency Papers and Collection of Rough Letters to the Governor General of India from the Resident at Poona,. L. No. 151 of 10th August 1799.

140. Poona Residency Papers and Letters.. L. No. 127,, dated 11th January 1799.

the 6,500 men of the British subsidiary forces which were with the Nizam, but an equal number of the Nizam's infantry and a large body of irregulars participated. The Nizam's troops were placed under Mir Alam and he for a second time co-operated with the British in their Mysore campaigns. The Nizam's armies joined the British forces under General Harris at Nellore and assisted in the subsequent siege and capture of Srirangapatam. In this battle Tippu died fighting in the defence of his capital. The Marathas did not participate in this war.

After the death of Tippu, Wellesley, appointed a commission consisting of General Harris, Col. Wellesley, Henry Wellesley and Lt. Col. Kirkpatrick and Lt. Col. Barry to settle the Partition Treaty of Mysore.

[141]By this treaty, the Company procured a territory yielding an annual revenue of 69 laks consisting of Malabar, Coimbatore, Dharapuram, all the heads and passes, Forts and Ports that lay between the Company's eastern and western coasts, including the Fort of Srirangapatam and the district of Wynad.

The Nizam got Gutty, Gurramkonda, the Jerimulla Taluk in Chitaldoorg, Nandidoorg and Kolar.

A territory yielding an annual revenue of 2.6 lakhs Pagodas was reserved for the Marathas but as they refused to be a party to this treaty it was decided to give two thirds of their share to the Nizam, while the remaining one third was appropriated by the British.

The much reduced Kingdom of Mysore was given back to the Rajah, belonging to the Wodeyar dynasty, which was originally displaced by Hyder Ali. The Rajah was given altogether an area yielding an annual revenue of 13.5 lakhs Pagodas.

The treasury of Srirangapatam was reserved for the British army on the ground that they stormed the Fort of Srirangapatam. Mir Alam did not like this but he had to put up with the decision of the Governor-General.

While making the Partition Treaty of Mysore Wellesley deliberately, saw that the portions procured by the British were more advantageous and of greater strategic importance than the portions given to the Nizam[142].

In fact the restoration of the Mysore Kingdom to the Hindu Rajah reduced Mysore to the position of a British protected territory. As a matter of fact Kirkpatrick described the new set-up in the following manner:

[143]"Purnaiyah considered the country to be the Company's and the Rajah a mere puppet".

141. Aitchison - Vol. IX., p. 21

142. Fraser. p. 223.

143. J. R. R. S. 1952, p. 132., Additional M. S. S. British Museum.

The Nizam was also not quite pleased with the partition treaty but he had to put up with it.

The Maratha Government viewed with jealousy this rapid growth in the British power.

Wellesley, realising that sooner or later, hostilities with the Marathas were inevitable, sought to strengthen the British alliance with the Nizam by entering into a new agreement with him in the year 1800.

Wellesley wrote to the Court of Directors:

[144]"The jealous and almost hostile spirit with which the Mahrattas regarded our operations against Tippoo,and the conflicts with which the Southern part of the Peninsula was threatened, from the weak and distracted condition of the Peishwa's government, pointed out the urgent necessity of adding, by every practicable means, to the efficiency of the alliance with the Nizam as that became the chief and after the defection of the Peishwa, the only means of protecting the British possessions, and those of its allies, in a state of peace and tranquillity."

In view of this necessity the British concluded a treaty with the Nizam on the 20th October, 1800.

The preamble to this Treaty declared that the Nizam and the Company "are in fact become one and the same in interest, policy, friendship and honour."

By this Treaty the strength of the subsidiary forces with the Nizam were increased. Apart from the regular six battalions, the Nizam was given in addition two more battalions of Sepoys, one regiment of cavalry with a due proportion of guns and artillery men, thus increasing the total strength of the British forces to eight battalions of Sepoys, and two regiments of cavalry with the requisite equipment of Guns, European artillery men etc.,

To meet the cost of these troops the Nizam ceded to the British East India Company in perpetuity, all those territories he had gained by the Treaty of Srirangapatam and by the Treaty of Mysore concluded on the 18th March 1792 and 22nd June 1799 respectively.

In order to give contiguity to the British acquisitions the Nizam agreed to retain with him Koppal, Gajendragar and other places in return for which he gave Adoni and the surrounding districts to the South of Tungabhadra and Krishna to the Company.

These ceded territories were to be under the exclusive management of the Company.

144. " Memoirs and Correspondence of the Marquess of Wellesley., " p. 370.

Commenting about this clause, Wellesley, wrote that the cession of territory was deemed desirable as it would make the alliance permanent[145].

Pearce, commenting about this arrangement writes: "An end would undoubtedly be put by its adoption, to that constant recurrence of irritation, which must always be expected to attend large pecuniary payments from sordid or extravagant courts. The resources upon which the support of a large English Force must depend would be placed in the hands of the British Government instead of being in those of another State whose imprudence, distress or treachery might at any critical moment endanger the general safety, and, the wish which, it was possible a future or fickle administration at Hyderabad might entertain, of freeing that State from a connexion from which it might think it had derived all the benefit that it could expect and the expense of which continued a burden, upon its finances, would cease to operate when it had, by a cession of territory paid in perpetuity, and by advance, for the services of the Corps by which its dominions were protected"[146].

By the treaty of 1798 the Nizam was not entitled to use the subsidiary troops against the Marathas, but according to this new treaty the British agreed to extend their protection to the Nizam against any power in India with whom he happened to be at war[147].

The Nizam, by this treaty, agreed not to commit hostilities against any other State and in case of differences arising with any other power he agreed to submit himself to the Company's arbitration and to acquiesce in the justice of its decision.

Thus by the Treaty of 1800 the Nizam was reduced to the position of a subservient ally. He not only lost his external sovereignty, but even his internal surzerainty was impaired to a great extent on account of this subsidiary alliance. The Subsidiary Force was a great drain on the economy of the country. As a matter of fact, soon after the conclusion of the treaty of 1798, Azim-ul-Umara realising that the maintenance of the subsidiary troops would be a strain on the finances of the State, tried to make reductions in the Nizam's army, but Wellesley prevented him from doing so, saying that such a step was inadvisable on the eve of the Mysore War[148].

Azim-ul-Umara was so eager to get the better of the Marathas that without sufficiently ruminating over the full consequences of the Subsidiary Treaty, he committed his master to the Subsidiary Alliance.

---

145. "Memoirs and correspondence of the Marquess of Wellesley"., p. 369.
146. Ibid.
147. Wellington's Despatches, pp. 20-21.
148. "Selections from State Papers" - Bombay Maratta Series., Vol. 1. Letters from the Earl of Morrington - L. No. 5., p. 613.

At this juncture Azim-ul Umara became so jealous of the ascendency gained by Mir Alam in the British friendship that he contrived temporarily to get Mir Alam, banished from the Nizam's court[149].

In the year 1802 the British entered into a Commercial Treaty, with the Nizam. By this treaty, it was agreed that the goods produced or manufactured in the territories of either power should be allowed to enter the territories of the other on the payment of a 5% duty. The duties on the British imports were to be levied at Hyderabad and from henceforth they were exempted from all other *rahadari* duties[150].

In August 1803, Nizam Ali Khan, died at Hyderabad, and his death was followed by that of Azim-ul-Umara in the year 1804.

When Wellesley arrived in India, he found the Nizam sullen and more or less alienated by the "Policy of Non-intervention" followed by Sir John Shore. It goes to the credit of Wellesley's statesmanship that he soon won over the Nizam, to the British alliance (the steadfastness to which, earned him the title of the "Faithful Ally") and made him a subservient ally of the British.

No wonder Sir John Austruther wrote to Wellesley saying:

"You found the British influence in the Dekkan gone, you have planted its power in the very centre of the mountains which hold India together"[151].

---

149. After his mission to Calcutta, and the Tripartite Alliance against Tippu Sultan, the Court of Directors on the recommendation of Lord Cornwallis granted to Mir Alam a pension of Rs. 1200/- per mensem in appreciation of the services rendered by him to the Company-Political Letter to Court, Fort William., dated 25th June 1795., para 26.

150. Aitchison., Vol. IX., pp. 72-74.
Rahadari duties are transit duties levied by the Zamindars through whose districts the goods had to pass.

151. Martin.-"Wellesley's Despatches."

CHAPTER VI

Nawab Sikandar Jah and The Subsidiary Alliance.

From the day the Subsidiary Alliance Treaty was concluded a subtle change took place in the relations between the Nizam and the British. By concluding the treaty of 1800, the Nizam lost his external sovereignty; but the British were not satisfied with merely taking away the external sovereignty of the Nizam. They wanted to make their presence and influence felt in the internal administration of the State also, though, they had solemnly declared in Article 15 of the Subsidiary Treaty of 1800": "The Honourable Company's Government on their part hereby declare that they have no manner of concern with any of His Highness's children, relations, subjects or servants, with respect to whom His Highness is Absolute"[1].

In order to bring the internal administration of the State into their grip the British always saw that only a person who was dedicated to their interests was chosen as the Diwan of the State. In trying to achieve this object, the Resident did not pause to consider whether his actions told upon the internal sovereignty of the Nizam. Nawab Sikandar Jah naturally did not like the Resident, to infringe on his internal sovereignty; yet on account of the vicious grip of the subsidiary forces over his country, he could not openly object to the Resident's action. His helplessness against the British ultimately produced in Sikandar Jah a state of indifference towards State affairs and it is said about him that he had "always entertained and seldom failed to express the most inveterate jealousy of the British power and of its particular influence over the councils of the state and considered every man to be his enemy who was attached to the British Government and every man to be his friend who was hostile to the British[2].

The utter helplessness of the Indian Prince who had entered the subsidiary alliance could be envisaged from the following letter of the Court of Directors to the Bengal Government. It says; "The subsidiary force absolutely constitutes a part of our own army, is entirely under our own control, and can be changed, or even withdrawn at the discretion of our own Government, and although it is supported at the expene of our allies, affording them protection and authority, whilst in amity with us, it gives them no strength in the event of hostile disposition[2-A]."

Sikandar Jah ascended the throne in 1803. At the time of his accession he promised in return for the British support, to respect all the

1. Aitchison.- Vol. X. Treaties, Engagements and Sanads.
2. Hyderabad Residency Correspondence. Vol. 29-L. No. 18, para 20.
2- A. Secret letter to Bengal, dated 3rd April 1815, from the Court of Directors.

treaty engagements that were hitherto concluded between Hyderabad and the English East India Company[3]. On Sikandar Jah signing an instrument sent to him from the Governor General, confirming all the treaty engagements, the British decided to support him, and his ascession to the throne was smoothy effected.

Shortly after his ascession, war broke out in 1803 between the British East India Company and the Marathas under the Scindia and the Bhonslay. The war is called the second Maratha war. According to the stipulations of the treaty of 1800, the Nizam was expected to assist the British with a force of 6000 infantry and 9000 cavalry. But Sikandar Jah, who at heart disliked the association with the British, did not send the full quota of troops. Even those troops he had sent under Rajah Mahipat Ram, the Governor of Berar and a close friend of the Nizam, were indiscipilied and they consisted mostly of the erstwhile French corps that were disbanded on the insistence of the Resident, J. A. Krikpatrick. Naturally the loyalty of these troops to the British was rather luke-warm.

Mahipat Ram, who was also not favourably inclined towards the British alliance, beguiled the British General, Arthur Wellesley saying that he was waiting for the supply of funds from the Nizam, to increase the quota of troops that had come to assist the British, but actually he never increased his army even by a single man.

Apart from Mahipat Ram, Salabat Khan the Nawab of Ellichpoor and Rajah Sukradar were placed in command of the Nizam's forces during this campaign against the Marathas. The general behaviour of the Nizam's commandants and their men throughout this campaign was rather obstructive than helpful[4].

In spite of this the Marathas were defeated on the 23rd September 1803 at Assaye.

During this battle the Mughal forces, instead of assisting in the war against the Marathas, were actually engaged in plundering the baggage of their allies, the British.

Shortly after the conclusion of the battle of Assaye, Major General Wellesley wanted to send the sick and wounded among his troops to the Fort of Doulatabad. But the Qiledar of the Fort refused to admit these troops into the Fort, saying that his instructions did not permit him to do so. This was not the only incident which revealed the general dislike among the Mughal nobles against the British.

The Qiledar of Badnapur in Aurangabad District fired on the British detachment that was on its way to join General Wellesley; during the course of the campaign Rajah Sukradar who was in charge of procuring

3. Fraser, p. 225.
4. Major R. G. Burton.—"A History of the Hyderabad Contingent", p. 16.

grain and fodder for the army in his district, caused vexation to the British by his tardiness. Seeing these obstructive tactics of the Mughals Major General Wellesley complained to Major Kirkpatrick, the Resident at Hyderabad, in the following manner:[5] "I am concerned to be under the necessity of making a formal complaint of any of the officers in the service of the Subahdar of the Deccan, but justice to the troops under my command and to the service, the conduct of which is entrusted to me obliges me to do so.

Some time ago- - - - I desired Colonel Stevenson to remove the hospital to Doultabad and to place the sick in the lower fort. Application was accordingly made to the Qiladar - - - and he positively refused to receive them- - - -. I think it proper to mention the subject to you now, as the consequence of this refusal to admit the sick and the wounded troops into Doultabad at present is that I must either send them to Ahmednagar and thereby delay my operation for a month, or I must leave these brave men exposed in an open place to the violence and ferocity of a barbarous enemy.

While writing upon this subject, it is proper that I should inform you that I am by no means satisfied with Rajah Sookroodoor. He throws all kinds of difficulties in the way of my people sent into the districts under his management to purchase supplies of dry grain".

It was not only the Qiledar of Doultabad and Rajah Sukradar who were unco-operative, but even the Qiledar of Dharore, when General Wellesley asked him to give asylum to a battalion of British troops that were passing through his territories, refused to provide them with the necessary shelter saying that he could not do so unless he got specific orders to that effect from Hyderabad[6].

Wellesley, the Governor General, took a serious view of these inimical proclivities of the Mughal nobles and he conveyed his disapproval in a strongly worded despatch dated 25th November, to the Resident at Hyderabad in the following manner[7]. "It appears - - - - 6thly that the existing connection with the British power is viewed by almost all ranks and discriptions of people in the Subahdari dominions with jealousy, distrust and aversion. 7thly-That His Highness the Subahdar himself is supposed to be not altogether free from this contagion, and that he was known to be indisposed to the British Government previously to his accession to the musnud, 8thly-That His Highness the present Soubahdar distinctly asserted that the British Government exercised a degree of interference in the internal concerns of his Government inconsistent with the provisions of the treaty, that the British Government was not entitled by the terms of the treaty of Hyderabad concluded in the year 1800, to make representations to him respecting the mis-conduct of the Qiladar, in time of joint war, and that it was a matter

5. Gurwood-Wellingtons Despatches, Vol. II, pp. 346-348.
6. Ibid., p. 357-359, para 8.
7. Burton—" A History of the Hyderabad Contingent, "pp. 14, 150.

of indifference whether His Highness's Qiledars did or did not admit the British troops into his forts in the time of joint war, under the general defensive alliance- - - - - -

If his Highness the Subahdar really entertains the sentiments ascribed to him, it must be inferred that His Highness secretly approves the late conduct of his officers. At all events, His Highness must either be considered to be responsible for the conduct of his public officers in points affecting the mutual obligations of the subsisting alliance, or if the Government of Hyderabad does not possess sufficient energy to control their conduct, His Highness must transfer to the British Government such a degree of authority over those officers as may secure the due fulfilment of the obligations imposed on His Highness by the stipulations of the alliance between the two States.

Either these stipulations must be distinctly acknowledged and faithfully fulfilled on the part of the State of Hyderabad or the alliance must be considered to be dissolved- - - - - - .

The Governor-General in Council deems it expedient that these sentiments should not only be fully explained of His Highness the Soubahdar, but that they should be openly and publicly declared. The Governor-General in Council, therefore, directs that you will immediately demand an audience of His Highness and that you will address to him a remonstrance in public Durbar, founded on the following topics which comprise the detail of the sentiments of the Govenor-General in Council on the subjects to which they refer - - - - - - .

A distinct intimation to His Highness Sikandar Jah that he owes his elevation to the musnud and that the owes his life entirely and exclusively to the support of the British power - - - - - - - .

That although the peculiar situation of Sikandar Jah at the period of the late Nizam's decease added to the existence of the claims which the Company possessed to compensation as above described and would have justified the demand of concessions from Sikandar Jah as the condition of our supporting his succession to the musand, no such demand has been made upon him - - - - - - .

That the State of Hyderabad has not in any instance fulfilled its part of the obligations of the Treaty, by affording the aid of the forces and the sources of the State for the prosecution of the war to the extent required by the obligations of the alliance, so far from it, that the conduct of its officers has been actually hostile to the British Government. In this place it will be proper to state the conduct of Rajah Sukrudar and the Killadars of Daulatabad, Badnapur and Dharur - - - - - - .

His Highness the Soubahdar should be required to state distinctly whether he avows the principle which he is said to have maintained to the Minister, as described under the 8th head - - - - - - .

That the maintenance of that principle will be a direct violation of the spirit of the alliance and will place the State of Hyderabad in the condition of a public enemy to the British Government - - - - - -.

That His Highness the Soubahdar neither adheres to the spirit or even to the letter of his defensive engagements, when he justified the officers exercising his authority, not only in refusing their aid and co-operation, but in committing acts of decided hostility against the power with which he is in alliance, and which he is united in the prosecution of a war for the preservation of his own possessions, rights and interests, and those of his allies and against the troops to whose exertions he owes the acquisition and actual possession of his present power."

On the receipt of the above strongly worded despatch from the Marquess of Wellesley, the Resident Major J. A. Kirkpatrick, conveyed the sentiments of the Governor-General to the Nizam in open Durbar.

As a result of this public remonstrance on the part of the Resident Nawab Sikandar Jah concluded a supplementary Treaty on the 15th December 1803 with the British by which he confirmed all the hitherto existing treaties between Hyderabad and the English East India Company[8]. [9]On the 9th January 1804, an additional Article was added to the Treaty of 1800 by which it was agreed that in the time of war all the forts and territories belonging to either of the allies would be available, to the armies of the allies. It was also agreed that the officials, civil or military, belonging to either of the allies should also co-operate with each other whole-heartedly in carrying on the various operations of war.

As a result of the victory gained by the second Maratha war the Nizam got as his share the territories lying between the Ajanta hills and the river Godavary together with the districts ceded by the Rajah of Nagpur situated to the west of the Wardha River and South of the Satpura Range. The territories thus acquired comprised the whole of the present Berar. As a result of this arrangement the Hyderabad State received a large increase of territory and obtained a compact and well defined boundary[10].

Shortly after the conclusion of the above treaty Azim-ul-Umara died on the 12th April 1804, [10-A] and the Resident feeling that "any advantage to be derived by the British from an alliance with the Hyderabad State depended on placing its resources under the control of a Minister who should owe his elevation exclusively to their influence", recommended the appointment of Mir Alam to the vacant post of the Diwan.

---

8. Briggs.—Vol. I, p. 296.
9. Ibid, p. 297.
10. Fraser, p. 226.
10-A. Administrative Files, S. No. 21 A1/a4 } Central Record Office, Hyderabad.

Sikandar Jah had not yet recovered from the effects of the strong remonstrance from the Governor General; so he was reluctant to cause fresh annoyance to the British at this juncture. Hence, he acquiesced in appointing Mir Alam as the Diwan. But Mir Alam's appointment was made under duress, and from the moment Sikandar Jah appointed him as his Diwan, he tried to nullify its effects by trying to appoint his own friends to positions of trust and responsibility in opposition to Mir Alam.

The Nizam knew that Mir Alam enjoyed the confidence of the British. He did not like the idea of his Diwan having free access to the British Residency and being the sole channel of communication between him and the Resident. So he endeavoured to get his trusted friend Rajah Mahipat Ram appointed as the Naib of Mir Alam[11].

Soon after the conclusion of the second Maratha war, Mahipat Ram returned to Hyderabad, on the 3rd October 1805. After his arrival he exerted himself in trying to gain the favour of the Resident by telling the latter, that he would see to it, that the Nizam became fully aware of the benefits from the alliance with the British.

Shortly after this the Nizam invited the Resident one day, apparently, to see the new palace he was constructing. During the course of the visit the Nizam told the Resident that owing to the efforts of Mahipat Ram, he had been able to perceive clearly the benefits of the subsidiary alliance. By saying so, the Nizam wanted to convey indirectly to the Resident that he had a very high opinion of Mahipat Ram, and that the latter should be entrusted with a reasonable post, and should be made the channel of confidential communications between him and the Resident. The Nizam was willing to keep Mir Alam as the nominal Diwan but he wanted Mahipat Ram, his own friend and confidant to wield the actual power in the State.

The Nizam, by speaking to the Resident in the above manner, hoped that the latter would convey this inclination on the part of the Nizam, to the Governor General and obtain the latter's consent to the appointment of Mahipat Ram.

Two days later, on the 10th October, Mahipat Ram sent a message to the Resident to the effect that the latter should convey to the Governer-

---

11. Hyderabad Residency Records Vol. 29. L. No. 7, Para 8. Rajah Mahipat Ram was a Gujrati Khatri. He was first noticed by Azim-ul-Umara, and soon gained the confidence of that Minister as well as that of Nizam Ali Khan, and of Sikandar Jah. He became a close friend of the latter and exercised considerable influence over him. He earned the gratitude of Sikandar Jah by supplying him with money and encouraging him when the latter lived in disgrace for some time during the life time of Nizam Ali Khan. After the disbandment of Raymond's Corps, these troops were reorganised by Mahipat Ram and were entertained by him. He was shortly afterwards appointed as the Governor of Berar.—Central Records Office, Hyderabad.

General the high opinion that the Nizam entertained about him (Mahipat Ram)[12]. But these manoeuvres of Mahipat Ram did not succeed with the Resident.

Mir Alam grew greatly alarmed at the influence of Mahipat Ram on the Nizam, and he began to press the Resident to ask Mahipat Ram, to return to his Subah of Berar. The Resident assured Mir Alam that he need not entertain any fears and that as soon as the wedding ceremony of Mahipat Ram's daughter was over, he would ask him to return to Berar.

The Resident knew that it was the intention of the Nizam to retain Mahipat Ram at Hyderabad, by conferring on him some important post; yet, he pretended to be not aware of the wishes of the Nizam in this respect.

At this juncture, the office of the Peishkar fell vacant. The Nizam desired that Mahipat Ram should become the Peishkar and wield extensive political influence in the State[13]. Apart from Mahipat Ram there were two other candidates who were also anxious to become the Peishkar. These were Munir-ul-Mulk, the son-in-law of Mir Alam, and Maharajah Chandulal.

Mahipat Ram to keep up friendly appearances informed the Nizam that the suggestion for his becoming the Peishkar must also come from Mir Alam who was the Diwan. Mir Alam perforce had to speak about Mahipat Ram to the Resident, but while mentioning about Mahipat Ram's anxiety to become the Peishkar, he also pressed the Resident to bring about the latter's speedy departure to Berar.

Mir Alam was jealous of the influence of Mahipat Ram over the Nizam, and was always afraid that given a free hand Mahipat Ram might try to undermine his influence with the Resident. So Mir Alam, never encouraged the visits of Mahipat Ram to the Residency, and on one occasion when the Resident visited the house of Mahipat Ram, Mir Alam tried to post spies at the latter's residence.

Apart from his jealously of Mahipat Ram, Mir Alam wanted to confer the office of the Peishkar on his own son-in-law, Munir-ul-Mulk[14]. While matters were in such a state, Mahipat Ram invited the Resident to his house and informed him that it was the intention of the Nizam, to associate him in the administration of the State by appointing him as the Peishkar. Mahipat Ram, also informed the Resident that in the event of his becoming the Peishkar, he wanted to exercise his powers without any undue interference from Mir Alam. Commenting about this, the Resident wrote to the Governor-General; "By the information which I have now had the honour to submit to you, you will perceive not only that it is the object of His Highness the Subehdar to effect the removal

12. Ibid., para 13.

13. Ibid. L. No. 8. Dated 23rd October 1805. From Henry Russell to the Governor-General.

14. Ibid.

of Mir Alam from his present station, but that the ambition of Mahipat Ram has at length aspired to the highest office of the State"[15].

The object of Mahipat Ram, in informing the Resident, of his aspiration was, that he wanted the latter, to inform the Governor- General of the Nizam's wishes and obtain, if possible, the sanction of the Governor-General for his appointment as the Peishkar. The Nizam hesitated to bring about such drastic changes in the administration of the State without formal sanction from Calcutta.

But the Resident felt that though Mahipat Ram might exert himself to strengthen the bonds of friendship between the English and the Nizam, he would under all circumstances be more loyal to the Nizam than to the British and ultimately he might impair the alliance rather than strengthen it, by not supporting it in an unstinted manner;

The Resident conveyed his opinion to the Governor-General in the following manner;

"I am strongly inclined to think that the elevation of the Rajah would prove beneficial to the interest both of His Highness and the Honourable Company's Government-----. But I am decidedly of opinion that the inordinate extension of his views ought not to be encouraged by the British Government and that the removal and disgrace of Mir Alam ought not to be accelerated by that power to whose influence and support he is indebted for his elevation to the office of the Prime Minister. If, on the contrary, Rajah Mahipat Ram should succeed in effecting the removal of Mir Alam and in obtaining for himself the exercise of an unlimited authority at Hyderabad, I am strongly inclined to apprehend that our influence would naturally become precarious and insecure. It is probable that Mahipat Ram would confine his sense of obligation to him alone on whose pleasure he would depend for the maintenance of his power and I am decidedly of opinion that Sikandar Jah should even find a minister in whose attachment and devotion he could implicity rely for the accomplishment for his purposes, it would become impossible for the British Government to maintain even the original principles and objects of the alliance without a constant and invidious interference in the internal affairs of the administration at Hyderabad and without exciting a degree of jealousy and dissatisfaction in the mind of the Subedar which it is on all accounts desirable to avoid"[16].

While such was the opinion of the Resident, Mir Alam, also tried to counteract the influence of Mahipat Ram over the Nizam by winning over to his side the widows of Nizam Ali Khan, Bakshi Begum and Tyneat-un-nissa Begam, and also two leading nobles of the court for whom the Nizam had great respect, namely Umzud-ul-Mulk and Ihtisan-ul-Mulk[17].

15. L. No. 16. Dated 20th December 1806.
Letter from H. Russell to the Governor-General, George Barlow.

16. Ibid. Para 12, 13.

17. Ibid. L. No. 10.

The Begams were greatly under the influence of Rajah Raghotam Rao,[18] who was opposed to Mahipat Ram and was in favour of Mir Alam. So it did not take a long time for Mir Alam to win over the Begams to his side. Mahipat Ram at first tried to win the favour of Rajah Raghotam Rao, but when he found that the latter was vehemently opposed to him, he also started openly to oppose Rajah Raghotam and tried to counteract his influence in the palace.

The Begams exerted their influence with the Nizam in favour of Mir Alam and on their recommendation the Nizam agreed to receive a *Wajib-ul-Arz* (written petition) from the Minister, in which the latter put down his demands.

Mir Alam pleaded in the petition that the Nizam should give him his confidence and also support him in the various measures that he might initiate for the welfare of the State.

In that petition Mir Alam also pleaded that he should be given the power to appoint the Peishkar and also a Minister for English affairs.

This petition was presented to the Nizam, by the Begams. On the receipt of the petition, the Nizam, after having gone through the various Articles in the petition, professed the greatest respect for the Minister, and told the ladies that he would return the petition duly signed, sometime later. The Begams pressed the Nizam to sign the petition in which the type of answers that were expected were already written down, immediately. But this the Nizam obdurately refused to do, and after the departure of the Begams sent for Mahipat Ram, Ismail Yar Jung and other friends and consulted them about the attitude he should adopt towards the *Wajib-ul-Arz.*

Mahipat Ram and his friends advised the Nizam not to sign the petition. Rajah Raghotam Rao whose opinion was also sought concerning the petition, urged the Nizam to sign it without any hesitation.

On the advice of Mahipat Ram, the Nizam altered the terms of the *Wajib-ul-Arz* and sent it to Mir Alam for consideration. But the altered *Wajib-ul-Arz*, rendered the original document completely nugatory. So Mir Alam refused to consider it.

The Nizam asked Umzad-ul-Mulk to suggest a way out of the stalemate. Umzad-ul-Mulk advised the Nizam to sign the *Wajib-ul-Arz* without any hesitation and thus put an end to all the intrigues at the Court. When Mahipat Ram found that even Umzad-ul-Mulk had gone against him, and that the Nizam was inclined to accept the advice of that nobleman, he himself started urging the Nizam to sign the *Wajib-ul-Arz*, and thus tried to placate Mir Alam. But the latter was not to be won over so easily.

The Nizam ultimately signed the *Wajib-ul-Arz.* Immediately after its ratification, Mir Alam presented another petition to the Nizam in which

18. Peishkar in the time of Nizam Ali Khan.

he urged the desirability of asking Mahipat Ram to return to Berar. The Nizam gave the necessary orders for Mahipat Ram to return to Berar. Prior to his departure Mahipat Ram sent a petition to Mir Alam in which he urged that he might be allowed to visit the court once a year to settle his accounts, and that his previous revenue statements should not be examined by the ordinary *mutsaddies*. He also requested that he should have full authority with regard to the management and payment of the *silladari* forces. Mir Alam fearing that if the Rajah was allowed to visit the capital even once a year, he might utilise that opportunity to win over the Nizam, refused to sign the petition presented by Mahipat Ram[19].

Mahipat Ram, knowing that all these above steps were taken by Mir Alam with the tacit support of the Resident, while taking leave of the latter, asked him, how he should endeavour to gain the favour of the British.

Capt. Thomas Sydenham, who was the Resident during this period, pointed out that Mahipat Ram should maintain the army in an efficient manner so that they might be in a fit condition to co-operate with the subsidiary forces whenever required. Secondly, he should try to promote the prosperity of the province of Berar by not extorting oppressive taxes; and thirdly, by not indulging in clandestine correspondence with the court with a view to impairing the happy relations that now existed between the Nizam and the Minister.

Shortly after the departure of Mahipat Ram to Berar, Maharaja Chandulal was appointed as the Peishkar[20].

Even after the dismissal of Mahipat Ram from the court, discontent prevailed among the nobles of the court against the British alliance, owing to the resultant loss in the powers of the Nizam.

Some of the leading nobles in the court who were greatly dissatisfied at the British connection were Rao Rambha Nimbalkar, and Nur-ul-Umara. These two noblemen tried to tamper with the loyalty of the subsidiary forces that were stationed in Hyderabad.

The Resident came to know of these activities quite accidently. The sepoys who were dissatisfied with the British alliance began to desert from the corps of the subsidiary forces and join the standards of either Rao Rambha or Nur-ul-Umara[21]. Incitement against the British power was carried on in the most secret manner. The sepoys were made to believe that the British were aiming to convert the Indians to Christianity, and to subvert the Musalman power in India. Therefore, they were asked to leave their ranks in the subsidiary corps and join the ranks of Rao Rambha Nimbalkar or Nur-ul-Umara. In their anxiety to wean the sepoys away from the subsidiary forces, the conspirators, the chief among whom were Ghulam Siddic Hussain and Khadir Beg, allowed it to be known that Rao Rambha would give Rs. 24/-

19. Ibid. L. No. 13. Dated 30th May 1806-From Sydenham to Barlow.
20. Ibid. L. No. 12., Para 15. Sydenham to Barlow Dated 15th May 1806.
21. Ibid. Vol. 71. Secret consultation., Dated 9th October 1806.

to every sepoy that might join his standard. They were also promised the patronage and protection of the Bakshi Begam. Rao Rambha's agents also spread the rumour among the sepoys, that the English were about to force the European headgear and dress on the Indian sepoys.

The Resident, Capt. Thomas Sydenham, came to know of the existence of this conspiracy, when a sweeper in the palace of the Nizam, who was in the secret pay of the British discovered a petition which was forwarded to the Nizam. The sweeper who was paid to pass on any papers that he might discover in the inner apartments of the Nizam, just passed on the paper to the agent of the British, who in his turn sent it over to Col. Montressor of the subsidiary troops.

Col. Montressor duly sent the paper to the Resident, who discovered, that it was an appeal to the Nizam made by Siddic Hussain on behalf of the discontended sepoys of the subsidiary troops to lend them his assistance and sympathy. They wrote that the British intended to christianise them and to impose the European dress on them and so they looked towards the Nizam, a Musalman Prince for their protection. They appealed to the Nizam in the following manner; "We will not consent to depart from the faith of Islam or to enhance that of the hat wearers; that we consider Your Highness to be our master, and therefore we represent that if your Highness will honour us with your orders, or communicate your intention of going on hunting excursion or to the Fort of Golconda - - - five days after that concerted signal, we will extirpate the English, everyone and all by murdering them - - - -. If our designs, should meet with your Highness's approbation let the orders be issued. Otherwise let this transaction be kept secret."

The Resident on reading the above appeal was filled with consternation. The fact that the Nizam obviously did not respond to the appeal did not console him. Knowing the disposition of the Nizam, he thought the latter was just awaiting developments and had adopted a neutral attitude. The Resident was afraid that the malcontents might be in communication with the disgruntled elements among the sepoys at Vellore. He started making vigorous enquiries and was amazed to see the strict veil of secrecy about the whole conspiracy. In the interests of the public and the personal safety of the informants, as well as the morale of the sepoys he decided to hold no court martial or any public enquiry, but to send away the suspected characters to centres outside Hyderabad. He also decided to insist on the dismissal of the Rao Rambha, and Nur-ul-Umra from the Nizam's Court, without informing the Nizam of his awareness of the plot. The Resident decided that the Nizam, if he had not read the paper and was ignorant of the plot, should under no circumstances be enlightened about [illegible] that were going on.

The Governor-General and the Council on being apprised of the plot were dubious about its existence, but they too advised, the Resident, to keep

22. Ibid., Vol., 71. From Edmonstone to Sydenham, dated 14-10 1806.

the Nizam ignorant of the plot[22]. The Resident, in order to put down every sign of discontent among the sepoys, asked Col. Montressor to inform them that it was not compulsory for them to wear the turbans that the British had thought of introducing among them. This satisfied the sepoys a great deal. Then the Resident called Mir Alam and informed him of the machinations of Rao Rambha Nimbalkar and Nur-ul-Umara and how the two had tried to tamper with the loyalty of the Indian soldiers, the former with the subsidiary sepoys and the latter with the native troops[23].

Mir Alam disapproved of the manner in which the British were trying to introduce changes in the dress of the Indian soldiers saying that it was a very imprudent step. He said, "I know that you wish to make the men look like European soldiers only because you think they will fight better, but the natives ascribe these changes to your desire to make them look like Christians. However, courage resides in the breast and not in the dress and be assured that your sepoys will be more attached to you, in proportion as you foster and promote their distinctive and favourite prejudice of religion, custom and appearance."

The Resident who knew that Mir Alam was sincerely attached to the British, listened to the Mir's remarks carefully, Mir Alam also dismissed the idea of the Bakshi Begam being connected with the conspirators sayingthat it was preposterous, and that he knew the Begam's disposition very well from Chandulal who kept himself informed of the various developments in the Mahal. Mir Alam confirmed the suspicions of the Resident regarding Nur-ul-Umara and the Rao Rambha's enmity towards the English, saying that the latter had even carried on correspondence against the English with Holkar and Scindia[24]. Then Mir Alam suggested that Chandulal should also be taken into confidence and consulted about the future procedure. So the Resident sent for Chandulal. The latter on hearing of the whole plot, said that for sometime he too had been hearing of a conspiracy in the ranks of the subsidiary forces and had also suspected that some sirdars belonging to the subsidiary troops were visiting the house of Rao Rambha!

When Mir Alam and Chandulal asked the Resident what steps he would like to be taken against Rao Rambha and Nur-ul-Umara, he replied that as it would be difficult to bring definite charges against them, he would advice the Minister to take such steps as would be necessary, in the interests of the security of the State. Mir Alam and Chandulal were in favour of confining Rao Rambha in the fort of Golconda, but the Resident cautioned them against taking such extreme measures as might it result in grave repercussions in the State[25]. So it was decided that the Diwan should apprise the Nizam of the activities of these noblemen and consult his opinion about the steps the Government should adopt against these Chiefs.

23. Ibid., Vol. 27., dated 31st August 1806. - From Sydenham to Barlow, L. No. 17.
24. Ibid., para 5.
25. Ibid., para 9.

The Minister, on the following day in an interview with the Nizam, informed him of the various developments, and urged the Nizam to take the necessary steps. The Nizam, who was greatly alarmed, asked Mir Alam what steps he should take against these Chieftains. Mir Alam replied that the Rao Rambha should be confined in the fort of Golconda, while Nur-ul-Umara should be dismissed. He proposed, that the Nizam should go on an excursion to Golconda and that Rao Rambha should be asked to accompany the Nizam, and once the party arrived at Golconda, Rao Rambha should be seized and thrown into prison. The Nizam who needed time to recollect his thoughts and think coolly, pretended to agree to this suggestion of the Minister and dismissed him. But the moment the Minister was gone, he ordered all the leading Omrahs, and the Paigah Chiefs to come to him with their respective forces and guard his palace. Then he informed Mir Alam that as the family of the Rao Rambha had served the Asafia dynasty, faithfully for several generations, he did not like to imprison the Rao Rambha. Moreover, he said that if the Rao Rambha tried to tamper with the loyalty of the sepoys, it would be more dangerous to the security of the Nizam than to the British. Therefore, he said the British had no cause to be alarmed. The Nizam at the same time being reluctant to force issues with the Resident, asked Mir Alam, to inform the Resident that he was willing, if the Resident so desired, to dismiss Rao Rambha from the capital.

The Nizam, the next day called the Resident to him, and asked him to narrate all the events. After hearing the Resident's report of the various events, the Nizam asked him what steps he would advise the Nizam to take against the conspirators.

The Resident replied that it was impossible for him to prove the guilt of Rao Rambha and Nur-ul-Umara, but nevertheless he hoped the Nizam would adopt the necessary measures in the interests of the State's security.

The Nizam replied that looking at the *prima facie* charges that were brought against the Rao Rambha, the only measure he was prepared to take against that nobleman was to ask him to retire to his jaghir.

However, the Nizam said, if the Resident could specifically prove the guilt of the Rao Rambha, he was willing to take more drastic steps. At this juncture, Mir Alam, intervened and said that considering the serious nature of the allegations that were made against the Rao, the Nizam should try to take appropriate steps irrespective of the fact whether the charges against the Rao were substantiated or not[26].

The Resident replied that ever since the assurance from Col. Montressor, that it was not compulsory for them to wear turbans, the Indian sepoys were pacified and so he did not apprehend any danger from the activities of Rao Rambha. But he also pointed out to the Nizam, that he should show by his

26. Ibid., para 14.

actions and demeanour that he disapproved of such activities on the part of his subedars. This, he said, could be shown by asking Rao Rambha to return to his Jaghir. The Resident also showed his disapproval of the Nizam stationing the Paigah troops in his place.

The Nizam duly dismissed his Paigah troops, and agreed to issue the necessary orders for the dismissal of Nur-ul-Umara from service and for the retirement of Rao Rambha to his Jaghir.

The Nizam in accordance with his promise asked Rao Rambha to return to his jaghir. He also confined Digambar Rao Pandit and Narsing Rao, two other Chiefs who were suspected of intriguing with the sepoys in the fortress of Malkhed. Nur-ul-Umara who belonged to Delhi, expecting his dismissal, camped with his troops near Golconda. In the meanwhile he sent a secret letter of appeal to Rajah Mahipat Ram and also appealed to the Nizam's foster brothers, Asaf Yar Jung and Jaffir Yar Jung, to exert their influence with the Nizam in his favour.

Mahipat Ram, in spite of his dismissal from the Court was still continuing clandestine correspondence with the Nizam, and with his tacit acquiescence, was also carrying on secret negotiations with chieftains like Scindia and Holkar on behalf of the Nizam against the British[27]. Mahipat Ram on receiving the appeal from Nur-ul-Umara, sent to that Chief a sum of Rs. 30,000/- for his immediate relief and also asked him to rest assured, since, he would ask the Nizam, to revoke the orders of dismissal regarding Nur-ul-Umara.

Shortly after this, the Nizam informed Chandulal and Mir Alam that he desired them to inform the Resident that instead of dismissing Nur-ul-Umara from his service, he had decided to ask him to retire to Ellichpur. The Nizam gave a draft to Chandulal, and asked Mir Alam to write a letter to the Resident on the basis of the draft informing him of the Nizam's decision. At first Mir Alam refused to draft the letter, but on the Nizam angrily insisting through Chandulal on the Mir writing a note to the Resident, he agreed. The Resident, on receiving the note from the Minister, expressed his surprise at the sudden change of attitude in the Nizam, and said that if the Nizam felt favourably disposed towards Nur-ul-Umara he could show his favour by granting a pension to him, but that he should be dismissed nevertheless. He also wrote to the Minister saying that as he had already intimated the Governor-General in Council regarding the action contemplated against Nur-ul-Umara, it should be implemented without fail.

When Chandulal read to the Nizam the reply of the Resident, the Nizam angrily exclaimed, especially when he heard that the Resident had communicated with the Governor-General regarding his intended action against Nur-ul-Umara, "What is it to me that he (Resident) received such a

27. Ibid. L.No. 18.

communication. Of course he did, and he wrote it to the Governor-General for every Resident is an *Akbar navees.*"

On hearing the Resident's tone of reproach in the letter which said that since the Nizam had already promised to dismiss Nur-ul-Umara, he should not go back on his word, and if he were to do so it would harm his own interests, the Nizam exclaimed saying: "What is that to the Resident? I may give a hundred Paúndauns of leave a day, and take them back again, if such be my pleasure - - - - . Who is to judge of my interests and dignity but myself? How do they concern the Resident? If I choose to hurt and degrade myself, I alone can suffer it. It was of no consequence to any other person."

Chandulal, on seeing this attitude of the Nizam, become nervous and said that Mir Alam would come and explain to him the letter of the Resident and the propriety of the advice given by the latter. On hearing this the Nizam flew into a rage, and after abusing Mir Alam, said in a threatening manner that Mir Alam should better take care of himself before he ventured to advise him; after this the Nizam dismissed Chandulal from his presence. Chandulal, was too glad to be allowed to depart, and he hurried to the residence of the Minister to narrate the particulars of his interview with the Nizam, Mir Alam became nervous, and he sent for the Resident. On the arrival of the Resident, he once again made Chandulal narrate all the particulars of the interview with the Nizam.

After Chandulal had concluded his report Mir Alam exclaimed to the Resident : "The present Nizam has always entertained and seldom failed to express the most inveterate jealousy of the British power and of its particular influence over the councils of the State. When a prince, he reproached the conduct of his father and the late minister in placing the Government under the influence of the English, and in addition to his personnel enmity towards the late Minister, he detested him as a creature of the British Government and considered him to be a traitor to the Asafphia state - - - - - . His Highness came to the throne with a predetermination to extricate himself from the controlling influence of the British Government, and it is still the prevailing and favourite object of his most anxious desire. On his first accession to the throne there were insurmountable obstacles to the accomplishment of his wishes. His Highness's authority and the extensive influence of the late minister, the decided interposition of the late minister, the decided interpositions of the Resident, and the general system of Lord Wellesley's Government. To these circumstances may be added the novelty of His Highness's situation, and the successful war with the confederated Mahratta chieftains - - - - - -. His High Highness would have been rejoined if you had been defeated in which case, he would readily have combined with the Mahrattas to complete your defeat and expulsion.

Mir Alam, after further dilating on the inimical attitude of the Nizam, towards the English, also informed the Resident saying that the anti-British feelings of the Nizam were further encouraged by Mahipat Ram and Rajah

Raghotam, who pointed out to the Nizam the desirability of asserting his independence, as Scindia, who was also a subsidiary ally had done. It was also revealed to the Resident that secret negotiations were going on between the Nizam and the Maratha Powers like Holkar, Scindia and Ghate, with Mahipat Ram, acting as the channel of communications. These transactions were carried on, without any reference to Mir Alam. Mir Alam further told the Resident that Mahipat Ram had written a letter to the Nizam admonishing him for the late measures he had adopted against Rao Rambha and Nur-ul-Umara, and also informed the Nizam that if the Nizam continued to abide by the advice of Mir Alam, it would be impossible for any loyal servants of the state to serve their master loyally. It was on the receipt of the above letter from Mahipat Ram that the Nizam withdrew his orders of dismissal against Nur-ul-Umara.

On hearing this, the Resident asked Mir Alam if he could not persuade the Nizam to change his attitude, upon which Mir Alam replied that as long as Mir Alam was in favour of the British allience, it was impossible for the Nizam to like him, because the Nizam regarded all those as his friends who where against the British, and those who were in favour of the British as his personal enemies. After saying this Mir Alam appealed to the Resident to arm him with more plenary powers, so that he might dismiss anyone who stood between the Nizam and the British. He also appealed to the Resident to report the particulars of the various developments to the Governor-General, and to persuade him to exert the British authority in a firm manner and make the Nizam realise his actual position.

Mir Alam said that he owed his elevation entirely to the British and to the favourable opinion entertained by Lord Wellesley of him. He said he was willing to resign his office it it would resolve the deadlock between him and Mahipat Ram. Then he appealed to the Resident to use his authority in order to save his master from the harmful influence of Mahipat Ram, Holkar, Ghate etc., Mir Alam, who perceived the subtle change in the relationship between the Nizam and the British after the subsidiary alliance, but was in no way anxious to retrieve the lost sovereignty of his master, declared; "I do not know how far such decided interposition on the part of the British Government may be consistent with the change which has taken place in the political system of the Company, but I am confident that no other measure but that of decided interposition and the most vigorous control can check the progress of His Highness's disposition to relinquish all the benefits of his alliance with the Company, and to abandon himself to the destructive friendship of Holkar and Ghatge."

On hearing this the Resident asked the Minister to arrange an interview for him with the Nizam. On being apprised of this request of the Resident, the Nizam declared to the Minister that he was willing to see Capt. Sydenham if he agreed to the retirement of Nur-ul-Umara to Ellichpur[28].

28. Ibid., Vol. 29, Note No. 1., L.No. 17.

On receiving this reply, the Resident, got irritated and wrote back saying that the Nizam should not attach any conditions for granting an interview, to a person holding the rank of a Resident and who was the bonafide representative of the British Government. He further declared in his note that he would see the Nizam only if the interview was unconditional, upon this, the Nizam declaring, he was fully conscious of the unity of interests that now existed between the Nizam and British granted the interview to the Resident. In this interview the Resident endeavoured to convey to the Nizam the desirability of his dissociating himself from his profligate companions. Then, knowing that the more anxiety the British showed to bring about the expulsion of Nur-ul-Umara, the more anxious the Nizam would be to protect the latter, the Resident adopted a neutralistic attitude and pretended indifference towards the fate of that chief[29].

The Nizam, who had been upholding Nur-ul-Umara as a matter of principle, seeing this indifference of the Resident, lost his interest in that chief. Later on, Nur-ul-Umara was sent to Ousa, at the behest of Mir Alam. Nevertheless, the Nizam realising that Mir Alam had throughout these negotiations been supporting the Resident against him, began to evince a greater dislike for Mir Alam than before.

In the meanwhile the Governor-General, instructed the Resident, to impress upon the Nizam at a suitable opportunity, the necessity of giving up, such of his friends as were definitely known to be opposed to the English, and to take the Minister into his confidence. The Governor General declared; "If contrary to expectations His Highness should be persuaded to resist the force of these communications, the British Government will be prepared to adopt such measures as circumstances may appear to be indispensably requisite for its security[30]"

The Governor-General, Sir George Barlow, also addressed a letter of remonstrance, to Nawab Sikandar Jah, in which he reminded him of the close ties that existed between the two powers. He reminded the Nizam of the magnanimity of the British in not demanding fresh territorial grants at the time of his accession, even though the Nizam was willing to give up the *Peishcush* from the Northern Circars. The Governor-General also wrote that as the British did not desire to impair the resources or authority of the Nizam they did not ask for territorial grants. He also reminded the Nizam that the British, much as they desired, the introduction of the *Silledari* horse, did not insist on its establishment when they knew that the Nizam was not in favour of it.

After duly reminding the Nizam of various instances of British nobility and magnanimity, the Governor-General reminded the Nizam of the absolute

29. Ibid. L. No. 22. Dated 11th October 1806-From Sydenham to Barlow.
30. Ibid. Vol. 33, Letter dated 25th October 1806—Edmonstone to Sydenham.

necessity of adhering to the principle of the Subsidiary Alliance. He declared - - -. "A perfect union of interests and views between the two States constitutes the vital principle, and essence of the Alliance, and can alone secure its advantage to both. Deprived of this vital principle it becomes a source of danger for the removal of which the application of an adequate remedy is indispensably necessary".

The Governor-General further reminded the Nizam that the only way in which he could preserve the principles of the alliance was by taking into his confidence, and entrusting the administration to those in whom the British had trust. Otherwise he declared that the British might find it necessary to directly intervene in the internal affairs of the State in order to preserve the principles of the treaty alliance.

While sending this above letter of remonstrance to the Nizam, the Governor-General conveyed to the Resident that there was no question of the British withdrawing from the alliance, and if the Nizam persisted in his obstinacy, the Resident should take all the necessary measures to preserve the alliance on its proper footing. While advising the Resident, about the measures he should adopt, the Governor-General declared: "I am aware that the adoption of such a measure involves a deviation from that system of non-interference in the internal concerns of His Highness's administration which has been established as a principle of wise and equitable policy but the adoption of that system necessarily presupposed a just conception on the part of His Highness of the true principles and solid advantages of the alliance - - - - unsupported by this just and reasonable presumption that system is deprived of its sole foundation and the change is adopted not from choice but from necessity - - - ."

The Governor-General also asked the Resident to insist on the Nizam depriving Mahipat Ram of the command of the Berar troops. He also instructed the Resident to observe the utmost circumspection in making these demands and to see that Mir Alam did not incur any danger during the course of these transaction[31].

The Resident knew that the dislike of the Nizam for his minister did not emanate from any personal hatred but was due to the minister's enthusiasm for an alliance with the British. He cryptically remarked; "I have every reason to conclude that this indisposition of the Nizam towards the minister is founded on his aversion for his connection with the British Government, and I am confident that if Mahipat Ram himself were minister, and were to act on any unison with the British Resident, Mahipat Ram would become as obnoxious to the Subedar as Mir Alam is and Aristo Jah was, during the period of his administration".

31. Ibid. Vol. 33., L. No. 24, Dated 24th November 1806-Barlow to Sydenham.

Nevertheless, he decided to take every precaution against any possible danger to the life of Mir Alam. He first sent his munshi with a note to Mir Alam expressing his desire to speak to the Nizam. On the Minister conveying the note to the Nizam, the later, sent Mir Alam to the Residency.

Mir Alam visited the Residency accompanied by Chandulal, Munir-ul-Mulk and Munshi Ali. From there the Resident conducted Mir Alam to a building set apart for him in the grounds of the Residency known as the Rang Mahal. He informed Chandulal that as he wanted to discuss with Mir Alam the Governor General's communication Mir Alam would remain in the Residency for some days as his guest. He also posted two companies of sepoys outside the Rang Mahal. Then Sydenham, sent to the Nizam, a memorandum of his demands through Maharajah Chandulal.

The Nizam on the receipt of the memorandum consulted his foster-brothers, and Ismail Yar Jung and sent word saying that the Resident could communicate the Governor-General's sentiments through Mir Alam. Instead, the Resident replied that trusted Omrahs of the Court must be sent to him so that he could convey the Governor-General's sentiments through them. The Nizam sent secret instructions to Omrahs like Umzad-ul-Mulk to refuse the invitation of the Resident to visit him. So when they were asked to do so they excused themselves. Seeing this, the Resident decided to personally convey the Governor General's letter to the Nizam and so he demanded an interview with the Nizam.

The Nizam agreed to receive the Resident. Sydenham, visited him on the 28th November 1806, He saw that the whole palace was surrounded by troops. He was conducted to the Durbar by Maharajah Chandulal. The Resident demanded a private interview with the Nizam at which he also insisted on the presence of Umzad-ul-Mulk. The Nizam with great reluctance retired to an antechamber in the hall accompanied by the Resident, Umzad-ul-Mulk, Ihtisan-ul-Mulk and the munshi of the Resident, Zia-ul-Mulk.

The Resident at this interview expressed his regret at the conduct of the Nizam, which betrayed ill-will towards the British. Sikandar Jah tried to contradict the Resident saying that the latter was under a misconception but the Resident forthwith declared that it was a well known fact that the Nizam was surrounded by only those persons who were inimical in their attitude towards the British.

The Resident also regretted the fact that no noblemen were sent to receive the Governor-General's communications and that he was ultimately forced to come personally to the Nizam to convey the message. He also mentioned that he would gladly have made Mir Alam the channel of communication between the Court and the Residency in this matter, but finding that the Mir who was so essential for the welfare of the country, did not enjoy the confidence of the Nizam he had desisted from doing so [31-A].

31-A. Ibid., para 41.

On hearing this the Nizam remarked that he had implicit trust in his ministers. Taking advantage of the remark of the Nizam the Resident joined in saying that Mir Alam had a very clear and just conception of the alliance that existed between the Nizam and the British and therefore, he was the only qualified person to promote that alliance between the two Powers. After saying this the Resident made his Munshi to read out the letter of the Governor-General. After hearing the letter to the end the Nizam complimented the Resident on the tone of the letter and ultimately declared ; " What have I to do with Mir Alam and Chandu Lal, my business is with the Company." On hearing this the Resident pointed out that " Mir Alam was the link which connected the two States." Thereupon the Nizam enigmatically declared : "You are the link which connects me and Mir Alam. Do you be my friend and I care for nobody else"[32]. Then the Nizam remarked that he failed to understand the reasons that might have been responsible for creating the apprehension in the mind of the Governor-General that the alliance between the two Powers was in jeopardy.

The Resident then desired the Nizam to take the Governor-General's *Khareeta* with him, so that he could study it leisurely and consult his Omrahs and the Begams about the letter. He also informed the Nizam that he would once again see him on the 4th December, and would come with a Memorandum on various points about which the Governor-General was anxious for a clarification from the Nizam.

After the termination of this interview the Nizam once again consulted his associates. Sikandar Jah was jealous of guarding his sovereign rights. On the advice of his friends like Ismail Yar Jung, he sent instructions to various Sardars like Mahipat Ram, Asad Ali Khan, Nur-ul-Umara and Shams-ul-Umara to be ready with their forces. He also sent orders to Shahyar-ud-Dowla a nobleman, to raise an army of 1000 men. In spite of adopting the above steps, the Nizam who was now acting against the definite wishes and advice of the members of his family including the two Begams and the leading nobles of the Court began to feel timorous.

The Resident, seeing these activities of the Nizam, also rose to the occasion and he sent secret instructions to the subsidiary forces to be prepared for all eventualities. On hearing of these militant preparations on the part of the Resident, the Nizam after consulting Umzad-ul-Mulk and the Begams decided to drop the idea of opposing the British openly and to sign the Memorandum presented by the Resident. So when the Resident visited him on the 4th December, he duly signed the Memorandum presented to him by the Resident.

By this the Nizam agreed to transfer Mahipat Ram from Berar to Sagar which was far off from Hyderabad, and to appoint to the administration of Berar, only, those persons who enjoyed the confidence of the Minister

32. Ibid., para 48.

and that of the Resident. He agreed to grant all interviews in future to the Resident without any conditions. He also cheerfully acquiesced in all the just demands of the British "On many points of details which though not very important - - - - - are necessary to the harmony and efficiency of our political intercourse."

Another interesting feature of this agreement was that the Nizam agreed to the posting of military guards at the residence of Mir Alam who felt "that after the menaces which were held out against his life by the attendants of the Nizam, in His Highness's presence, he could not return to the city without his person protected by a guard of British troops". The Nizam also promised to act on the advice of his Minister, and to submit himself to the arbitration of the British Resident in case of disputes between him and his Minister[32-A]: As a gesture of his goodwill towards Mir Alam the Nizam visited the Minister at his residence. Mir Alam on his return to power appointed Rajah Govind Baksh, the brother of Chandulal, as the Governor of Berar. The Resident also insisted on the Nizam dismissing the troops he had ordered to be raised and also on the dismissal of Asad Ali Khan. The Nizam was so much dejected and demoralised, by the strong attitude of the Resident that he denied having summond Asad Ali Khan, to the capital and asked him to go back.

In order to create an impression of ready compliance with the wishes of the Resident, and of his friendship towards the British he addressed his friends in the presence of the Resident in the following manner[33]; "You will understand that the safety of my State depends upon the friendship of the British Government, and that it is the just wish of my heart to cultivate and improve the alliance which connects us. You have witnessed in the example of Mahipat Ram and Ismail Yar Jung the dangerous consequences of opposing the united interests of this State and that of the Company. You will be careful to conduct yourself in such a way as may not render yourself liable to the suspicion of the British Resident whom I consider to be my best friend. Be careful what you say and what you do and bear in mind the examples of Mahipat Ram and Ismail Yar Jung."

In spite of the apparent denunciation of Mahipat Ram, Sikandar Jah could not overcome his feelings of friendship and sympathy for his friend and he requested the Resident to depute the Assistant Resident, Charles Russell, to Mahipat Ram to assure him that no harm would befall him. The Resident granted the request of the Nizam.

Mir Alam did not live long to enjoy his triumph over the Nizam. He died on the 28th February 1808, and his death once again revived the tussle

---

32-A. Ibid., Vol. 29., L. No. 26, para of the Memorandum.

33. Ibid., L. No. 28.

33-A. Administrative Files.—Central Records Office, Hyderabad. (Vide p. 208).

between the Nizam and the Resident over the crucial problem of the appointment of the Diwan[33-A]. It was indeed an indirect struggle for internal supremacy in the State between the Nizam and the British.

The Nizam was reluctant to appoint anyone to the position of the Diwan, who was likely to become a pliable instrument in the hands of the Resident, ready to be used against the Nizam. The death of Mir Alam, gave rise to a keen competition in the State for the vacant post of the Diwan, in which the British Resident evinced a great deal of interest and triedto mould the situation in the State in favour of the British.

Soon after the death of Mir Alam, Mahipat Ram once again tried to depute one Mir Khan at the head of an army, obviously to assist the Nizam in the administration of the country. In the meanwhile, the Nizam through the Resident formally informed the Governor-General of the death of Mir Alam and asked his advice with regard to the appointment of the future Diwan.

The Governor-General after examining the pros and cons, of the question, decided in favour of Shums-ul-Umara[34] But besides Shums-ul-Umara, there was also another aspirant to the post of the Diwan. This was Munir-ul-Mulk, the son-in-law of Mir Alam. Prior to the death of Mir Alam, Munir-ul-Mulk had contrived to obtain the Diwan's seal and prevailed on the sick man to sign a paper to the effect that after him, the Diwanship, should be conferred on his young grandson, Asadullah Sahib, the son of Munir-ul-Mulk, and that Chandulal should be continued as Peshkar [34-A].

Commenting about this arrangement the Resident wrote to the Governor-General[35]. "This effect of this arrangement would be to direct the attention of the Nizam to his own affairs, to oblige him to discuss in person with the Resident, all subjects of importance to the mutual interests of the two States and to leave the internal administration of the country to the general superintendence and control of Chandulal - - - - -. Of all the men of any consequence at this court, the peshkar is the only person in whom I can place any confidence. He is the only man at Hyderabad who appears to me to have formed a perfect conception of the principles and objects of an alliance with this State and a just estimate of the nature and extent of our power in India. Whoever might be the Minister it would be for our interest that Chanduial should profess the largest share of active influence in the administration and as long as he held a confidential situation about the Nizam we might almost be assured of the security of our interests at this Court - - - - - -.

However, the Governor-General decided in favour of Shams-ul-Umara. The Governor-General in fixing his choice on Shums-ul-Umara had two

34. Ibid., Vol. 39., dated 17th February 1809.—Minto to Sydenham.
34-A. Ibid. Vol. 36., L., No. 14, dated 25th November 1808.
35. Ibid., para 7., Section 4.

objects in view namely that as he was a mediocre in administrative capacity; all the authority would be vested in Chandulal. Secondly, by choosing Shums-ul-Umara as the Minister, the British would be able to gain the support of one of the most powerful parties in the Court.

But, no sooner did the Nizam hear of the British choice, than he decided to support the candidature of Munir-ul-Mulk to the post of the Diwan. Munir-ul-Mulk was trying to gain the goodwill of the Nizam through his niece Jehan Parvar Begam who was the consort of the Nizam and also through Chandni Begam, another wife of the Nizam, to whom he offered Rs. 50,000/- as present. The Nizam's mother Tyneat-un-nissa Begam was also in favour of Munir-ul-Mulk.[36] In spite of the strong support of the Begams the Nizam had a great dislike for Munir-ul-Mulk. But now the mere fact the British set him aside in favour of Shums-ul-Umara, made him decide in favour of Munir-ul-Mulk, and all the exertions of the Resident through his friends Chandulal and Shums-ul-Umara would not shake him in his decision.

When the Resident, capt. Sydenham, saw this firm determination of the Nizam, he decided to give way to the Nizam's will, and asked the latter to send a letter to the Governor-General formally informing him of the appointment of Munir-ul-Mulk as the Minister.[37]

The Nizam at first agreed to do so, and sent to the Resident the draft of the letter that he proposed to send to the Governor-General, in which he declared that he was determined to confer the office of the Diwan on Munir-ul-Mulk. Upon the Resident objecting to the tone of the letter, and suggesting suitable alterations, the Nizam promised to re-draft it. But by this time the Nizam had found out that the British had no real objections against the appointment of Munir-ul-Mulk and that on the contrary, they favoured him as he happened to be the son-in-law of Mir Alam. So, now he began to hesitate about appointing Munir-ul-Mulk to the office of the Diwan.

The Nizam now decided to do away altogether with the appointment of a Diwan in the State and instead to appoint a Council of Advisers to run the administration. In order to appease the Resident he sent word through SikanderYarJung his favourite that the Resident could nominate some members to the Council.[38]

The main object of the Nizam in devising this plan was to prevent the possibility of any single individual becoming too intimate with the Resident, and thus act in opposition to the Nizam's wishes as Mir Alam had done on certain occasions. He knew that the considerable influence gained by Azim-ul-Umara and Mir Alam in the affairs of the State was mainly due to the British support. Hence he thought if there were to be a Council of Advisers, it would not be possible for any single individual to attain that ascendancy

36. Ibid., Vol. 36., L. No. 15, dated 15th January 1809.
37. Ibid. L. No. 20. dated 20th June 1809, Sydenham to Minto.
38. Ibid. L. No. 38.

that was gained by Mir Alam in the state affairs. The Resident on hearing of the plan clearly informed Sikandar Yar Jung that he could not entertain such a plan. Then he also sent word through his Munshi to the Nizam that hereafter he would like Chandulal to be the channel of communication on all important State matters between the Residency and the Durbar. By sending this message the Resident obviously wanted to convey that no matter who became the Diwan, the actual power within the State would be wielded by Chandulal who from henceforth would enjoy the special patronage of the British. The Resident through the Munshi also indirectly hinted that the Nizam in order to show his regard for the representative of the British Power should occasionally visit the Residency. The Nizam conveyed his approval of the plan but continued to postpone the appointment of a Diwan.

It was nearly six months since Mir Alam had died, and there was no successor to the office of the Diwan. So the Resident now tried to bring pressure on the Nizam by personally visiting him and speaking to him on the absolute necessity of appointing a successor to Mir Alam. On hearing the Resident's remonstrance the Nizam categorically declared: "I must have a Minister who holds no great office in the State, who will not dispute with me, and who will conduct my affairs with regullarity." The Resident on hearing this hastened to add, "and who will exert himself to preserve and improve the alliance between the two States[39]...............thus indirectly hinting that only those candidates who are in favour of the British Alliance should be preferred.

The Nizam of course in order to keep up appearances of friendship with the British, assented to what the Resident said. Then the Resident insisted that Munir-ul-Mulk must solemnly affirm that in his capacity as the Diwan he would not by his acts try to jeopardise the alliance of the Nizam with the British. On the Nizam agreeing to this, drafts were prepared about the appointments of Munir-ul-Mulk and Chandulal for the offices of the Diwan and Peishkar and the respective powers to be wielded by them.

The Resident addressed Munir-ul-Mulk and Chandulal respectively in the following significant manner. He said to Munir-ul-Mulk : "If it should be your good fortune to become the Minister of this State; you will do well to attend to two objects, one to consult the wishes and pleasure of the Nizam and to preserve the favour and confidence. The other to improve the friendship, harmony and union which happily subsists between your soverign and the British Government."

Then he said to Chandulal "As you possess the confidence both of the Nizam and the British Government, I have only to tell you that it is the Nizam's pleasure, that the administration of his affairs should be conducted on the same footing as it is at present, and that you are held responsible that no changes shall take place in that system. It will therefore be your peculiar duty to lay before His Highness continual representation of the conduct of

39. Ibid. L No. 22;

affairs and to report any deviation that may take place in the management of the State."

Thus, in a very subtle manner the Resident made Chandulal, the Peishkar, responsible for the administration of the State and the medium of contact between the British and the Nizam. The Nizam agreed to this arrangement with apparent good grace.

Capt. Sydenham suspected that Mahipat Ram had indirectly encouraged the Nizam, to evade appointing a Diwan after the death of Mir-Alam. He had also heard that Mahipat Ram was intriguing with the Holkar on behalf of the Nizam, So Sydenham, also wrote a letter to Holkar with the approval of the Nizam denouncing the activities of Mahipat Ram.[40]

The loss of power under the arrangement made by Sydenham rankled in the heart of Munir-ul-Mulk and he tried to poison the mind of the Nizam against the Peishkar. In this he was greatly encouraged by the Tyneat-un-nissa Begam and Rajah Raghotam Rao, her protege and an aspirant for the Peishkarship.[41]

The Nizam, who heartily disliked any one who was on terms of intimacy with the British, did not require a great deal of persuasion to dislike Chandulal. Taking advantage of the retirement of the strong handed Resident, Capt. Sydenham the Nizam demanded that Chandulal should render all the accounts of the State from the time he assumed the office of the Peishkar. The Nizam made this demand in order to intimidate Chandulal. But the British were of the opinion that "any specific measures either to limit the authority of Chandulal's office or openly to fix upon him the weight of the Nizam's avowed displeasure must be considered to constitute an unquestionable prognostick of his downfall and cannot therefore be allowed to pass without manifest injury to the stability of our interests.[41-A]

So the Governor-General-in-Council sent two letters to the Acting Resident Mr. Charles Russell one in the name of the Nizam and the other in the name of the Minister Munir-ul-Mulk remonstrating against their treatment of Chandulal. But the Resident, Henry Russell, advised his Assistant Charles Russell, not to deliver those letters unless matters assumed a serious turn and Chandulal's power was in danger of being subverted. Henry Russell took charge of the Residency early in 1811. Soon after his arrival finding that the Nizam and Munir-ul-Mulk had not ceased to harass Chandulal, he decided to visit the Nizam and remonstrate against the manner in which Chandulal was treated. Accordingly, when the Resident visited him, the Nizam asked the Resident to be seated, without observing the etiquette of embracing. The Resident finding that the Nizam had deliberately omitted

40. Ibid. Vol. 36. Enclosure to letter No. 18.
41. Ibid. Vol. 44 L. No. 2, dated, 21 May, 1811.
41. A. Ibid. Vol. 177. L. dated, 12th October, 1810.

the embrace and was thus remiss in his courtesy towards the English representative, demanded an explanation from the Nizam through Chandulal. The Nizam at first tried to evade the issue by saying that it was not customary for the Nizam to embrace the Resident except on the occassion of important festivals like *Idd.* Khan Jehan Khan, one of the old courtiers of the Nizam who was present on the occassion, tried to substantiate the Nizam's stand by saying that it was never the custom for the Nizam to embrace the Resident and that the late Nizam Ali Khan used to shrink with evident distaste at the mere touch of a European. But now Chandulal being sure of the British support, pointed out, to the Nizam, that in the olden days the etiquette of embracing the Resident was scrupulously followed, and that it was discontinued by Sikandar Jah after the retirement of Sydenham. The Nizam admitted that it was so, saying that the offensive custom was introduced by Aristo Jah. Then he asked Chandulal in an exasperated manner if there was any treaty Article that bound the Nizam to embrace the Resident?

Ultimately finding that Russell was quite adamant on the issue he sent word through Chandulal saying that he would hereafter follow the custom of embracing the Resident when the latter came to visit him provided the Resident did not revive the topic.

But the Resident refused to accept the imposition of any conditions for his interview with the Nizam. He conveyed his feelings through Chandulal in the following manner[42]: "It was both irregular and improper for the Nizam to precribe any condition to the forms of intercourse between His Highness and the British Government.:.......I, therefore steadfastly resist it, as an innovation, subversive, of the friendly intercourse which had hitherto subsisted at the court and derogatory from the dignity of the representative character in which I had the honour to be placed. After telling Chandulal his real feelings in the above manner the Resident demanded an unqualified answer from the Nizam to the effect that he would embrace the Resident on every occasion he happend to visit the Durbar."

Before this determined attitude of the Resident, Sikandar Jah, ultimately gave way and agreed to observe the practice of embracing the Resident, whenever the latter visited him. But this latent struggle against the British power and its failure and the feeling of helplessnes told on the nerves of the Nizam. It produced on him a state of melancholy and he fell seriously ill. After the recovery of the illness he stopped taking interest in the details of administration[43].

Commenting about this Russell wrote: "His original defects of character, the habits of his life, his dislike of his own Ministers and his

42. Ibid., L. No. 1, dated. 27th, April, 1811, Vol. 44.
43. Ibid., L. No. 7, dated 31st October, 1811.
44. Memoirs and correspondence of General Fraser. P. 184.
45. Hyd. Residency correspondence Vol. 44 L. No. 7.

jealousy of our control have gradually withdrawn him into a sullen and total seclusion[44]." He also wrote[45]: :The Nizam's obstinate retirment from public business of every kind rather strengthens Chandulal's authority than otherwise. It compels everybody to look up to him alone for the adjustment of any business they have to transact and constitutes him in fact, though not in name, the sole and for ordinary purposes the absolute Minister of the Government. But the entire stop that has been put to every appearance of show in State and the Nizam's sullen seclusion of himself from all established forms and ceremonies is very offensive to the whole body of Omrahs and to all those persons who have any feeling of either pride or interest in the parade and splendour of the court."

With the retirement of Nawab Sikandar Jah from active administration of the State the British through the Resident exercised absolute power in the State. No doubt, Barton while speaking of the effects of the subsidiary alliance says: "The Subsidiary Alliance decreased the self-respect in the ruler and his nobility, due to the loss of the attributes of sovereignty. The British did nothing to set up a new moral anchorage. Naturally many of the chiefs began to feel the presence of the British Resident or political agent at their courts as an irksome restrait on their old freedom of action.[46]

Chandulal became a mere tool in the hands of the Resident. In order to maintain himself in power he did not scruple to sacrifice the economic welfare of the State by entering whole-heartedly into any scheme that was proposed by the British Resident.

About the year 1810, Chandulal received a messenger from Maharajah Ranjit Singh informing him that certain potentates in India like Doulat Rao Scindia, Jaswant Rao Holkar, the Rajah of Bharatpur and Amrut Rao were intending to form a confederacy in association with Ranjit Singh against the British. Ranjit Singh sought the frank opinion of Chandulal about the efficacy of such a confederacy and his frank opinion of the English. Instead of giving his opinion to Ranjit Singh, of the British as became a friend of the latter. Chandulal went to the extent of showing that letter to the Resident and asking him about the nature of reply he should give. [47] This incident reveals the abject manner in which Chandulal was prepared to serve the British.

Shortly after his taking charge of the Residency and after having settled the issue between the Nizam and Chandulal in favour of the latter, Henry Russell took up the reorganisation of the Nizam's forces.

46. Barton. Princes of India.
47. Hyderabad Residency correspondence. Vol. 35

CHAPTER VII

The Hyderabad Contingent and Palmer & Co.

As early as 1804, General Wellesly had drawn the attention of the British Resident at Hyderabad to the general inefficiency of the forces supplied by the Nizam in the late Maratha War of 1803 and of the necessity of reorganising them on an efficient basis. [48]

So the Resident at Hyderabad, in view of this communication from General Wellesley, submitted a scheme to the Nizam in 1804, which ensured regular payment to the troops by appropriating the entire revenues of the province of Berar towards the maintenance of ten thousand *Silladar* Horse. But Sikandar Jah, who was averse to the idea of British interference with his troops, rejected the scheme. The British also did not like the idea of the Nizam's army being commanded by Europeans other than the English. They knew that most of the European officers who were rendered jobless after the disbanding of the Raymonds corps, were re-employed by Mahipat Ram and were in charge of the Nizam's troops at Berar. The Resident wanted them to be replaced by English officers who were already in the Nizam's service, and he made Mir Alam agree to these reforms. It was also decided that in order to enable the English officers to exercise the necessary influence, a British detachment should be stationed near Berar. This time the Nizam agreed to introduce these measures[49]. So two Battalions of British Infantry were sent to Basim under the command of the Assistant Resident, Charles Russell in 1807. This was the period when Capt. Sydenham browbeat the Nizam into agreeing to keep Mir Alam as the Diwan and to send Mahipat Ram to Sagar. The Nizam's troops at Berar consisted of 11 battalions of 850 each and their maintenance cost him Rs. 15 lakhs per month. There was much to be desired regarding the discipline of the troops. The condition of the cavalry was still worse. On accountant of their inefficiency the countryside was a constant prey to freebooters and marauders like the Pindaris and the Bhils. Many of the zamindars also took advantage of the ineffectualness of the Nizam's army and carried on depredations in the countryside.

While things were in such a deplorable condition, Henry Russell, became the Resident in March 1811. Soon after his assumption of office, he drew the attention of the Bengal Government to the turbulence of the zamindars in the Nizam's dominions. In view of the fact that the subsidiary

48. Gurwood. Wellington's Despatches., pp. 346–48.
49. Burton. History of the Hyderabad Contingent., p. 23.

troops could not be used to quell the internal disturbances in the Dominions of the Nizam, he wanted to reorganise the Nizam's troops on a more efficient basis to put down the depredations of the zamindars.

Russell, suggested that in order to maintain the efficiency of the Nizam's corps, the number of British officers in them should be increased, their pay regulated, that they should be disciplined on the English model, and that the Nizam's should be made to purchase arms and ammunition for them, only from the British stores. Russell, did not like the idea of the Nizam's Chief Army officer in the pay of the English to be stationed at Berar, who would send him from time to time factual reports of the progress of the army[50]. He also wanted these newly organised forces to be under the general control and supervision of the British. Russell set about initiating the reforms by supplying arms and ammunition to two regiments of infantry that were newly raised by Rajah Govind Baksh and Maharaja Chandulal. These were placed under the command of Mr. Fraser and Mr. Becket respectively.

Commenting on this, Barton blandly remarks: "The Nizam's Government was not in a position to raise the crops unless the British intervened to assist him in raising them. They could only do so by straining Articles 12 of the Treaty of 1800............that was the logic of the Policy"[51].

The Nizam who by this time was not even allowed any option as to the continuance or removal of a Minister allowed the Resident to have his own way.

While these reforms were being introduced, two rebellions broke out in the Nizam's army, one in the Infantry regiments stationed near the Residency, who tied their Commander, Major Edward Gordon, to the muzzle of a gun and threatened to blow him to pieces unless their arrears of pay were cleared. Gordon was subsequently released and the ringleaders of the mutiny were executed.

Another muiny also broke out at Indur (Nizamabad).

It was felt that though the reason given by the mutineers for their rebellion was their growing despair at not receiving their arrears of pay, the real reason for the outbreak of the mutiny was the dislike of the people of Hyderabad for the Reforms that the Resident was contemplating to introduce in the Nizam's army. Evidently the people were averse to the idea of the Indian troops being officered by British officers who were responsible for the discipline of the corps not to the Nizam's Government, but to the British Resident.

However, the mutiny of the Nizam's troops in 1812 hastened the for-mation of a "Russell Brigade" that subsequently developed into the Hydera- bad Contingent.

---

50. Ibid., P. 53.
51. Burton, P, 170,

The mutiny of Gordon's detachment and of the mutiny of the detachment at Indur forced the hands of the Hyderabad Government in sanctioning the raising of two popular infantry battalions which were to be trained on the model of the Company's troops. After the mutiny of 1812, the Hyderabad Government could give no vaild reason for the postponing of reforms. The two battalions that were now raised were known by the name of the Russell Brigade and they were placed under the command of Mr. Becket and Mr. Larride respectively[52]. They subsequently constituted the 1st and 2nd Infantry division of the Hyderabad Contingent. Side by side with these the reorganisation of the army at Berar and that under Salabat Khan at Ellichpur was also undertaken, and thus six more battalions were reorganised under the new scheme.

In April 1814 Lieutenant Hare was appointed to the command of the Brigade at Hyderabad. The Court of Directors on hearing of this reorganisation of the troops belonging to Indian powers expressed their apprehensions, in the following manner[53]..............."We are led to apprehend more dangers from the extension of the European system of military discipline amongst the troops of the native powers than we can expect to derive from their services. To this superiority of European discipline is to be attributed the establishment of the British Empire in India, and in proportion as that discipline is extended amongst the natives not in our service; we must consider the powers we have acquired exposed to hazard."

However, in spite of the above apprehensions of the Court of Directors, the plan for the rapid reorganisation of the Nizam's army went on. It was taken up not only with regard to the Nizam's infantry but with regard to the cavalry also; and the Government of India finally gave its approval to the schemes on the 22nd February, 1816.

The general superintendence and direction of the troops was placed under the control of a Company's officer known as the Commandant who was to be assisted by five other Company's Officers, one of whom had to act as the Staff Officer of the Commandant[54].

Reporting the formation of the reorganised troops which became famous as the Hyderabad Contingent, Russell, wrote to Sir Thomas Hyslop Commander-in-Chief of the Madras army on the 14th June, 1817 in the following manner[55] "The two battalions at Hyderabad compose the Russel Brigade which is commanded by Captain Hare of the Company's army The enclosed return exhibits the strength and composition of this corps The men are chiefly Hindus; natives of the Company's territories in Hindustan. They are disciplined, clothed, armed and equipped in all respects like our own troops. They are paid regularly every month out of the Resident'

52. Burton, p. 28
53. Hyderabad Papers. Secret letter to Bengal dated 3rd April 1815., p. 1. 3.
54. Burton. 34.
55 Papers Relatives to certain Pecuniary Transactions of Messrs: William Palmer & Co., with the Govt. of H. H. the Nizam—Bengal. Pol. Consult. D-1-1-1820.

treasury. They do, no duty, in the city or with any other troops in the Nizam's service, nor have they any sort of communications with any branch of the Nizam's Government. In fact, they belong to the Nizam's army in name only ; they consider themselves as Company's troops and for all practical purposes they are as much so as those on our own immediate establishment."

In view of the apparent benefit to the India Government accruing from the formation of these corps, it was decided that British officers in charge of these corps should draw their salary from the Company's treasury but they were also given a monthly allowance from the Nizam's treasury.

Shortly after the formation of the Russell Brigade, these troops were called upon to put down the rebellion of the Nizam's son, Mubariz-ud-Dowla.[56]

The Nizam Sikandar Jah had three sons, namely, Nasir-ud-Dowla, Shams-ud-Dowla and Mubariz-ud-Dowla. Of these Mubariz-ud-Dowla was destined to play an important role in opposing the British interference in the internal affairs of the Nizam. Mubariz-ud-Dowla and Shams-ud-Dowla were further encouraged in their antipathy towards the English by their cousin, Imtiaz-ud-Dowla.

The Princes started openly defying the constituted Government by setting up an independent tribunal where they tried cases, punished people whom they regarded as culprits and also executed deeds of money. The Resident in vain, tried to keep a check on the actions of these princes.

At last things headed towards a crisis when a tailor belonging to the Residency was arrested at the order of the princes. A servant of Mubariz-ud-Dowla by name Sheereen had a quarrel with a tailor belonging to the Residency.[57] The tailor threatened the life of Sheereen, who sought asylum with Mubariz-ud-Dowla. Mubariz-ud-Dowla got the tailor arrested. Since the tailor belonged to the Residency Bazaar, Russell took an interest in the case and he made a complaint to the Nizam concerning the conduct of the princes. The Nizam empowered Chandulal and the Resident to take the necessary action against the princes.

So Russell, ordered Capt. Hare to proceed at the head of 700 men and two guns of the Russell Brigade and mount guard over the palace of the princes. Capt. Hare started on 20th August 1815;[58] and while he was half a mile from the house of the princes, their men who were concealed in the upper stories of the houses on either side of the streets, opened fire on the British troops. In spite of this, Capt. Hare proceeded with his men, blew open the gates of the house and even tried to set fire to the house, but the prince's men repulsed the English attack and compelled Hare to retreat.[59]

56. Burton. p. 31.
57. The Freedom struggle in Hyderabad. Vol. I p. 120.
58. Burton. p. 31.
59. Hyderabad Papers – Bengal Secret Consultations dated, 20th September, 1815.

Seeing this Russell sent Major Macdowell at the head of all the available British forces at Hyderabad.[60] This open fight between the English and the princes with the Nizam's troops on the side of the British created a great stir in the city. The people, the nobles and even the Nizam, were greatly alarmed; they feared the outbreak of an insurrection at any time and the likelihood of the city being destroyed by the English.

But Russell realised that the position of the English was rather weak and that the number of the British troops was insignificant (316 Europeans, 412 sepoys with some canon), compared to the armed population of the city consisting of the turbulent pathan elements near Chenchalguda. So he ordered Mr. Macdowell to withdraw and wrote for reinforcements to Bellary and Akola.

Chandulal, who was conscious of his own unpopularity on account of his popularity with the British, never dared to move out of his house during these eventful days. Nawab Sikandar Jah, who feared that the British might avenge the defeat of Capt. Hare and that it would deepen the crisis all the more, got his two sons Shams-ud-Dowla and Mubariz-ud-Dowla along with their cousin Imtiaz-ud-Dowla removed to his own palace on the 23rd August 1815.

Russell demanded that the princes should be confined in the fortress of Golconda and their adherents severely punished.

The Nizam was in the beginning reluctant to confine the princes in the fort of Golconda, and he informed the Resident that apart from his feelings as a father, the Begams, the Nizam's mother and his wife were in the way of his imprisoning the princes. But Russell, remained adamant, and so the Nizam had ultimately to give way. The Begams, by way of protest against the princes's confinement, accompanied the princes to the fort of Golconda. Ultimately, the princes were released in 1820. i. e. after a period of five years.[61]

The Hyderabad Contingent also participated in the Maratha War of 1818 and played a notable part in the suppression of the Pindaris and in the capture of Nagpur.[76] The cavalry of the Contingent played a considerable part in bringing about the surrender of Peishwa Baji Rao to the British. Among the crops of the Hyderabad Contingent the Russell Brigade distinguished itself for its discipline and effective action. It earned the thanks of the Commander-in-Chief especially for its discipline and gallantry.

After the conclusion of the third Maratha War in 1818, the British exempted the Nizam from the payment of *Chouth* to which they were now entitled as the successors of the Peishwa. The taluka of Vaizapur and Kannad that were taken from the Peishwa, and the taluka of Ellora and Aurangabad that were taken from the Holkar, were now added to the

60. Russell to Hastings L. No. 124, dated 23rd August 1815.
61. Palmer Papers - Extract - Bengal Secret Consultations dated 20th Sept. 1821.
62. Ibid., pp. 56, 57 and 59.

Nizam's Dominions, One of the direct results of the Maratha War of 1818 as far as it concerned the Nizam was that it freed him perpetually from the domination of the Marathas, In spite of this, rebellions by the local zamindars continued to occur in different parts of the State and the Contingent from the year 1818 to 1826 was employed in putting down these local rebellions. As a result of this the State was greatly impoverished and cultivators unable to bear the burden of the taxation, fled to the nearby jungles.

In the meanwhile expenditure on the Contingent was rapidly increasing. Realising the potential usefulness of the Contingent, which for all practical purposes was attached more to the British than to the Nizam, the British wanted to expand it. As a result of this the expenditure that was incurred on the maintenance of the Contingent became exorbitantly high, This was too much for the already tottering finances of the State, The staff consisting of the British officers in the Contingent was overpaid, The commander received a salary £5000 while the salaries of the other officers under him were also proportionately high,

On account of the high salaries, people vied with one another to get employment in the Contingent forces, and they pressed the Resident, with their applications, very often the applicant in order to get this coveted job resorted to underhand means such as bribing the officers concerned, The joke "Nizzy pays for all" became a current phrase during this period.[63]

The finances of the State during this period were disorganised. The Government was always forestalling the revenues, and in order to raise finances somehow or other, they resorted to oppressive taxation, Instead of assessing the actual yield of the land and fixing the taxes in a proportionate manner, Chandulal, just fixed the sums he needed from a particular area in an arbitrary manner, and rented the land to the highest bidder,

These bidders were given the power of life and death and the poor farmer was not empowered to appeal against their decision, This was not all, Once, the crops were harvested and ready, the collectors just took whatever they wanted, ignoring the settlement deeds, This gave rise to the saying that "the farmers in Hyderabad after concluding a settlement with the Government returned to their fields looking backward over their shoulders to see if their successors were already following them."[64] On account of this deplorable state of affairs, there was depopulation and the cost of living was very high, nearing famine prices, This led to disturbances and turbulence throughout the country and the Contingent troops whose maintenanee was partly responsible for the general misery were used to put down these local rebellions,

Russell justified the action of the Hyderabad Government and his own attitude in the following manner,[65] "Exaction is the necessary vice of every

63. Kaye. "Life of Lord Metcalfe". Vol. II. p. 16.
64. Thomson. Life of Charles Lord Metchalfe. p. 190.
65. Ibid. pp. 190, 191.

Government which derives its principal revenue from the direct rent of land, It seems to be universally acknowledged that the assessment is too high in every country in India, the Government demands too much from the fear of receiving too little - - - - Even our own Government with a system the most elaborate and expansive, has hitherto been unable to afford adequate security to the inferior classes of its subjects, Every Indian Government subsists upon its immediate means, it is always from hand to mouth", While justifying the Hyderabad Government's actions in the above manner he tried to justifying himself saying "In some degree the weakness and disorders of the Nizam's Government are the necessary consequence of his political situation, An alliance with us upon the subsidiary system, however it may contribute to the advancement of our own power, leads inevitably to the ultimate destructiun of the State which embraces it - - - - - - . The Nizam is dying comatose while the Peishwa has expired in convulsions, but the destiny of both originated in the same cause, and necessarily tended to the same termination, If we owe the foundation of our empire in the country to the weakness in which we found the native powers, we ought not to complain of the evils which that weakness necessarily produces, If we have reaped the benefits we must submit to witness the inconveniences which are its inseparable attendants."[66]

But even the phlegmatic Russell, realised that it was impossible for the tottering finances of the Hyderabad State to support the payment of the salaries of the Contingent officers and soldiers. So he devised a new method by which the Contingent forces could be paid regularly, He came to an understanding with the commercial Firm of William Palmer & Co,, and the Firm of Palmer & Co, was made responsible for the payment of the salaries of the Contingent forces,

From the day Russell made Chandulal enter into an agreement with Palmer & Co,, for the payment of the Contingent Troops, the Firm of Palmer's came into prominence. The sinister influence wielded by the Commercial House was coveted and feared by one and all, People identified it with the British Government, and it loomed large in the political horizon of Hyderabad State till at last nemesis overtook it in the shape of the Resident, Sir Charles Metcalfe, and the Firm collapsed like a house of cards.

The rise and fall of this commercial firm is a matter of interesting study against the background of the 19th century politics in Hyderabad.

The founder of the Company was one William Palmer, son of General Palmer by his Indian wife.[67] William Palmer started his early career in the military service of the Nizam in 1799, He was the first British subject to have entered the Nizam's service and he rose to the rank of a Brigadier, He seems to have retired from the Nizam's service about the year 1812, in pre-

66. Remarks on the volume of Hyderabad Papers.
Russell to Hastings. Dated 24th Nov. 1819.

67. Burton. p. 22.

ference to a commercial career in Hyderabad. From that time onwards the firm carried on various commercial transactions in the Nizam's Dominions.

It first drew the attention of the British Government when it applied on the 30th March 1814, to the Governor-General in Council for permission to open a banking agency in the State of Hyderabad, and also to exploit the timber yields on the banks of the Godavary for building ships.[68] The application was duly forwarded by the Resident, Henry Russell. The Governor-General and Council finding no legitimate grounds for objection, permitted the Resident, to allow the House to open a banking house.

At this time the firm was apparently constituted by the following members: William Palmer, Hastings Palmer, William Currie the Residency Surgeon, and Bankati Das a Hindu millioniare, and Samuel Russell.[69] The last mentioned person was a friend of the Resident, Henry Russell, to whom the latter had entrusted his money to invest in business. Samuel Russell without any hesitation invested the Resident's money in the House of Palmer. But the actual membership of the house consisted apart from the above-mentioned persons, of the Resident Russell, his brother Charles Russell, Russell the Engineer, Southby, the Assistant Resident and one George Lamb an Englishman. The membership of the Residency officials was kept a close secret which was unearthed only towards the end by Metcalfe, the successor of Henry Russell.[70] Thus the Resident Russell when he forwarded the application of the firm to open a banking agency in Hyderabad was an interested party; when subsequently charged with this he denied his knowledge of his money being invested by Samuel Russell, in the firm of Palmer and Company, but we have the irrefutable evidence of John Palmer of Calcutta, the elder brother of William Palmer, who admitted to Fendall, one of the members of the Governor-General's Council, that Russell lent his money through the frm to the Nizam at 48% interest.[71]

Thus, the firm of Palmer & Co. stepped on the ladder of commercial prosperity under the patronage of the Resident, who was supposed to be interested in promoting the welfare of the Nizam, the ally of the British.

The opening of this Commercial House at Hyderabad marked the beginning of the economic exploitation of the State. The patronage of the Resident sheltered it from all danger. Its offices were located within the precincts of the Residency building which added to its prestige. Russell used his influence to procure for the firm customers and funds from private sources.

The firm used to borrow money at 12% and lend it at 25%.

---

68. Palmer Papers. p. 3.
69. Ibid. p. 70. para 5.
70. Ibid. pp. 732, 734 and 736.
71. Hyderabad Residency Correspondence – Vol. 173.
    L. B. Adam to Metcalfe dated 3rd June 1822.
    Palmer Papers. pp. 30, 31.

Finding the Company growing in prosperity day by day, many of the European servants belonging to the Company, hastened to invest their funds in the firm.

Finding that the Resident was obviously interested in promoting the interests of the firm, many of the nobles in Hyderabad including the Minister Chandulal, coveted the friendship of the firm.

At this juncture Russell, perhaps finding that the location of the firm within the precincts of the Residency, could not be reconciled with his position as a public official, asked the firm to remove its offices from the Residency.[72] He also withdrew his membership from the House. This action of the Resident gave rise to the apprehension that the firm might lose the prestige which it commanded hitherto. At this critical juncture in April 1815, William Palmer by a shrewd stroke of diplomacy brought into the firm, a new member in the person of Sir William Rumbold. Commenting on this, Metcalfe, wrote to his friend Adams, a member of the Governor-General's Council in the following manner;[73] "It was then a masterly stroke of policy on the part of W. Palmer to bring in Sir William Rumbold which gave an accession of influence superior to that of the Resident, an influence of which the Resident himself was a fraud, courting it at the same time and to which Minister knew no bounds of subservience and sacrifice. From that time the affairs of the firm have gone on more swimmeringly till it has reached a point of undue influence and profit never I suppose before heard of in any mercantile concern."

The power and influence wielded by the Company was so great that Metcalfe wrote: "They have contrived also to identify themselves with the British name and when I am in districts the pillage of which goes to their shop, people always talk as if our Government were a party concerned. Their chaprasis range the country with the double power of the Nizam's and the British Government and one source of their profit is the buying up at a heavy discount of debts which the rent creditors cannot collect, but which they can by the means of these authoritative messengers."[74]

Sir Willim Rumbold, was an unscrupulous adventurer, who accompanied the Governor-General, Lord Hastings to India in 1813, with a view to acquiring riches. The Governor-General, Lord Hastings, evinced a greate interest in promoting the welfare of Sir William Rumbold, as he had married one of his wards for whom he had a deep affection.[75]

Ever since his arrival in India, Rumbold was exploring various avenues for becoming rich. Ultimately his choice fell on Hyderabad and

---

72. Palmer Papers. pp. 30, 31.
    Hyderabad Residency Correspondence, Vol. 173.
    L. B. Adam to Metcalfe dated 3rd June 1822.
73. Palmer Papers. pp. 732–734.
74. Ibid.
75. Ibid.

he became interested in Palmers'. Finding in the Company a congenial means to realise his ambition he duly informed the Governor-General of his intention to become a partner in the firm of the Palmer & Co., and obtained the Governor-General's consent.[76]

The accession of Sir William Rumbold increased the prestige of the firm immensely and its affairs went on more "swimmeringly" in the words of Metcalfe. The belief among the general public was that Rumbold was the son-in-law of the Governor-General, Lord Hastings. Even the Resident Henry Russell harboured this opinion, and he now began to exert himself assiduously to gain the goodwill of Palmer & Co., and of Sir William Rumbold in particular.

Palmer & Co., knew that the inclusion of Europeans as binding partners in a commercial concern carrying on trade with a Native State was illegal. Hence it felt the necessity to obtain the necessary exemption form that rule from Lord Hastings. Russell who was anxious to win the favour and good opinion of the Governor-General by serving Rumbold through the firm came forward at this juncture with the suggestion that Palmer & Co., should advance money to the Nizam's Government towards the regular payment of the Contingent forces.

The Palmers had already applied on the 30th March 1814, and also obtained permission from the Governor-General to obtain a banking agency in Hyderabad and to exploit the timber yields on the banks of the Godavary.[77]

Now, on the 27th March, 1816, after Rumbold joined them, Palmer & Co., once again applied to the Supreme Government to allow them to lend money to the Nizam's Government and thus alleviate the distress of the latter. While forwarding this application they also took the precaution of asking in advance for exemption from the provisions of the Parliamentary Act that prohibited British subjects to advance money to the Native Princes.

Russell, while forwarding the application of the Company wrote to the Governor-General urging him to grant the necessary sanction so that the Contingent could be placed on an efficient footing in view of the impending war against the Marathas.

On first hearing of the decision of William Rumbold to join the Firm of Palmer & Co., the Governor-General wrote to him assuring him of his approval and support to the Palmers, in preference to any other British firm. He wrote to Rumbold. "The partners speculate, that you being one of the firm will interest me in the welfare of the house, to a degree which may be materially beneficial to them. It is a fair and honest calculation - - - - perhaps a more distinct benefit may attend the firm from the consequent discouragement to competition with you, by another British partnership to

76. Ibid.
77. Burton. p. 22.

which a similarly professed sanction would not be granted. It is on the ground of the service to the Nizam, at the request of our Resident, that I have consented to let the good wishes of Government for the prosperity of this firm be signified. No new establishment would have such a plea[78]."

As the Governor-General was already inclined favourably, towards the Palmers as the above letter reveals, it was not difficult for the Palmers to obtain the necessary sanction. Nevertheless, the Supreme Government took the precaution of asking Russell, if their approval would indirectly imply the giving of any guarantee on the part of the British Government, on behalf of the Nizam's Government for the regular payment of the loan received by the latter from Palmer & Co.[79] On Russell, assuring the Supreme Government that no such guarantee was involved on the part of the British Government, the Governor-General in Council gave the necessary sanction. The Supreme Goverment, after consulting the opinion of the Advocate-General, Mr. Strettell also exempted Palmer & Co. from the restrictions imposed on the trade of the British Subjects by the Parliamentary Act of 1797, 37th Geo. 3. Section 28[80]. The Supreme Government also gave their permission to Palmer & Co. to advance money to the Nizam's Government at more than 12 per cent.

Russell, while informing the Palmers that they should not expect any guarantee from the British Government, for the loans they advanced to the Nizam's Government, assured them at the same time saying; "I consider you to have entered into it under the assurance of receiving from the Resident that support which is essentially necessary to the security of your transaction[81].

Raja Govind Baksh on first hearing of this new arrangement with the Palmers, objected to it saying that there was no necessity for the firm to supply money for the payment of the troops as he was in a position to pay them regularly. As a matter of fact the real reason for Govind Baksh objecting to the new arrangement was that he feared that it would lessen his own influence and that the Firm might build up an undue influence in the State. The Firm, on hearing of the Rajah's objection, offered to withdraw, Russell broached this subject with Chandulal. The latter who knew that not only the Resident but even the Governor-General was now interested in the Company, naturally did not like to take the risk of incurring the displeasure of the British by saying "No" to such an arrangement. On the other hand he was anxious to entrench his position more securely as the *de facto* Diwan by heartily co-operating with the Resident and falling in line with his policy and by implementing all the measures proposed by him. So Maharaja Chandulal in a very enthusiastic manner informed the Resident that he was highly satisfied with the new arrangements made with Palmer & Co. He told

78. Hastings to Rumbold. Dated. 4th January 1815. Palmer-Papers.
79. Palmer Papers. p. 2.
80. Ibid. pp. 5, 6.
81. Ibid. p. 13. Russell to William Palmer & Co., dated 22nd April 1819.

the Resident "that an efficient system having at length with a great deal of difficulty been completed, he was unwilling to forego any part of it[82] - - - - -.

The firm after obtaining this permission, agreed to advance two lakhs per mensem, stipulating that the Nizam's Government should assign to it the revenue of certain districts in Berar[83]. The districts assigned to Palmer & Co., yielded 30 lakhs annually, i. e., six lakhs more than what the Palmers gave to the Nizam.

This was done with a view to covering any contingency that might arise "such as defects in revenues to cover interests and to give facility to the establishment to make the required monthly payments." Thus the actual interest levied by the firm on the loans it advanced to the Nizam's Government amounted to 25 per cent. The firm, in order to facilitate regular payment to the troops, opened a Banking House at Aurangabad also.[84]

It can be said without any hesitation that from this time onwards the "virtual plunder of the Nizam began." The phrase that "Nizzy pays for all" became a current saying in all the dominions of the Company.

Chandulal, for all practicable purposes was a creature of the British. He was the instrument through which the British hoped to mould the internal and the external policy of the State to promote their own interests. Commenting on him Lord Hastings wrote; "Chandoo Loll has reposed his existence wholly on our good faith. I lay it down as the basis of every procedure, that we must act up inviolably to the pledges either specific or implied, which have induced him to promote our views at the risk of his own fortunes. He must be at all events upheld - - - - -. This invariable attention to the interests of Chandoo Loll (to which we are in honour bound) and the maintenance of the reformed troops are essential for us.[85]

While the British Government was prepared to uphold Chandulal at any cost, the latter was also equally anxious to remain in their good books. Chandulal's supreme passion in life was to hold power and in order to maintain himself in power he did not hesitate to sacrifice the welfare of his country and people.

Knowing the Governor-General's predilection towards the Palmers he assiduously cultivated their friendship. He gave regular pensions to the members of the Palmer family from the State treasury. These pensions amounted to nearly Rs. 80,000/- per month.[86]

Later, when this was discovered by the Resident Metcalfe, William Palmer tried to explain the cause of his receiving pension from the Nizam's

82. Ibid. p. 21 (Extract) Bengal Political Consultation 12th Dec. 1819. Russell to Bengal Govt., 15th October 1819.
83. Ibid., pp.12, 16
84. Ibid.
85. Kaye's Life of Lord Metcalfe. Vol. II p 85
Hastings to Russell. Dated 26-10-1819
86. Thomson's Metcalfe, pp. 214, 215.

Government by giving the specious reason that Chandulal was greatly pleased at William Plamer's efforts to bring about the "Russell Reforms" and that he wanted to reward "William Palmer the benefactor of the State" in an appropriate manner. On Chandulal asking William Palmer how he could manifest the gratitude of the Nizam's Government, towards William Palmer, the latter suggested that the education of his two sons might be financed by the Nizam's Government.

But this specious argument put forward by William Palmer deceived no body in view of the facts discovered about the dealings of Palmer & Co. with the Minister. It was discovered that apart from paying monthly pensions of Rs. 1,200/- to each of the two sons of Williams Palmer who were studying in England, Chandulal also paid a monthly pension of Rs. 1,000/- to Hastings Palmer, the brother of William, while William Palmer himself, received a monthly gratuity of Rs. 2,000/-.[87]

Thus the pensions paid to the Palmers was nothing but gross bribery on the part of the Minister to gain their good-will.

This was not the only method by which Chandulal sought to gain the good-will and support of the all-powerful British. In order to win the favour of the Residency officials he granted them clandestine allowances. The expenses for the maintenance and upkeep of the Residency building which according to Metcalfe was a "shameful monument of rapacity, built and furnished by the poverty-stricken State", were borne by the Minister. The expenses incurred for the maintenance of building came to nearly Rs. 2,000/- per month.

Apart from this the Residency officials were always kept in good humour by the Minister who sent them "*dallies*" of fruits, dinners etc., which made Metcalfe, the successor of Russell, remark that they "came in such quantities as to give them the appearance of regular supplies, instead of being merely complimentary."[88]

This ignoble conduct of the Minister, coupled with the unscrupulousness of the Residency officials, drove the country to the verge of total ruin.

The Palmers managed to take the entire financial resources of the country into their vicious grip. The firm began to grow like a grangrene. Its powers increased to such an extent that it could employ armed troops to storm the villages for extorting taxes from the poor inhabitants. From a mere banking agency it rose to the position of receiving commissions, and acted as an agency to collect any one's debts. On account of the prestige and power commanded by the Company, the Palmers were regarded as identical with the British Government; where even the Nizam's Government failed to collect the revenues the firm very often succeeded in extracting

87. Palmer Papers. p. 132.
88. Palmer Papers. p. 132.

them out of the poor peasentry. People thought that it wielded more power than the Resident or the Nizam or even the Governor-General himself.

The firm gradually appropriated for itself the role of being the sole commission agency in the State, and no Native Firm was allowed to have direct relations with the Nizam's Government.[89]

The Firm could lay its hands on the entire revenues of the State, the inevitable result of this was that the country groancd under oppressive taxation. The oppressive methods adopted by Palmer & Co., to wring out payment from the debtors, made the people flee to the neighbouring jungles, thus making entire villages depopulated. Malcolm, while depicting the condition of the peasantry during this period, describes them as "broken and oppressed,[90]" while Thomson the biographer of Metcalfe, categorically remarks that "their condition was a pestilence which could not be altogether isolated and restiveness spread to contiguous regions." While the desolation of the State was going on the Supreme Government in Bengal remained blissfully ignorant of the doings of Palmer and Company.

Meanwhile, the firm feeling that it would be safer to obtain the Supreme Government's guarantee for their various monetary transactions in the State, induced Chandulal to obtain the permission of the Supreme Government for taking a fresh loan of sixty lakhs of rupees annually.

Chandulal applied in 1819 to the Supreme Government, to allow him to borrow 60 lakhs from the Palmers so that he might clear "certain debts, advance *taccavi* loans to cultivators". He also affirmed that he would improve the administration by curtailing unnecessary expenditure to the extent of 25 lakhs of rupees annually.

This request of Chandulal was duly forwarded to the Supreme Government by Russell, along with his own proposals for effecting further reforms in the Contingent troops. This new proposal of Chandulal to borrow a further sum of Rs. 60 lakhs from the Palmers created a stir in the Governor-General's Council. Some of the members of the Council had already heard rumours about the Palmer transactions. So this fresh application for a loan from the Palmers created grave apprehensions in their minds. So these members headed by James Stuart, demanded that a detailed account of the Palmer transactions with the Nizam's Government should be placed before them. These members also insisted that once again the Supreme Government should seek the opinion of the Accountant-General on the validity of the Palmer transactions.

The Governor-General, Lord Hastings, acceded to the wishes of his Council and the Political Secretary Lord Metcalfe, was asked on the 14th September, 1819, to demand from the Palmers a detailed account of their various transactions with the Nizam's Government.

89. Palmer Papers – p. 28 (Extract) Bengal Pol. Consultations dated. 1st January 1820. Suart's Minute.

90. Thomson – Metcalfe. p. 195.

But Palmer & Co., who corresponded with the Governor-General's Council through Rumbold, replied to this demand of the Supreme Government saying that for the firm to reveal the accounts of its constituents would be inconsistent with the confidence reposed in them by their customers.[91] So the Resident and the Palmers appealed to the Governor-General to relieve them "from the painful state of anxiety in which we are now placed".[92]

Lord Hastings sympathised with the position taken by Sir William Rumbold and his colleagues, but the Council differed from the Governor General. It declared "that in demanding information respecting a particular measure, sanctioned by the Resident and submitted by him to the notice of the Government the Supreme Government was in no way asking the Palmers to infringe on the confidence placed in them by their constituents."

Commenting in a sarcastic manner about the scruples of the Palmers in this respect, James Stuart declared:[93] "The circumstances, that at a capital like Hyderabad, native bankers cannot be found possessing adequate funds to make an advance to the Government of two lakhs of rupees monthly, secured upon the growing revenue of the country, and the consequent utter dependance of the Resident and the Nizam's Government for the payment of the troops upon the only British house of agency established in the country is in itself sufficiently extraordinary and alarming - - - - We are quite at a loss to conceive in what manner the production of figured statements, comprising particulars of a pecuniary arrangement concluded with the Nizam's minister, under the sanction of the Resident, for the public service of the Nizam's Government, could be thought to involve a disclosure of the affairs of the constituents of the house and a breach of private confidence. We had not imagined that, in speaking of their constituents, Sir William Rumbold could possibly have alluded to the Nizam's Government - - - - Sir William Rumbold has, in his letter, dwelt with some emphasis upon the willingness of the house to disclose to the Resident any part of their transactions with the Minister. The faith due to the constituents then, was no impediment to any disclosures to the Resident. It is to be opposed only to the demand of this Government for information."

Thereupon, Rumbold with the active support of the Governor-General personally attended the Council meeting and tried to convince them of the bona-fides of Palmer & Co. All the members except James Stuart expressed their satisfaction. Stuart, protesting against the attitude adopted by the Governor-General, snggested that the Supreme Government should advance money to the Nizam's Government from its own treasury.

---

91. Palmer Papers. p. 26.
92. Thomson. Metcalfe. p. 195.
93. Palmer Papers (Extract) Bengal Pol. Consultations Stuart's Minute dated. 9th November 1819

Stuart, pointed out that it was hardly justifiable on the part of the British to make the Nizam pay for the Contingent troops which for all practical purposes belonged more to the British than to the Nizam. To this Lord Hastings replied saying; "It is perfectly true that these troops are in fact more ours than those of the sovereign by whom they are maintained ---- Now would it be consonant with wisdom, and to the trust reposed in us by the Honourable Company that we should sacrifice such a security to a casuistical point of equity?"[94]

Adams, another member of the Council, also supported Stuart's resolution for granting a loan from the British Government's Treasury. He declared: "I have been struck by a passage in Mr. Russell's letter, viz., that the Minister cannot obtain the requisite funds by any other means than the assistance of Messrs. William Palmer & Co., whose circumstances enable them to secure a combination of the native monied interests. If this be so, I am so far from considering it as a motive for giving the additional strength to such an influence which it would derive from the proposed loan, that it seems to me to form a powerful reason for abstaining from any measure calculated to confirm a monopoly from which no good can result either to the Nizam's Government or the commercial interests of the country."[95]

The Accountant-General, Sherer, on being asked to give his opinion on the Palmer dealings declared them to be dubious.

The Governor-General did not relish this attitude of his Council and he declared that "to implicitly refer to the Accountant-General as a political oracle would be rather an extravagant abandonment of our judgement and our duties.[96]" After contemptuously demolishing the opinion of the Accountant-General in the above manner, he also turned down the proposal of his Council for advancing a loan to the Nizam's Government from the State treasury declaring it to be illegal and tantamount to interference in the internal administration of the Nizam.

Then Hastings, decided to grant the necessary permission to Chandulal to take the loan of sixty lakhs from the Palmers and the Resident was duly informed of the Governor-General's decision.[97]

Hastings at this Juncture also came out with the novel suggestion that the Nizam should be asked to contribute at least four lakhs annually for a period of four months towards the construction of a cathedral at Calcutta,[98] as a token of his gratitude for having exempted him from the payment of Chouth which he had been paying to the Marathas. As an

94. Ibid. pp. 31. 32. Governor-General's Minute dated. 10th Nov., 1819.
95. Ibid. pp. 55. Adams - 1st minute, dated. 16th June. 1820.
96. Ibid. p. 35. Governor-General's minute dated. 10th Nov. 1819.
97. Ibid. p. 55. Metcalfe to Russell. Dated. 15th July 1820.
98. Thomson's Metcalfe. p. 200.

inducement, the Resident was asked to hint to the Nizam that a royal title would be conferred on him if he so desired.[99]

But the Council could not reconcile itself with the stand taken by the Governor-General and it decided to put the issue to vote. Hastings at first assumed the role of an offended dignity and refused to take part in the voting lest he should be regarded as an interested party.[100]

Staurt, in the meanwhile demanded clarification about the rate of interest at which the Palmers were allowed to advance loans to the Nizam's Government. He was also able to win over to his point of view the remaining members of the Executive Council like Adams etc. All these members now demanded to know whether the said loan could not be either advanced from the British treasury or floated elsewhere at a lower rate of interest.[101]

The Governor-General, though at first had signified his unwillingness to participate in the voting on this issue, now decided to participate in the voting, realising that his abstention might result in the vetoing of the loan. He now not only participated in the voting but even exercised his casting vote in favour of the Palmers. This resulted in the Supreme Government permitting the Palmers to advance the loan of 60 lakhs to the Nizam's Government in six yearly instalments at the rate of 18 per cent.[102]

In the meanwhile, the Court of Directors having been informed about the entire Palmer transactions, strongly criticised the Supreme Government for having granted the licence to Palmer & Co. to establish monetary dealings with the Nizam's Government.[103] They wrote to the Governor-General in the following manner:[104] "We can by no means approve of the indulgence which you have extended to Messrs. Palmer and Co., and we positively direct that the instrument by which that indulgence was conveyed, may be, immediately upon the receipt of this despatch, revoked and cancelled - - - - -. If any discussion shall at any time arise between the Nizam's Government and the House of Messrs. Palmer & Co., respecting any pecuniary transactions which may have taken place between them, you are hereby positively prohibited from inter-posing, in any way whatever, the name, the authority, influence, or good offices of any sort of the British Government, for the furtherance of any demand which these gentlemen may bring forward."

Declaring that the original sanction given to Palmer and Co., was illegal, the Court of Directors in their letter dated 28th November 1821

99. Palmer Papers – Bengal Secret Pol. Consultations —Metcalfe to Russell dated. 22nd January 1820
100. Palmer Papers. pp. 50–51. Minute of the Governor-General dated. 16th June 1820.
101. Ibid. Stuart's minute.
102. Palmer Papers. p. 55.
103. Ibid. p. 6. para 10 12.
104. Ibid.

commenting on the membership of Rumbold and George Lamb said:[105] "There cannot surely be a doubt (at least there is none on our minds) whether an enactment of the legislature can be set aside by a deed of partnership. If a native of India voluntarily limits his rights by associating himself in trade with British European subjects, he has no ground either in law or equity to complain of a limitation which is the result of his own choice."

The Court of Directors further questioned the actions of the Governor-General in the following manner:[106] "The arrangement for the payment of the troops in Berar did not take place until near the end of April 1818; it could not therefore materially conduce to the success of the war, which was then drawing to a close, but whatever may have been its influence upon the fate of the war, it was clearly contrary to the spirit of your instructions to continue it after the war was over - - - - from circumstances to which we shall here- after advert, we are but imperfectly informed of the particulars of the arrangement entered into with Messrs: Palmer & Co., and which in consideration of stipulated monthly advance on the part of the house, of two lacs of rupees, for the payment of the troops in Berar, it obtained assignments of revenues to the extent of thirty lacs per annum. Yet enough is disclosed to satisfy us, that the terms of the convention were the very reverse of moderate. No person can read the agreement without seeing that the stipulation was highly favourable to the lenders and of course proportionately unfavourable to the borrower. In truth, you have in substance, if not in form lent the Company's credit in the late pecuniary transactions at Hyderabad not indeed for the benefit of the Nizam's Government but for the sole benefit of Messrs. Palmer & Co." The Court of Directors also disapproved of the tendency on the part of the Palmer & Co. to monopolise all the economic resources of the Seate.

After receiving such a strongly worded letter from the Court of Directors, Load Hastings had no other choice than to readjust his policy towards the Palmers. But the Governor-General and Council realised that if they were to withdraw the licence that had been already granted to the Palmers, according to the latest instructions of the Court of Directors it would result in the total ruin of the Company, and would be a bad reflection on the Government of India's good faith. So Lord Hastings and his Council decided to forbid Palmer & Co. henceforth, to have any financial dealings with the Nizam's Governmen [107].

[108]Though the Nizam had conveyed his apparent willingness to contribute money towards the building of a cathadral at Calcutta, the Court of Directors also forbade Lord Hastings to levy any contribution from the Nizam for the benefit of "British spirituality".

105. Ibid. pp. 70, 71, 72. Pol. letters to Bengal (Secret).
106. Ibid. pp. 32, 36, 40.
107. Pamler Papers Bengal. Pol. Consultations, dated. 16th Dec. 1820. para 2. p. 70.
108. Ibid. Secret letter to Bengal, dated. 5th Dec. 1820. p. 103.

Lord Metcalfe, in the meanwhile, succeeded Henry Russell, as the Resident of Hyderabad in December 1820. Metcalfe, on his arrival found the finances of the State at the lowest ebb. He also saw that the people unable to bear the oppressive taxes were fleeing enmasse to Nagpur across the Wardha border.

Realising the urgent necessity of reorganising the finances of the State, Metcalfe asked Chandulal to furnish him with a complete statement of the State's finances. On a careful scrutiny of the accounts submitted, Metcalfe, discovered that many of the evils that prevailed in the State could be traced to the hold of the Palmers on the country. He realised that the only way of relieving the oppression of the people was by rescuing the country from the clutches of the Palmers. Hence, Metcalfe suggested to the Supreme Government that it should raise a loan at Calcutta at 6% interest for the Nizam under British guarantee, so that the Nizam's Government might pay off its debts to Palmer and Company.

Metcalfe also undertook a tour of the country. He saw to it that nearly 300 villages were repopulated, and appointed European Superintendents and settlement officers to protect the collectors. He also made it clear that if there were any complaints, the Resident would hear them and try to redress them.[109]

The Palmers and the Peishkar Chandulal found these various proposals of the Resident acutely disagreeable. They decided to foil the attempts of Metcalfe. So they represented to the Governor-General through Rumbold, that the Resident was bent upon ruining them.

Hastings, at once hastened to the help of the Palmers by writing to Metcalfe in a warning tone, saying : "Any ill will on your part towards the House of William Palmer & Co. must necessarily be an idle imagination." He also made it plain to Metcalfe that the latter should change his attitude towards Chandulal. The Governor-General wrote : "I must thence not let a day slip in observing to you, that I am personally pledged to the support of that individual.[110]"

The Governor-General, also turned down the proposal of Metcalfe, for raising a loan at Calcutta under the British guarantee, saying that such a loan together with the reforms recently introduced by Metcalfe, would amount to blatant interference on the part of the British in the internal administration of the Nizam, thus openly curtailing his internal sovereignty.

The Governor-General felt that "the placing of the Resident at the head of a body of creditors of the Government wholly dependent on him for protection would be to furnish him with an instrument of oppression - - - - Mr. Metcalfe has in effect, taken upon himself the whole Government of the country, not by secretly working on the devotion of the Minister but by a

109. Thomson. Metcalfe. p. 205.

110. Idid. Hastings Metcalf 4. dated. 27th, August 1821. p. 205.

direct and avowed superintendence of the territorial settlements - - - - system of sway over the concern of an ally, is so irreconcilable to the maxims reiterated, impressed upon us by the Honourable Court - - - - that I must see with jealousy anything which tends to prop its silent operations, after we shall have professedly retired from the interference.[111]"

Such was the hold that the Palmers had on the Governor-General. Metcalfe, at once hastened to assure the Governor-General that the Palmers had nothing to fear from him and that on the other hand he had every reason to be afraid of them. He didnot hesitate to write plainly to the Governor-General: "I lament the connexion between them and Rajah Chandulal, because it tends to draw them quite out of their sphere of merchants and makes them political partisans - - - I lament the monopoly established in their favour by the sanction and virtual guarantee of the British Government because it deprives the Nizam's Government of the power of going into the European money market, where with the same sanction it might borrow money at less than half the rate of interest which it pays to Messrs. Palmer & Co."[112]

During the course of these recriminations, Metcalfe, discovered that the loan of sixty lakhs advanced by the Palmers to the Nizam's Government was nothing but a fiction. Instead of levying 18 percent interest according to the Supreme Government's instructions, the firm levied its usual rate of 24 percent interest; but what was more alarming was that 9/10 of the so-called loan of 60 lakhs was actually made up by the transference of an already existing debt of 40 lakhs, and by further reducing the burden of the new loan amount by another 14 lakhs in the shape of fictitious bonuses.

Seeing all this, Metcalfe began to entertain suspicions about the Residency officials. The Palmers would not take things lying down. Taking advantage of the Resident's temporary absence from the capital they drew up an affidavit saying that no public functionary was connected with the firm. This affidavit was solemnly affirmed in the presence of Sotheby, the Assistant Resident, and duly forwarded to the Supreme Government.[113] William Palmer, sensing trouble from the attitude of the Governor-General's Council when the 60 lakhs loan was proposed, had asked Sotheby, to withdraw from the firm. So now, the firm with consummate skill played the part of a much abused martyr, the victim of Metcalfe's unfounded suspicions

After seeing the affidavit, the faith of Lord Hastings, in the bona-fides of Palmer & Co. increased all the more, and he got the affidavit recorded in the proceedings of the Council.

Taking advantage of this, Palmer & Co. started working against Metcalfe, through Maharajah Chandulal who, seeing that the Governor General's sympathies were with the firm, and believing that the firm's

111. Palmer Papers p. 115, 116. Hastings Case-20th October, 2822.
112. Thomson. Metcalfe. p. 223.
113. Palmer Papers. P. 132. Thomas Metcalfe. p. 214

support was essential for his remaining in office, duly sent reports against Metcalfe. Due to these machinations of Palmer & Co., the Governor-General was highly incensed against the Resident and even talked of recalling him.[114]

Metcalfe protested against the unconstitutional methods of the Governor-General in receiving reports against the Resident through the channel of a private firm. In this he was supported by the members of the Governor-General's Council, Adam, Fendall and Bayley. So the Governor-General had to discontinue this practice.[115]

On Metcalfe charging Chandulal, of having worked against him, the latter abjectly apologised to Metcalfe and told him that he was coerced by the Palmers to do so, on the threat that they would require him to pay five lakhs more if he did not act in their interest.

Metcalfe, wrung out more particulars from Chandulal concerning the debts to Palmer & Co., and by July 1822 he came to know that the total debt to the Company amounted to 83½ lakhs, while the State's remaining debts to the native bankers amounted to another 17 lakhs. He also made the startling discovery that most of the Residency officials including Russell, the former Resident, and his Assistant Sotheby, were originally secret partners in the firm and had derived immense profits.

Taken aback by this stunning discovery, he hesitated to directly report about it to the Governor-General as it would involve the integrity of high Residency officials. However, he informed his friend Adams, who was in the Council, of this and asked him to privately acquaint the Governor-General, of the plunder carried on by the firm with the active support of the Residency officials.

The Governor-General was so much taken in by the guile of the Palmers that he took a long time to see the truth. Ultimately, Adams succeeded in making the Governor-General see the real state of affairs. The latter, convinced now of the malpractices of Palmer & Co., declared; "The conduct of the house of William Palmer & Co., with respect to the bonus is considered by the Governor-General in Council to be in the highest degree reprehensible; and the concealment both by the house and by the Minister, of the real condition of the loan - - - - - admit of no excuse or palliation, and justifies the influence of a culpable collusion between these parties[116]".

After expressing his disapproval in the above manner, Lord Hastings agreed to the request of his Council to guarantee a loan to the Nizam's Government on the security of the *peshcush* of the Northern Sarkars for twelve years.

---

114. Hyderabad Residency Correspondence Vol. 173 Adam to Metcalfe. D. 22nd Sept. (foreign) 1820.
115. Ibid. Palmer Papers. p. 178. Hastings to Chandulal dated 24th August 1822.
116. Ibid p. 187

Shortly after this Lord Hastings left India, in the begining of the year 1823 and was succeeded by Adams, the seniormost member in the Council. Adams and his Council cut down the debt to 80 lakhs and paid off the debt to Palmer & Co., from the British Resident's treasury.

The Council disallowed the illegal bonus and the illegal allowances that the members of the firm were hitherto getting, along with all the interest that accrued on them. They condemned these spurious transactions by intimating to Metcalfe in the following manner[117]; "You will be pleased to acquaint Messrs: William Palmer & Co., that, under the above circumstances the British Government never could sanction by its countenance so shameful and criminal misappropriation by the Minister of the public funds as the liquidation of the demands of the house on account of the bonus and arrears of allowances, and in the event of Chandulal taking upon himself to satisfy these demands from the coffers of the State you are authorised and instructed to make a representation to the Nizam himself demonstrating against such misapplication of the public money".

In view of the British Government having discharged the Palmer debt, the Nizam was made to cede seven lakhs of *peshcush* of the Northern Circars to the British Government perpetually. He surrendered his claims to the *peshcush* of the Northern Circars to the British on the 4th November 1823 A. D.

Chandulal, anxious to absolve himself of his own part in the Palmer transactions, made it appear to the Nizam that the cession of these fertile regions was more due to the connection of the Nizam with the British, on account of which he had to undergo heavy expenses by participating in the Maratha War, than due to the fraudulent dealings of the Palmers. So while asking the Nizam to cede the Northern Sarkars to the British completely, Chandulal in his most suave manner explained: "Although I, who am but your Chobdar (shoe-bearer) was obliged by extreme difficulties during the war to contract a debt, yet what I have done has been for the prosperity and stability of your Highness's Government."[118]

The Company, anxious to put an end to the painful episode wrote: "Up to the date of the late treaty there was an excess in the collection of the districts ceded by the Honourable Company to His Highness the Nizam. above those of the districts ceded by the Nizam to the Company, estimated at twenty lakhs of rupees. Consequently credit has been taken for the above sum out of the one crore sixteen lakhs, sixty-six thousand, six hundred and sixty-six rupees, given in exchange of the *peshcush*. Agreeable to your desire, the sum of seventy-eight lakhs, seventy thousand, six hundred and seventy-rupees. nine annas, has been paid to them from one crore sixteen lakhs, sixty-six thousand six hundred and sixty-six rupees given in exchange

---

117. Palmer Papers p. 824

118. p. 824

for the *peshcush*". No demand on account of the debt to them has ever been made by the Honourable Company, and none ever will be made, the Honourable Company having no concern whatever in the affair." [119]

Within a year of the Nizam discharging his debts this Leviathan Firm that threatened to bring about the total ruin of the State, became bankrupt, "not from any run upon it, but merely from want of funds to meet ordinary demands."

119. Ibid p. 825

CHAPTER VIII

Metcalfe's Reforms.

When Metcalfe took charge of the office of the Resident in Hyderabad in 1820, he found the conditions in the State deplorable. The economy of the country was at a low ebb. On account of the oppressive methods of revenue administration adopted by Chandulal, the poor cultivator left off cultivation and fled to the neighbouring territories. The oppressive administrative system very often goaded the peaceful peasantry to open rebellion or banditry. Life in the countryside was unsafe; there was no security of life or property, and the name of the Government remained only in name. It was in such conditions that the Hyderabad Contingent was created ostensibly with a view to strengthening the internal administration of the Nizam by suppressing all rebellions. It was also on account of such conditions that Palmer & Co. was able to carry on its nefarious activities.

Chandulal, instead of basing the revenue administration of the country on a careful assessment of the land, merely fixed the revenues of each taluq according to his requirements, and farmed them out to greedy and vicious contractors who made the highest bids.[1] The bidders or contractors had the power of life and death and there was no appeal against their decision.

While the peasantry remained oppressed, the contractors realised huge profits by sub-letting the land to farmers and sent tax-collectors to extort money from the cultivators at the bayonet's point.

Seeing the distress of the people growing day by day, Russell after the conclusion of the Maratha war drew the attention of the Supreme Government saying that administration was "in so lamenatable a condition that it would not long continue to endure the extortions which were practised upon it by the avarice and rapacity of its governors."

Russell realised that many of the disorders and the general weakness of the administration in the State were due to the political alliance with the British. Describing the condition of Hyderabad in a graphic way, Russell wrote about the court and the people in the following manner. "They have no objects of hope or ambition. The splendour of the court has faded with decay of the Government. The distinction which arose from the notice of the prince, and from the intercourse between him and his nobles have been lost - - - - More than one half of the country is a desert; and even where there is cultivation, the farmer has no interest beyond the supply of his immediate necessities. He must provide himself and his children with

1. J. W. Kaye. Metcalfe, Vol. 01. pp. 10. 00.

bread to eat and more than that he knows he would not be suffered to retain out of the fruits of his utmost industry - - - -

The administration of Justice, and the collection of the revenues, which are nominally committed to the same hands are equally neglected and oppressive - - - - The officer who has the charge of district is considered to do his duty according to the amount of his remittances to the capital. He makes the most he can in a short time both for the Government and for himself; and the inhabitants are left without even the shadow of a security for their lives and property - - - - Evils produce one another. As a Government becomes weak, it becomes rapacious. It demands more, as it can enforcé less - - - - Although the restriants of our alliance did produce the mischief, the removal of them would not correct it - - - - Therefore we must either continue the same control which we now exercise, or we must lessen it, or we must increase it - - - - of these three cases, the last is, perhaps, the most likely to occur." [2].

So Russell realising that British intervention was a necessity in order to ameliorate the distress of the people, and also to tone up the gene: adminitration in the State, suggested certain reforms of a comprehensive nature.

While suggesting these reforms, Russell bore in his mind the avowed professions of the British that they would not interfere in the internal administration of their ally. So Russell tried to increase the British sphere of influence in the State without actually interfering in the administration of the State in a direct manner. This he sought to do, by exercising his will through Chandulal who for all practical purposes was the Diwan of the State. Under the new scheme of Russell, Chandulal was to be the instrument for implementing the reforms that Russell proposed to undertake. By evolving such a plan, Russell tried to increase the British sphere of influence in every field without openly intervening in the domestic affairs of the State; in the words of Kaye, the technique was, "In fact to be everything and nothing at the same time".[3]

Russell, while discussing the implementation of the proposed reforms, wrote to the Governor-General; "I am persuaded that nothing short of a close vigilant and decided control over the internal administration of the country will be attended with any real or lasting benefit. But this control should be exercised through the medium of advice and influence and not by exertions of authority. We should improve and direct the implements of the country and not introduce new ones of our own. I would rather enlarge the sphere, than increase the degree of interference."[4]

---

2. Hyderabad Papers—Russell to the Court of Directors Appendix B. P. 2., para 41, 43 & 48.
3. Kaye. Metcalfe. Vol. II. p. 18
4. Hyderabad papers p: 90. Russell to Hastings Nov. 24, 1819.

The Governor-General, Lord Hastings, concurred with the views expressed by Russell and he gave him the necessary sanction to implement his proposed reforms.[5]

Russell based his reforms on the following lines, namely: (a) reduction in public expenditure by retrenching useless and unnecessary troops. (b) selecting men of integrity as Taluqdars on the recommendation of the Resident and reorganising the land system on the basis of Inami land system.[6]

In order that the Nizam might be induced to grant his sanction to these schemes readily, Russell, requested the Governor-General to permit him to set free the Nizam's sons who were confined in the Fort of Golconda from the year 1815.

Chandulal, whose primary aim in life was to please the Resident, readily agreed to implement this new scheme of Russell under which a special tribunal consisting of a Hindu Pandit and a Mussalman Qazi was set up to administer Justice and to redress the grievances of the people. Russell himself exercised personal supervision over the administration by receiving petitions. A special tribunal was also established at Aurangabad, to redress the grievances of the people, and even officers commanding the several stations of Nizam's troops were authorised to receive petitions from the oppressed peasantry.[7]

Russell was busy throughout the year 1820 in implementing these reforms. But the distress of the people was not lessened by the operation of these reforms. While the receiving of petitions for redressal of grievances by the officers under the auspices of the Resident, and the appointment of taluqdars on the recommendation of the Resident was tantamount to direct interference in the State administration, the appointment of collectors to collect the revenues in no way solved the difficulties of the people. Chandulal about whom Metcalfe wrote that "extortion was the minister's chief vice", nullified the effectiveness of the Russell reforms by making the collectors responsible for supplying the state treasury with specific sums. This made the position of the collector more or less similar to that of the contractor, and the collectors levied taxes from the people in an arbitrary manner. There was no authority to check such actions.[8]

Moreover, the taluqdars were not given regular salaries. They only received a commission for having collected the revenues and a percentage to cover the cost of administration. It was also not necessary for the taluqdars to reside in the taluqa headquarters, with the result, that they preferred to reside at the capital, entrusting the taluqa administration to their deputies or *Naibs*. The *Naib* was a mere officer backed with limited

5. Ibid p 98
6. Ibid Russel to Hastings D/24th Nov 1819 p. 90
7. Ibid pp 214-215
8. Hyderabad Papers—pp. 214-215-Enclosure in Bengal Political- Letter 20th Dec. 1822.

authority and inadequate salary, but he was the only official referree and representative of the Government to whom the people could refer. The talukdar was appointed only on his paying a *nazar* or a large fee, and sometimes a whole year's revenue was accepted in advance as *nazar*.

Naturally this system of Taluqa administration led to the perpetuation of great abuses. While Russell was still busy trying to tackle these evils he was succeeded by Lord Metcalfe, as the Resident, in December 1820. Metcalfe, after taking charge of the Residency saw the urgent necessity of the Government to relieve the sufferings of the people. He undertook a tour of the Nizam's Dominions to gain a first hand knowledge of the conditions in which the people lived.[9] After studying the living conditions of the people, Metcalfe, became convinced that if the people were to be properly protected, British intervention is absolutely necessary. Hence, we find him writing to the Supreme Government in the following manner:[10] "After I had taken charge of the Residency I found that the very peculiar circumstances of the Nizam's Government increased, if possible, the claims which the people had on us for protection, and even called on us to interfere for the sake of the sovereign himself - - - - - -.

In, as much as it was certain whether the Nizam's virtual abdication might not, in part proceed from our known support of the actual minister, the situation of the prince seemed to constitute an additional claim to our care, lest the welfare of his dominions should suffer from the misrule of the servant sustained by our power."

He further wrote : "The only refuge of a people intolerably vexed, is emigration or insurrection, and as we secure the Nizam's Government against rebellion, it seems to be incumbent on us to save his subjects from grievous oppression."[11]

Feeling that it was a moral obligation on the part of the British to restore the prosperity of the land, Metcalfe decided to bring about salutary changes in the administration. With this object in view, he demanded from Chandulal a factual statement of the revenues and expenditure of the State, and also an account of the actual yield of the Khalsa, Jagheer and Jaidad lands, and whether their revenues were managed by collectors, farmers or by any other authority.

Metcalfe also, wanted Chandulal, to inform him about the number of troops in the employment of the Nizam's Government, and also, in the employment of the various Jagheerdars and other military chiefs. He also elicited information regarding the various pensions paid by the State to several persons.

---

9. J. W. Kaye—Metcalfe. Vol. II P. 31.
10. Palmer Papers pp. 214-220,–Para 9, 10. Metcalfe's Letter D-31. August 1822.
11. Ibid para 3.

After making the above enquiries Metcalfe discovered that there was a total deficit of 10 lakhs in the revenues of the State, and that the expenditure exceeded the income.

In order to make good the deficit in the state revenues, Metcalfe decided to introduce land reforms on the village settlement basis as an experimental measure for a period of 10 years[12]. Chandulal as usual readily concurred with the proposal made by the Resident. Metcalfe, in order to prevent the possibility of the collectors oppressing the peasants while the taxes were collected, decided to fix the exact amounts of revenue that the Government expected from the cultivators of each village. Government officers were sent to each district to assess the land value of every village. In some districts, European officers, were appointed to make the assessment, while in the remaining districts Chandulal sent his own officers to make the assessment of land.[13]

Wherever Chandulal undertook to appoint officers to make an assessment of the land, he deliberately tried to foil the effectiveness of the proposed reforms by merely turning the existing taluqdar into a farmer, and the village settlement he made was far from reliable. This was deliberately done with a view to leaving the door open for governmental interference and extortion in future.

Seeing that Chandulal was silently trying to thwart his reforms, Metcalfe, devised a novel scheme. Under this scheme he appointed European officers as Supervisors to receive complaints from cultivators, and also to prevent the officers of the Nizam from oppressing the people by effectively supervising over them. The cultivators were empowered either to appeal to the local authorities or to the Nizam's Government through the Resident directly.[14]

The European Supervisors were also empowered to put down the depredations of robbers and other crimes. Metcalfe also appointed hereditary police officers.[15]

The introduction of the European Superintendents over Indian officers, and empowering them with the right to receive applications and to put down rebellions and depredations, amounted to nothing short of active interference on the part of the British in the internal affairs of the Nizam's State. It made the ruler as well as his people, and Ministers aware that the British were infringing on their internal sovereignty in an open manner. But Metcalfe felt that if the people were to be saved there was no alternative except to interfere with the administration of the Minister.

On account of the salutary reforms he introduced, the population that had migrated to the neighbouring provinces of Bombay and Madras

12. Kaye. Metcalfe. p. 24.
13. Palmer Papers (Hyderabad aper) p. 214 dbara 20, 21.
14. Hyderabad Papers pp. 215-216. para 22-24.
15. Ibid.

started coming back, and once again took up their old occupations such as cultivating the land.[16] The prices of foodgrains also came down and this benefited the poor people a great deal.

Justifying his conduct in introducing European supervisors, Metcalfe wrote to the Supreme Government: "At present, therefore, the state of our relations with the Nizam's Government on this subject is as follows. We interfere avowedly for the protection of the people from extortion and depredation and for the security of the Nizam's revenue against destruction ------ The only doubt which it seems to me, we have to combat is that which attaches to any interference whatever in the affairs of a foreign country. That doubt I might consider as set at rest by the authority conveyed to the Resident by the orders of the Governor-General in Council. Moreover, an interference at this Court is not of recent date, but in one shape or another of long standing, and if it be right to interfere on behalf of our own interests, by imposing a Minister on the country it cannot surely be wrong to interpose for the interests of the people, with a view to their protection against his rapacity. ---- Were I to attempt to define briefly the nature of our present interference, I should describe it as a healing of the wounds inflicted by misrule and a nursing of the country for the benefit of the people and the Sovereign." [17]

Chandulal was at heart not in favour of the reforms, and tried to sabotage them by spreading the rumour that the Supreme Government was not in favour of the reforms introduced by Metcalfe. Finding the obstructionist policy of the Minister a great handicap, Metcalfe addressed the Supreme Government at Calcutta in the following manner; "The policy, generally, of exerting our influence, either for the election of a Minister, or for the support of any minister, actually in power, seems to be better suited to other times and circumstances than to those which at present exist. ---- Such a policy may have been wise and necessary in times of political contentions; It may also have been right and inoffensive, when the several princes of India were masters over their own ministers and strong enough to choose their own line of policy ---- At present by imposing a minister on a Prince and supporting that Minister during our pleasure we make the sovereign subject to his servant; we make the minister tyrant over his master; we patronise a virtual usurpation, and if the man whom we choose for our own purposes be a vicious ruler we sanction by our countenance all the evils of his misrule ------ The conduct therefore at this court which I should conceive to be best suited to our present circumstances in India would be to court the good will of the prince himself in preference to that of any of his servants, to act cordially, with any minister of his selection and to fix our attention on measures rather than men".[18]

16. Ibid p. 217.
17. Ibid para 41, 42.
18. Ibid para 48, 50, 52, 54. pp 229, 220.

However, this active policy of interference in the internal policies of the Nizam's Government was not approved by the Supreme Government. It was not prepared to follow a policy of direct subversion of the Nizam's power, even though it might be in the interests of the people. So Lord Hastings made his approval of the Metcalfe's measures conditional. He allowed Metcalfe to experiment with his reforms for the time being, but informed him that the European supervisors should be withdrawn as soon as conditions appeared favourable in the State for their withdrawal.

The Supreme Government made it's policy clear to Metcalfe in the following manner;[19] "In the second paragraph of your letter you say, that you suppose our interference in the Nizam's affairs to be not merely right, but also a duty, arising out of our supremacy in India - - - - . The assumption of our possessing an universal supremacy in India, involving such rights as you have described is a mistake - - - - Although a virtual supremacy may undoubtedly be said to exist in the British Government from the inability of other States to contend with its strength, the making of such a superiority a principle singly sufficient for any exertion of our will, would be to misapply that strength, and to pervert it to tyrannical purposes.

The argument of supremacy having been set aside, nothing but the tenor of some special engagement could render us liable to the call or allow to us the title for such interposition. Our treaties characterising the Nizam as an independent sovereign, authorise no such latitude, when for our private views, that Prince was constrained to support a body of our troops, to be stationed near his capital, the then Government disguised the interested oppressiveness of making him a portion of our army for holding him in thraldom, by a sturdy declaration, that His Highness had spontaneously sought the aid of a subsidary force, to secure his person and territories. The veil thus thrown over our policy, required that any stipulations which could mark the prostration of his power should be forlorn, so that in appearance, he legitimately retained his freedom. This measure, however, really placed him at our mercy. It was hardly to be imagined that our advantage would not be abused but it was abused - - - - The unequivocal encroachments on the Nizam's just authority were perceived by the Honourable Court, and a more becoming system was enjoined. The Governor-General in Council laboured to introduce it - - - - and having established an understanding with Raja Chundoo Lal for the correction and future conduct of affairs, (this Government, in return binding itself to support that minister), the Resident was directed to adopt a course of conciliatory counsel instead of those starts of despotic dictation which has before been in use. That limited degree of interference would still be objectionable, but for the common interest between the two Governments, that His Highness's territories should be restored to prosperity. Yet even that excuse would be insufficient were not our influence to be managed with delicacy and to be unavowed. Such is the distinct

19. Ibid. P 224. Letter from Swinton. Secretary to Government to Metcalfe. Enclosure No. 4 in Bengal Pol. letter d 20th December 1822.

nature of our relations with the Nizam, and a disregard of its terms would be no less repugnant to general principles than to the orders of this Government."

The Governor-General also informed Metcalfe, that it was difficult to determine whether conditions in the State really warranted British interference because the degree of anarchy that prevailed in the State was a matter of personal interpretation, and the opinion of the Nizam's Government and that of the Resident might be at variance in the matter. The Governor-General reminded Metcalfe of the obligations of the British towards Chandulal and asked him to uphold the Peishkar's authority under all circumstances. The Governor-General pointed out that the empowerment of the European Superintendents to receive applications and to put down local disorders would tell not only against the powers of Chandulal, but might also prejudice the Nizam against the minister for having given his ready assent for the implementation of such a scheme.

After making its views clear on the various issues in the above manner, the Supreme Government under Hastings, reluctantly consented to the introduction of the reforms of Metcalfe. The Supreme Government said,[20] "Much as the Governor-General in Council regrets a step so completely at variance with the principles which we had laid down, he is aware that it cannot be restricted suddenly without the alteration being attributed to a disapprobation notified by this Government. As it is the Governor-General's wish that your possessing his entire confidence should never be doubted, the arrangement must remain as it is for so long as it shall be thought by you really necessary according to your views and its abrogation hereafter should be gradual." After his coming to Hyderabad, Metcalfe also on behalf of the India Government entered into a new treaty with the Nizam in 1822, by which the boundaries of territories acquired by the Nizam and the East India Company after the last Maratha War were defined. and the India Government, which had lately succeeded to the position occupied by the Marathas, released the Nizam from the obligation of paying Chouth.

Lord Metcalfe left Hyderabad in 1825, and his successor, Martin, tried to palliate the feelings of Chandulal by consulting him on all important matters of administration, before giving his decision.

Nawab Sikandar Jah died on the 21st May 1829, and he was succeeded by his eldest son Nawab Nasir-ud-Dowla. The India Government, while recognising the title of Nasir-ud-Doula to the throne, also took the opportunity of changing the style of their letters while addressing the Nizam. They also directed the Resident, Martin, to request the Nizam's Government to modify the tone of their letters to the Governor-General accordingly.[21]

Hitherto, it was the custom of the State Government to address their letters to the Governor-General in the form of a *Parwanah*, and the Nizam

20. Ibid. Para 7.
21. Hyderabad Residency Correspondence. Vol. 67 (Foreign) L. dated 30th May 1829. pp. 323-326.

in these letters usually styled himself as the *Mahbe-Doulat* i,e., Our Royal-self, while the Governor-General referred to himself as a '*Niaz-mund*', a title indicative of inferiority in rank. Subsequently the Governor-General dropped this style of humility in his letters, but Nawab Sikandar Jah did not reciprocate by making a suitable alteration in addressing the Governor-General.

As the India Government did not like to irritate the Nizam, Sikandar Jah, whose dislike for the British was well-known, it did not raise the matter during his life time.

Now that Nawab Sikandar Jah was dead, the India Government informed the Resident that henceforth the form of address adopted in the letters between the two Governments must be on terms of perfect equality. It also told the Resident that if the Nizam's Government was not amenable to the suggestion, the Resident must decline to forward the Nizam's letters to the Governor-General. If the Nizam still obstinately preferred to cling to the old form of address, it was made clear that the Governor-General might retaliate by adopting the style of superiority which had hitherto been assumed by the Nizam.

Soon after his accession to the throne, Nawab Nasir-ud-Doula, on the advice of the Minister Chandulal (Munir-ul-Mulk having died), requested the Resident to withdraw the European Superintendents who were introduced under the reforms ushered in by Metcalfe.[22]

Lord Bentick, was the Governor-General during this period. He was a strict believer in the policy of non-intervention and so he readily assented to the request of the Nizam. The Governor-General expressed his opinion about the Nizam's desire in the following manner:[23] "This desire is considered by the Governor-General in Council to be natural and reasonable, and His Lordship is readily disposed to accede to it."

The Governor-Genral, carried away by his enthusiasm for a policy of non-interference, also informed the Nizam that he was free to choose his own minister. Of course Nasir-ud-Doula after his accession had hinted to Martin, the Resident, that he would not like to be kept in the same state of thraldom in which his father was placed. So the Supreme Government hastened to tranquillise the ruffled nerves of the new Nizam by assuring him thus: "The Governor-General-in-Council embraces this opportunity to place our relations at the Court of Hyderabad altogether on a footing more consistent with the dignity and independence of the Nizam, than that which has existed since the accession of the late prince, twenty-five years ago. During the whole of this period the State of Hyderabad has been ruled by a minister maintained by our influence, without regard to the

22. Ibid. Vol. 67 (Pol. Dept.,) pp. 323, 326.
23. Ibid. pp. 379–386.

pleasure of his nominal master and for the most part without being responsible to anyone - - - - - - The Nizam himself as well as his ministers - - - - - - be made clearly to understand that it is the determination of the Governor-General-in-Council to leave to His Highness the uncontrolled choice of his ministers, with regard to those now in office, he may either continue his favour to them, or remove them and substitute others at his pleasure.[24]

The Governor-General also offered to absorb the Hyderabad Contingent provided the Nizam paid 20 lakhs, but the Nizam once again under the influence of Chandulal refused the offer.[25] Even though the Governor-General had assured him that the Nizam was free to choose his own ministers, the Nizam, who had a shrewd idea of British policy, was not elated by such an assurance.

Commenting on the withdrawal of the European Superintendents St. Nihal Singh pithily remarks : "A proposal emanating from the British Residency would if carried out have meant the virtual extinction of the Nizam's rule. Control exercised through a subservient minister appeared however to be a better policy, and the Company's agents humoured the Nizam by abandoning all idea of direct administration and withdrawing all British officials in the districts.[26]

But this withdrawal of British interference in the internal administration of the State in no way removed the various ills with which the State was suffering during this period. Taking advantage of the withdrawal of the European Superintendents, many of the local zamindars refused to pay the full amount of revenue to the State. They threatened the life of the cultivators if they cultivated the land, and collecting all the money available in the local treasury, they fled to the neighbouring British territories like Masulipatam and Bellary which were on the borders of the Nizam's dominions, thus openly flouting the authority of the Nizam's Officers.[27] As it was the policy of the Company not to hand over any person who sought refuge in their territories to their native allies, these refractory zamindars carried on depredations into the Nizam's territories in a blatant manner.[28]

The zamindars of Moongal, Amapalam, Mensoor, Chintaganee, Hingolee carried on these depredations in such a impudent manner that the Minister was forced to request the Resident to send the contingent troops to put down rebellions in the Hingoli division. On account of the depredations carried on by these zamindars, the taluqas were once again deserted and depopulated. The zamindars whose lands lay in the Nizam's territories entered them and looted entire villages, and when they were attacked by the

24. Ibid. Pare 5, 10, 11.
25. Meadows Taylor. The Story of My Life. P. 68.
26. The Nizam and the Brittsh Empire.
27. H. H. R. Foreign Dept. Misc) Vol. 223. L. No. I dated 14th July 1832 and L. No. II.
28. Ibid.

Nizam's forces, fled into the Company's territories, knowing that the Nizam's troops could not pursue them there and open fire on them.[29]

The rebellion of Tulajee the Zamindar of Gouligaon, and of Jayaram the Zamindar of Mudkal were a great menace during this period. But, However, they were put down by the Contingent forces.[30]

Seeing disorderliness prevailing everywhere and the consequent oppressive policy adopted in the State, J. Stewart who became the Resident in 1830 wrote: "I can perceive a general spirit of insubordination and violence which will constantly demand the employment of the troops under our control in the whole country." Stewart deplored the withdrawal of British interference in the civil affairs of the State. On receiving such reports the Government of India asked the opinion of several European officers who were in the service of the Nizam's Government to give their opinion on the effect of the withdrawal of Metcalfe's reforms in the State. The opinions of the officers no doubt varied, but the majority of them were of the opinion, that the withdrawal of the European Superintendents was responsibie for so much anarchy in the State.

As a matter of fact, after the withdrawal of the European Superintendents, the Nizam's Government appointed in their place Indian Supervisors called Amins or Mansabdars.[31] But these Amins proved very inefficient in putting an end to the oppression of the Talukdars. So, wherever there were local rebellions the services of the Contingent troops were requisitioned to put them down.Metcalfe,who had become a member of the Governor-General's Council, described the position of the British saying, "The embarrasment to which we are liable in the Nizam's territories on the consequence of our withdrawal from interference in the civil concern of the Nizam's country and partly of the continuance of our interference in its military concern - - - - -. The real state of the case is that it is scarcely possible to maintain a military interference which leads to our taking part against the people in the event of rebellion, and at the same time to abstain altogether from civil interference, for, if we do not ascertain before we act against the people that they have not been driven into resistance by intolerable oppression, we make ourselves the tools of the most iniquitous tyranny."[32]

So Metcalfe, in order to prevent the British from becoming an oppressive machine of tyranny at the disposal of the Minister, wanted the British to help the Nizam in putting down the rebellions; At the same time he wanted the Resident at Hyderabad to be empowered to receive complaints from the people and to settle their disputes justly so that the sufferings of the people might be ameliorated.

---

29. Ibid. L. No 4.
30. Ibid. L. No. 21 of 1832.
31. Ibid. Vol. 230 (Foreign Misc.) from Ravenshah dated 2nd Nov. 1830. Vol. 233 (Pol. Dept.)
32. Ibid. (Pol. Dept) L. dated 9th August 1830.

Metcalfe also, in his capacity of Vice-President of the Governor-General's Council put up a note against the intended reduction in the size of the Hyderabad Contingent saying that it would in no way cure the chronic economic ills of the Hyderabad State. On the other hand, the advantages derived by the British on account of this force would diminish without bringing any substantial benefit to the State. Metcalfe felt that as long as the method of revenue administration in the State was not changed, the sufferings of the people would continue. While speaking against any reduction in the strength of the Contingent, Metcalfe described the nature of the Contingent troops thus;[53] "The Contingent furnished by the Nizam being found inefficient, we gradually assumed the management of it until we finally established a force in bringing it completely under our own control.

This we were enabled to do by the subserviency of the Minister who was the creature of our ascendency but who also saw in the existence of the force the measure of maintaining his own power against rival nobles as well as refractory subjects.

This is the footing on which the force stands at present. It is the personal interest of the Minister to maintain it; and it is therefore maintained; were it otherwise we should long ago have had applications for its abolition as in the case of our interference in civil matters which was contrary to his sense of his personal interests and therefore always unpalatable. Since the formation of this force exclusively neither the late nor the present Nizam has taken cognizance of it. They have both left it like other matters of their Government to the management of their minister, being either unwilling or unable to interfere with his controlled administration of their affairs. It is in reality a joint concern between Rajah Chandulal and us, in which the Nizam himself takes as little interest as in other affairs of his Dominions, being completely excluded from all share in his government either by actual disinclination for businesss or by hoplessness of success in any attempt to assume the power properly belonging to him, but now and for the last thirty years, almost entirely exercised by the Minister."

So with no reductions made in the strength of the Contingent, and no proper revenue administration, the dominions of the Nizam during this period were in a state of anarchy and chaos.

As a matter of fact the chaos that existed during this period, on account of rebellions in the various parts of the country like the rebellion of Dharamji Pratap Rao the Zamindar of Bhir, the Hatkar rebellion, the rebellion of Nowsaji Naik of Nowah, Veerappa Naik of Kopal, Venkat Narsimha Rao of Amalapaliam, Kapu Raja Rao of Chintagance, Jalagani Venkat Ram, Jagganat Rao of Moongal, and the rebellions of the zamindars of Sirancha and Mahdevpuram, and the Bhil rebellions in the Aurangabad District, could be traced to the mal-administration in the country even when the

53. Ibid. (Foreign Misc.) Vol. 65. S. No. 232 Pol. Dept L. Dated 1st March 1832.

European Superintendents of Metcalfe were employed, as Dighton. one of the European officers frankly admits.[33A]

The Talukdar exercised supreme authority in the districts and utillised his power to levy fines to oppress the people. The innocent and the guilty were indicriminately charged with crime, and criminals were unscrupulously allowed to go free, because they provided a means of revenue to the state. As a result of this the country-side was full of murders, highway robbery and loot. The zamindars convived at these depredations, as very often than not, they were also shareholders in the booty brought to them by highway robbers.

Seeing such abuses perpetuated in the country, Metcalfe appointed his superintendents and also restored the ancient police system. The superintendents to a certain extent protected the poor cultivator from oppression, and also settled the disputes between the zamidar and the ryot in an amicable and just manner. But even this system was not quite satisfactory because the time taken for the assessment of the villages was too short, and as was natural with all hasty measures, it gave rise to conflicting and contending interests, and involved the rights of the talooqdars, the zamindars, the village headman and the cultivator of the soil. Their conflicting claims over the land could not be reconciled; so naturally they all combined to deceive the European Superintendent. These contending parties took full advantage of the divided authority that was established under Metcalfe's scheme and tried to set the Superintendent against the Minister and vice versa. Naturally Chandulal after the accession of Nasir-ud-Doula took the earliest opportunity to recall these European Superintendents. With the withdrawal of these European Superintendents, the *Kouls* given under the Metcalfe scheme were ignored and once again conditions in the State reverted to anarchy and confusion.

The recalcitrant zamindars raised their heads once again and the Contingent troops were employed against them. These troops which were always used to suppressing the aspirations of the common people as well as the zamindars, were regarded by the people as dragons of tyranny, which had come to suppress their aspirations.

The troops themselves do not seem to have been very satisfied with their lot at this juncture, as was revealed by the mutiny that took place at Mominabad in 1827, in which Lt. Col. Evan Davies, the commanding officer in charge of the troops was assasinated. The officer in charge of the sepoys, wanted to introduce changes in the uniform of the sepoys, and also insisted on their shaving their beards. The sepoys refused to comply, with this and they shot their commandant.[34]

In 1835, the Court of Directors, their attention having been drawn to the unsatisfactory conditions in the Hyderabad State, directed the Govern-

---

33-A. Ibid. Docket No. 3.
34. Burton—P. 109.

ment of India, to intimate through the Resident to the Nizam, that they would not for long remain indifferent to the unsatisfactory conditions of administration in his State and also advised him to change the Minister if necessary so that the the administration in the country might be improved.[35]

Chandulal, on hearing this communication, at once conveyed his willingness to the Resident, to restore if necessary the European Superintendents and also to appoint European officers to look after the Judicial administration. He was prepared to do every-thing short of giving up his control over the revenues of the country. Though Chandulal apparently agreed to bring about these changes, he secretly advised the Nizam not to accept these proposals as their implementation would tell against his internal sovereignity in an adverse manner. So the Nizam did not approve of these measures, and the system of administration through Indian amins was continued.

In the meanwhile the anarchy in the State continued to grow day by day. Hyderabad during this period was also a victim of Thuggee as revealed in the writings of Meadows Taylor, an officer in the Nizam's Service.

While things were in such a sad plight General Fraser became the Resident in 1838.

35. Briggs. Vol. II. P. 107.

CHAPTER IX

The Wahabi Movement.

General Fraser was appointed the Officiating Resident at Hyderabad in 1838; soon after his arrival his attention was engaged in unearthing a widespread conspiracy against the British Government known as the Whahabi movement. The Hyderabad State was the focus of attention; when this conspiracy was discovered it was found that prince Mubariz-ud-Doula was deeply involved in it.

The Wahabi movement was originally started among the Mussalmans of Northern India by one Syed Ahmed Brailvi. By 1820 the movement was widely prevalent in Bengal, the Northwest Frontier, United Provinces and it spread even in Southern India up to Madras. The movement was originally directed against the predominance of the Sikhs in the Punjab by Syed Ahmed and his followers—Syed Ahmed Brailvi had also written a letter to Nawab Sikander Jah appealing to him as a Muslim ruler to help the followers of Syed Ahmed who were known as "*Mujahids*", with [1] proper funds and men in order to enable them to carry on their struggle not only against the Sikhs but also aginst the Europeans who had come to wield political suzerainty in India.

Syed Ahmed died in the year 1831; but the Wahabi movement continued. Moulavi Vilayat Ali and Salim, two of the followers of Syed Ahmed, came to the Deccan in 1838, and they also spread the movement in Bombay, Bangalore, Madras and other places in Southern India through their agents During the course of these activities they succeeded in gaining the confidence of Mubariz-ud-Doula who was accepted by the Wahabis as their leader in India.

After his release in 1820, Mubariz-ud-Doula returned to his palace in the city, but did not give up his antipathy towards the English. In the year 1829 he once again raised an insurrection against the Government, and once again the Contingent forces under the command of Col. Stewart were sent against the prince [2].

The prince was arrested and he was once again confined in the fortress of Golconda. There he tampered with the loyalty of the garrison and tried to appropriate the treasury at Golconda by preventing the Nizam's men from taking away the treasury. Once again, the Nizam had to seek the help of the Contingent troops to retrieve the treasury [3]. Later on through the

---

1. The Freedom Struggle in Hyderabad Vol. 1 Page 126.
2. Burton P. 116.
3. Meadows Toylor, Story of My life PP. 77–81.

efforts of Capt. Meadows Taylor, the prince was reconciled to his brother and on his request that he should be given the residence of the late prince Ali jah, he was released and allowed to take up his residence in the city[4]. Soon after this the prince got interested in the tenets of Wahabism and he joined the movement. The Wahabi leaders, recognising the potential importance of Mubariz-ud-Doula, recognised him as their leader in India, by conferring on him the titles of "*Rais-ul-Muslimin*" and "*Umar Bin Abdul Aziz*", Naib of the Martyred Syed Ahmed[5].

The British during this period were engaged in the Afghan wars, and the rumour was widely spread in India that the Russians were advancing through Central Asia towards India. This resulted in the growth of increased activity on the part of the Wahabis in India. Their spies began to swarm about in the streets of Madras, Bangalore, Kurnool, Bombay etc.,

The attention of General Fraser at Hyderabad was drawn to the menace of Wahabism and the probable complicity of Mubariz-ud-Doula, by the Madras Government on the information gathered by Mr. Stonehouse the Magistrate of Nellore.

However, General Fraser, decided not to precipitate matters till he had some specific knowledge of Mubariz-ud-Doula's complicity in the matter [6]. He set about gathering information about the activities of Mubariz-ud-Doula. On the information supplied to him by Capt. Malcolm that Mubariz-ud-Doula had ordered a seal to be made for him with the little "*Rasi-ul-Muslimin*" engraved on it, he decided to draw the attention of the Nizam's Government to the dangerous proclivities of Mubariz-ud-Doula.

General Fraser, made the Nizam send to him his confidential Munshi, Rasheed-ul-Mulk and informed the Nizam through him about the activities of Mubariz-ud-Doula, without disclosing the names of the various other Indian Princes involved. As a matter of fact it was discovered through the revelations of a Sikh spy, Dhoom Das, that Ranjit Singh, the rulers of Jodhpur, Satara, the Nawab of Bhopal, the prince of Sagar and the Nawab of Kurnool were also parties to this conspiracy and that all these princes were waiting for a suitable opportunity to strike at the English. General Fraser placed a memorandum dealing with all these particulars in the hands of Rasheed-ul-Mulk, to be conveyed to the Nizam.

The Nizam on the receipt of the news called general Fraser for an interview, and both of them in concert with Chandulal, decided to confine prince Mubariz-ud-Doula in the Golconda Fort [7].

4. H, R. R. (Foreign Misc.) Vol. 1 Docket No. Nil L. 24th Nov, 1831.
5. Ibid.
6. H. R. R. Vol. 75 L. No. 8 d. 16th March 1839.
7. Ibid L. Dated 29th May 1839 No. 8.

The memorandum submitted to the Nizam revealed that Mubariz-ud-Doula used to contact the various princes in India through two of his confidential emissaries, Lall Khan and Fakeer Mahomed.

Lall Khan was sent to Sind to contact Moulavi Asif, who was originally expelled from Hyderabad, and from Sind they both arrived at Sholapur via. Bombay to preach the tenets of Wahabism to the people there. After carrying on his propaganda at Sholapur, Lall Khan returned to Hyderabad on the 24th April, where he was arrested.

The memorandum submitted by General Fraser also stated that Mubariz-ud-Doula was corresponding with the Nawab of Tonk and the Amirs of Sind. Mubariz-ud-Doula in order to further his plans usually employed Moulavis who went about the country preaching the tenets of Wahabism; Of these Moulavi Salims's name is worth mentioning because, he played a prominent part in influencing Mubariz-ud-Doula in favour of Wahabism, and also in maintaining correspondence with the various princes in India.

General Fraser, on receiving information about the confidants and friends of Mubariz-ud-Doula, surrounded their houses with troops and placed them under arrest.[8] Apart from Moulavi Salim, Lall Khan, Moulavi Jaffar, Sunder Pandit the *Mutsuddie* of Mubariz-ud-Doula, and Pokarmal the banker who supplied funds to Mubariz-ud-Doula were also arrested.

While making these arrests General Fraser made it clear that they were made on account of these people's suspected plot against the Government of the Nizam, as well as that of the Company and not because they professed the tenets of Wahabism.

Prince Mubariz-ud-Doula on receiving the message of the Minister that he should proceed to the fort of Golconda in accordance with the Nizam's orders, refused to go there unless the charges against him were proved. He said that if the charges against him were substantiated, he would himself set out on foot to the Fort of Golconda. In the meanwhile pressure was brought on the Nizam by the ladies of his family headed by Jahan-Parvar Begum the Nizam's step mother, on behalf of Mubariz-ud-Doula.

The Nizam, not wishing to appear in the garb of a tyrant to his own family, sent one of his confidants, Muhammad Hafeez, and Wahid-ud-Doula to persuade Mubariz-ud-Doula to proceed to Golconda peacefully. But finding his brother adamant, he began to waver in his decision.

Finding this attitude of the Nizam quite unhelpful General Fraser in a interview with the Nizam, at which Chandulal was also present, complaind against the delay in effecting the arrest of Mubariz-ud-Doula. This remons-

8. Ibid.

trance on the part of the Resident led to the Nizam issuing orders for the arrest of the prince. While issuing the orders, Chandulal calling the *Urzee Beg* told him that he should proceed to the palace of Mubariz-ud-Doula and inform him that he was being arrested on the orders of both the Governments.

General Fraser, who was about to take leave of the Nizam, on hearing this pointed out to Chandulal, that the orders for the arrest of Mubariz-ud-Doula emanated solely, from the Nizam's Government and not from the India Government. He added: "I have communicated to the Circar whatever information I possessed, but I have left it to H. H. to adopt such measures as he deems proper. The British Government gives no order in the case, nor do I presume on its behalf to dictate to H. H. what ought to be done"[9].

This statement of the Resident shows that though the British did everything to bring about the arrest of Mubariz-ud-Doula by more or less applying pressure on the Nizam, they were reluctant to throw away the mask. They wanted to keep up the facade of the internal sovereignty of the Nizam, lest they should become unpopular with the Indian princes and the Indian people.

Shortly after this interview, the house of Mubariz-ud-Doula was surrounded by the Nizam's armies, and the prince was removed to the Fort of Golconda under strong guard.

After the arrest of the Prince the Resident once again visited the Nizam who told him that personally he would have cared little if his brother had acted treasonbly towards him, but since he acted in a treasonable manner against both the Governments he had to arrest him however painful the task was. The statement of the Nizam shows that he obviously wanted the British Government to be associated with him in having brought about the arrest of his brother. Left to himself, the Nizam perhaps would not have put Mubariz-ud-Doula in confinement since the charges that were levelled against him, of plotting to overthrow the Nizam's Government, were not definite.

After the arrest of the prince, on the initiative of general Fraser, a Commission was appointed to look into the charges levelled against the prince and his associates. Fraser wanted the Commission to be a joint Commission consisting of Indians and Englishmen appointed by the Resident, so that the people might feel that an impartial enquiry was being made to prove the innocence or guilt of the prince Mubariz-ud-Doula. General Fraser nominated Major Armstrong as the President of this Commission of Inquiry, while Captain Malcolm and Captain Hutton were appointed members of the Commission. On behalf of the Nizam's Government he asked Chandulal to nominate three more members to the Commission[10].

9. Ibid L. No. 40.

The Nizam's Government nominated Yazaz-ud-Doula, Khurshid Jung Bahadur and Benazir Jung Bahadur as members of this Commission. The Commission first met on the 20th June 1839. and continued its sittings from the 20th June 1839 to March 1840. The sessions were held in the Residency building.

The enquiries made by the Commission revealed that there was a general discontent against the British among the Indian princes, and some of them wished to bring about the downfall of the British. With this object in view Mubariz-ud-Doula had corresponded with the various Indian Chief's like the Nawab of Tonk, the Nawab of Rampur, the Nawab of Odiyagiri and especially with the Nawab of Kurnool who not only collected troops for the cause but also converted his palace gardens into arsenals[11].

The Commission also discovered that Moulavies who were in the pay of Mubariz-ud-Doula had tried to tamper with the Muslim sepoys belonging to the subsidiary forces stationed at various places like Kurnool, Mysore and Srirangapatnam.

The spies who were in the pay of the Wahabi leaders used to wear a steel ring on the finger of their left hand and also steel bangles. They also kept figured papers as amulets.[12] These were recognised as the tokens of their being Wahabi spies. When the spies were in need of money or any other necessary article they got it on showing these steel rings or bangles.

The Commission's enquiries also revealed that Mubariz-ud-Doula was the chief link between the discontented elements in the North and the South, and that the Wahabi's in India also procured a letter from the Sharif of Mecca eulogising their efforts against the foreigners.[13] In the course of their investigation the Commission also found that a general opinion was prevalent among the Wahabi Muslims that the Mughal Emperor and the Mughal heir apparent were also behind the Wahabi movement. It also learnt that allowances ranging from Rs. 12 to 100 were paid every month, to all persons who joined the movement.

As a result of these discoveries the Commission came to the conclusion that Mubariz-ud-Doula was guilty of having carried on treasonable correspondence with Indian Potentates like the Nawabs of Tonk, Kurnool and the landlords of Odiyagiri and Chnnapatnam with the object of overthrowing the British power in India. They were also of the opinion that Mubariz-ud-Doula was guilty of having tried to tamper with the loyalty of the Indian soldiers to the British and that he wanted to organise a planned rebellion against the British.

10. Ibid. Note 3—Fraser to Chandulal.
11. H. Fraser—Members and Correspondence P. 56 of General J. S. Fraser.
12. Report of the Commission of Inquiry. Section 21, 35.
13. Ibid Section 28.

The Commission however admitted that most of the letters of the Moulavis to Mubariz-ud-Doula spoke of a *Jihad* against the Sikhs, rather than against the British.

A report of the findings of the Commission was sent to Chandulal, upon which the Nizam's Government decided to intern the prince at Golconda. On hearing about this decision the Supreme Government at Calcutta gave its opinion of the trial and confinement of Mubariz-ud-Doula in the following manner.[14] "The Governor-General in council cannot concur with you that there is a proof upon these proceedings of the existence of a very extended spirit of dissatisfaction towards the British Government. There appears to His Lordship in council to be evidence only of some very wild and unsupported attempts on the part of the adherents of a peculiar sect to raise a spirit of disturbance, at a time which seemed to them to be extraordinarily favourable to their endeavours."

The Supreme Government as well as the Court of Directors also felt that the charges against Prince Mubariz-ud-Doula were inadequate, but they supported the decision of the Nizam's Government to keep the prince in detention.

The Supreme Government instructed General Fraser to send troops against the Nawab of Kurnool. The Resident despatched a detachment of the Nizam's Contingent forces to co-operate with the Madras troops in reducing the Nawab. The troops succeeded in defeating the Nawab of Kurnool, and the Nawab was duly deposed by the British and Kurnool was absorbed in the Presidency of Madras.

Mubariz-ud-Doula died a state prisoner at Golconda on the 25th June 1854.[15]

The trial of Mubariz-ud-Doula and his associates left a feeling of dissatisfaction even among Englishmen; and some of the News Papers of that period wrote articles in their periodicals urging the Supreme Government to set free the Wahabis. They criticised the appointment of Major Armstrong and Capt. Malcolm as members of the Commission in view of the fact that these two police officers were primarily responsible for unearthing the alleged Wahabi conspiracy.

The contemporary opinion also was that the Indian officers appointed to the commission by the Nizam's Government lacked independence of spirit.

The "EXAMINER", one of the English News Papers, lamented the fact that the Commission and the European Officers who took a prominent part in the trial, instead of sentencing the prisoners had left the matter in the

14. H. R. R. Vol. 75 L, No. 427 Para 6, 2.
15. H. R. R. Vol. 93. L, No. 71 of 26th June 1854.

hands of Chandulal who, it felt, was solely interested in pleasing the Resident rather than in doing justice.

Commenting on Chandulal's anxiety to please the British, the "Examiner" wrote; [16] "Of the Ministers' implicit deference to the supposed wishes of a Resident, in cases like the present, we cannot give a better proof than by relating (we speak only from recollection) a circumstance which occurred during the Residency of Mr. Russell. A native had slain another either in absolute self-defence or under circumstances of the very gratest provocation. He surrendered himself to an English gentleman, and the Resident ultimately sent him to the Minister to be tried. The Cazee on hearing the case acquitted him, but the Minister sent back the prisoner saying, 'What do you mean by not executing him ? The Resident sent him to be punished!' The Cazee remonstrated, but the Minister sent them word that they should at least sentence him to lose an arm. Fortunately the Resident heard what was going on, and informed the Minister that so far from wishing for the man's execution, he thought the court quite right in acquiting him. He was released immediately".

In spite of such public agitation against the prolonged imprisonment of the Wahabis, and several appeals by the prisoners themselves against the rigours of their imprisonment and the indefinite period of confinement, they were not set free. The invariable reply given by Chandulal to these charges was that he would release them only on the receipt of specific instructions from the Resident to that effect; when an appeal was made to the Resident, the usual reply that the prisioners received from the Residency was, since the prisoners were imprisoned by the Nizam's Government the Resident could not interfere in this matter [17].

Once, when Mubariz-ud-Doula appealed to the Nizam against the severity of his punishment, the Nizam was alleged to have replied, "You have committed no fault against me; I am helpless; The Feringees have confined you". Upon this Mubariz-ud-Doula appealed to General Fraser to intercede on his behalf with the Nizam.

The Resident on receiving this appeal asked Chandulal if it was true that the Nizam had expressed his helplessness in the matter saying that the English were responsible for his brother's imprisonment. The redoubtable Chandulal who was anxious to please the Resident and to avoid controversy with him promptly replied: " The disaffection of Moobariz-oo-Doulah is known to the world. There is no necessity for recapitulating all that was written in the numerous notes I have been favoured with from you,.........what assertions has Mobbariz-Doula ever made approaching or near the truth there should be any grounds of truth in what he has written. The note is returned enclosed for your perusal"[18].

16. Hyderabad Affairs, Vol, V, pp, 4, 6
17. Hyderabad Affairs Vol. V, pp, 86, 87,
18. H, R, R, Vof, 75 L, N, 34,

The result of this was that Mubariz-ud-Doula languished in the prison till his death on the 25th June 1854; The rest of the Wahabi prisoners were set free during the course of that year.

The conspiracy of the Wahabis in Hyderabad against the British power indicates the deep resentment felt by certain sections of the people about the loss of political power by the Indians. The Wahabi movement is a prelude to the events that happened in 1857.

CHAPTER X

The Cession Of Berar.

After the suppression of the Wahabi conspiracy, General Fraser turned his attention to the chronic economic distress in the country. The Supreme Government as well as the Court of Directors as we have seen had not accepted the recommendation of Col. Stewart for the reintroduction of European Supervisors.

The Court of Directors felt that the reintroduction of European Supervisors would amount to a direct assumption of Government in the State, without the advantages that naturally go with the exercise of sovereignty. Hence they felt that the economic disorders of the Hyderabad State "must speedily work its own extinction when the financial embarrassments of the Government and the wretchedness of the people would constitute a case which would justify, and in fact compel, a resort to the ultimate remedy contemplated by Col. Stewart, viz., that of taking the administration, both financial and judical entirely into our own hands." Yet they did not want to appear as though they had deliberately allowed the economic conditions in the State to drift to such an extent that the British assumption of the administration in the State became inevitable. So they asked the Resident to warn the Nizam that the Supreme Government could not remain indifferent to the economic ailments in the State and the Nizam was also advised to change the Minister if he felt it was necessary in the interests of State.

This warning given by the Resident did not result in any beneficial results, because as Stewart admits, the real responsibility for the mal-administration that had set in the State, lay more with the British, than with the Nizam's Government. Col. Stewart reporting about the chronic economic ailments in the State, wrote to the Supreme Government in 1834 in the following manner:—

"Those who have witnessed the course of our policy at this court for the last thirty years, who have seen how we put up creatures of our own as Ministers, and supported them against their Sovereign, how we have obtained the control of all the effective country, can hardly feel a doubt, least of all on the Nizam himself that we have considered ourselves as the actual rulers of the country. Many of the evils that exist in the State are unquestionably the almost unavoidable result of the anomalous nature of our connection with it. It seems hardly fair, therefore, to hold either the Nizam or his Minister responsible for the evil, situated as they are. I do not think that they had the power to correct them. In fact, we may, perhaps, more properly be regarded as responsible for them, having the power in our hands to remedy them, and having shown that we are in no way scrupulous about making use of that power when we think fit to do so."[19]

The Supreme Government at Bengal, as well as most of the Residents at Hyderabad, realised that one of the main reasons for the State of indebtedness from which the Nizam's Government suffered was the maintenance of the Hyderabad Contingent. They knew fully well that legally they had no right to insist on the maintenance of the "Contingent" forces, yet they were loth to make any reductions in its size and thus relieve the burden of the Nizam's Government because, the maintenance of the force gave them a definite political advantage in the State. Apart from that they found in it a convenient source for extending patronage to their favourites and relatives.

Even Lord Dalhousie who ultimately demanded the cession of territories to discharge the debts of the Nizam's Government, debts that were mainly incurred towards the mainteance of the Contingent forces wrote: "The debt to the British Government which burdens the Nizam has been produced by the Contingent. The monthly subsidy, for which the Resident at Hyderabad maintains a perpetual wrestle with the Dewan, and which transforms the representative of the British Government by turns into an importunate creditor, and a bailiff in execution is the pay of the Contingent. Were that sort of demand and dispute once adjusted, there is no Native State in India whose relations with the British Government would, as far as we know, be more friendly and unruffled. The Nizam has been our ally for much more than half a century."[20]

As a matter of fact Nawab Nasir-ud-Dowla, on his accession to the throne had not only expressed his desire to abolish the system of European Supervisors but also he expressed his desire to remove the European officers of his "Contingent" and to appoint Indians instead. The Nizam was also of the opinion that the Contingent troops were unnecessary. Chandulal who found European supervision over the revenue administration of the country irksome, encouraged the Nizam in his demand to abolish the European supervisors. But when it came to the question of either abolishing or reducing the size of the Contingent, Chandulal would not agree with the Nizam, because he knew that the maintenance of the 'Contingent' alone would win for him the favour and patronage of the Resident.

Hence the Minister dissuaded the Nizam from insisting on either the reduction or the abolition of the Contingent.

Shortly after this Col. Stewart visited Calcutta in 1837 and apprised Lord Auckland of the situation in Hyderabad. On his return to Hyderabad, Col. Stewart received a letter from the Supreme Government in which he

19. H. Fraser. Memoirs and Correspondence of Gen. J. S. Fraser. p. 86.
20. Ibid. pp. 64, 65.

was exhorted to see that the Contingent was maintained, and if possible to secure the assignment of special districts towards the pay of the Contingent troops, so that the Contingent could be free from being "dependent on the caprice of either the Ruler or the Minister of Hyderabad, the means for paying the force being vested permanently in our Government."

While matters were in such a state General Fraser arrived in Hyderabad as the Resident in 1838. Shortly, after his coming to Hyderabad the Supreme Government on the receipt of a proposal from the Court of Directors wrote to General Fraser asking if the Nizam's Government could not be persuaded to pay the salaries of the European officers also. which were hitherto paid by the Company besides the regular emoluments, it was paying uptil now to the European officers. The expenses incurred by the Nizam on the Contingent amounted to nearly 38,00,000 lakhs of Rupees par annum. So realising that the imposition of an additional burden on the already overstrained finances of the State, in shape of regular pay to the European officers would not be relished by the Nizam's Government, General Fraser opposed the scheme. He wrote to the Governor-General on the 17th January 1840, in the following manner: "I have already offered generally my opinion to your Lordship on the subject of the proposal of the Court of Directors, that the Company's officers in the service of Native Governments shall receive that portion of their allowances which is technically termed 'Pay' from the States under which they serve. It would be particularly unpalatable here, because the Nizam's Government already view with dislike the Native Army we have officered, and would most willingly get rid of the heavy expense which it involves. The Army is always four months in arrears; and even in this way, they pay it with so much difficulty that any additional expence might be expected to become the subject of serious remonstrance, more especially when this expense has no reference either to the amelioration of the Army, or the security of the Nizam's country, but is merely to be incurred as a measure of relief to the Company's finances. The very Army itself exists but upon sufferance, and if any decided objections were made to it, however we might be able to insist upon its maintenance, we should find it difficult to justify this act by a reference to treaties, or to any agreement which has ever been passed, on the subject between His Highness the Nizam's Government and our own. I think, therefore, it were advisable to abstain from proposing a measure of which the justice would certainly not be perceptible to the Native State, and which might give rise to questions and propositions regarding the Army itself which it were, perhaps, as well avoid".[21]

Finding the economic distress in the State increasing day by day General Fraser proposed to the Bengal Government that the Supreme Government should agree to the Resident advancing a loan of a million Sterling to the Nizam's Government at the rate of six percent interest. General

21. Ibid. p. 90.

Fraser proposed to clear the arrears due to the irregular troops of the Nizam consisting mostly of Arabs and Rohillas, with this loan. He also intended to make suitable reductions in the size of these irregular troops of the Nizam instead of in the well-disciplined Contingent, because the maintenance of these troops cost the Nizam's Government nearly 90 lakhs of rupees per year.[22] In order to realise the money lent to the Nizam's Government General Fraser proposed to take over temporarily under his control the management of the Nizam's territories, and he proposed to administer these territories through men approved by him, preferably Indians, and not by Europeans as it was in the time of Metcalfe.[23] The Resident realised that it was impossible to implement these reforms as long as Chandulal remained in office, and as the Supreme Government felt that Chandulal was indispensable, his scheme was not taken up. So, General Fraser as an alternative suggested that he would appoint capable native agents in the revenue department to assist the Minister in his revenue administration. But this proposal was also not approved by the Governor-General-in-Council.[24]

In the meanwhile conditions in the State began to take a turn for the worse and the economic crisis in the State began to deepen during the years 1841 and 1842.

While matters were in such a state, the chieftain of Deodrug, Narsing Rao with the help of the Arab Chief, Koharan, rose in rebellion. Deodrug was in the Raichur district. The insurgents rose in rebellion and took the Fort of Badami that belonged to the Company and plundered the town. The rebellion however was put down by the Contingent troops and Badami was retaken. Rumour attributed the rebellion of these Chieftains to the incitement they received at the hands of the emissaries of the ex-ruler of Satara.

General Fraser finding that it was difficult to obtain an authentic account of the finances of the State from Chandulal, suggested to the Supreme Government the advisability of removing the Minister from office on the plea of old age and appointing a new Diwan or to sanction the power to the Resident of appointing a Committee of Enquiry into the finances of the State. But these suggestions of the Resident were turned down by the then Governor-General, Lord Ellenborough.

Lord Ellenborough soon after his assuming office had issued a directive to the Resident on the 26th of April 1842, in which he stated that the Resident must show the utmost respect to the Native Princes, and that the Resident when called upon to exercise his authority, must exercise it in such a courteous manner as to not to hurt the feelings and dignity of the Native Potentate in whose court he resided.

Lord Ellenborough declared "You will distinctively understand that the further extension of its dominion forms no part of the policy of the

22. Ibid. p. 95.
23. Ibid. p. 100. L. to J. R. Colvin, Private Secretary to Lord Auckland.
24.

British Government; that it is desirous on all occasions of respecting the independence of Native States; and that, satisfied with the extent of its own rule, it has no other wish than that every State within the limits of India should freely exercise its rights as recognised by Treaty, and contribute, by the maintenance by its own means of peace and good government within its dominions, to the general happiness of the whole people."[25]

Lord Ellenborough not only sent this circular to the Residents but also got it translated into the Persian language and sent it to the various princes in India with whom the British had political relations. Buoyed up by the receipt of this circular the Nizam as well as Chandulal began to set aside the advice of General Fraser in the internal affairs of the State.

General Fraser noting this tendency on the part of the Nizam and his Minister especially intimated to the Supreme Government the danger that might arise to the very existence of the Contingent forces if this tendency was allowed to develop. He wrote to the Supreme Government "If the Nizam is permitted to retain this impression it is not improbable that, beside other evils which may arise; we shall experience one of very considerable magnitude in a proposition on the part of His Highness for the disbandment of the Contingent, to which he is known to be averse, and of which neither the continued maintenance nor the original organisation is provided for by any existing treaty. In the year 1833 His Highness actually stated his objections to the continuance of the force; and the expenses attending it has ever been a source of complaint from the Minister."

This letter of the Resident made Lord Ellenborough realise the danger of allowing the native princes to indulge in dreams of internal independence. He at once wrote a letter of remonstrance to the Nizam on the 1st October 1842 saying "I am sorry to learn that the Minister of Hyderabad does not act according to the counsels of the Residents as he has done hitherto. It is expedinet that you direct the Minister to attend to the wishes of the Resident. It is a great pity if anything contrary to the former friendship and concord between the two Governments should occur."[26]

After strengthening his position by means of the above letter General Fraser once again tried to impress upon the Supreme Government the necessity of either displacing Chandulal who had proved himself to be incapable of looking after the administration, or to appoint a person or body of three or four persons independent of the Minister, as Financial Advisers to look after the finances of the State and to introduce the necessary salutary reforms, under the guidance of the Resident.

He wrote to Lord Ellenborough. If it is the intention of the British Government to maintain the system of non-interference in the affairs of this and other Native States, we must look for frequent commotions and disturbances of one kind or another throughout India. If, on the otherhand, it is our object to establish a well-regulated and uniformly organised Govern-

25. Ibid. p. 152.
26. Ibid. p. 166.

ment, maintaining peace and good order in every part of the Empire, with the hope, if not the immediate realisation of great improvement, then instead of non-interference our best policy may be one of interference, by which I mean the imposition of our advice, guidance, and support to the utmost limit which good faith and adherence to existing treaties will allow. Any essential or permanent change for the better in the Nizam's country is quite hopeless under the present constitution of affairs, for as long as Chandulal remains in the office of Dewan, he will never cease to retain or endeavour to retain, in his own feeble grasp the exclusive power of the Government."[27] In spite of all these remonstrances on the part of the Resident, still the Governor-General in Council adhered to thei roriginal decision of not intervening directly with the decision of Chandulal.

Chandulal in the meanwhiie tried his level best to grapple with the deteriorating economic situation in the State. But finding that he could not cope with the situation, he ultimately came forward in February 1843, with the request that the British Government should advance him a sum of Rs. 75 lakhs to relieve him from his pressing and more urgent financial embarrassments. He proposed in lieu of this loan to cede to the British, in perpetuity, districts yielding an annual revenue of Rs. 450,000/- in any part of the Nizam's Dominions which the British might choose say either Raichur, Bhir or Berar.[28]

Chandulal promised to discharge the arrears due to the irregular troops of the Nizam with the help of the money that the British might advance to him.

Upon Capt. Malcolm, the Assistant to the Resident, to whom this proposal was made, asking him if the Nizam would like to sell a portion of his territories to the British towards the discharge of his debts, Chandulal gave this cryptic reply by saying that it was useless to inform the Nizam of this proposal till the views of the British Government were known, and that once the British Government agreed to the proposal, he could obtain the consent of the Nizam. General Fraser on being informed of the proposal insisted that for such an important scheme the prior consent of the Nizam was necessary.

So Chandulal perforce had to intimate the Nizam about the latest proposals he had made to the Resident. The Nizam on hearing of these proposals refused to be a party to the scheme.

Hence Chandulal made an alternative proposal to the Resident, saying that instead of ceding territories in perpetuity, he would assign the revenues of the districts to the British till such time as the loan with interest was gradually cleared.[29] Inspite of his repeated appeals to the Resident to

27. Ibid. p, 168.
28. H. R. R. Vol. 8 Foreign & Secret Dept. No. 17 of 1844.
29. H. Fraser-Memoirs and Correspondence of J. S. Fraser, p. 175.

recieve him from his financial distress, Chandulal never gave to the Resident a factual report of the actual indebtedness of the State inspite of the latter requesting him several times to do so.

Upon General Fraser making private enquiries from the local *sowcars*, he learnt that the debts of the State ran to the extent of two crores of Rupees apart from the pay of the Contingent troops which was in arrears for nearly five months.[30]

Finding that he could not manage without some substantial monetary help Maharajah Chandulal made a formal proposal to the Resident in April 1843 asking for a loan of a crore of rupees in lieu of which he promised to assign territories yielding seventeen lakhs of rupees per year as security for the payment of principal and interest.[30-A]

But the Government of India replied to this appeal of the Minister saying that it would not advance money on a commercial basis. It said unless it had some political object in view it would not advance any money. At the same time the Supreme Government at Calcutta wanted to prevent the possibility of the pay of the Contingent falling heavily into arrears. In case of such a contingency arising it wanted to intervene in the internal administration of the Nizam and also to aid his Government with the necessary monetary grant. So it instructed the Resident that in case of such an emergency arising, to advance the necessary sums to clear the arrears of the pay of the Contingent troops and to take over the management of some districts belonging to the Nizam as a security for the repayment of the principal of the loan within a period of five years.

The pay of the Contingent troops was in arrears for the last six months. So the Resident demanded of the Minister, the payment of at least two months salaries of the troops, This made the Minister to make a desperate appeal to the Nizam, asking him to advance money from his private treasury to discharge the arrears of pay of the contingent troops as well as the other debts of the State.

The Nizam refused to accede to the request of the Minister, so Chandulal finding his position quite untenable tendered his resignation,

Past experience having made him realise that it was not wise on his part to interfere with Chandulal the Nizam refused to accept the resignation of the Minister lest it might offend the British.

To find a way out of this stalemate Chandulal suggested that the Resident should countersign on the bonds that he would give to the *sowcars* if they were to lend him money to discharge the arrears of the Contingent troops. But the Resident refused to countersign the bonds as it would imdirectly make him responsible for the money.

30A. Ibid. p. 178, 179.

30. H. R. R. Vol, 79, L, No, 87 of 1843 pp, 72, 73,

Seeing this attitude of the Resident, Chandulal suggested that he should write to the Nizam asking him to adopt some definite course of action in order to end the deadlock. The Resident accordingly wrote to the Nizam requesting him to find a way out of the stalemate.[31]

On the receipt of above communications from the Resident, the Nizam sent his confidential secretary Rasheed-ul-Mulk to the Resident, and conveyed through him the Nizam's willingness to accept the resignation of Chandulal provided it was recommended by the Resident. General Fraser also realised during the course of his conversation with Rasheed-ul-Mulk that the Nizam was afraid even to examine the financial accounts of the State as long as the Minister remained in office.

Upon Fraser telling Rasheed-ul-Mulk that the Nizam should decide about the choice of a successor to Chandulal, Rasheed-ul-Mulk replied saying that for the time being the Nizam would assume all executive power in the State, and when the time for appointing the future Diwan came he would make the appointment after consulting the Resident.

On hearing that the resignation of the Minister must be sent through the Resident for the Nizam's acceptance, General Fraser asked Rasheed-ul-Mulk, why the Nizam would not accept the resignation of the Minister straightway. To this Rasheed-ul-Mulk gave the enigmatic reply saying "He wishes it to be done through you."[32]

This reply of the Munshi is quite revealing. It showed the fear of the Nizam that he might incur the displeasure of the British if it were to appear that he was eager to accept the resignation of the Minister, even though he felt that it was Chandulal who was responsible for the economic ruin of the country.

General Fraser replied to Rasheed-ul-Mulk saying that in such an important matter, as forwarding the resignation of the Minister he would have to consult the Governor General in Council, but he advised him to inform the Nizam to accept Chandulal's resignation, and also to appoint immediately a Diwan or a Commission to look after the administration in the State.

The Supreme Government on hearing of the resignation of Chandulal, conveyed to Fraser their acquiescence to Chandulal being retired from service,[33]

Chandulal inspite of his proferred resignation still tried to retain power by complaining to Lord Ellenborough against General Fraser saying that the latter was inimical towards him, but the Governor-General-in-Council did not take cognisance of his complaints against the Resident. On

31, Ibid P, 31,
32. H. R. R. Vol. 79. L. No. 76 of 1843 pp. 91-101.
33, H. R. R. Vol. 80, L, No, 17 of 1844 date 3-4-1844.

the other hand they sent back to the Resident, the letters written by Chandulal to the Governor-General, against the Resident saying that as the Resident was the proper channel of communication between him and the Supreme Government, at Calcutta, those letters should be duly returned to Chandulal.[34] After receiving this rebuff Chandulal resigned himself to his fate.

In the meanwhile General Fraser finding that Chandulal and even Rasheed-ul-Mulk who was actually a partisan of the Minister were intriguing against him, not only refused to have any communication with them but even refused to recognise Chandulal as the Minister.

The Nizam there upon appointed Rajah Ram Baksh a nephew of Chandulal as the Peishkar and Siraj-ul-Mulk the son of Munir-ul-Mulk the former Diwan of Hyderabad, as his vakil and the channel of communication between him and the Resident.

Fraser acquiesed in this arrangement in the hope that Siraj-ul-Mulk would ultimately be appointed as the Diwan by the Nizam.

[35] The Supreme Government apart from expressing their acquiesal in the resignation of Chandulal also conveyed to Fraser, their wllingness to advance a crore of rupees to the Nizam's Government upon certain conditions.

These were that the Nizam should hand over the administration of his country to the Resident till such time his debt to the British Government was discharged with compound interest at the rate of 5% per annum, and till the Resident was certain that similar economic embarassments would not arise in the future.[35-A]

The Supreme Government also wanted the Nizam to allow the British Government to appropriate any surplus revenue that might come on account of the efficient administration of the country under the direction of the Resident, The Supreme Government also wanted the Resident to insist on the punctual payment of the Contingent.

These proposals were embodied in the form of a draft treaty and were sent to the Resident for implementation.

The Court of Directors on hearing of this, recorded their opinion of the clause pertaining to the utilisation of the surplus revenues of the Nizam's state in the following manner.[36] "We cannot however approve of the conditional provision which you were desirous of making for the appropriation of surplus revenue to the general purposes of India. No surplus revenue, could of course exist while any debt remained unliquidated and the stipulation, therefore, could apply to no case but that of our retaining the management after all our advances had been repaid with compound interest. This,

34. H. Fraser – Memoirs & Correpsondence of J. S. Fraser P. 196. Chandulal to Ellenborough dated 20th Oct. 1843.
35. H. R. R. Vol, 80 L, No, 17.
35-A, L. No, 95 of 1843, Vol. 79 Note 1-P, 146 Note 2,
36, Ibid Para 13, 14,

under the proposed treaty, we could only do on the ground of our not be satisfied that the country could be properly governed by the Native authorities, and this ought not to be presumed before hand, nor ought we to ad a provision which would bear the appearance of a preconcieved determi tion not to relinquish the management".

However, this draft treaty sent by the Supreme Government never implemented because the Nizam did not apply to the Resident, for a pecuniary aid. He met the financial needs of the state by advancing necessary money from his treasury at Golconda.

Finding that by the resignation of Chandulal, he had escaped frc the tutelage of the British, he was reluctant to be shackled once again appointing a Diwan of the Resident's choice.

Seeing this evasive attitude of the Nizam, Lord Ellenborough, expressed his dissatisfaction to the Resident by writing to General Fraser in the following manner, "I cannot but regret that Chandulal was definitely put o of office before all arrangements had been made for the appointment of successor of whom you approved, and for the payment of the more pressin debts of the State, including the arrears due to the troops, Chandulal havin gone with your consent, I fear the chief hold upon the Nizam is gone too and that relieved from the incubus he will trifle and delay, and do nothing i the way of reform.

Your expectations that Sooraj-ul-Mulk will be made Chief Ministe seem to be just, but I should have been more satisfied had he been appointe Minister at once".[37]

The Court of Directors also showed their disapproval at this delayin tactics of the Nizam by saying[38] "It is a matter of much regret that befor our consent was given to the deprivation, of Chandulal, efficient arrangements were not made for the purpose of carrying on the future administration of the country".

Chandulal inspite of his retiring from Office continued to exert his influence on the Nizam and tried to throw obstacles in the way of his appointing a Diwan. At his instigation the Nizam informed the Resident that as far as the revenue administration of the country was concerned he considered the powers vested by him in Ram Baksh the Peishkar as quite sufficient.

Lord Ellenbourough wanted to directly communicate with the Nizam on the advisability of appointing a Diwan in accordance with the wishes of the Resident that the Nizam's Dominions could no longer be considered as constituting a separate unit since they formed "a component part of a

37. H, Fraser Memoir and Correspondence of General J, S, Fraser P, 194,
38. H, R, R. Vol, 80 L, 17 Para 21,

powerful Empire, in which unity of thought and purpose are essential to the well being of the whole."[39]

But Lord Ellenborough left India in June 1844 and he was succeeded by Sir Henry Hardinge as the Governor-General.

In the meanwhile the pay of the Contingent troops again began to fall into heavy arrears. So Lord Hardinge, sent a letter of warning to the Nizam dated the 11th April 1845, saying that he would not permit the pay of the Contingent troops to fall into arrears for more than four months, and if that were to happen the Nizam should borrow from the Residency to pay the Contingent troops, on the terms laid down by the Resident.

A year after this friendly warning of the Governor-General, the Nizam sought the assistance of the Contingent troops to punish some refractory zamindars, but the Resident informed Siraj-ul-mulk the Vakeel of the Nizam, that the services of the Contingent troops could not be lent to the Nizam unless their arrears were paid and one months salary was given to them as advance ? He also informed Siraj-ul-Mulk that the Contingent could not be moved against any rebel or defaulters merely at the request of the Nizam "unless the reality of the offence had been ascertained" !

The irony of the situation could be fully appreciated when we remember that the Contingent was originally formed by the Nizam to assist the British with a Contingent force of 6,000 Infantry and 9.000 cavalry in the event of war, according to the stipulations of the treaty of 1800!

The Resident however called the accused zamindars and settled the disputes between them and the Nizam. At the same time he refused to assist the Nizam in expelling the bands of Rohillas that infested the Nizam's dominions until their claims were adjusted. The Nizam meekly put up with this unjust attitude of the British Government.

General Fraser, finding that the Nizam was delaying the appointment of the Diwan pressed the Nizam to make the appointment. But the reply he got was that Chandulal who had resigned was only a Peishkar, and as Ram Baksh had already been appointed in his place as the Peishkar, and was now discharging the duties that were performed by Chandulal there was no need to appoint a Diwan, an office that was lying vacant ever since the death of Munir-ul-Mulk.

This subtle reasoning of the Nizam's Court exasperated General Fraser and the irate Resident urged the Governor-General to send a letter of remonstrance to the Nizam asking him to appoint a Diwan immediately.[40]

The Resident also impressed on the Nizam and his nobles that though Maharajah Chandulal's official designation was only that of a Peishkar to

39, H, R, R, Vol, 79 L, No, 110 pp, 165-166,
40, H, R, R, Vol, p, 162 of 1846,

the Diwan, yet for all practical purposes he exercised the full powers of the Diwan, and that he was usually referred to as the Minister in all the correspondence of the British, the word Minister in the English language being synonymous with the term Diwan.

He also wrote to Siraj-ul-Mulk to inform the Nizam that "the appointment of a Diwan is the preliminary step which must precede any other or more general arrangement for the future better regulation of the affairs of the State".

In the meanwhile a letter arrived from the Governor-General in the name of the Nizam asking him to appoint a Diwan without any delay.

Armed with this letter, General Fraser sought an interview with the Nizam on the 2nd November 1846, and impressed upon the Nizam the necessity of appointing a Diwan.[41] The Nizam on hearing this declared his intention of appointing Shums-ul-Umara as the Diwan. But Shums-ul-Umara though belonging to one of the noble families in Hyderabad happened to be too old to take up the responsibilities and rigours of the office of Diwanship. So General Fraser told the Nizam that he could not agree to the appointment of Shums-ul-Umara as the Diwan.[42]

Thereupon the Nizam asked General Fraser to suggest any one, whom, the latter thought suitable for occupying the post of a Diwan in the Hyderabad State. Fraser suggested Siraj-ul-Mulk as a suitable candidate for the office of Diwanship. The Nizam accepted the suggestion of the Resident.[43]

Fraser, while recommending the name of Siraj-ul-Mulk, knew fully well that certain courtiers at the Court of the Nizam had tried to poison the mind of the ruler against Siraj-ul-Mulk by saying that if Siraj-ul-Mulk were to become the Diwan he would take the earliest opportunity to surrender the whole country to the British Government. So the Resident tried to dispel the fears of the Nizam by assuring him in the following manner, "that in the event of Sooraj-ool-Mulk being invested with the office of Diwan, if ever he forgot that his first duty was to his Sovereign, and that the primary object of his future life was to be that of maintaining intact the honour and independence of his country, I should myself be the first to denounce and abandon him."[44]

The Nizam after investing Siraj-ul-Mulk as the Diwan, conveyed the news of this appointment to the Governor-General in the following manner "I said to that undoubted well wisher of the nobles of this court Major-General James Stuart Fraser Bahadur whom do you consider qualified for the appointment of Diwan? This undoubted well-wisher spoke highly of

41, H, R, R, Vol, 83 Mis. L, No, 127 of 1846 p, 151,
42, Ibid L, No, 128 of 1846 pp, 151-59.
43, Ibid Para 30-33,
44, Ibid 32,

the capacity of that exalted in dignity and rank, that receptacle of courage and excellence, that faithful and wise servant, Sooraj-ool-Mulk, Bahadur, as adapting him for that office. I, therefore, having assented to this, and considering it proper, have elevated the aforesaid Bahadoor to the dignity, of Madar-ool-Muham.[45]

The Indian Government on the receipt of this letter noticed, that the Nizam had tried to lay stress on the fact that Siraj-ul-Mulk had been appointed Diwan only on the specific recommendation of the Resident. Since the British at this time professed to follow a policy of non-interference in the internal affairs of the Native States the Governor-General and his Council while sending the *Kharita*, recognising the appointment of Siraj-ul-Mulk as the Diwan, had it so worded that it gave the impression of the Nizam appointing Siraj-ul-Mulk as the Diwan of his own free will after consulting the Resident,

In spite of the appointment of Siraj-ul-Mulk as the Diwan matters did not improve in the State, Siraj-ul-Mulk soon after his becoming the Diwan had sent a *Kharita* to the Governor-General, informing the latter of his appointment. The Governor-General neglected to reply to this letter of the Minister, and later on wrote to General Fraser disapproving of the style in which the letter was addressed. In that letter Siraj-ul-Mulk called himself as "the friend and well wisher of the British, The Governor-General expressed his disapprobation by writing to General Fraser, "The circumstances of India have greately altered since his predecessor, Mir Alam, received the address forty years ago, which is now cited as a precedent, and the relative position of the Governor-General of India and the Minister of Hyderabad renders it no longer advisable that the representative of the British Government should be addressed in terms approaching equality by the Minister of a protected and subsidised State".[45]

Commenting about this H. Fraser says, that it was the British Government that was a "subsidised state instead of the Nizam's Government on account of the fact that the Nizam's Government never received any subsidy from the British, but on the other hand paid for the British subsidiary force.

Hastings Fraser's no doubt was correct in his argument, but the importance of the letter lies in the fact that it reveals the true state of things. For all practical purposes the Nizam's Government was subservient to the British. Naturally the British who were conscious of their power did not scruple to call the Nizam's State a "subsidised State".

This negligence of the Supreme Government to reciprocate by sending a complimentary letter to Siraj-ul-Mulk was construed in the court circle as lack of goodwill on the part of the Supreme Government towards the Minister. This gave them the courage to thwart not only the Minister

45, H, Fraser-Memoirs and Correspondence of General J, S, Fraser p, 217,

but also the Resident in their attempts to introduce any economic reforms in the State, by way of retrenchment in the irregular forces of the Nizam.

The Resident could think only of retrenchment in the irregular army of the Nizam, for he knew the jealous manner in which the Supreme Government safeguarded the interests of the Contingent Forces.

General Fraser wanted the British Government to empower the Resident more explicitly, to intervene in the internal administration of the State and to introduce salutary reforms if necessary. He wanted the Supreme Government to warn the Nizam to reinovate his administration through his Minister under the able direction and guidance of the Resident, but the Supreme Government, did not deem it necessary to do so, so long as it received regularly the salaries of the Contingent forces; Complaining about this the Resident wrote to his friend Major Oliphant, a member of the Court of Directors in the following manner :"[46] - - - - the expulsion of the Arabs and other foreign mercenaries, whose presence here has been so injurious for a long series of years might have been accomplished if I could have inspired the Government of India with the requisite determination and energy on this subject.

Everything else that I had planned might in a similar manner have been done, and the Hyderabad country might at this moment have been progressing, But the Governor-General, as I have said above, was otherwise occupied, and I could not prevail on him to act, or to attend to Hyderabad affairs. He thought that force alone was requisite, and told me that his troops were engaged elsewhere. It was in vain that I assured him they would not be wanted. No military force would ever have been required; but even if it had been, I had in the Contingent and the Subsidiary force more than enough to overcome any resistance that could possibly have been offered anywhere. I repeat however that such a contingency was not for one instant to be apprehended.

The present Governor-General, deterred, perhaps, by the fear of counteraction at home, or by some other motives I cannot fathom, pauses and heistates when we ought to be moving on. He permitted me, after I had been urging the point for three years. to insist upon the appointment of a Minister. But the advantage of a Diwan has been nullified by the same hesitating and undecided spirit of which I have already complained. He is not supported by the Supreme Government, but quite the reverse; and with every corrupt agency in active operation at Hyderabad to put him down, besides the unfavourable disposition of the Supreme Government to contend against it, it is utterly impossible he should succceed. The determination of the Governor-General to allow the Nizam to have his own way, leaving him to glide down the slope that leads to destruction, I will not venture to

46. Fraser, Memoirs & Correspondence of J, S, Fraser Letter to Oliphant d, 7th Oct,1847 pp, 226-229,

dilate upon, because I could hardly avoid being disrespectful to the Government I serve; but I may at least be permitted to say that I know not how to reconcile the instructions of Government with its declared wish to maintain the independence of the Hyderabad State. While professing to uphold Treaties that subsist between us and the Nizam, resolutions are adopted by the Bengal Government which must necessarily produce a disruption of our present relations with the Nizam, and the downfall of his independence."

While matters were in such a state, Lord Dalhousie arrived in India in 1848 as the Governor-General; Lord Dalhousie's attention soon after his arrival in India was fully engaged by the affairs in Northern India and he too assumed an indifferent attitude towards the deteriorating situation in Hyderabad.

He was indifferent whether matters drifted from bad to worse in the State; In vain did General Fraser remonstrate with him, time and again to actively support the Minister and the Resident against the intrigues that were afoot in the court. Lord Dalhousie in one of the despatches to the Resident declared "This Government disclaims not only the intention but the wish of doing any act by which the independence of the Nizam can be in any degree impaired. The Treaty itself offers a bar to any such design, by declaring in the most emphatic terms, that the Government of India binds itself in no way to interfere with His Highness's subjects, servants or concerns."

If at all Lord Dalhousie's interest was to be roused, it could be roused only by the fate of the Contingent forces, and we find him later on in 1853, the great annexationist that he was, annexing certain parts of Hyderabad towards the maintenance of the Contingent forces. The Contingent which consisted of 9,000 men, for all practical purposes, belonged to the British. The Resident assisted by ninety English officers was virtually its commander, and it was on his recommendation after consulting the Supreme Government that promotions and transfers were effected.

All matters of expenditure, discipline and internal economy were decided by the Resident, while the expenditure was borne by the Nizam's Government. Only in matters of employing the troops and stationing them in different parts of the country, the Resident communicated with the Minister and the Nizam.

The cost of the Contingent during this period came to nearly forty-two lakhs of rupees per annum,[47] and this was a heavy drain on the finances of the Hyderabad State. Members of the Court of Directors like Sir James Lushington and even the Residency officials like Col. Low, Assistant Resident, realised the injustice that was done to the Nizam and they contemplated reducing the size of the Contingent in such a way that its maintenance charges would not amount to more than twenty lakhs of Rupees per annum.

47. Ibid p. 247,

They felt that a reduction in the size of the Contingent would in no way affect the security of the Nizam's Dominions, because ever since 1819 there was no external war. The services of the reduced Contingent could be utilised in an effective manner to put down local rebellions created by the turbulence of the Arab mercenaries etc.[48]

Col. Low, while writing to Sir James Law Lushington speaks of the Contingent forces as - - - - -. "We have been guilty towards the Nizam's Government in keeping up for so many years the continued drain upon the revenues of this country of no less than forty lakhs of rupees per annum for the pay of the Contingent in other words, for the purposes of our own, not of the Nizam.

Ever since 1819 there has been profound peace in the Deccan, and therefore as it is only during 'war between the contracting parties and any other power' that we can claim to be joined by 6,000 infantry and 9,000 Horse of His Highness's own troops', We have had no right by Treaty to demand a single rupee for a Contingent during the whole of that period, upwards of twenty-eight years. In the course of that time, however, we have actually drawn from the Nizam's treaty (not reckoning forty-two lakhs now due to us for advances to the Contingent) the enormous sum of eleven crores and twenty lakhs of Hyderabad rupees, of which a large portion has gone out of the Nizam's territories for ever - - - - - - so that this huge drain not only exhausts the Nizam's treasury, but tends to impoverish his people by diminishing the amount of specie in his Dominions - - - - - - -. Under all these circumstances, I know my assertion to be a correct one, that a Contingent costing twenty lakhs of rupees per annum would be to the full as useful to the Nizam as the present one costing forty lakhs. My plans would be to annul that part of the Treaty requiring the Nizam to join us in time of war with 6,000 infantry, and 9,000 cavalry and instead of it to bind him to keep up at all times a force that would cost twenty lakhs per annum. And if I could get a cession of territory for the payment of the Contingent, I would think that, so great an advantage that I would be quite satisfied with lands that yielded seventeen or eighteen lakhs only, making the Contingent of a corresponding strength. This would put an end to the continual pressure upon the Durbar for money - - - - 'give, give and give more' is the word perpetually in the Resident's mouth here, and it tends much to destroy his influence in all other matters.

But you talk of 'disbanding'. Now, much as I detest this drain upon the Nizam, I would never advise the sudden breaking up and dispensing of the Contingent. I would not do so - - - - - - for although we are very chary in affording the use of the Contingent, as I explained above, yet the Talukdars think that if they were to be guilty of rebellion, they would assuredly be punished by those very troops, known as they are to be ready for service

48, Ibid p, 256,

at all times, and posted in five or six different parts of these territories. Their presence, therefore operates as a check against insurrection."[49]

But this suggestion to reduce the size of the Contingent was ultimately not taken up and the Governor-General recorded his dissenting opinion by observing,[50] "I cannot perceive or acknowledge that the British Government commits any injustice or practises any extortion whatever on the Nizam's Government in requiring that this force, fully manned, equipped, and disciplined, shall be maintained in His Highness's territories and at his expense.

The Treaty of 1800 gave us a right to demand at any moment 15,000 troops from the Nizam - - - - - - we rightly and justly construed the Treaty to mean that we were to be supplied with the specified number of effective soldiers; and we therefore with unquestionable equity may and do demand of His Highness that certain precautions should be taken up on foot a regular force paid by him and officered by us, which shall be available for the maintenance of peace in those central districts of the Deccan, and we demand only 800 instead of 15,000 men.

Thus - - - - - - at the same time I agree with Col. Low, in thinking that we cause the Contingent to become a much heavier burden on the Nizam's finances than it ought to be. The staff in my humble judgement is preposterously large; the pay and allowances and charges of various kinds are far higher than they ought to be."

Thus, though the Governor-General did agree with Col. Low, that the Contingent was a huge drain on the resources of the State he was at this juncture not prepared to effect any reductions in the size of these troops; on the otherhand he preferred to interpret the subsidiary treaty of 1800 in a technical and literal manner without troubling to look into the prevailing conditions under which that treaty was drawn up.

Finding the distress of the Nizam's Government still unrelieved the Assistant Resident, Col. Low, who feared that Lord Dalhousie might assume the management of administration ultimately wrote: " - - - - - - for the sake of our own good name among the Native States of India, I sincerely hope that Hyderabad may be kept up as a Native Government, and it is undoubtedly possible that it may be so kept up, if ihe Nizam and his Minister will act according to Fraser's counsel in the principal arrangements of the Administration" - - - - - - I feel quite confident that Lord Dalhousie will never assume the direct management of the Hyderabad country if his Lordship does not honestly think the measure to be absolutely necessary, but our Native allies - - - - - - at a distance will never believe that there was any such necessity - - - - - - . They knew that there has been profound peace in this part of India for at least eight and twenty years. They know that this

49, Ibid pp, 248-251,
50. Burton "Hyderabad Contingent",

reigning family have been quite subservient to us for several generations, and if they shall ever hear of our reducing the Nizam and his Minister and nobles to ciphers, and of our managing the whole country and collecting its revenues by instruments of our own selection, made responsible exclusively to English officers, our allies will most assuredly ascribe the whole proceedings to our ambition and our supposed innate aversion to all Native sovereigns in India. And hence there will be no trifling increase to the suspicion, and fear and dislike of us that now exist in the minds of a great many chiefs in other Native States, while the Nizam and almost all the families of high rank in his country, and most of the military classes among his subjects, will of course most cordially detest us. They will forget their former miseries, and remember only the vexations they will be subject to under our rule; for the Natives of this country are, after all, not different in one respect from the inhabitants of all parts of the known world, in that they like their own way better than those of foreigners."[49]

Some of the members of the Court of Directors like Sir Henry Willock, General Caulfield, Colonel Sykes were also of the opinion that the Contingent was indeed an unbearable and unjustifiable expense that the British had tagged on to the Nizam's Exchequer.

Sir Henry Willock in a Minute dated 19th November 1851 declared that "by the gradual transformation of the Nizam's best irregular troops into the well disciplined Contingent, "completely under our control," the Prince was deprived of the services of those who had been his personal guards, and who constituted the force relied upon by the Collectors of revenue and officers of police, to maintain peace and order in the country, and was thus necessitated to organise another and very objectionable force composed of Pathans, Rohillas and Arabs, to enable him to carry on the administration, and support his own authority."

Col. Sykes, Major Moore and General Caulfield also recorded their opinion supporting the views of Sir Henry Willock by saying [51] "We impose an unnecessary expense of 42 lakhs of rupees annually upon the Nizam in maintaining a contingent, organised, disciplined and officered by us to peform those duties which by treaty devolve upon the subsidiary force, and we have withheld its services from the Nizam on grounds that cannot be defended' thereby rendering it necessary for His Highness to maintain at a heavy charge a large and inefficient force, with a view to avoid vexatious interference, and to afford employment to those of his adherents who have no other means of living."

But these members were in a minority. The majority of the members of the Court of Directors supported the views of the India Government, with the result no changes were made in the size or even the expenses of the Contingent forces.

---

49. Ibid p, 255, 50. Papers Relating to the Nizam L, No, 234 of 859 p, No, 1.
51. Ibid p, 21.

Unable to have his own way here, General Fraser turned his attention in the direction of the irregular forces of the Nizam.

On his advice Siraj-ul-Mulk tried to reduce the size of the irregular forces of the Nizam, and also introduced the Zilladari system of administration in the country. Under this system the Zilladar was expected to remain in the district headquarters where he was posted and not in the capital, as they were doing hitherto.

Siraj-ul-Mulk also wanted to make an enquiry into the feudal tenure, and the pay of the troops, that were in the employment of the various jagirdars. Naturally, this created a great panic in the minds of the various nobles of the Court. All the Mansabdars, Talukdars, Jaghirdars were now united as one man to rouse the ire of the Nizam against the Diwan, who they accused was trying to introduce European interference in the administration of the country.

The Nizam who had bitter experience of the Diwan running the administration on the advice of the Resident in the past, viewed with disfavour the reforms that were introduced by the Diwan. The Nizam looked upon the retrenchments in his irregular army as a measure to diminish his internal power and sovereignty.

Seeing the prejudice of the Court against his measures General Fraser wrote to Lord Dalhousie at least to sanction the scheme that was proposed by Lord Ellenborough, namely that of advancing a crore of rupees to the Nizam at 5% compound interest per annum and to assume the administration of the country for a temporary period. But Lord Dalhousie did not accept this recommendation of the Resident saying:[52] "If then H.H. chooses to take advantage of the power which we recognise him to hold, and disregarding our counsel, should take some other incapable person to be his Minister, he must bear his fate when it comes. But whatever may happen, or may not happen, the Government of India can undertake no great political reforms, can neither organise nor instruct a political revolution in the Kingdom of Hyderabad, until the war with the Punjab is concluded, and the affairs of that part of the country are settled. If the Nizam chooses to precipitate his crisis in the meantime, he must go to the dogs his own way, for the Government of India has no time just now to take care of him --------"

The only concession that Dalhousie was prepared to make at this juncture was to levy only 6% interest on the money advanced by the Resident to the Nizam's Government towards the payment of the salaries of the Contingent forces. In the meanwhile the nobles at the court of the Nizam started intriguing not only against the Minister but also against the Resident, and to effect his removal, for apparently, it looked as though he did not receive the support of the Supreme Government for his various schemes.

52. Ibid P, 268.

General Fraser who got an inkling of the intrigues that were afoot informed the Governor-General of the same; Lord Dalhousie in his characteristic manner assured the Resident of his full support by saying -------- "I am not disposed to attach much political importance to his interference, especially if the tenor of his communications is to any such effect as that reported, regarding the Governor-General immediateiy removing you, or any other Resident on the mere complaint of the Prince to whom he is accredited. If H. H. sends any impudent letter of that kind to me, I will make his knucles so smart as never Nizam's knuckle's smarted before."[53]

Though the Nizam did not report against the Resident, he dismissed his Diwan Siraj-ul-Mulk from office on the 10th November 1848. In his place he appointed Rajah Ram Baksh the nephew of Chandulal as the Peishkar on the latter promising to pay a sum of fifty lakhs of rupees as *nazrana* to relieve the state of its immediate financial stringency.

Though the office of the Diwan was at first conferred on Amjud-ul-Mulk, later on the Nizam appointed Nawab Shums-ul-Umara as the Diwan.

General Fraser who disapproved of the measure at first wanted to absent himself from the Court at the investiture ceremony of the Diwan but he was counselled by Lord Dalhousie not to adopt such a course.[54]

On the receipt of the news of the Diwan's dismissal, Lord Dalhousie expressed his pain and surprise at the news and further wrote to the Nizam saying; "[55]The Governor-General does not desire to dictate to His Highness the person whom he shall employ in his service as Diwan. His Highness the Nizam is an independent Sovereign. The British Government desire that he should continue to be so and will rejoice to see his country made happy and his people prosperous. But the Governor-General is desirous of impressing upon the mind of His Highness the grave importance of the circumstances in which he is acting and the fatal consequences to His Highness dignity and realm which may be the result of his acting unwisely at so critical a time.

The State of Hyderabad is oppressed with heavy debt. The advances made by the British Government for the payment of troops are largely increased.

The Governor-General desires clearly and distinctly to warn His Highness that within a short space of time his treasury will be bankrupt, and his whole Kingdom in disorder and confusion. - - - - - - - - - - - - - - - - - -

In such a state of things the British Government would probably feel itself compelled to exercise a peremptory interference in the internal administration of His Highness' Dominions ---- The Governor-General

53, p, 282,
54, Ibid p, 283,
55, Ibid p, 285,

sincerely trusts that His Highness will give heed to these friendsly words, and that regard for the honour and interests of his own realm will induce him to act as to avert the adoption of such measures by the British Government as must tend to lower His Highness' dignity and to reduce his power."

After receiving such letters, the Nizam naturally could never by any stretch of imagination think that this very same Lord Dalhousie would demand territorial concessions from him without any justification.

By the middle of 1850 the debt due to the East India Company on account of the "Contingent Troops" charges, stood at sixty four lakhs of Rupees.[56] The Nizam was told specifically that he should discharge the interest regularly, and that the Diwan should be instructed to discharge the principal debt also as early as possible. The Nizam was also told that the British Government would not allow hereafter any arrears to accumulate in the pay of the Contingent troops. If it were to happen, the Governor-General warned the Nizam that he would have to adopt such measures as would be necessary to secure the British interests. But even now the Governor-General did not indicate the direction in which his mind was working.

But inspite of this warning the Nizam's Government could not keep up the regular payment of the Contingent troops. At the time of his assuming office, Shums-ul-Umara had assured General Fraser that he would pay 17 lakhs of rupees every four months towards liquidation of the Nizam's debt to the Company. Later on, he assured Fraser that he would pay the interest every month, and five lakhs of rupees per year beginning from April 1850 towards the clearance of the debt. General Fraser doubted very much the ability of the Nizam's Government to keep up this promise. Moreover, calculated at the rate proposed by Shums-ul-Umara it would take eleven long years for the Nizam's Government to clear the whole debt, and the Resident was afraid that the Supreme Government might not be amenable to such a plan.[57]

So General Fraser once again pleaded that the Resident must be empowered to initiate reforms in the State with the aid of the Diwan, to bring about a curtailment in the expenditure of the State.

But this the Governor-General would not allow. Shums-ul-Umara very soon realised the difficulties of the situation in which he was placed. He submitted the receipts of the revenue that was expected for the ensuing year, and expressed in an interview to the then Assistant Resident Capt. C. Davidson, that it was impossible for him to settle the whole debt at once. He said that if he wanted he could at once pay fiftyfour lakhs of rupees and clear off the debt due to the Company, but it would not be of advantage to

56, Ibid p, 289,
57. Ibid, P- 193.

Nizam's Government, unless the Minister was taken into the confidence of Nizam, and was invested with full powers. The Diwan also told Capt. Davidson that the court nobles and the Nizam were jealous of any signs of growing intimacy between the Diwan and the Residency, and that they secretly worked against the growth of such an intimacy, So, Shums-ul-Umara pleaded that he should be supported by the Resident in the administrative measures he wanted to introduce.

Upon Resident Fraser informing the inability of Shums-ul-Umara to pay up the debt, the grandieloquent reply he got from Lord Dalhousie was "I am sorry that the Nizam is bent on breaking his own head apparently, but if he is resolved on doing so, I shall provide that the interests of this Government are fully cared for - - - - "In short, my hands are likely to be full enough of these booby potentates for sometime".

He also wrote "I say nothing of the debt until the answer of the Minister comes ; - - - - - - - I must have those sixty lakhs prompt payment - - - - I am in earnest in it; and you may, therefore, feel secure, when communicating the message to His Highness, in employing such earnestness of expression as may let him know that I will infalliably do what I say.

Purposely I have avoided specifying any particular measure; but he may make up his mind that there will then be decided action on the part of this Government."[58]

Finding that it was impossible to carry on the administration against so many odds Shums-ul-Umara tendered his resigantion of which the Resident was informed by the Nizam on the 6th July 1849.[59] During Shums-ul-Umara's short tenure of office, nearly a period of five months, the monthly pay of the Contingent was paid regularly. But after his resignation, Rajah Ram Baksh who was the Peishkar again allowed the payment of the Contingent forces to fall into arrears.

So Lord Dalhousie finding that the time to adopt a more stern attitude with the Nizam was drawing near demanded that the whole debt must be liquidated by the 31st December 1850. He also declared that if the Nizam's Government failed to do so he would be forced to take more decided steps.

It was well understood what the decided steps would be, namely, the exaction of territorial security towards the payment of the principal and interest.

When Fraser, at one time had written to Lord Dalhousie saying it was a moral obligation on the part of the British to promote the material welfare of the Native States with whom they were at alliance Dalhousie replied saying[60] "I will rigidly act upto the requirements of the Treaty with him. I will give him aid and advice. I will effectually take care that if he chooses

58. Ibid. PP. 291, 296. L. D/6th July 1849, & 30th May 1849.
59. Ibid. P. 298.

to ruin himself in spite of aid and advice, he shall not disturb the peace of British territory, or either injure or play with British interests. But I will not contravene the treaty on the pretence of protecting the Nizam, and I disavow the doctrine of our having any moral or political obligation to take the Government of his country into our own hands, merely because he mismanages his own affairs; and I recognise no mission entrusted to us to regenerate independent Indian States, merely because they are misgoverned."

Lord Dalhousie in the name of the sanctity of the Treaty of 1800, refused to intervene in the internal administration of the Nizam, but he had no scruples to entertain while demanding territorial cessions, for the existence of a force which had no legal basis, and we find him blandly writing to General Fraser to let him know what districts would be suitable for the British to take over. He wrote "I do not care much about the liquidation of the principal of the debt, or even about the regular payment of the interest in the intervening period from November 1849 to December 31st, 1850, but I am quite disinclined to recur again to the periodical advance of the pay for the contingent implying as it does, previous inconvenience and hardship upon the troops; as well as a gradual increase of the already existing debt.

The Nizam will force me, in such a case, to take possession of territory at once, whereby the means of paying the contingent with certainity and regularity will be placed in the hands of this Government, virtually pledged to ensure such payment.

It would not be expedient yet to make this announcement definitely to the Minister. It's necessity, however at an early period, appears to be probable, that I beg to have, confidentially, your views on the particular districts which may be most conventiently mortgaged, as it were, for this purpose, clearly, one adjoining to our territories at some point would be desirable."[61]

When we read this letter of Lord Dalhousie we could assuage how the mind of this arch imperialist was working from the beginning. He was abiding his time to snatch territory at a favourable opportunity from the Nizam. Since there was no likelihood of the Nizam declaring war against the British in a bold manner, the only way by which Lord Dalhousie could appropriate territories from this subservient and docile ally was under some pretext and that pretext was found in the accumulation of the arrears of pay of the Hyderabad Contingent, a Contingent which the Nizam was not bound to maintain at all.

He never bothered to consider that the subsidiary troops was the only British army that was entitled to be maintained by the Nizam, and towards whose maintenance the latter had already ceded territories.

---

60. Ibid, 291.
61. Ibid, 303.

General Fraser who was under the impression that the cession of territories that would be demanded from the. Nizam would be only for a temporary period recommended the Berar Payen Ghat and the Balaghat along with the districts of Bassim.

He estimated the revenue of these three districts at Rs. 39,89,000 while the annual expense of the Nizam's Army, i. e., the Contingent he estimated at Rs. 38,26,500/-.

Speaking about the Berar Payen Ghat he wrote, "Berar Payen Ghat is the richest and most profitable portion of the Nizam's dominions both in an agricultural and commercial point of view - - - - I believe there is no part of India superior to it for the production of cotton - - - - - - - - - .

"The three Talooks I mention are compactly situated, forming nearly a square of parallelogram, of which the North and Northwest boundary would be the chain of hills on which the forts of Narnull and Gauilghur are situated, adjoining the Company's districts on the Nerbudda a portion of Scindia's country and part of Khandesh. The North East boundary would be the Warda river which separates the Nizam's dominions from those of the Rajah of Nagore."[62]

General Fraser also suggested that in case the actual revenue yield of these districts fell below the estimation made by him, the British could demand additional adjoining districts on the Nanded side, keeping in view not only the pay of the Contingent, but Appa Dessaye's Chouth and the allowance given to Mahipat Ram's family which amounted altogether to Rs. 1,26,000/- per month, besides the interest of Rs. 3,24,000/- that accrued every year on the Nizam's debt.

Though he made the above recommendation, Fraser also informed the Supreme Government that if the Nizam was faced with the choice of ceding territories, or discharging his debts to the Company from his private treasury by mortgaging his jewels the Nizam would prefer to follow the latter course.

Rajah Ram Baksh though he was invested with the office of the Peishkar did not possess ony independent powers. The Nizam who had bitter experience of his connection with the British, viewed with jealousy any attempt on the part of either the Diwan or the Peishkar to carry on any administrative measures on the advice of the Resident.

He deliberately thwarted every action of the Peishkar. He wanted to enforce his own personal rule, and also wanted his Diwan or Peishkar to receive orders about administrative matters directly from him and not from the Resident.

62. Ibid P. 306

The Resident resented this attitude of the Nizam and wrote in exasperation to the Supreme Government "It is my deliberate opinion, formed after considerable experience of the character of the Nizam, that nothing less than a decided British administration will save this country as long as the present Sovereign remains on the musnud."[63]

During this time such was the general dislike for the British among the people that Nizam's officers and men tried to thwart the British whenever and wherever it was possible. They found it rather convenient to give vent to their latent resentment against the British by harassing British subjects who came as travellers to the Nizam's country and also the Company's detachments that wanted to ford the rivers or ferried across into the British territory.

When the Resident armed with a letter from the Supreme Government went to remonstrate with the Nizam about this, the Nizam after assuring the Resident that such incidents would not happen in future, told the Peishkar in the presence of the Resident, very pointedly, that the Peishkar should take his instructions from the Nizam. Then the Nizam while professing his friendehip towards the British, and the mutual advantage derived by both the powers on account of this friendship and alliance pointedly drew the attention ofGeneral Fraser to the acquisitions made by the British by virtue of their alliance with the Nizam. General Fraser wrote to the Supreme Government, "He asked me if I had ever known him to do an oppressive act or whether I ever heard complaints of his own personal proceeding; and after this he spoke at considerable length regarding the relations between his Government and ours, and the advantage we had received from our connection with him, epeciaily our possession of the Northern Circars, the Ceded Districts and more recently, the District of Kurnool."[64]

This pointed reference of the Nizam to the various territorial gains made by the British East Indian Company in the name of their alliance with the Nizam shows that the Nizam, Nasir-ud-Doula, was conscious of the injustice that was done to him. But at the same time he was also conscious of his helplessness against the all powerful British. Being a shrewd man, he tried to strike his bargain by friendly mediation and timely subservience. Nasir-ud-Doula tried as far as possible to lessen the interference of the British in the internal affairs of the State. He looked upon with jealousy any growing intimacy between the Resident and the Diwan or even the Peishkar. We can attribute to this dislike of his the dismissal of both Siraj-ul-Mulk and Shums-ul-Umara. Whenever Fraser reminded the Nizam of the necesstiy of having a proper Diwan and entrusting him with responsible powers to carry on the administration, the Nizam used to ask

63. Ibid P. 308.
64. Ibid P. 309

Fraser, if Mr. Martin, the former Resident in Hyderabad (1825-1830) had not assured him that he was free to appoint and dismiss his own Diwans.

All these tend to show the anxiety of the Nizam to preserve his personal rule and internal sovereignty but the odds were too strong against him. He had to contend against the cankerous encroachments of the British, whose interference spread in his State administration as a gangrene and ate up his internal sovereignty.

Rajah Ram Baksh, at the time of his appointment as the Diwan, had promised to furnish the Nizam with fifty lakhs every year towards the maintenance of the Contingent, and also to advance a sum of sixty lakhs to tide over the immediate financial difficulties of the State. But the Peishkar quite naturally was not able to keep up the promise.

Now that the Nizam had heard rumours that the British might demand territorial cessions from him for the money due from his Government to the British towards the payment of the Contingent, the Nizam at first proposed that he would advance ten lakhs of rupees from his treasury and then pawn his jewals for the remaining amount. Finding that it was not feasible and that the Peishkar had not kept the promises he made at the time of his appointment, the Nizam dismissed Ram Baksh from the office of the Peishkarship on the 7th October, 1850. In the meanwhile, the time laid down by Lord Dalhousie for liquidating the debt due to the Company was fast approaching.

So the Nizam deputed Siraj-ul-Mulk to inform the Resident that the Nizam intended to clear off the debt to the British in instalments of twelve lakhs of rupees per annum, and the Resident was requested to recommend the proposal to the Government of India.

By January 1851, the Nizam's debt to the British East India Company stood at 70 lakhs of rupees, and there was no sign of the debt being cleared in spite of the promise made by the Nizam earlier to clear the debt in yearly instalments of twelve lakhs of rupees.

So General Fraser waited on the Nizam on the 25th January, 1851, and in the interview with the Nizam tried to impress him with the necessity of appointing a regular Diwan; he also informed the Nizam that his proposal to clear the debt by paying 12 lakhs every year would not meet with the approval of the India Government because it would mean a delay in the realisation of the debt. According to the Nizam's proposal it would take six years for him to clear the debt if he was to make regular payments. But the Nizam has yet, had not kept his promise of even paying off fifty lakhs of rupees by the 8th October, 1850.

The Nizam after hearing the Resident, expressed his regret at his inability to keep to his promise, which he attributed to the failure of his negotiations with the Sowcars; and hinted to the Resident that he had family jewels worth about one and a quarter crore of rupees. But the Resident gave him no hope to suppose that the Bitish Government would approve of such a security.

About the appointment of Diwan with regular powers, the Nizam tried to evade the issue by saying that the office entailed a large salary and heavy establishment charges. On hearing this, the Resident suggested that the salary of the Diwan could be reduced from Rs. 25,000/- per month to Rs. 10,000/- per mensem, but the Nizam was too shrewd to commit himself to a specific manner.

The fact was, the Nizam felt that the only way to preserve his authority was by not appointing a Diwan lest he might become a second Chandulal and try to dictate terms to the Nizam, banking on the support of the Resident.

General Fraser was of the opinion that the only way to restore order in the administration of the country, and to preserve the nominal sovereignty of the Nizam was by introducing effective reform in the State through a pliable Diwan who would carry out the instructions of the Resident without any hesitation.

Finding the attitude of the Nizam quite unhelpful in this respect, the Resident wrote to the Governor-General urging him to address a strong letter of remonstrance to the Nizam, depicting the general chaos in the country owing to the existence of swarming bands of Arabs and Rohillas in the country and asking the Nizam to hand over the administration of the country for a temporary period, to the exclusive management of the British, as his attempts to administer the country without the help of a Diwan had failed, or if the Nizam did not like to hand over his country to British management even for a temporary period, to appoint a Diwan, empowering him to work in concurrence with the British Resident.[65]

These letters of Resident Fraser to the Supreme Government, show that the Resident was anxious to preserve for all outward appearances the facade of the Nizam's suzerainty.

Since Lord Dalhousie had asked General Fraser to suggest districts yielding nearly thirtyfive lakhs of rupees annually, for the British to take over, and enable the Nizam to discharge his debt within a period of three years, Fraser suggested instead a scheme of introducing European officers into the civil administration of the country and renovating the revenue administration. Fraser, in order to achieve this object wanted to take over for a temporary period of at least five years, the administration of the State into his own hands. He hoped to implement his reforms through a Diwan, who would act in accordance with the instructions of the Resident, but who would owe his allegiance to the Nizam.

65. Ibid pp 329, 331, L. dated 12th March 1851 and 14th March 1851.

Lord Dalhousie who had ulterior motives in allowing things to drift to a final catastrophe in Hyderabad did not approve of the recommendations made by the Resident. In the meanwhile, the Nizam appointed one Ganesh Rao as his Peishkar on the 25th February 1851..

Fraser was furious on hearing of the appointment of Ganesh Rao, and he showed his disapproval by refusing to have any communications with the Peishkar. Seeing this attitude of the Resident and knowing that the predilection of the Resident lay towards Siraj-ul-Mulk, the Nizam cancelled the appointment of Ganesh Rao, and deputed Siraj-ul-Mulk once again as his vakeel with the Resident without conferring the office of the Diwan on him.[66]

In the policy that General Fraser adopted towards Ganesh Rao, and the appointment of a regular Diwan in Hyderabad, the Supreme Government not only gave him little encouragement but adopted a very unhelpful and indifferent attitude, towards the whole problem.

The Resident who did not want to perpetuate any injustice on the Nizam by divesting him of his territories for an unjust cause was exasperated by this attitude of the India Government, and began to entertain doubts about their good faith. Referring about this matter to his friend Major Moore one of the members of the Court of Directors, he tartly remarked [67]"I am ashamed of the weakness and irresolution of my own Government, and I would add a still meaner quality, but that it is just possible they did not speak with deliberate hypocrisy—although it has that effect—in professing a wish to maintain the Nizam's independence, while obstinately refusing to adopt or encourage the measures which alone could have promoted that object"

By April 1851, the Nizam's debt to the British increased to seventy five lakhs. So now Lord Dalhousie deeming that the time to remonstrate with the Nizam had come addressed a *Kharita* to the Nizam on the 6th June 1851. The Resident was expected to deliver this *Kharita* to the Nizam, and to demand the cession of districts for the temporary management of the British till the debt of the Nizam was completely cleared. In this *kharita* Lord Dalhousie not only expressed his strong disapproval of the State of affairs in Hyderabad but he told the Nizam not only of the absolute necessity of appointing a Diwan, but laso of maintaing the Contingent troops as an obligation imposed by regular treaty rights. The Governor General also warned the Nizam to check the indicipline of his Arab mercenaries, and prevent them from insulting and harassing passing British detachments lest he might incur the British displeasure. Describing about the indignation felt by the Government of India the Governor-General wrote that the Government

66. Ibid. P. 330–335
67. Ibid. P. 389–L. D/. 4th May 1851

of India's power was such that it could crush the Nizam at it's will. These were strong words which could hardly be applied against an equal ally. These words when translated into the persian language as was very often done in case of all *kharitas* sent in the name of the Nizam, were interpreted as "the Government of India whose power can make you as the dust under foot, and leave you neither a name nor a trace"

The Nizam realising his utter helplessness quietly put up with this insulting letter. The only way in which he could show his hurt feelings was by trying to evade sending a reply to the Governor-General for the *Kharita.* In accordance with the instructions of the Governor-General, he promptly appointed a Diwan. Nawab Siraj-ul-Mulk was reinstated as the Diwan once again on the 29th June 1851·

The Nizam also promised to pay the Contingent Forces regularly, and by way of assurance and his good faith he paid on the 15th August 1851, Rs. 34,08,485-11-4 ie. more than half his debt to the British, leaving a balance of Rs. 32,97,702-9-2 to be cleared. This balance he promised to pay off before the 31st October 1851.

In view of the Nizam having paid up more than half of his debt to the India Government, the latter did not insist on the transfer of districts from the Nizam.

This action of the India Government and the Resident, made the Nizam so confident that he thought that though the India Government might threaten him saying that it would divest him of his territories, it would never carryout its threat by demanding actual cession. That is why we find him at a later date telling his Diwan Siraj-ul-Mulk[70] "Don't be afraid. The British Government never can take from me districts to pay troops, I am not bound to support by treaty ----" I am aware that the days when my alliance was useful or desirable to the British Government are well nigh at an end, but I fully rely on the performance of the different articles of the Treaties existing between the two Governments".

But whatever might be the real feelings of the Nizam concerning the maintenance of the Contingent troops, from henceforth, he dare not express any desire for the abolition of the Contingent Forces. On the other hand he hastened to assure General Fraser that he regarded the Contingent Forces as indispensible for the tranquillity of the country, adding of course the pregnant remark that [71]"Mahrajah Chandoo Lall had repeatedly impressed upon his mind the importance of maintaining the Contingent and regularly paying it as an indispensible means of preserving the peace and tranquillity of the country".

---

68. Ibid. pp. 344

70. H.Fraser. Memoirs and Correspondence of J. S. Fraser p. p. 374, 375

71. H. R. R. Vol. 116 L. No. 214 1851

The Nizam also conveyed his willingness to make reductions in his own personal troops. Upon General Fraser expressing his surprise at the Nizam maintaining such an ill clad and indiciplined forces, the Nizam gave the tart reply "These troops are, as you say, worthless, and have not the clothing and discipline of yours. But what can I do? If I were to proceed to clothe, and discipline, and organise them more regularly, what would your Government say, and what ideas would it entertain"?[72]

To this direct and heart searching question of the Nizam the Resident had no suitable reply to give.

In the meantime the Diwan Siraj-ul-Mulk in order to raise the funds for clearing the debt of the Nizam, asked the India Government to allow the Nizam to enjoy the excise revenues of the Secunderabad Cantonment City.[73]

Originally the subsidiary forces were camped at Jalna and Secunderbad, and these forces were also exempted from the excise duties, along with the native servants and employees.

To avoid any possible disputes the Nizam's Government, placed Secunderabad under the jurisdiction of the Resident, and he was held responsible for the receipt of excise duties, and for paying an equal amount to the state.

Later on during the incumbency of Maharajah Chandulal, the Resident was exempted from remitting any money to the treasury of the Nizam, and from henceforth, a lakh of rupees that was levied as excise duty in Secunderabad went to the Residency treasury and not into the treasury of the Nizam.

Commenting about this one of the writers remarks about Chandulal "meagre in physique, very humble in his manner, but ruthless in extortion he was the prototype of Uriah Heap.

Though he wasted Hyderabad by his rapacity he made provision for the diversion of some of the state revenues into the Company treasury.[74]

The Nizam now owed nearly thirty three lakhs of rupees to the British. The Company has been enjoying the excise duties of the Secunderabad and Jalna Cantonments for nearly forty years, which calculated at the rate of one lakh of rupees per year amounted to forty lakhs of rupees in all. So now Nawab Siraj-ul-Mulk hoped to clear off the remaining debt of the Nizam by asking the British, to deduct thirty three lakhs from the excise revenues that they were unduly appropriating from the Cantonment areas.

Lord Dalhousie on hearing this claim of the Diwan through the Resident summarily dismissed the claim of the Nizam's Government saying "His Lordship thinks there is no ground for the claim to the tax on the part of

72. H. Fraser P. 374.
73. Ibid. P. 348.
74. A. P. Nicholson. "Scraps of Paper. India's broken Treaties." P. 176.

the Nizam. It is a check established for the maintenance of order, sobriety and discipline among the troops in Cantonment, and as such is not claimable by his Highness, but belongs to the Power whose troops they are and who are placed in such Cantonment by virtue of treaty[75].

But when we consider the fact that the Nizam had already ceded perpetually territories that he had acquired by the Treaties of 1792 and 1799, to meet all the expenses and requirements of the Subsidiary Force, we have to admit that the argument of Lord Dalhousie was based more on force than on principles of justice and equity.

The British on the other hand were to be blamed for not adhering to the Treaty of 1800 by surreptitiously decreasing the strength of the Subsidiary Forces. By doing so they gained a surplus in the amount allotted to the subsidiary troops, which went into the savings account of the British India Government. The work that was expected of the Subsidiary Forces namely the maintenance of law and order was performed by the Contingent troops for which the Nizam was coerced to pay an additional sum.

But there was no one to say "no" to the decision of Dalhousie.

Inspite of his promise to clear the whole debt by the 31st October 1851, the Nizam was able to pay only Rs. 873,547 towards the end of 1851. So the Nizam in order to make up the reminder gave his personal jewels worth about 30 lakhs of Rupees to the Diwan, so that he could raise money on them from the local *Soucars*. The Diwan finding his hopes for acquiring the excise revenues of Secunderabad dashed to pieces now tried with the help of the leading *soucars* of the city to open a Bank, which would lend money to the Nizam on the security of his jewels.

The people responded with fervour to this scheme, and very soon the necessary capital was subscribed, and the bank was able to advance a loan of forty lakhs at six percent interest to the Nizam. The Diwan was filled with joy at the prospect of paying off the debt of the Nizam, and he informed the Resident about the formation of the bank, with one Mr. Dighton as the Director of the Bank.

The Resident duly informed the Governor-General of these latest developments at Hyderabad.

The Governor-General who had ulterior objects in veiew was filled with anger on reading the report. He not only forbid the formation of the banking house under the direction of Mr. Dighton but threatened to persecute Dighton under the Parliamentary Act 37. George III Chapter 142, Section 26, that forbid an European to enter into any financial transactions with a Native State[76].

---

75. H. Fraser P. 364.
76. Abid. P. 390.

By doing so, Dalhousie foiled any attempts on the part of the Diwan and the people of Hyderabad to redeem the Nizam and his country from being in a state of indebtedness. Dalhousie was also furious with the Resident for having given his tacit approval for the scheme.

He instructed the Resident to make arrangements from the Residency treasury for the regular payment of the Contingent and also not to press for the payment of the principal debt, for, Dahlousie, who knew that there were no regular grounds on which the Contingent could be maintained, wanted to regularise it by concluding a treaty with the Nizam based on territorial cessions.

So we find him writing to General Fraser in the following manner[77], "The Government of India frequently speaks of the obligation to maintain the Contingent imposed by Treaty, because for forty years the Nizam has admitted practically the application of such an interpretation to the 12th Article of the Treaty of 1800. If, however, the Nizam should turn round upon us, and deny the obligation existing by Treaty, I am bound as a public man to say that I could not honestly agree that there was any other warrant than that of practice for upholding the Contingent. I could argue and have argued, that His Highness'sconduct has hitherto given that construction to the Treaty, and that till it is rejected and resisted, there is an obligation upon him to support properly the Force which, under that construction he has allowed us to organise but if he was to take his stand upon the Treaty I could not agree that either the letter, or the spirit of it, bound the Nizam to maintain 9,000 troops, of a peculiar and costly nature, in peace, because it bound him to give 15,000 of his troops on the occurrence of war. The question cannot be allowed to remain any longer in a state of uncertainity.

The specific demand which we must make, supported by the reasons to which I have adverted, is that the Contingent shall be put upon a clear and secure footing by means of a Treaty, supplementary to that of 1800 which must be concluded for the purpose, the amount of the Contingent, its duties, etc., must be distinctly specified, and for its payment territory must be made over to the British Government. This territory shall be assigned only, not made over in perpetuity.

"Notwithstanding, therefore, the formal declaration in 1851 of his wishes for the maintenance of the Contingent he may be so sincere as to repudiate that wish now, as he has lately attempted of specific revenues for its payment. He may take his stand on the actual Treaty, and deny his obligations to uphold the Contingent in its present form, when he sees it about to be permanently established in that form. He may be so unreasonable as (while willing to render the Contingent permanent) to object to the assignment of territory for its payment, though this is essential to its permanency.

77. Ibid. P. 375-380.

If he shall do so, the question will become more grave than it has ever yet been. At this moment I do not wish to commit myself to any declaration as to the course the Government of India would, under such circumstances, feel itself called upon to take. But assuming that the Government should resolve to admit his repudiation of the Contingent (Whatever it may think of the conduct of a prince who could act so dishonestly), still the Contingent must be provided for at the present moment, and for some time to come.......

If then the Nizam should refuse to give his consent to the continuance of the Contingent, provision must still be made for its maintenance, while it is in the course of being gradually absorbed with a view to its ultimate extinction. For that purpose an assignment of territory will be as indespensable as in the other case. The Nizam must be prepared to give it. If he refuses, the British Government will not submit to such an outrage upon all justice, and will take temporary possession of the territories by force, for the purposes already indicated".

This letter amply revealed the way in which Lord Dalhousie's mind was working. It showed that he was under any circumstances prepared to take territories from the Nizam, and that he would give no option to the Nizam in that matter.

Even the Resident, General Fraser was taken aback by this determined attitude of the Governor-General and he wrote to the India Government in the following manner; "Your Lordships argument in support of the Nizam's obligation to maintain the Contingent is founded upon the fact that for forty years he has practically admitted the application of such an interpretation of the 12th Article of the Treaty of 1800....... But when your Lordship proceeds to observe that the Nizam's consent has hitherto been given to this construction of the treaty, I may be permitted to remark that the consent, if given at all, has been a tacit one. for as far as I am aware or can recollect His Highness never expressed any direct judgement in favour of the maintenance of the Contingent until he did so in my interview with him in October 1850, which was immediately afterwards reported to the Government,

As regards ourselves, the Justice of this proposed arrangement cannot be impunged; but as regards the Nizam, I consider it to involve his certain ruin, and the utter extinction of his power as an independent Sovereign"[78]

After having expressed his disapprobation, of the measures proposed to be adopted by Lord Dalhousie, one could expect that the days of the Resident at the Residency were numbered.

The Governor-General not only differed from the Resident diametrically with regard to Hyderabad, but he showed his dislike of the general

78. Ibid p. 380-381. LDt 29th Sept 1852

by censuring his conduct with regard to certain military trials held in Hyderabad.

This attitude of the Governor-General made Fraser resign his office on the 12th November 1852[79].

In his place Colonel John Low was appointed as the Resident. Low, took over the charge of the Residency on the 7th March 1853.

With the arrival of Low, as the Resident matters began to move at a greater acceleration at Hyderabad. The debt of the Nizam now stood at more than 45 lakhs and the pay of the Contingent forces was in arrears for more than seven months.[80]

On the 12th March 1853, the Resident informed the Nizam "It is necessary that I should tell you that my Government is determined no longer to rely upon promises - - - some substantial arrangement must be made that will produce the monthly sum required to a certainity and I really know, no other, that can be relied upon excepting assignment on the revenues of the districts for that specific purpose"[81]

The Nizam who was taken aback by the bluntness of the demand and was smarting at the injustice of the whole transactions pertinently asked the Resident[82] "Colonel Sahib, I want to ask you a question about that Contingent? - - - In the time of my father the Peishwa's of Poona became hostile both to the Company's Government and to this Government and Sahib Jung (meaning Sir Henry Russell) organised this Contingent and sent it in direction along with the Company's troops to fight the Maharatta people and this was very proper - - - the Company's army and my father's army conquered the ruler of Poona - - - after that there was no longer any war, so why was the Contingent kept any longer than the war"?

So, the question anticipated by Lord Dalhousie over which he had already passed irrelevant strictures on the conduct of the Nizam anticipating this very question, was atlast asked by the hapless Nizam. But there was no one to support his case or do him justice; The only answer he got from the Resident was the bland reply[83] "I don't see why your Highness should expect me to answer questions about events that occurred...six and thirty years ago[83]" Then Col. Low, lamely told the Nizam that the 'Contingent' continued to exist because the previous Nizam had not objected to it. Then in a magnanimous manner he informed the Nizam that if the latter desired to reduce the expenses on the 'Contingent' the Governor-General was willing to accept it, provided the Nizam made some permanent arrangement for the regular payment of the 'Contingent'.

---

79 Ibid. P. 408

80. H. R. R. Vol. 116. L. No.346 of 1852.

81. H. R. R. Vol. 91 (Foreign Dept) L. No. 58 of 1853.

82. Ibid L. No. 58 of 1853 Para 6.

83. Ibid. Para 7.

Upon the Resident saying that the Contingent existed because the previous Nizam had allowed it to exist the Nizam interrupted him saying "Do not say my father—say the Maharajah"—meaning Chandulal. Finding that it would not absolve him of the necessity of ceding territories the Nizam declined to make any changes in the 'Contingent'.

Anxious to get a a secure footing for the 'Contingent' Troops by obtaining territories by means of a treaty the Resident began to dilate upon the advantages that would accrue to the Nizam by the conclusion of such a treaty. On hearing this the Nizam exclaimed "God forbid that I should suffer such a disgrace", I don't want any new treaty at all, how much so ever you or any other person or persons may fancy it to be advantageous to my interests".[84]

[85] Finding the attitude of the India Government adamant he irritably asked the Resident "Did I ever make war against the English Government? nor intrigue against it? or do anything but co-operate with it... and be obedient to its wishes that I should be so disgraced- - -" "Two acts on the part of a Sovereign Prince are always reckoned disgraceful - - - one is to give away unnecessarily any portion of his heriditory territories and the other is to disband troops who have been brave and faithful in his service".

Then he pleaded with the Resident, to inform the Governor-General that the Nizam would personally see that the debt to the Company was paid and the payment of the Contingent troops regularised. He also informed the Resident that the *Soucars* of Hyderabad are prepared to stand surety for the Nizam's words.

Then after making the Resident read out the draft treaty to him the Nizam pathetically declared. "Gentlemen like you"- - -who are- - -sometimes employed in Government business, at other times as soldiers- - - and at other times even engaged in commerce- - -cannot understand the nature of my feelings in this matter - - - I am a Sovereign Prince, born to live and die in this Kingdom, which has belonged to my family for seven generations. You think I could be happy if I were to give up a portion of my Kingdom---it is totally impossible---I should feel that I was disgraced- - -I have heard that gentlemen of your tribe, considered that I ought to be quite contented and happy if I was put upon the same footing as Mohamed Ghouse Khair (meaning the Nawab of Arcot) to have a pension paid to me like an old servant and have nothing to do but to eat and sleep and say my prayers"- - - Then the Nizam angrily said to the Resident "you are not quite so preposterous in your way of judging me as that but you too don't comprehend the nature of my feelings as a Sovereign Prince for instance you talk of my saving atleast eight lac of rupees per annum by making this treaty as something that I ought to

84. H. R. R. Vol. 91 (Foreign Dept) L. No. 70 of 1853.
85. Ibid. L. No. 71—of 1853.
86. Ibid. Para 17, 18.

like - - - now I tell you that if it were quite certain that I could save four times eight lacs of rupees I should not be satisfied because I should loose my honour by parting with my territory".

After speaking in a plaintive manner about the loss of the *peishcash* from the Northern Sarkars and the denial of his legitimate share in the Carnatic country. the Nizam told the Resident, that henceforth, he would see that - - - the Contingent was regularly paid and in case he failed to do so the Governor General after waiting for a period of four months could demand the cession of territories.[87]

On hearing this the Resident insisted on the immediate payment of all the debt including the principal and interest, and an additional sum of 3 lacs of Rupees towards the arrears of the Contingent Troops upto January 1853 and the transfer of some taluks to the British to ensure regular payment of the Contingent Troops in future.[88]

The only point on which the Resident was prepared to make some concession was that since the Nizam did not like the idea of ceding his districts in perpetuity, these districts he said should be handed over to the management of the British and that they would acknowledge the Nizam's Sovereignty over them by submitting annual accounts of the revenues of the ceded districts after deducting the cost of the Contingent, Appah Desaye's Chouth and the allowance to the family of Mahipat Ram, the balance would be paid into the Nizam's treasury.[89]

He firmly told the Nizam, when the latter tried to procure the guarantee of the principal nobles for the regular payment of the troops ;

"I am not permitted by my Government to make any change in that part of the plan which prescribes that districts must be made over to our exclusive management to provide for the monthly pay of the Contingent whatever the strength of the Force may be.[90]

Then the Resident directly asked the Nizam to say "Yes" or "No" to his proposal. On hearing this the Nizam angrily asked "Suppose I were to declare that I don't want the Contingent ?"

To this the Resident replied saying that if the Nizam wanted the Contingent to be disbanded, it would be done but in gradual stages and till such time the whole force would be disbanded it was imperative on the part of the Nizam to lease temporarily territories to ensure the regular payment of the troops.[91]

---

87. Ibid Para 23, 24, 29.
88. Ibid. Resident's Memorandum.
89. Ibid. Vol. 91 L. No. 74.
90. Ibid. Para 14.
91. Ibid. Para 14.

To this answer of the Resident the Nizam argued that since the revenues of the districts ceded by him for the maintenance of the subsidiary troops was now yielding a surplus, the Contingent could be maintained out of those surplus revenues. This argument of the Nizam was quite logical and pertinent in view of the fact that the British were not maintaining their full quota of subsidiary troops in the Nizam's Dominions and were saving money on that account. But the Resident turned down this request of the Nizam, on the ground that the districts alluded by the Nizam, no longer belongd to him and as such the Nizam was not entitled to discuss about them.[92]

Finding the Resident quite obdurate, the Nizam sought the advice of the nobles who were present at the meeting. One of them, the second son of the Nawab Shums-ul-Umara, realising the hoplessness of the situation pointedly replied "If it is the Governor-General's determination to have districts for the pay of the Contingent what advice need we give ? Your Highness does not require our advice or any further consultations on the subject".[93]

On hearing this the Resident, pressed the Nizam for a specific answer, upon which the latter quite exasperated remarked "I could answer in a moment and what is the use of answering, if you are determined to take districts you can take them without my either making a new treaty or giving any answer at all"[94].

The statement of the Nizam, showed that he was conscious of his weakness and of the futility of trying to resist the British in their greed for power.

The Resident to pacify the feelings of the Nizam assured him that the British Government would not interfere in his administration, and that he was quite free to do anything that he wished, even including the choice of his ministers. On hearing this the Nizam exclaimed," "Yes, apparently that was the case and yet how was my Mutsuddy Ganesh Rao treated when I appointed him"?... I have tride much to please your Government in such matters[95]? After, all that was said on both sides, the Nizam was yet loth to part with his territories. Hence, he requested the Resident to give him time for two more days when he said, he would send a deputation to the Resident intimating his final decision.

On the appointed day the Nizam sent Nawab Shums-ul-Umara and Iqtidar-ul-Mulk the second son of Shums-ul-Umara, with the proposal that if the India Government would give him four months time he would not only clear all his debts but would also ensure the regular payment of the Contingent troops or in case the Government of India was reluctant to

92. Ibid. Para 15.
93. Ibid. para 20.
94. Ibid. Para 26.
95. Ibid. Para 25.

concede it, atleast that the proposed districts to be ceded should be under the joint management of the British and the Nizam's Government. It was suggested that on behalf of the Nizam, Nawab Shums-ul-Umara would be asked to take over the administration of these districts, and that he would be instructed to obey the Resident's directions implicitly.

The Resident informed Nawab Shums-ul-Umara that the Government of India might not approve of such an arrangement, and that he himself would never recommend such a course. When Shums-ul-Umara conveyed the desire of the Nizam to see the Resident in this connection, the Resident remarked emphatically "I will not refuse to visit the Nizam if he sends for me, but that I consider it useless - - - and that I must now immediately report his Highness's obstinacy and folly to my own Government, and if His Highness does not forthwith depart, from his present foolish conduct, he will assuredly hereafter have much cause to regret that folly - - - but that this will be no fault of mine"[98].

[99]The Resident also impressed upon the mind of the Diwan Siraj-ul-Mulk the necessity of the Nizam concluding the treaty with the British and also informed him that failure to comply with their demand might necessitate the employment of force. The Nizam was informed that unless he consented to sign the treaty, British troops would be ordered to enter not only the districts under discussion but also the capital.

The Resident instead of officially warning the Nizam adopted the tactics of making the Assistant Resident write an informal letter to the Minister Siraj-ul-Mulk about the action the Resident proposed to take.

Major Davidson the Assistant Resident wrote to Siraj-ul-Mulk in the following manner;

"My dear Nawab,

I believe the Resident requires your attendance this evening, to inform you that his negotiations with the Nizam are at an end, and he applies to the Governor-General to more troops by today's post.

His Highness asked for four months' delay, which was refused, not even in that time positively stipulating to pay the troops. Had he however, done so, this would have been refused, as contrary to the instructions of the Governor-General.

His Highness next offered to place forty lakhs worth of talooks in the hands of Shums-ul-Umara for the pay of the Contingent. The Resident said, 'No' as he could not be assured that there would be no other interference on the part of his Highness's Government, or his other officers, but

95. Para 25
96. Ibid. L. No. 78
98. Ibid. L. No. 79
99. Ibid. L. No. 81

if the talooks were made over to the Resident and Shums-ul-Umara, or any other officer of the Hyderabad Government as Commissioners-they to have the entire management and control of these districts, only furnishing accounts yearly to His Highness-he would refer to propositions to Calcutta, but without the slightest expectation that the Governor-General would agree to it.

His Highness has refused to agree to the above, and therefore he has lost a chance of obtaining a remission of what was disagreeable to his ideas of dignity. The terms first proposed are now renewed and with an unfriendly feeling that would, in my opinion drive matters to extremites. Indeed I have a letter from my nephew at Poona, mentioning that the 78th Highlanders and H. M's 86th Regiment have received orders to be in readiness to march on Hyderabad. Don't suppose military operations will be confined to the districts; and if you are a friend of his Highness, beg of him to save himself and his dignity by complying at once with what the Governor-General will most assuredly compel him to accede to[100]".

During this time a British officer was asked to survey the ramparts of the city in an ostentatious manner.

Realising that he had no option, the Nizam agreed to enter into the Treaty of Berar and the Treaty of Berar was concluded on the 21st May 1853. By this Treaty the province of Berar and the districts of Osmanabad and Raichur were ceded to the British.

During the course of these transactions the Nizam at one time sarcastically remarked that all the vexation had arisen due to the "high value that the British Power Placed upon money[101]".

To this the Resident hastened to reply "My Government had no desire to gain for itself in the arrangement, whatever surplus money we can make by the good management which His Highness talks of, will go into coffers of His Highness himself by the plan which I now offer to him of having districts only made over to our exclusive management and not transferred to us as our property[102]."

Inspite of this lofty demeanour of the Resident subsequent events have fully borne out the worst fears of the Nizam. Not only was great unhappiness created over the rendering of accounts, but Berar was never returned to the Nizam.

With the conclusion of the Treaty of Berar the "Contingent". forces of the Nizam were converted into a British auxiliary force, officered by the British and it was henceforth called as the "Hyderabab Contingent". Thus the existence of the force was formally recognised. The strength of this

100. P. 414
101. H. R. R. Vol. 91 L. No. 74
102. Ibid.

"Hyderabad Contingent" was to consist of not less than 5000 infantry and 2000 cavalry and four field batteries of artillery.

Shortly after the conclusion of the Treaty of 1853, the Diwan Siraj-ul-Mulk died on the 23rd May 1853. It was believed that the death of the Diwan who was ailing for some time was accelerated by the strain and humiliation of the Treaty of 1853.

The Nizam appointed Nawab Salar Jung, the nephew of the late Diwan, to the office af the Diwan and Rajah Narrainder to the office of the Peishkar[103]. These appointments were approved by the Resident. Subsequent to the signing of the treaty on the 21st May 1853, it was found that some of the western districts in Berar did not yield as much revenue as it was estimated by the late Siraj-ul-Mulk, so some more villages in the Berar were added to make up the deficiency and a fresh treaty was signed on the 6th June 1853[104].

The areas that were now ceded consisted of the Valley of Berar yielding a revenue of Rs. 30,60,309/-, Balaght yeilding Rs. 5,48,601/- western districts yielding Rs. 2,29,588/- and Raichur district, yielding a revenue of Rs. 11,51,342/- altogther yielding a total revenue of Rs. 49,89,840/- out of which a sum of Rs. 9,07533 were deducted as *Sar-fe-khas*, and a sum of Rs. 40,82,307/- remaining as balance.

The Government of India placed on record its appreciation of the services of Col. Low the Resident, and Major Davidson the Assistant Resident, for bringing about the Treaty of 1853 to a successful conclusion. The entire transactions that lead to the signing of the Treaty of Berar by the Nizam, were based on injustice and coersion. Realising the Nizam's aversion to cede the districts in perpetuity to the British, the Governor-General gave his consent to the Resident to obtain those districts in assignment for a temporary period[106].

This was done obviously to lull the fears of the Nizam. The British had their own views with regard to the treaty, for we find Col. Low writing on the 19th June 1853 to the Governor-General regarding some Jaghirs in Berar[107]". I suppose that General Fraser excluded these Jaghirs partly to please the Minister, and partly because the General then expected that the whole of the districts would then remain only a short time in our hands; but, as I knew that those districts are to be permanently in our hands, I thought that those jaghirs should at once come under our own exclusive management".

Even Lord Dalhousie though he recognised the unwillingness of the Nizam to cede the districts in perpetuity, records in his farewell minute

103. Ibid. L. No. 61 of 1853
104. Ibid. L. No. 92 1853
105. Ibid. Para 4
106. Ibid. Vol. No. 98 L. No. 102 of 1853, Consultations.
107. Ibid. Vol. 92.

reviewing his own administration on the 28th February 1853, wrote "By a treaty concluded in 1853, His Highness the Nizam has assigned in perpetual Government, to the Honourable East India Company, the Province of Berar and other districts of his State. for the permanent maintenance of the Hyderabad Contingent.[108]

Thus the whole transactions that lead to the conclusion of the Treaty of Berar were based on force and fraud.

Many members among the Court of Directors were conscious of the injustice of their demand on the Nizam, but they did not take the trouble to rectify matters.

Bruce Norton, commenting about the Treaty of Berar, pithily remarks, "Cotton stuffed the ears of justice, and made her deaf as well as blind.[109]

The prospects of acquiring the rich cotton growing land of Berar seemed to have dulled the British sense of justice.

108. Minute by the Marquis of Dalhouse (245 of 1856)P. 7

109. J. Bruce Norton. The Rebellion in India.

CHAPTER XI

Hyderabad And 1857

Within four years of the cession of Berar the War of 1857 broke in India, and the whole of Northern India was plunged into a great upheaval. One of the unique features of the rising of 1857 was that while Northern and Central India were the main theatres of war during this period, Southern India remained more or less aloof.

The part played by Hyderabad during the great war of 1857, was mainly responsible for keeping Southern India free from the embers of war. The British also recognised the importance of Hyderabad and the friendship and good will of the Nizam during this period, and we find the Governor of Bombay writing to the Governor-General, to the effect "If the Nizam goes all goes".

The usual impression about the part played by Hyderabad during the struggle of 1857 is that the State was completely immune from all anti-British feelings during this period. But when we look closely at the history of Hyderabad we find that the State was far from immune. The Wahabi Conspiracy was a fair pointer to the real feelings of the people. People all over the State were greatly agitated by the events in the north and they were anxious that they and their ruler should also participate in the national struggle for emancipation from the British control. But their aspirations could not be realised due to the pro-British attitude adopted by Nawab Afzal-ud-Doula and the Minister Salar jung I. More-over the people could not get the right kind of leadership from the feudal nobles that surrounded the court of the Nizam. Hence this lead to only sporadic risings in the State, and these were put down by the British with some difficulty. Nawab Nasir-ud-Doula died on the 16th May 1857[1].

During the course of his long reign Nawab Nasir-ud-Doula seemed to have realised the futilty of trying to resist the British. So he advised Nawab Afzal-ud-Doula, prior to his death, to adhere to the British alliance.

Afzal-ud-Doula, though he had his own grievances against theEnglish over the question of Berar and the subversive influence exercised by the Resident in the State affairs, decided, during this momentous period in Indian history to remain firm in his alliance with the British inspite of various indications from his subjects that they expected a contrary behaviour from their ruler.

This decision of the Nizam, coupled with the strong sense of loyalty displayed by the feudal nobles headed by Shums-ul-Umara, in Hyderabad,

1. H. Traser.

and the exertions of Salar jung the Diwan prevented a violent and a serious outbreak of rebellion in the dominions of the Nizam. Nevertheless a close study of Hyderabad history during this period, would convince the reader that the people in the State were eagerly awaiting for some one to guide them and lead them against the British, but that eagerly awaited leader, could not be got. The lack of proper leadership, a man in whom the people could have implicit trust, and for whom they could sacrifice everything, stilled the enthusiasm of the people, to a great extent. If at all they had to rebel against the British, they had to rebel in the name of the far off Nana, whom they had never seen, and about whom they had a vague knowledge based only on rumours, while their natural leader the Nizam, for whom they were prepared to rise, lay inert.

The attitude adopted by the Nizam during the great rebellion of 1857 proved very decisive. It prevented the embers of war engulfing the whole of South India.

It not only succeeded in preserving an uneasy peace in the Deccan, but was also responsible for maintaining general tranquillity in the South.

The policy adopted by Salar jung and the Nizam was responsible for making Southern India secure, to the British. The reconstituted Hyderabad Contingent by playing a decisive role in the battle fields of Malwa and Central India brought the first war of Independence of 1857 to a speedy conclusion.

The anti-British struggle in Hyderabad during the war of Independence in 1857, could be traced in the following manner; namely rebellion in the capital, rebellion of the Contingent forces at Aurangabad and rebellion and conspiracies in the various districts and zamindaries.

The news of the outbreak of the war in Delhi created excitement among the people of Hyderabad. Placards began to appear on the walls of mosques and other public places exhorting the ruler to raise the standard of revolt against the British in the name of the Delhi Emperor and in the name of Islam.[2]

It was generally expected that the people would rise in revolt on the 10th June; one of the persons who took a prominent part in inciting the people to rebel was one Maulavie Ibrahim. On the apprisal of the Resident about the Moulavie's activities, the Nizam personally called the Moulavie to his presence and gave him a severe warning asking him not to indulge in seditious activities, and his movements were put under restraint,

Inspite of this, attempts were made to incite the people to rebellion, especially the army. On the 12th June a Fakir was apprehended at Bowenpally while addressing the people of that locality, asking them to rebel in association with the Contingent forces that were stationed there. This Fakir who later on it was discovered was a camp follower of the Bowenpally

2. H. R. R. Vol. 92 L. No. 85 of 1857.

Fouj was put in irons and sent to the Residency by the Minister for interrogation.

Apart from this Salar jung also prevented the reading of the Qutba at Mecca Masjid when an attempt was made to proclaim Jehad; He also removed all placards that were pasted on the walls of the Mosque asking the ruler to join the revolutionaries, and sent them to the Resident for perusal. Some of the placards were to the following effect.

(1)

"The oath of the Almighty is on him who does not read this paper"

The aid of the Almighty and his prophet is present with Afzul-Ood-Doula Bahadur who should not fear or be apprehensive. If fearful he should wear bangles and sit at home".

"If Afzul-Ood-Doula does not act on this paper another Soobah will be ready from Delhi".

This proclamation *(Izaharanamah)* is written for the faith and Islam of Mahomad Mustapah Sullulallo Allah Wo Salum for the stability of the Reign in the Deccan and war (Jehad) against the infidels.

In the month of Ramzan the sword fell on Delhi, besides ten other places, but up to the time there is laxity (delay) in the region of the Deccan. What is the reason of this? It would appear that the re-establishment of the Delhi throne (Takhta) by the followers of Islam is not congenial to the feelings of the people of the Deccan but it is necessary and appears desirable that without any delay the zamindars, Cazees etc. should be brought together and after giving them courage and confidence they should be ordered to make war with the infidels. If not in a year or two hence Afzul-Ood-Doula Bahadur and Salarjung will have to work on the roads. If as stated above the order for War is not given, your life will be cursed and your minister's (Dewan) rank and pedigree (Asubo nus fubo) will be repudiated. If any Moulavi or Alim does not give a futwah on what I have said, his seven generations will be cursed and repudiated. If after reading this paper or hearing of it, a represention is not made to the King or his Dewan the oath of the Swine is on him and if in the case of a Hindu the oath of the cow.

Yah Allah, increase the faith of Islam, if this paper is removed from this place the curse of God and his Prophet will rest on the person removing it.

Amen Amen Amen"

While some of the placards were written in the above style, others were written appealing to the people Hindus and Muslims, to raise against the alien Christian power.

3. Unpublished Records in the Central Records Office. Freedom Struggle in Hyderabad. Vol. II PP. 9. 10.

They wrote[5] "In the Name of God Almighty the most Gracious and benevolent of all".

"It is a greeting from God to all the Muslims that success and God's help is fast approaching. A Muslim who resolves to kill a kafir, i.e. a Christian and delays will be cut off from the society and called a descendant of the parish caste, of a pig and of a dog. He will be a descendant of Yazeed and Shumar. It is an oath on God to a Muslim whether he is rich or poor, or the Dewan or spiritual head, or Moulvi, Kazi, Mufti Suba or Kootwal, to participate in the task and get the blessings of God. If he succeeds he will be called a victor (Ghazi). If he dies he will be counted among those who dies in the holy wars and will get a place in the Bliss. God's command is unquestionable. He commands to kill the unbelievers wherever they are found. So why do you hesitate and delay and lose precious time ? You will repent for it afterwards we don't worry whether you take part in it or keep aloof. But you should take courage to start with all your power. So gather under the Holy flag, and start on that mission, the unbelievers will be overpowered and fly away with great panic. In Delhi, this mission has been started for twelve miles (Manzil) in the name of the King. It is essential and befitting for the Chief of this place, Mir Tahniat Ali Khan Bahadur, Afzul-ud-Doula to undertake the mission by collecting all the Muslims, and suppress the Kafirs and then advance to Delhi. Otherwise great panic will come to this place. The Muslims have been informed to take their own course. They should gather on Friday, 25th Shawal 1273, at the Mecca Masjid, and start agitation from there so that we may also join them from our place. Whoever will remove this poster will be called a descendant of the great unbeliever Yazeed".

Attempts were also made by one Moulavie Akbhar to incite the people who had congregated at the Mecca Masjid to offer prayers, to rebel and the people also made an attempt to raise the standard of revolt at the mosque by hoisting the flag but they were put to flight by the strong guard of Arabs posted by the Minister Salarjang.

These various incidents in the city greatly disturbed the loyalty of the subsidiary troops also, and they gave went to their feelings in their conversations with the city people.

Reporting about this Col. Davidson wrote to the India Government "I regret to report to the Government of India that my opinion of the loyalty of the native troops of the subsidiary force has completely altered since I despatched my letter No. 35 of the 13th and I believe our only reliance for continuance of peace in the Deccan must be placed on the fidelity of the Native Government and I sincerely trust that after the present crisis has passed over the British Government will not forget what it has owed to his Highness the Nizam and his most able Minister.

4. Hyderabad Affairs. Vol. III. PP. 213, 214.
5. H.R.R. Vol. 93 L. No. 37 of 1857.

Cavalry and Infantry sepoys from the Hyderabad subsidiary force have of late been in the City without their officers' leave and without passports, preaching that this is the time to rise and offering to make common cause against all Europeans. These are not only the assertions of the Native Government but, of men who are if anything hostile to it, and whose correct intelligence I have tested for years. I have taken measures, to prevent this sedition for the future, but there is not a doubt, although now checked, it exists in all its nakedness.

I have had people lately in Secunderabad who were instructed to converse freely and elicit in whatever way they could, the feelings of the Native troops. All that we could depend upon apparently was that in the event of rising they would not march against the City but they would defend their own camp, the meaning of which was that they would fight for their own houses, as each Madras sepoy has his family in his hut and he therefore cannot afford to burn down his lines according to the practice of his Bengal brother. This, in my opinion with few exceptions, is the sole hold we have upon their fidelity. I acknowledge it is a great one, but we must not be blinded by such expressions, as the bad feeling only exists among a few bad characters, in each corps'.

The oportunity and a leader are all that I believe to be wanting to extend the North-West revolt to the Deccan and all Southern India. Our Sepoys have dared to judge in what cause they will fight and in what not. After that how can they be considered good and trustyworthy soldiers.

I have still no fear of the resutlt or that there will be any serious outbreaks here.

Should the seditious language they used to the crowd in the city when they were on escort duty with me on Monday the 18th instant, be brought home to them, I should concieve, although the particular Trooper may not be identified, that the Native Officer and the whole Escort should be dismissed - - - as such conduct is not only mutinuous and seditious but has caused it to appear in the eyes of the Native Government that the Governor-General's representative at the court of His Higness the Nizam cannot trust his own immediate escort. It is after the maturest consideration and after incessant investigation and secret enquiry through agents in whom I can thoroughly rely that I have formed this opinion of the State of feeling of the Madras Sepoys. It may be good policy not to scrutinise too narrowly what is going on at the present time and I shall not let it appear that I have withdrawn my confidence from the Native Troops" - - - -

Disaffection towards the British was not only rampart among the subsidiary troops stationed at Secunderabad but also among the Contingent troops stationed at different headquarters. This feeling of resentment against the British took a serious turn at Aurangabad among the 1st Cavalry of the Hyderabad Contingent.

The third Cavalry of the Hyderabad Contingen't was sent to Malegoan at the requisition of the Bombay Government. In it's place the 1st Cavalry of the Contingent troops was moved from Mominabad to Aurangabad, under the command of Captain H. D. Abbot, on the 11th June 1857.

While the 1st Cavalry was at Chota Pimpalgoan a viliage about 14 miles from Aurangabad, the troops heard about the setbacks received by the British in the North. From Chota Pimpalgaon they reached Aurangabad on the 9th June and encamped between the Kala Chabutra and the Cavalry lines[6].

Fearing that they might be asked to go to Delhi the first Cavalry declared that they were primarily recruited to serve in the Deccan, and as such they would not proceed to the North and fight against their ruler the Mughal Emperor.

On hearing about this development from a non-commissioned Sikh officer, Capt. Abbot intimated the Risaldar that he would come to the Cavalry lines in the evening. Thinking that the visit was preparatory to a march, the troops declared that they would kill Capt. Abbot, Lt. Dowker and the Risaldar if they came to the lines in the evening.

Inspite of this, Capt. Abbot in the company of Lt. Dowker and the various Risaldars inspected the Cavalry lines, and he also tried to assuage the ruffled feelings of the sepoys over an incident that happened a few days previously.

While on their march to Aurangabad, on the 5th morning, Capt. Abbot, had ordered all the troopers after they had rested for a while, to put on their regimentals and mount on their horses and form lines for march ahead. Then he espied a sepoy near a local *nullah* still washing himself. On asking what he was doing Capt. Abbot was informed that the man was preparing himself for prayers.

On hearing this Capt. Abbot ordered the man to put on his regimentals and fall in line, saying, that was not the time to offer prayers.

This roused the umbrage of the sepoys, who took this action of Capt. Abbot as tantamount to interference with their religious practices.

Capt. Abbot now tried to assuage their doubts by making Risaldar Mahomed Baroon, one of the senior Risaldars to assemble all the troop officers and explain to them the whole incident. On hearing that the 3rd Cavalry was refusing to go north and fight against the Emperor, he assured the troopers that there was no likelihood of their being asked to go north[7].

6. The Freedom Struggle in Hyderabad Vo. II. P. 24.
7. H. R. R. Vol. 668. L. No. 628. Charles Ball. A History of the Indian Mutiny Vol. I. PP: 427, 428.

Inspite of these assurances the 2nd Cavalry men plainly told their Risaldar that they would not go beyond the Nizam's frontiers and take up cudgels against their religion and co-religionists. *Nizam Ke Serhud* Ke *Bahir Naheen Jangy. Aur deen ke upper Kamar Naheen Bandiggy)*[8]

On hearing this reply Capt. Abbot asked all the musket masters and Jamadars to come and see them, but to this he got the reply saying that if at all they were coming, they would make their own arrangements.

However about 9°, clock on the 14th morning the Jamadars and troop officers visited him but finding their replies, and general attitude unsatisfactory, and also owing to the rumour that the city men were congregating in large numbers and the Cavalry was intending to leave for Ambah in contravention of Capt. Abbot's orders. So Capt. Abbot, selected a suitable place for his infantry troops and placed his infantry men at strategic places keeping the river Kaum as the dividing place between the cavalry lines and the infantry.

He also got some felled trees placed across the bridge, as well as on the ascents on either side of the bridge. The Captain also took the precaution of sending away the ladies and families of non-Commissioned officers to places of safety. He also applied to Poonah and Nuggur for reinforcements.

But signs of disaffection began to appear in the infantry lines also. There were secret visits and meetings between the infantry and cavalry lines.

The European officers in charge of the divisions lived in an atmosphere of fear and mistrust, nevertheless, maintaining a calm appearance outwardly.

Everyday there were rumours of intended massacre of all the European Officers and their families.

On the 14th night one Burhan Bux a trooper of the 3rd Cavalry came and informed Capt. Spied to whose family he was deeply attached that the Cavalry had hoisted the green flag of religion and that it intended to attack the cantonment at day break[9].

On receiving this information Capt. Spied the Commandant of the Infantry at once put his wife and children along with some other ladies in a bullock cart, tying *purdah* on either side of the cart so that it would be mistaken for a Muslim family, and sent them along with Burhan Bux to Ahmednagar.

In that night the green flag hoisted by the cavalry was blown away due to gusts of wind and torrential rains and the cavalry gave up its intended attack taking that as an illomen.

8. Ibid. PP. 428-429.
9. C. Wilmot and Bilgrami-Historical and Descriptive Sketches of H. H. the Nizam's Dominions Vol. II. PP. 335-338.

But the next morning the Europens officers heard another wild rumour that the local men of the city intended to attack them. On the receipt of these news Capt. Abbot assembled two companies of infantry and asked them to hold the bridge across the river Kaum that divided their cantonment from the Cavalry lines.

The cavalry mistaking these preparations as directed against them mounted their horses and threw pickets in the direction of the cantonment. However the troop officers on behalf of their cavalry divisions expressed regret for their behaviour.

Capt. Abbot conveyed his willingness to accept their apology provided they submitted unconditionally and agreed to do or go whatever or wherever they were asked to go.

The cavalry agreed to this condition and duly submitted.

The Resident who had by this time received reports of the developments at Aurangabad, ordered that troops should be sent from Ahmednagar under Major General Woodburn, to the assistance of Capt. Abbot, so that all signs of mutiny could be put down and the ring leaders among the mutineers court martialed.

But sings of disaffection in the infantry were also becoming quite obvious by 17th June, because a cavalry trooper informed Capt. Abbot that an infantry sentry had told him to the effect that a "portion of the Regiment were with them; and how was it that they had done nothing;" meaning that some of them shared the feelings of ill-will towards the British and were sorry that the cavalry had given in.

This feeling of resentment against the Europeans affected the Artillery Corps also, because, the Commandant of the Artillery, Capt. Sinclair was told by his Subahdar that some of the Artillery men might refuse to load their guns if asked to do so against the cavalry.[10]

On receiving these various reports Capt. Abbot visited the corps and was greatly impressed by the surly behaiour of most of the men. He informed them that Major General Woodburn's force was due to arrive and appealed to them to remain quiet and do their duties. Capt. Abbot also sent away the 3rd Cavalry to Buldhana on the 18th, on the request of Brigadier Hill, who was in command of the Hyderabad Contingent[11].

Major General Woodburn arrived at Aurangabad on the 23rd June 1857. Soon after his arrival Capt. Abbot after having made arrangements for the protection of the cantonment preceded Major General Wooburn, to the ground occupied by the mutinous cavalry. They were asked to fall in at foot parade and were asked to give up their arms. Then the Risaldars

10. Burton–History of the Hyderabgd Contingent P. 171.
11. H. R R. Vol 93 L. No. 194 of 1857.

of the 1st Troop were asked to read the names of those men whose conduct was blameworthy and were implicated in the mutiny.

Jamedar Amir Khan's name was read out first, who on hearing his name pronounced, became very violent, and asked his men to prime and load. Several sepoys while loading ran off the parade ground and saddled their horses, inspite of every endeavour on the part of Capt. Abbot to make them stop and hear what was said to them, with difficulty the greater portion of the men were persuaded to fall back in rear of the force, but the remaining dispersed among the lines refusing to return.

General Woodburn opened fire on them, upon which they fled. The dragoons pursued them with little effect. Amir Khan took refuge in the city under the protection of the Subha of Aurangabad. Most of these men belonged to the 2nd Cavalry, so Capt. Abbot could disarm only the men that belonged to the 1st Cavalry.

Out of the men belonging to the 2nd Troop only five men remained, Risaldar Muhammad Hashim being one of them. While the 1st Troop was being disarmed a Duffadar, Mir Fida Ali discharged a pistol at Capt. Abbot but missed him. He was secured, and during the course of the night a gallows was erected for him in front of the lines.

The next morning Major General Woodburn's force was paraded, Mir Fida Ali was brought out and tried by court martial, and hanged.[12] The Native Infantry and the Artillery were made to march past the gallows. It was also witnessed by a large number of people from the city and the adjacent villages.

On the whole the number of men arrested and disarmed during the course of these incidents, consisted of 1 Risaldar, 3 Jamadars 9 Duffadars, 76 Troopers, and 4 Trumpeters. Apart from them, 3 Duffadars, and six Troopers were also arrested at Mominabad. Out of these 21 persons were shot dead, 3 were blown away from guns. Describing about their trial Capt. Abbot wrote[13] "We have already disposed of a goodly number of the ninety four prisoners we took in the first haul of the net. One has been hung, four shot, one blown from a gun a frightful sight indeed! his head ascended about twenty yards into the air, and his arms were thrown about eight yards in either direction. I was astonished to see how cooly they received intelligence that they were to suffer death. The man who was blown away only said, that witnesses against him would have to answer for this in the next world and begged of them not to tie him to the guns, as he would not flinch at all. The fellow who hung said, that having washed his hands of life he has washed away all his sins, and the sooner he went to paradise the better (We have yet plenty of this work before us", (he added). Of the prisoners taken in this affair, two were blown from guns; seven shot by the

12. Charles Ball. Vol, I P. 430
13- Ibid. P. 430, 432

dragoons; four cut down in the charge; several hung; between thirty and forty transported; one hundred disbanded and turned out of the station; and some fifty or sixty others flogged and otherwise punished".

While these incidents were taking place at Aurangabad, even the 3rd Cavalry that was sent away to Buldhana did not remain unaffected by the various events in the country. In order to put down all signs of disobedience in the 3rd Cavalry a detachment under Capt. Gall consisting of one Squadron, 14th light Dragoons, two guns, and the 4th Light field Battery and the Bombay Artillery, two flank Companies of the 25th Bombay Native Infantry, two guns of the 4th Company Artillery of the Hyderabad Contingent under Sinclair and one Company of the 2nd Infantry of the Hyderabad Contingent under the Lieutenant Lennox were sent to Buldhanna. On hearing of the approach of Capt. Gall with these reinforcements, the Risaldar, 2 Jamadars, 3 Duffadars, 7 Troopers and 2 Trumpeters fled towards Hyderabad while of the remaining 1 Duffadar and 10 Troopers were arrested.[14]

Commenting about this the deputy Commissioner T. H. Bullock wrote to Capt. Gall in the following manner",

"Although the immediate object of your march to this place had been partly anticipated and partly rendered ineffectual by the flight of mutinous men of the 3rd Troop of the 1st Cavalry, Hyderabad Contingent, yet I am of opinion that the temporary presence of an European force of this place will have had a very useful effect upon the turbulent classes in Nort Berar as it will show that we are within the reach of Military (Aid) and if it should fortunately happen that Major General Woodburn's force could be spared to fix its Headquarters some where in the neighbourhood of Aurangabad it would afford protection to a large extent of (the) frontier country, where there is not at present a single European soldier. Jalna as Headquarters would secure Aurangabad, Mominabad, Hingoli, Booldhana, and even Elichpur would feel the influence of this force.

Therefore at least 20,000 armed men, Mussalmans principally are ready for any cut throat service in North-Berar and although I do not hear of any overt acts on their part, there are reports that they are secretly preparing their weapons and watching for adverse news and therefore what is safe and quiet today may be a moving mass of insurrection tomorrow"[15]

While these incidents were taking place at Aurangabad and Berar, events were also moving at a fast pace at Hyderabad. Ultimately these events culminated in an attack on the Residency building, the symbolical citadel of British power on the 17th July 1857.

The Sepoys that deserted from Buldhana, about thirteen in number arrived at Hyderabad under Jamedar Cheeda Khan with the hope of recei-

14. H. R. R. Vol. 93 L. No. 188
15. Ibid.

ving protection from the Hyderabad Government. The Hyderabad Government offered a reward of Rs. 3000/- for catching Cheeda Khan.

But as soon as Cheeda Khan arrived in Hyderabad Salarjung got him arrested and sent him over to the Residency for trial. This created a great commotion in the city and the people congregated at the Mecca Masjid on the 17th July 1857, and they resolved to send four Movlavis to the Nizam with the request that Cheeda Khan and his associates might be freed. In the event of the Nizam refusing to accede to their request they also resolved to attack the Residency. On hearing of this news brisk preparations were made at the Residency to put it in a strong defensive position[16].

Salarjung, on being apprised of the congregation at the Mecca Masjid sent a body of Arab Guards to disperse the croud, and he informed the Resident that he need not apprehend any danger. But on hearing the news towards the evening that a body of about 300 Rohillas are heading towards the Residency under the leadership of Moulavi Ala-uddin and the Rohilla leader Turrabaz Khan, Salarjung at about 6 P. M. in the evening sent word to the Resident that there was a danger of the Residency being attacked by the people.[17]

The Minister further sent word that the Resident should try to defend himself, till the Minister could assemble the Nizam's troops, and send them to the assistance of the Resident.

The Resident on the receipt of the above news posted strong guards at every gate. The Rohillas headed by Turrabaz Khan, and the infuriated masses marched towads the Residency building form the west i.e., from the Sultan Bazaar area, the road connecting Hyderabad and Secunderabad. After arriving at the Residency the insurgents occupied the upper stories of two large houses belonging to the local *Soucars*, Abban Sahib and Jaigopal Das, thereby commanding an advantageous position over the gateway towards Putli Bavli and Dilsook gardens.

The insurgents after occupying these houses called upon the guards who were on patrol duty to deliver Cheeda khan and his companions into their hands. On seeing this Ismail khan the Risaldar of the 2nd Cavalry belonging to the Hyderabad Contingent went to remonstrate with them. The insurgents who had expected that the sepoys on duty would join them and make common cause with them were infuriated at the conduct of Ismail khan and opened fire on him, seeing which he galloped away.[18]

The defence of the Residency was placed in the hands of Major S. C. Briggs, who was at that time the Military Secretary to the Resident. Major Briggs, as it was already dark, decided not to disturb the Rohillas, and to

16. H. R. R. Vol. 668 L. No. 773.
17. H. R. R. Vod. 668 PP. 134, 138 Hyderabad Affairs, Vol. 3 PP 214, 215.
18. Ibid.

allow them to remain in the occupation of those houses, - but posted Arab guards around them. But he was forced to open fire on them when the Rohillas, advanced by breaking through the partition wall of the adjoining house belonging to one Azim Ali Khan[19]. The Rohillas succeded in tearing off the hinges of the gateway towards Putli Bavli, while keeping a constant fire for about twenty minutes from the housetops of the houses that they had occupied. But they had to give way before the heavy firing kept up by the English till about 4 o'clock in the morning. Finding the English cannon fire too severe, the Rohillas during the course of the night evacauted the houses with the help of the very Arab guards that were posted around their houses to prevent their escaping[20]. The Rohilias carried away their wounded with them leaving behind 4 dead.

Turrabaz Khan the Rohilla leader who lead the attack on the Residency was subsequently apprehended at Mogulguda while trying to escape, and was placed under arrest. During the scuffle the Rohilla leader received a severe wound. The Government had announced a reward of Rs. 5,000[21] for any one who assisted them in bringing about the arrest of Turrabaz Khan and Moulavi Ala-ud-din.

Reporting about the incident to the India Government Col. Davidson the Resident also speakes of the general feelings of disaffection among the people and the sepoys in the following manner.........[21] temper of the whole of the lower classes and the impression generally of the population that our rule is at an end.........Neither the minister nor the noblemen of the Nizam's durbar can at the present moment control their followers and the only way is to meet force by force. I should have no hesitation in meeting the whole armed population of Hyderabad with every armed retainer and follower the nobles could bring into the field with the present Subsidiary Force, were we certain of the native troops but we must not close our eyes to the fact that they have been tampered with and although the Madras Army has as yet remained faithful there is no knowing what might happen in case of continued reverses—............... with this subject I am informed a certain Moulavi warned Syed Ahmed still was meetings with the sepoys at a mosque between the city and Secunderabad and that the party who attacked us were assured by him that they would be joined by the Native Horse Artillery and had nothing to fear on their part.

The Arabs cannot be relied on and will evidently oniy be on our side as long as we are successful,"

While, H. C. Brigge the official Historian on the Nizams of Hyderabad commenting about the conditions in Hyderabad during this period wrote;

19. Ibid.
20. Ibid Para 6, 7.
21. Hyderabad Affairs. Vol. III. P. 227.
22. H. R. R. Vol. 93 Poras. 6, 7.

"Had any of the Moglaee princes or nobles of Delhi taken the initiative instead of Tantia Topee in stirring insurrection, Hyderabad must have given away. I firmly believe that the opportunity was alone wanting to make Hyderabad go like Delhi, Lucknow, and other Mohommedan cities. It was simply by maintaining a firm attitude while the populace and the seditious were waiting to see how affairs progressed elsewhere that enabled the Residency to tide over the storm." [23]

After arresting Turrabaz Khan, three persons namely Karamat Ali the Magistrate of the Criminal Court, Fazlullah the Magistrate of the Civil Court and Ghalib Jung were deputed to take his statements. Turrabaz Khan was tried and was sentenced to transportation for life. But he contrived to escape from confinement on the 18th Jannary 1859! The Government announced a reward of Rs. 5000 to any one who would apprehend Turrabaz Khan. He was once again rearrested with the help of Kurban Ali, near a village called Toopran where in the scuffle that ensued he was shot by the British soldiers. The body was subsequently brought to Hyderabad and was hung up by chains in a public place [24].

Moulavi Ala-ud-din who actcd as the standard bearer of the people who lead the attack on the Residency on the memorable evening of the 17th, fled to Bangalore where he was subsequently arrested at a village called Mangalapalli, brought to Hyderabed, tried and was sentenced, for transportation for life to the Andaman Islands, on the 28th June 1859, He died in the Andaman Islands in the year 1884 [25].

The statement given by Turrabaz Khan during the course of his trial was something noble and inspiring. He took the full responsibility upon himself for having attacked the Residency. He told the jury, that he joined the rebellion in the name of his religion, to drive away the British from India. He denied the fact that he was followed by any other Rohilla, or of of having known Moulavi Ala-ud-in previously and of having concerted the attack on the Residency in unison with him. As a matter of fact he said that he did not know Moulavi-Ala-ud-din's name. He took the sole responsibility for having attacked the Residency and tried not to involve the name of his patron Buddhan Khan in this affair.

The incident on 17th July, the attack on the Residency, was the only major incident that took place in Hyderabad proper, but it does not mean that the closing of that episode put an end to all disputes between the people and their alien rulers Great tension prevailed among the various sections of the people in the city and this uneasy situation continued upto the year 1860. The situation in the state was very

23. H. G. Briggs. Vol. II. PP. 81, 82.
24. Freedom Struggle in Hyderabad, PP, 83, 84.
Unpublished files in the Central Records Office.
25. Ibid. PP. 64, 65,

critical, expecially when the emissaries of Nana Sahib, Tantia Tope and Rao Saheb Peishwa moved among the people. The discontent against the British rule in India took a more concrete form, in the form of rebellions in the various districts and parts of the state, the most notable among them being the rebellion of Rajah Venkatappa Naik of Shorapore a tributary of the Nizam.

The state of Shorapore was a small principality in the Gulbarga district, and a major portion of its population consisted of the Bedar community, the Rajah himself being a Bedar. At the time of our narrative Rajah Venkatappah Naik an young man of about 24 years was ruling over Shorapore. During the minority of the Rajah, Capt. Meadows Taylor acted as the political agent of the State, and he looked upon the Rajah as his own ward, and gave him a good training in administration. The Rajah was invested with full govering powers in 1853 and Capt. Meadows Taylor left Shorapore for Hyderabad[26].

Shorapore was originally a feudatory State under the Marathas, but later on it came under the Nizam's hegemony. When the war of 1857 broke in India, Venkatappa Naik, could not resist the lure of asserting his independence against the British. Emissaries from Nana Sahib and from zamindars of the Raichur district tempted the Rajah to rebel against the British, promising to make him the ruler over the whole of the Southern Maratha country, stretching from Shorapore to Rameshwar[27].

The Rajah apart from yielding to the natural feelings of patriotism that were inherent in an individual, could not resist the pressure of his own people who wanted to rebel against the British. He confessed later to Meadows Taylor in the following manner, ---- And then my people rebelled against me and called me a coward and a fool because I would not let them go".

The Rajah soon after the mutiny broke out in India started raising Arab and Rohilla recruits. He also sent agents to Bombay and Belgaum to raise men for his armies. When the British questioned him regarding his activities the Rajah denied that he had any evil intentions towards the British but continued to levy Arab, and Rohilla mercenary forces of about 600 strong[28],

Finding the Rajah implacable, Col. Davidson made the Nizam's Government to issue a proclamation by beat of drum to the effect, that, if any person happened to take service with the Rajah of Shorapore. he would run the risk of being severely punished and his property confiscated.[29] Major

26, Meadows Trylor-Story of my life p. 273.
27. Mcadows Laylor. Storp of my life p. 400.
28. H. R. R. Vol. 94 L. No. 139 Hpderabad Affail Vol. 3 p. 217.
29. Ibid.

Davidson further sent Capt. Rose Campbell in January 1858 to Shorapore hoping that the presence of Capt. Campbell might influence the Rajah to the extent of giving up his anti-British activities. At the same time Major Davidson took the precaution of calling a force from the Bombay Presidency under Col. Malcolm, and locating it at a point equi-distant between Shorapore and the Southern Mahratha country. He also ordered a force from Madras and asked Major Hughes to keep a eye on the eastern frontier of the Shorapore country, while a part of the Hyderabad Contingent consisting of 400 men and two guns were sent from Hyderabad under Capt. Wyndham to Lingasagar, so that in case of necessity all these three forces could act in concert and paralyse the Rajah's strength in no time. [30].

After stationing the forces in the above manner Major Davidson instructed Col. Campbell to demand of the Rajah, the expelling of the mercenary troops that he had levied, from Shorapore. But the Rajah was hardly in a position to do so. Davidson. became so irate, at this conduct of the Rajah that he suggested to Col. Campbell, that the Rajah must be made to appear before a Military Commission, presided over by Lt. Col. Malcolm, and answer for his conduct, during the past few months.

He also instructed that Col. Malcolm should be instructed with the task of clearing Shorapore of the presence of the mercenary soldiers. [31].

Meanwhile, intrigues were afoot in Shorapore to put an end to the life of Col. Campbell. [32] The Rajah who had been trained and brought up by Col. Meadows Taylor, could not entirely overcome his friendly feelings towards Gol. Campbell who belonged to the same race as Taylor. So the Rajah sent secret agents to Campbell to warn him of the danger to his life. [33]

Finding the situation growing critical Col. Campbell ordered Capt. Wyndham to march on Shorapore. Wyndham arrived at Shorapore, on the 7th February 1858. On his arrival the Rajah sent men to receive him properly, who advised Wyndham to choose a valley between two lofty hills as his camping ground. But Wyndham was too shrewd to fall into the trap and he chose an open plain to encamp with the troops [35].

In the same night Wyndham was attacked by the Rajah's troops consisting of Bedars, Arabs and Rohillas. The attack continued throughout the night, but the next morning Wyndham received reinforcement under Major Hughes, consisting of two Companies of the 74th Highlanders and the Madras Cavalry.

30. Hyderabad Affairs. Vol. III. P. 365.
31. H. R. R. Val. 94.
32. Meadows Taylor-Story of My Life pp. 401, 402
33. Ibid.
34. Ibid.

The attack on the English side was lead by Capt. Newberry; in the fight that ensued between the two armies Capt. Newberry lost his life, while his Subaltern, Lieutenant R. C. Stewart was severely wounded.

The forces of the Rajah were driven into the town, and Wyndham, decided at this juncture, to await the arrival of reinforcements under Col. Malcolm, before he could take further action against the Rajah.

The Rajah finding his troops dispersed, fled to Hyderabad with the hope of meeting Col. Meadows Taylor, his former guardian. He reached Hyderabad with only two followers and then tried in vain to gain the protection of the Arabs. Ultimately he was apprehended and taken to the Diwan Salar Jung, while wandering in the bazar. The latter handed him over to the Resident, Major Davidson.

In the meanwhile the English forces occupied Shorapore, and Col. Campbell took over the administration of the State.

Major Davidson kept Rajah Venkatappah Naik a prisoner at Secunderabad and had him tried by a Military Commission. During the course of the trial, Col. Meadows Taylor was deputed by the Resident to visit the Rajah, who was his former ward.

Though the Rajah was overwhelmed by feelings of grief and affection at the sight of Taylor, he firmly refused to divulge the names of his assocciates and other people, who were responsible for making him join the conspiracy against the British. He took the entire responsibility on himself by merely saying to Meadows Tayior "They promised, by their incantations to raise me to be Rajah of all the country—from Shorapore to Rameshwar and if I marched at the head of my twelve thousand they said all the country would rise, and we should be conquerors, Then Marathas from Poona, from Sattara, from Kolapoor, from Mungood, from Bheem Rao, who had secured all the disaffected people of Raichore persuaded me to join them, and offered me what I pleased if I did so; but still I did not go. I was......still... ..true to you......And then my people rebelled against me and called me a "Coward and a fool" because I would not let them go. Arabs and Rohillas now came around me, and one man, worse than all the rest, swore to me on the Qoran that the Arabs and Rohillas of Hyderabad, and all the Mussulmans, had declared a crusade against the English, that the Madras troops would not fight and that they would all come and join me if I would rise and these men led me into evil which I could not help".[35] On Taylor asking the Rajah if he would like to see the Resident, the Rajah spiritedly replied "No Appa, he would expect me to ask my life of him, and I won't do that, tell him, if you like, that if the great English people grant me my life, I and mine will be ever true to them, but I deserve

35. Meadows Taylor p. 401.

to die for what I did, and I will not ask to live like a coward, nor will I betray my people''[36].

On Taylor advising the Rajah to be bold and to speak the truth before the tribunal the young Rajah replied saying "I will surely tell all", but if they press me to disclose the names of those who excited me I shall be silent. Government is powerful enough to crush them if they rise. But what can they do ? Was I not the strongest among them? And yet where am I now? Shall I, who have to face death, be faithless to those who trusted me months ago, Never, Appa ! I would rather die than be sent over the black water, or shut up in a fortress always. Suppose they sentence me to that, I could not bear it. No, the meanest Beydur could not live if he were imprisoned and shall I, a Raja ?..

....

I shall not trouble when they tie me up to a gun......only one thing appa...... do not let them hang me, I have done nothing to be hanged for, like a robber. Tell the Residentt hat is all the favour I ask".

The Rajah of Shorapore, Rajah Venkatappa Naik was tried, and originally sentenced to death, but later on at the intercession of the Resident the Governor-General commuted his sentence to only four years imprisonment in the fortress of Chingleput near Madras.

But, the Rajah while he was being escorted to the south, taking advantage of the temporary absence of his guard who having taken off his belt containing a loaded revolver, had gone to have a wash, shot himself with the revolver, and died in order to avoid the humiliation of remaining a prisoner at the British hands.

Thus ended the sad and brief but brilliant life of Rajah Venkatappa Naik of Shorapore.

After the death of the Rajah, the Arabs and Rohillas that he had recruited dispersed in various directions. Among them one Tasaduq Hussain was taken to Shorapore, tried and was hanged in the market place on the 3rd July 1858 as a warning to others.

The State of Shorapore that passed into the British control during this period was subsequently restored to the Nizam on the 4th March 1861.

Apart from the rebellion in the Shorapore country other rebellions also took place in different parts of the erstwhile Hyderabad State. The most notable among them being the rebellions led by Bhim Rao Nadgoud the Zamindar of Mundargi in the Dharwar District and Kenchangouda the Desai of Hummigi when the British attempted to disarm the population in these parts.

36. Ibid P. 403.
37. Ibid. P. 404.

The attempts of the British to disarm them displeased them and the people of these parts readily joined Bhim Rao Desai's Standard when he raised the standard of insurrection against the British. Bhim Rao was also joined by the Zamindar of Sortoor.

Bhim Rao collected about 400 men under the pretext of constructing a tank at Dumbal, but the British who knew the real feelings of Bhim Rao towards them were not taken in by this ruse. Apart from that Mr. Kafman a Christian missionary had warned the Collector of Dharwar of the intended rebellion of the people both Hindus and Muhammedans under the leadership of Bhim Rao[38].

After collecting men Bhim Rao showed his animosity towards the British by preventing the collection of revenues in the State.

The Collector of Bellary on hearing news of the intended rising, ordered the head-constable of Dumbal to search the fortified enclosure of Kenchangouda at Hammigi. The constable discovered a large quantity of ammunition.

Realising, that the game was up, Bhim Rao gathering a few men, attacked the guard, killed the informant, and after securing the stores marched along with Kenchangouda and attacked the treasury at Dumbal. There he was joined by the local people, and from thence he proceeded to Gadag where on his approach the staff of the Post Office and the Electric and Telegraph office fled for their lives. As Bhim Rao was closely pursued by the Police, he along with his friends reached the neighbourhood of Koppal, and camped at a village called Kumar-raman Kunta about 6 miles from the Tungabhadra river.

The principal police officer on hearing of the approach of Bhim Rao went in advance to arrest them.

On hearing of this Bhim Rao went by a different route to Koppal and occupied it. On hearing of this the British sent troops from Dharwar, Bellary and Raichur with great haste. Major Hughes from Bellary reached Koppal on the 31st May 1858 and laid seige to the fortress. The British musketry played havoc on the garrison in the fortress. The next day Major Huge's forces were reinforced by the arrival of Lieut. Pindar of the Hyderabad Contingent. accompanied by Lieut Taylor, Assist. Commissioner of Raichur. Major Huges after the arrival of these reinforcements sent a letter to Bhim Rao Desai and his friends asking them to surrender. He gave Bhim Rao three hours notice to surrender but as Bhim Rao decided to face the British cannon fire rather than surrender, Major Hughes decided to storm the fortress of Koppal.

---

38. The Freedom struggle in Hyderabad. Vol. No. II. p. 11 (From information supplied by the Bombay State Committee, History of Freedom Movement in India Bombay.)

The Fortress was captured by Major Hughes on the 1st June 1858. Bhim Rao and Kenchanguda along with most of their followers fell fighting in the battle field. Only 150 men were taken prisoners.

At about the same time the Zamindar of Nargund, Bhaskar Rao Bhave rose in rebellion and killed Mr. Manson and the small body of soldiers he commanded. but later on the Zamindar was captured and his property was confiscated. [39].

The lands of Bhim Rao, Kenchangouda, Srinivas Venkatadri the Desai of Dumbal were also confiscated.

Out of the rebels that were caught about 75 of them were blown away from guns. [40].

From the statements made by Bhimappa the *Gumastha* of Bhim Rao it was revealed that the Chief of Nargund was in communication with Nana-Saheb, and that all these chieftains of the Bombay Karnatak country had planned to rise against the British on a fixed day, namely, on the 27th May 1858. They had also assigned to each one the roles they had to play against the British namely that the Zamindar of Nargund was to hold Nawalgund, the Desai of Dumbal was to loot Dumbal and Gadag, while the Thorgal Raja was to create a disturbance on his side. It was also decided that Bhim Rao along with Kenchangouda was to hold Koppal. [41].

The plan could not be worked out because Bhim Rao and Kenchangouda were forced to rise in arms earlier than the scheduled date.

Commenting about this the "Englishman" wrote "These risings are a part of a large conspiracy, which had appointed the month of July for its combined movements, as the ground being then under water our troops would find a difficulty in acting against them. The rising piecemeal, as the above two instances, is imputed to the fears of the conspirators, who, conceiving that disclosures respecting their conspiracy had been made by the late Raja of Shorapor, have been precipitated to take up arms prematurely as their only resource." [42].

During this period the Rohillas in Basmathnagar and Nirmal regions and the Bhils in the Ajanta region created grave disturbances in the state and indulged in loot and arson with a view to upset the British power in Hyderabad. The Rohilla disturbances in the Ajanta region were very serious throughout the year 1858 to 1859. till they were ultimately put down by Sir Hugh Rose. [43] However these Rohilla insurrections in the state continued upto the year 1860, Throughout this period Contingent forces

39. Hyderabad Affairs Vol. III P. 219.
40. Ibid.
41. Bombay State Committee "History of Freedom movement in India", Bombay.
42. Hyderabad Affairs P. 219.

were employed in quelling these disturbances and order was ultimately restored in the states by arresting and sentencing the Rohilla leaders to various terms of long imprisonment. The Rohillas called themselves the subjects of the Nana Sahib Peishwa, and posted placards in the market places of the villages they visited, to the same effect, so that they could win the symathy of the local people. The placards ran as follows.

"In the name of all the Rohillas, servants of Nana Sahib of Poonah. The Nizam (Mogullai) has allied himself with the British, and does not aid Nana Sahib. For this reason we are plundering the Nizam's country. The Soobah (or Nizam) has seized three of our brethern—it is immaterial. You are to forward this letter to the Chief Authority of Salona for transmission to Aurangabad so that its contents may be made known to the Nizam of Hyderabad. This letter is to be forwarded with all speed to Salona. We shall devastate all the Nizam's country. "

These swarming Rohilla bands devastating activities increased all the more when the rumours of Tantia Tope crossing the Narbada with a view to come to the Deccan became current in the country.

The British employed the Contingent forces against them under Brigadier Hill. Ultimately, they arrested and brought to trial the Chief of Javla and his brother, Shah Ghulam Hussain and Syed Hussain for having entertained 500 Rohillas in his service. His Jaghir was seized and he was ordered along with his brother to undergo two years imprisonment.[45]

The leading Rohilla and Arab Leaders were hanged, and the forts of Basmathnagar and Nageshwari the Rohilla strongholds were razed to the ground. [46]

Rohilla rebellions were also rampant at Nirmal in the Adilabad district. Here they were joined by Ramji Gond, the Gond leader.

A fight took place between the Collector and the troops on one side ann the Rohilla, Gond forces of about 500 strong on the other side, at Nirmal in April 1860. The Rohilla-Gond forces suffered casualties on account of the heavy artillery fire opened on them by the Collector. So they dispersed and Ramji escaped. However, he was subsequently caught, tried and hanged at Nirmal. [47]

The Bhils also rose in rebellion in 1857 in the Ajanta region under their leader Bhagoji Naik. The Bhil depredations continued upto 1859, and in these depredations they were greately helped by, the Deshpandes of

---

43. Hyderabad Affairs Vol. III. P. 225.
44. From Files kept in the Central Records Freedom Struggle in Hyd. Vol. I.
45. Ibid.
46. Hyderabad Affairs Vol. III PP. 226, 227.
47. Ibid. Freebom Struggle in Hyderabad Vol. II. P. 157.

Vaizapur. However, the Bhil depredations were brought under control by the effective employment of the Contingent forces against them.[48]

The disturbances created by the Rohillas, Gonds and Bhils and the fact that there were Indian chiefs ready to encourage them, indicates that the people and the chieftains of the Hyderabad State were far from reconciled to the British hegemony in India, and that they were eager to take advantage of the British troubles in the North, to wrench from them, the political power in the South.

Apart from the Rohilla and Bhil rebellions, another serious conspiracy was also hatched in the Nizam's Dominions, against the British in 1858.

The chief persons who were involved in this plot against the British were one Ranga Rao who acted as the agent of Nana Sahib, Rajah Deep Singh the Zamindar of Kowlas and Safdar-ud-Dowla, a Muslim nobleman closely connected with the family of Rao Rambha Nimbalkar, a nobleman of the Nizam's Court.

They wanted to raise the standard of rebellion in the name of Nana Sahib Peishwa, but they could not succeed in their plans due to lack of finances and co-ordination.

The British discovered about the existence of this plot during the course of their activities in putting down the Rohilla insurrections.[49] They searched the house of the Patels of Harlee for having given asylum to the Rohillas, and during the course of their search they came across letters written by the Rajah of Kowlas, Safdar-ud-Dowla etc.[50] Commenting about this the "Englishman", a contemporary newspaper wrote; "...... I belive many men to have been concerned in conspiracies against the English Government; and that the Resident and the Minister have never received direct information of it (for I confidently believe that would have been followed by the apprehension and punishment of the criminals) does not in my opinion negative the existence of an extensive conspiracy with numerous conspirators concerned in it, but is a proof that, that the whole country nearly colludes with them; of its sympathy there can be no doubt."[51]

The papers discoverd by the British revealed that one Sonaji Pandit, a Daftardar in the employment of the Raja Rai Rayan a nobleman in the Nizam's court, wrote to Nana Sahib Peishwa at Cawnpore as early as February 1857. Sonaji Pandit who was banished from Hyderabad and was residing in a Jaghir village, sent these letters to Nana Sahib through the village Patwari Ranga Rao Pagay. Ranga Rao seems to have visited Nana Sahib in the middle of 1857 at the Village of Berthwada.

48. Hyderabad Affairs. Vol. III, P, 240.
49. Hyderabad Affairs. Vol. III. P. 230,
50. Ibid.
51. Ibid. pp. 231, 232, 233,

of rebellion against the British in the State of Hyderabad. Nana Sahib also sent a letter addressed to the various patels and Kulkarnis in the districts of Nagar and Shorapur to co-operate with Sonaji Pandit and Ranga Rao to rise against the British.

The letter to the Patels and Kulkarnis ran as follows :—

"Let it be known that in Hindusthan the Hindus and the Mohammedans having been provoked to stand up together to defend their faiths, have attacked the camps of the Sahebs and they (the Sahebs) have been slain everywhere. In consequence, it is being made known to you by these present that Shri Ratnakar Page, Narkhedkar and Sonaji Pandit of Hyderabad have been charged with the responsibility of organising effective resistance in those parts. You are therefore enjoined to act in the name of your faith and destroy the Englishmen wherever they may be found. This is the only way in which Hindus and Mohammedans alike be able to preserve their faiths. Whosoever will lend his wholehearted support to this cause will live to see his prosperity and will earn our rewards too."[52]

Armed with these letters, Ranga Rao arrived at Aurangabad and delivered the letters of Nana to one Ghalib Khan but there he heard, that Sonaji Pandit had died on the 26th Fedruary 1859. From thence Ranga Rao proceeded towards Hyderabad. On his way to the capital he stayed at Kowlas, and after gaining access to the Rajah Deep Singh of Kowlas, in the garb of a medical man he narrated his mission and won the sympathy of the Rajah towards his cause.[53]

From Kowlas he proceed to Maniknagar asking the village patels he met on his way to comply with the orders of the Peishwa Nana Sahib. While still he was in this mission, the British having heard about his activities arrested him at Ankalska. In the meanwhile Ranga Rao had also communicated with Safdar-ud-Dowla and the latter conveyed his willingness to raise the necessary Arab troops if funds were supplied to him.[54]

But lack of funds proved to be the greatest hitch in the whole undertakings of Ranga Rao who wanted to raise an army of 10,000 in the name of Nana. His single-handed efforts to gain the necessary funds and equipment was of little avail before the swift and striking power of the British.

He was arrested and along with him the Rajah of Kowlas and Safdar-ud-Dowla and other associates were also arrested and tried.

Ranga Rao was transported to the Andamans. The property of Safdar-ud-Dowla was confiscated and he was condemned to life imprisonment.

52. Freedom Struggle in Hyderabad. Vol II pp. 162, 163.
53. Statements made by Ranga Rao and Santaji Rao pp. 166, 167, 168, 169.
54. Ibid. Statement made by Safdar-ud-Dowla.

Rajah Deep Singh was sentenced to three years imprisonment for having supressed the information regarding the activities of Ranga Rao Patwari.

The transportation of Ranga Rao Patwari to the Andaman Islands brings to a close the anti-British activities in Hyderabad during the years 1857 to 1859. But long after the so called Indian Mutiny was suppressed the embers of war continued to exist in Hyderabad as long as the year 1867 and popular resentment against the British took the form of the Bhalki conspi-piracy and an attempt against the life of the Diwan Salar Jung for having supported the British.

Commenting about the unity displayed by the Hindus and Muslims during this period the "Englishman" who could scarcely comprehend or appreciate the phenomenon that was taking place in India wrote as follows: —"It is curious to observe that easy transition with which the Mohemmadans who above all things are instructed by the precepts of their Koran to abhor idols and infidels, in regard to the last of which they have given us a bumper benefit, have passed into sympathising with the Hindus. How absurd to think that, notwithstanding their doctrines and their antecedents past and present, they expect to be believed; they certainly will be. Our taxes will improve in regard to all that may make against us, the easy credulity of the Hindus. There are few such as gentlemen whom I have described above because the Hindus will begin to hate us, they will begin to love the Mussulmans.[54]

Thus we find that during this period a greater part of India was engaged in fighting to overthrow the British rule in India. The people of Hyderabad also, inspite of absolutely no encouragement from their ruler and their Diwan, tried to oppose the might of the British in their own humble way. The History of Hyderabad during this period does not offer any luminaries like Tantia Tope to illumine the pages of history and the fight was waged by the people against aliens. Nevertheless, the humble efforts made by the people of the State shed a glowing light on the history of the period like the twinkling light emanating from the glow worms.

After the suppression of the 1857 movement, the British in appreciation of the stead-fast loyalty displayed by the Nizam and the services rendered by the Contingent forces restored to the Nizam the districts of Raichur Doab and Naldrug that were originally taken from him in 1853, retaining only the Berar districts.[55] Shorapur was also given back to the Nizam; and the British Government also cancelled a debt of 50 lakhs of rupees due from the Nizam to the British.

The British ratified these changes by entering into a fresh treaty with the Nizam in 1860. Presents worth about £10.000 and £3000 were sent to

55. Hyderabad Affairs. Vol. III. P. 239.

the Nizam and his Minister respectively. The Nizam as became his dignity sent to the Governor-General presents worth about £15,000 which were duly consigned to the Imperial Treasury by the India Government.[56]

In 1861, the order of the Star of India that was then recently instituted was also conferred on the Nizam.[57] The knighthood of the "Most Exalted Order" was conferred on the Nizam.

The Nizam in the beginning was reluctant to accept the order as the Persian Translator of the Governor-General's *Khareeta* referred to the order as a "towk" which when interpreted literally meant a collor worn by a slave. But on being told that even the Prince Consort, the Prince Albert also belonged to this order of the Knights, the Nizam finally accepted this honour. The title of "Faithful Ally" was also conferred on the Nizam in recognition of the loyalty displayed by him during the great rebellion of 1857.

Though the restoration of the Raichur Doab was received with delight, yet the retention of the Berar assigned districts under the control of the Resident of Hyderabad, and the transfer of their jurisdiction to the Commissioner of Nagpur was greaty resented by the peoble.[58]

The people also did not like the idea of the Nizam accepting the order of the "Star of India" and placards conveying their feelings were put up in the streets.[59]

But beyond expressing their general dissatisfaction they had little power in determining the policies of their feudal monarch.

57. Hyderabad Affairs. Vol. III. P. 243.
58. Ibed.
59. Administratibe files – Central Records Office Hyderabad.

BIBILIOGRAPHY

Aitchison (C. W) — Treaties, Engagements and Sanads. 9 vols.
Government Press.
Calcutta (1909).

Arnold (E) — The Marquess of Dalhousie's, Administration of British India. 2 vols.
66 Brook Street, Hanover Street
London, (1862)

Auber (Peter) — Rise and Progress of the British Power in India.
W. H. Allen & co
London (1837)

Authentic Memoirs of Tippoo Sultan by an Officer of the East India Service.
London (1800).

Barton (W) — The Princes of India.
(London 1934)

Beatson — On the War with Tippoo Sultan.
(London 1800).

Bilgrami and Willmott. — Historical and Descriptive Sketch of His Highness the Nizam's Domnions.
Times of India Steam Press
Bombay (1884)

Black (Lt. col. Valentine) — Memoir of the Operations of the British Army in India during the Mahratta War of 1817, 1818, 1819.
London (1820)

Blunt (Scawen) — India under Ripon—A Private Diary.

Briggs (H. G.) — The Nizam, His History and his Relations with the British.
(London 1861)

Burton (R) — The Hyderabad Contingent

Calendar of Persian Correspondence. 7 Vols. Govt. of India. Central Publications

Cambridge (R) — Account of the War in India.
London (1761)

Cardew (A) — The White Munity

Chirag Ali (Syed) — Hyderabad Deccan under Sir Salar Jang. 3 vols.
Bombay (1886)

The Chronology of Modern Hyderabad. (1720-1890)
Central Records Office Publication
Hyderabad, (1945)

Davis (C. Collin) Preliminary Report on the Russell Correspondance to Hyderabad.
(Archives-India)

The Private Correspondence of Lord Macartney, Governor of Madras (1781-85).

Dirom (Major) A Narrative of the Campaign in India which terminated the war with Tipu Sultan in 1792.
London (1790)

(Digby. W) India for the Indians and for England
London (1859)

Dodwell (H) Ananda Ranga Pillai's, Diary 12 vols.
Govt. Press. Madras. (1904-1928)

Calendar of Madras Despatches, (1744-1755)
Govt. Press. Madras. (1920)

Calendar of Madras Despatches (1754-1765)
Govt. Press. Madras (1930)

Dupleix and Clive The beginning of the Empire.
London (1923)

Warren Hasting Letters to Sir John Macpherson.
(1927)

Duff (James Grant) History of the Mahrattas. 3 vols.
Calcutta (1918)

East India Company Papers relative to certain pecuniary transactions of Messrs William Palmer & Co., with the Govt. of His Highness the Nizam.
London (1824)

Copies of Papers relative to George Pigot's arrest and the King of Tanjore.
London (1776).

Bengal, also Fort st., George and Bombay Papers relative to the Mahratta War in 1803. Presented to the House of Commons.
London (1804)

Charters granted to the East India Company from 1601. Also the Treaties and Grants made with or obtained from the Princes and Powers in India from (1756-72) Treaties and Grants from the Country Powers to the East India Company
London (1774)

East India Company — A short Examination of the Hyderabad Papers as far as they relate to the House of William Palmer & Co., in a letter addressed to the Proprietors of East India Stock, by an enemy to oppression,
London (1825)

Forrest (G. W) — Administration of Warren Hastings.
Calcutta (1895)

Selections from the State Papers of the Governor Generals of India-Warren Hastings- 2 vols. Basil Blackwell Oxford. (1910)

Selections from the State Papers of the Governor Generals of India–Lord Cornwallis.
Basil Blackwell. Oxford (1926)

Selections from the Letters, Despatches and other State Papers preserved in the Foreign Department of the Government of India. 3 vols. (1772-85) 1890.

Selections from the Letters Despatches and other State Papers preserved in the Bombay Secretariat vol 1.
Govt. Central Press,
Bombay (1887).

Selections from the letters, Despatches and others State Papers preserved in the Military Department of the Government of India (1857 58)
Military Department Press.
Calcutta (1893)

Bengal and Madras Papers. 3 vols. Imperial Records.
Calcutta (1928).

The Life of Lord Clive. 2 vols.
London. (1918)

History of the Indian Mutiny 3 vols.
Edinburgh. (1904-1912)

Fraser (Capt Hastings) — Our Faithful Ally the Nizam.
London (1865)

Memoir and Correspondence of General James Stuart Fraser.
London. 1885

Gleig. (G. R) — History of the British Empire in India. 4 vols.
London. (1830)

Memoirs of the Life of the Rt. Hon. Warren Hastings.
London (1841)

Gribble (J. D. B) — Manual of Cuddapah District.
Madras (1875)

Gribble (J. D. B). A History of the Deccan 2 vols. London (1924)

Gurwood.- (John) Despatches of the Duke of Wellington, 13. vols. (1799-1818) London (1837)

Halls. The Dalhousie-Phayre Correspondence (1852-56) Oxford University Press. Oxford (1932)

Hill (SE) Bengal in 1756-57. 3 vols. India Record Series London (1905)

Hindu (Correspondent) Hyderabad in 1890-91. Madras (1892)

Hodson (G. H.) Travels in India

Hollingbery (W) History of Nizam Ali Khan. Calcutta 1805.

Hunter (W) Indian Musalmans.

Bengal M. S. Records

Hussain (Yusuf. Dr.) Nizamul-Mulk Asaf Jah I Mangalore (1936)

Some Unpublished letters of Shah Nawaz Khan Samsamud Daulah (Proceedings of the Deccan History Journal.) Hyderabad Session 1945.

The Freedom Struggle in Hyderabad 3 vols. Government of Hyderabad. Andhra Pradesh (1956-60)

Imperial Gazetteer of Madras.
Imperial Gazetter of Hyderabad.

S. K. Iyengar. Historical Inscriptions of South India (1728-1803) Madras (1950)

Kaye. (J. W) A History of the Sepoy War in India. 3 vols. London (1878-1880)

Kaye Life of Lord Metcalfe. 2 vols.

Kirkpatrick (Col. W) Select letters of Tippoo Sultan London (1811)

C. A Kincaid and D. B. Parsinis- History of the Maratha People 3 vols. Oxford University Press. 1918-1925.

Kinnaird(Douglas Honb'le)	Remarks on the volume of Hyderabad Papers. London (1825).
Love (H. D)	Vestiges of Old Madras, 3 vols. Indian Record series. (1918–1925)
Lothian (Sir Arthnr)	Kingdoms of Yesterday. London (1951).
Lyall (R. C)	Rise and Expansion of the British Dominion in India. London (1919).
Malcolm(Sir John)	Sketch of the Political History of India from the introduction of Mr. Pitts Bill. London (1811).
	Life of Lord Clive, 3 vols. London (1836).
Malleson (Col. G. B)	History of the French in India. Edinburgh (1909).
	The Decisive battles of India (1746–1840). London (1914).
	Essays on Indian Historical Subjects. London (1876).
Mehdi Ali (Syed)	Hyderabad Affairs 11 vols. Bombay (1883).
Mehta (Mohan Sinha)	Lord Hastings and the Indian States. Bombay (1930).
Mill and Wilson.	The History of British of India. London (1858).
M. M. D. L. T	The History of Hyder Ali Khan, 2 vols. London (1724)
De, Montalembert, (M. Le comte)	A Debate on India in the English Parliament. London (1858).
Nainar	Tuzaki-Walajahi. Madras 1934.
	Narrative Sketches of the Conquest of the Mysore effected by the British troops and their allies in the Capture of Seringpatam and the death of Tipu Sultan. May 4th 1799. London (1800).
Nicholson (A. P)	Scraps of Paper – India's Broken Treaties. London (1930).

St. Nihal Singh — The Nizam and the British Empire. Bombay (1923).

News letters froms Sri Rangapatam and Chinnapatnam (1767 - 1796).
Ed. by Dr. Yusuf Hussain
Central Records office Publication Hyderabad (A. P.) 1950.

News letter from Bijainagar and Nagpur, Bombay.

Orme (Robert) — History of the Military Transaction of the British Nation in Indostan, 3 vols. Madras (1861-62).

Historical fragments of the Moghul Empire of the Morattoes and of the English Concerns in Indostan. London (1865).

Owen — Selections from Wellesely's Despatches. Oxford. (1827)

Pearce (R. R) — Correspondence of the Most noble Rechard Marquess of Wellesley. 3 vols. London (1846).

Philip. — The Correspondence of David Scott, Director and Chairman of the East India Company relationg to Indian Affairs, 2 vols. (1787).

Poona Residency Correspondence, 10 vols. (Ed by Dighe, Sardesai) Bombay (1936-1939)

Princep (H. T) — History of the Military and Political Transactions in India during the administration of the Marquess of Hastings (1813-1823). 2 vols. London (1825).

Ranade. (M. G) — Rise of the Maratha Power. Bombay (1900).

Rajwade — Marathi Itihas Sadhana.

Robert (P. E) — India under Wellesely. London (1929).

Robson. — Notes relative to the late transactions of the Marhatta Empire. London (1804).

Ross. (C) — Corn Wallis, 3 vols. London (1859).

Ross. (C)	Marquess of Hastings. London (1900).
Sajanlal. (K)	Studies in Deccan History. Madras (1951).
	Nizam Ally's relations with the Marathas (Typed thesis) Central Records Office. Hyderabad (1950).
	Sanpuri Bakhar. Central Records Office Publication Hyderabad (A. P.) 1950.
Sardesai (G. S.)	The New History of the Marathas. 3 vols. Bombay.
	Historical Papers relating to Mahadaji Scindia. Gwalior (1937).
Sen. (Surendranath)	Eighteen Fifty Seven. Govt. of India Publication. 1957.
Srinivasa Chari (C. S)	Ananda Ranga Pillai "The Pepys of French India". Madras (1940).
	History of Madras. Madras. (1939).
Taraporewala	Fort William India House Correspondence. India Record Series. Delhi. (1949).
Temple (Sir. Richard)	Journals kept in Hyderabad, Kashmir, Sikkim and Nepal. 2 vols. London. (1887).
	Men and Events of my time in India. London. (1922).
Thomson. (E)	Life of Charles Lord Metcalfe. London. (1937).
Thorontan (E)	General Sir Richard Meade and the feudatory States of Central and Southern India.
Wellesley	The Marquis of Wellesley's History of the Marhatta War London. (1804).
Wheeler (T)	Madras in Olden Times. Madras. (1882).
	Early Records of British India. London. (1878).
	Tales from Indian History. Calcutta (1890).

Wilks. (Col. Mark) — Historical Sketches of South India. 2 vols. London. (1869).

Wood (M) — A Review of the Origin, Progress and Result of the late decisive war in Mysore. London. (1800).

Woodruff. (J) — The Men who ruled India "The Founders". London (1935).

The Men who ruled India "The Guardians". London (1954).

Records of Fort St. George

Country Correspondence, (1743-1760) Public Department.
French Correspondence, 1751, 1752.
Diary and Consultation Books, 1742, 1743, 1744, 1745.
Political Despatches from England, 1744 - 1747.
Political Despatches to England, 1743 - 1746.
Secret Consultations, 1748 - 1760.
Military Consultations, 1740 - 1763.
Madras Local Records,

Oriental Manuscripts Library, Madras. Mackenzie Mss. (Telugu).

Kalingapatnam Hakikat.
Ganjam Hakikat.
Sarpavaram Kaifiyat.
Samalkot Kaifiyat.

Bandar Machilipatnam Kaifiyat.
Kaifiyat Pargana Bobbili - (Kalingam Sarkar).

Telugu Sources — Published.

V. R. Jagapati Varma — Samalkot Kaifiyat.
Pusapativari Kaifiyat.
Korukonda Kaifiyat.
Kimmoori Kaifiyat.
Mogaliturru Kaifiyat.
Peddapura Samsthana Charitramu.

Sri Rama Murti (G). Sri Ravu Vamsiya Charitra.

Records of Fort William.

Secret and Political Department Diary —vols 4 to 58. (1758-1797).
Public Department Diary — Vols 37 - 52.

Central Records Office Hyderabad (A. P.)

Unpublished Material; Persian :—

Kharitas — (Correspondence of Nawab Salabat Jung, Nizam Ali Khan, Sikandarjah, with the English — Darul Insha Section).

Mansarani—Mathiri Nizami. MSS.
Yusuf Muhammed Khan — Tarikhi Fathiya.

English :--

"The Trial of "Mubariz-ud-Doula" Translated into English MSS. from Persian.

Unpublished Administrative Files pertaining to correspondence between Sir Salar Jang and the Residents, Corderoy, Yule, Temple, Saunders Meade etc., regarding the treaties of 1802, 1853.

National Archives, Delhi. (Unpublished).

Hyderabad Residency Correspondence (Foreign & Miscellaneous). (1795 - 1858).

Urdu Books.

Alaamia Najmu'l Ghani Khan Sahib of Rampur - Tarikhi Riyasat Hyderabad (Dn).

Mir Dilawar Ali Danish — Riyaaze Mukhaariza

Rahvaare Farooqui — Nasirjang Shahheed.

Siraj - ud-din — Nizam Ali Khan - 2vols.

French.

Martineau (A) Dupleix et l'Inde Francaise. 4 vols. (Paris 1920.)

Correspondence du conseil Superieur de Pondichery.

INDEX